FASHION
from Concept to Consumer

GINI STEPHENS FRINGS

Designer, Koret of California and Solo Sport
and
Fashion Design Program Director,
Bauder College

Prentice-Hall, Inc.
Englewood Cliffs, New Jersey 07632

Library of Congress Cataloging in Publication Data

FRINGS, GINI STEPHENS.
   Fashion, from concept to consumer.

   Bibliography: p.
   Includes index.
   1. Fashion. I. Title.
TT518.F74   338.4′7391′00973   80–28625
ISBN 0-13-306605-3

© 1982 by Prentice-Hall, Inc., Englewood Cliffs, New Jersey 07632

Printed in the United States of America

10 9 8 7 6 5 4 3 2 1

Editorial/production supervision by Joan L. Lee
Interior and cover design and page layout by Judith Winthrop
Manufacturing buyer: Harry P. Baisley

Prentice-Hall International, Inc., *London*

Prentice-Hall of Australia Pty. Limited, *Sydney*

Prentice-Hall of Canada, Ltd., *Toronto*

Prentice-Hall of India Private Limited, *New Delhi*

Prentice-Hall of Japan, Inc., *Tokyo*

Prentice-Hall of Southeast Asia Pte. Ltd., *Singapore*

Whitehall Books Limited, *Wellington, New Zealand*

For Philipp

CONTENTS

2

INFLUENCES ON FASHION AND CONSUMER DEMAND *31*

3

FASHION CHANGE AND CONSUMER ACCEPTANCE *45*

APPAREL PRODUCTION   153

11

FUR AND ACCESSORY MANUFACTURING   171

12
WHOLESALE FASHION MARKETS AND DISTRIBUTION 183

PART FOUR
THE RETAILING OF FASHION

13
RETAIL STORES 199

14
RETAIL FASHION MERCHANDISING 213

RETAIL FASHION PROMOTION *229*

THE HOME SEWING INDUSTRY *241*

ACKNOWLEDGMENTS

The author wishes to thank the many friends and business associates who took time to answer questions, make suggestions, review chapters, and donate photographs during the creation of this book. The author is particularly indebted to:

Marchese Emilio Pucci, whose genuine interest and cooperation in the training of fashion students makes his foreword especially meaningful;

Claudy Stolz, Catherine Rousso at *Elle*, Sylvie Zawadski of the Fédération Française de la Couture, Bertrand Djian at Per Spook, and Bernard Danillon de Cazella at Pierre Cardin for information about the French fashion industry;

Sidney Burstein of Brown's, Tony Glenville and Linda Ballarian at *IM International*, Tricia Whitehead at *Faces*, Nancy Richards at the Wool Secretariat, Henry Shoot of the International Color Authority, Casey Tolar of the London Collections, and Annette Worsley-Taylor of the London Designer Collections for information on the London and European fashion scenes;

Massimo Ludovisi at the Los Angeles Italian Trade Commission for information on Italy;

Masako and Yosiko Hosaka of the Tokyo Fashion Group and Keiko Ishihara for information on Japan;

Chantal Tittley-Moreault of the Montreal Fashion Group for information on Canada;

Robert LaForce at Celanese Fibers Marketing Company and Duncan Lamont for their technical advice in the textiles area;

John Foster and Peter Kobel at Koret, Billie Sher of Habits, Jane Klein, and Steffan Aletti of the *American Jewelry Manufacturer* for specialized information on production;

Basab Basu at Koret for his input in the marketing area;

René Carrillo of Macy's for reviewing the retailing chapters;

Edna Goldenberg for her input in the home sewing area;

Debra Smith at Koret who patiently reviewed the entire manuscript with the author; Donna Atkinson and Mary Ann Stein for their editorial suggestions;

Laila Paris, Patrick Ciganer, Susan Thomas, and Linda Cox for their assistance;

Jessica McClintock, Karen Alexander, Jeanne Allen, Barbara Colvin, Terri Branch, Lydia Dresnek, and Al Malouf who have been so generous to my students;

Mervin Brown, now at Solo, Lee Brown, and Judye Marino at Koret, Fern Volkman, now at Belk Stores, Ruth Kettle at Bauder, and Mary Epstein, Drexel University, for confidence in my abilities and the opportunity to prove them;

My grandmother Ida Martin, my parents Ida and Russell Stephens, Elma McCarraher, Dolores Quinn, Eleanor Kling Ensign, Hazel Stroth, Krestine Corbin, and other dear friends for inspiration and encouragement throughout my education and career; and

Especially Philipp for his patience and support and for putting up with soup for dinner and nearly no social life for three years. An extra little thank you to KCK for keeping me company.

PREFACE

The purpose of this book is to tell the whole story of how the fashion business works, in sequential order from concept to consumer. The fashion business is a series of buying supplies, creating and developing a new product, and marketing that product to another consumer. This process is repeated on three levels: raw materials, manufacturing, and retailing. It is important for people in the fashion industry to know something about all levels, as all are interrelated. The fashion designer should understand the importance of selling garments, and what the consumer and buyer look for in a garment. The retail fashion buyer should know what happens before the garment arrives in the store, so that he or she is better able to make wise buying decisions and to be a more creative merchandiser.

The fashion business includes all the firms involved with producing apparel: fiber, textile, findings, and trimmings producers; manufacturers of the actual garments; wholesale markets; and the retail stores that sell the finished product to the public. In addition, this book covers related industries like fur and accessory manufacturing and home sewing. Many facets of the fashion industry besides designing and buying are both interesting and rewarding.

The objectives of the book are to trace the development of fashion and the fashion industry; to explore the fundamental concepts of consumer demand and fashion change; to trace the development, production, and marketing of merchandise from concept to consumer; to explain the interrelationship of each level of the industry; and to explain the various aspects of fashion as they relate to each of these levels.

Part I concentrates on fashion fundamentals. Chapter 1 gives a brief history of fashion and the fashion industry as a background to understanding why and how fashion changes. Chapter 2 discusses influences on fashion and consumer demand. Chapter 3 explains fashion change and consumer acceptance. Chapter 4 gives sources for design and merchandising information and analysis that aid people at all levels of the industry in product development or merchandising.

Part II covers the product development, production, and marketing of raw materials including textiles, trimmings, leather, and fur—the supplies needed for fashion manufacturing.

Part III traces the fashion manufacturing process through design and merchandising development, production, and sales. The first test of a successful fashion design is at the wholesale market, the meeting ground of manufacturer and retailer.

Part IV covers retail stores and how they identify with consumer groups. Chapter 14 follows the garment through the buying and selling process to the customer. The customer's acceptance is the final test of its success. Chapter 16 profiles the home sewing industry, which in many ways parallels ready-to-wear.

Each chapter contains lists of objectives, review questions, terminology, and projects to aid in reviewing the subject matter. The appendices include additional information on company ownership and career guidelines.

This book will be a valuable tool for an introductory course in fashion design, apparel production, clothing, merchandising, retailing, vocational education, or even business. In the fashion design field, this text would complement courses in clothing construction, textiles, sketching, and the history of costume, followed by pattern making and practice in garment design. In the merchandising field, complementary courses would include textiles, followed by thorough study of buying, personnel, merchandising, marketing, and business math.

This is an introductory book for specialists as well as for those who are taking only a single course in fashion. In fact, it will interest anyone who wants to know more about fashion and the fashion business.

FOREWORD

Fashion, I believe, is the visual representation of a given historical period.

Ancient civilizations identified the exercise of power—political, religious, or military—with visual elements related to the garb worn by kings, priests, or warriors. This practice continues at present in those countries where old traditions have been preserved, and in authoritarian societies, especially in Africa, where new rulers have established more or less absolute power.

As professions, arts, and crafts acquired importance, special ways of visually expressing such occupations were developed. This was particularly so in Florence, Italy, where, in order to "belong," citizens had to join and identify with associations. Each association has its own costume, often bearing the insignia of its purpose.

In later times fashion in its more primitive sense became generalized to larger groups of people, as society became organized in classes, each having a different role in economic, social, and intellectual development. In modern times, as the class system became less rigid, fashion became more generalized and an indication of the economic level of the people as well as of the surroundings in which they lived.

The twentieth century has witnessed a completely new situation: clothes, traditionally individually made, are now mass produced. Fabrics are more available and less expensive, and the garment industry has grown by leaps and bounds, becoming an extremely important economic factor worldwide.

At present, automation and the various technical and scientific developments of the post-industrial system are shaping the first classless society in many centuries. In this society, entertainers and champion athletes are the new idols of the young, who have adopted first the garb of the agricultural worker (blue jeans) and then the dress of tramps or hoboes to signify their rejection of aesthetic values connected with a hierarchical system. This trend was soon picked up by older men and women, signifying their urge to identify with the younger generation and to adopt their rejection of established values and their permissive life style.

How far will the trend go? Will it spread to all fields, such as architecture, home furnishing, and motor cars? Or, having reached the extremes it has attained in clothing, will it give way to a different attitude based on the appreciation of pure and absolute aesthetic values? Much depends on the philosophy of life that develops in the 1980s, as people become more aware that our limited natural resources mean that individuals will have to earn the right to enjoy life by their personal contribution to it.

Even more than in the past, designing in the future will be first and foremost a service to our fellow humans, by furnishing visual options in all fields of human activity. I say visual *options*, not authoritarian impositions, since we live in an era in which mass media have established an intellectual pattern of strong individual expression.

This book is a significant means of preparing to perform this service. Anyone entering the designing field should do so with great dedication and utter humility, for the real essence of designing is the ability to detect emerging trends and to interpret them according to individual means of expression, sensitivity, and feeling.

Emilio Pucci di Barsento
Florence, Italy

FASHION
from
Concept
to
Consumer

THE
FUNDAMENTALS
OF
FASHION

PART ONE

FASHION
DEVELOPMENT

1

Inspiration from the past:
a fashion show of historic costumes
(Courtesy of the French Apparel Center, Inc.,
New York City)

If I were allowed to choose from the pile of books which will be published one hundred years after my death, do you know which one I would take? . . . I would simply take a fashion magazine so that I could see how women dress one century after my departure. And these rags would tell me more about the humanity of the future than all the philosophers, prophets, and scholars.—Anatole France, French writer, 1844–1924

More than a designer's whim, fashion is a subtle reflection of the social, political, economic, and artistic forces of any given time. The changing styles that evolve from these forces tell of historical events as poignantly as textbooks, journals, or periodicals. Dressing room mirrors throughout the ages have reflected the trends in how people think, live, and love.

One way to study history is to look at photographs and paintings of the clothes people wore. We shall examine some major influences on fashion in recent history as a background to understanding contemporary fashion and anticipating future change. This chapter traces the development of the fashion industry in Europe and America from the seventeenth century to the present, emphasizing the last 100 years. It shows how fashion innovators, together with society, technology, economics, and politics, change fashion.

FRANCE AS THE CENTER OF FASHION

Fashion as we know it is relatively new. In ancient and medieval times, clothing styles remained practically unchanged for a century at a time. Fashion change began to accelerate somewhat during the Renaissance, as Western civilization discovered different cultures, customs, and costumes. As new fabrics and ideas became available, people craved more new things. "Nothing motivates change so well as change itself." [1]

Standards Set by the Court of Louis XIV

Until this time, people were segregated mainly in two classes: the wealthy, mostly land-holding aristocrats, and the poor, mostly laborers and farmers. Because wealth was concentrated in the land-owning class, these people were the only ones who could afford to wear what was considered to be fashionable. Royalty, at the top of both the social and the economic ladders, set fashion trends; while other members of the aristocracy followed their example in order to gain approval.

[1] Helen L. Brockman, *The Theory of Fashion Design* (New York: John Wiley & Sons, Inc., 1965), p. 31.

During the mid-seventeenth century, the interesting and talented people of King Louis XIV's court became the arbiters of taste, making Paris the fashion capital of the world. The textile industry grew in Lyon and other French cities, supplying the court with silk fabrics, ribbons, and laces. Dressmakers and tailors, sponsored by the wealthy, developed their skills to a high level on these beautiful materials.

Hand Sewing by Dressmakers and Tailors

It is hard for us to imagine that all sewing, even basic seams, was done entirely by hand. Shape was engineered by means of many intricate seams. This elaborate detail required an enormous amount of painstaking hand labor. All clothes were not only handmade, but also *custom* made. Each garment was made to fit the customer's exact measurements; each dress or suit was individually sewn by dressmakers or tailors to their employers' specifications.

Dressmakers were known in France as the *couture* (ko-tour'). A male designer was a *couturier* (ko-tour'-ee-ay); his female counterpart was a *couturiere* (ko-tour'-ee-air'). The identities of personal couturiers were secrets guarded by the wealthy. No one wanted to share the talents of clever dressmakers for fear of losing them. The first known couturiere was Rose Bertin (Ber-tan'), dressmaker to Queen Marie Antoinette, who made her the official court minister of fashion.

The poor, who were lucky to have clothes on their backs at all, sewed for themselves. Special occasion clothing, painstakingly embroidered, was passed from one generation of the poor to another and became the traditional peasant costume.

The contrast between the plight of the poor and the extravagancies of the court during the eighteenth century was one cause of the French Revolution in 1789. In response to a general revulsion against excess, fashion changed from elaborately decorated costumes to simpler garments.

Empire, the style created during Napoleon's reign in France (1794 to 1815), imitated the ideals of ancient Greece and Rome. The high-waisted line of the empire dress still carries the name of this period.

After a time of restoration of the monarchy, the Empire returned under Napoleon III. However, with the Germans' defeat of the French in 1871, Napoleon III was forced to abdicate. This marked the end of royal fashion dominance, except perhaps for Queen Alexandra's influence during the Edwardian period in England.

Beginnings of the Modern French Couture

With the end of royal fashion leadership, clients relied more and more on their couturiers' judgment about styling and fabrics. Some couturiers became not only creative forces but business people as well, directing salons with a staff of seamstresses and tailors. The independent modern couture is a bridge between the class-structured fashion of the past and the democratization of fashion today.

Fashion Trend Setter: Charles Worth

Charles Worth is considered the "father of the modern couture" because he was the first successful independent designer. Born in England, he came to Paris at age 20 in 1846 (the year Elias Howe patented his sewing machine). In Paris, Worth found a position as a clerk in a quality clothing shop. Customers admired dresses that he designed for his wife and ordered duplicates for themselves. From an original sample garment or a sketch, the customer ordered a dress custom made by a seamstress to fit her measurements. Worth was so successful that he was asked to be a partner in the store. In 1860, at the age of 34, he went into business for himself.

Even in those days, a Worth gown cost up to $2,500, and wealthy young society women needed as many as 40 gowns for a single social "season." [2] Worth attracted more and more prominent women as clients, until at last Empress Eugenie, wife of Emperor Napoleon III, purchased his designs. Other women of the European aristocracy, in an effort to copy the empress, were anxious to buy from Worth. Finally he had so many clients that he chose to sell only to the ones who were attractive and prestigious enough to show off his clothes to the best advantage.

---

[2] Ishbel Ross, *Crusades and Crinolines* (New York: Harper & Row, Publishers, Inc., 1963), p. 73.

Growth of the Couture

Other couture houses followed Worth, such as Paquin, Cheruit, Doucet, Redfern, the Callot Sisters, and Jeanne Lanvin. Lanvin is the oldest couture house still in existence in Paris.

From these beginnings, the international market grew for Parisian high fashion. In 1868 the couturiers of Paris formed a trade association. Other European capitals followed Paris' leadership, Vienna becoming the next in importance. Couturiers were the major influence on fashion design for over 100 years, setting style trends for all of Europe as well as the rest of the Western world.

Bringing French Fashion to America

Fashion dolls, dressed in miniature versions of couture gowns, were sent from France as a convenient means of publicizing fashion. Orders from wealthy women were mailed back to Paris, where the gowns were made to fit the customers' requirements. However, most people could not afford couture clothes but managed to copy them to some degree. By contrast, the pioneers on the western frontier wore simple clothes made of rough homespun fabrics and buckskins.

Madame Jeanne Lanvin (Courtesy of Lanvin Couture, Paris)

EFFECTS OF THE INDUSTRIAL REVOLUTION ON FASHION

Growth of the Middle Class

Great economic, social, and fashion changes throughout the Western world accompanied the Industrial Revolution in the late eighteenth century. Burgeoning trade and industry in turn created a middle class with money to spend on the luxuries of life, including better clothing. The wealth of the new industrial class made their life style comparable to that of earlier royalty. Money gave the middle class power, not only in business and society, but also to influence fashion trends. Fashion became a status symbol, a visual means to show off wealth.

Establishment of the Business Suit

Until 1800, men's and women's fashions had equal amounts of decoration. In Louis XIV's time, men's dress was at least as elaborate as women's. Elizabeth Ann Coleman, curator of costumes at the Brooklyn Museum in New York, explains that "it is only within the last 175 years that the patterns of male and female fashion have parted ways."[3] As the middle class grew, businessmen wanted to establish an image of respectability and dependability. At that point, "men's garb descended from brilliant finery . . . into bleak conformity."[4] Men adopted the conservative, dignified business suit with long trousers, jacket, vest, shirt, and necktie—"a permanent noose, you might say," and they have remained trapped in the same mold ever since. Men's wear has remained basically conservative with very few changes since.

Men's clothing as well as women's was originally custom made. Even recently, most well-to-do businessmen had their suits made by tailors. The finest tailor shops—such as Henry Poole and Company, established in 1843—were on Savile Row in London, which became the center of men's fashion.

Some ready-made men's clothing was made by hand in France in the late 1700s. In America, the first ready-to-wear suits were made for sailors so that they would have clothes to wear when they came on land. Naturally, these first clothing factories were located in seaport cities such as New Bedford, Boston, New York, and Philadelphia. The first record of a men's clothing factory is dated 1825.[5]

[3] Phyllis Feldkamp, "Men's Fashion, 1750–1975," New York Times Magazine, September 14, 1975, p. 66.

[4] Ibid.

[5] "Bicentennial of American Textiles," American Fabrics and Fashions, no. 106 (Winter–Spring, 1976), p. 64.

Employees outside Levi Strauss company headquarters in San Francisco about 1870 *(Courtesy of Levi Strauss & Co.)*

A few well-known men's retail stores that opened in the early 1800s are still in existence. Henry Brooks started his men's clothier business in 1818, which became Brooks Brothers in 1850. There Abraham Lincoln bought an overcoat for his second inauguration.[6] In 1824, Jacob Reed opened his first store in Philadelphia.

Growth of the Textile Industry

Early America had virtually no textile or fashion industry. Most materials were imported from abroad: silks from Italy, France, India, and China; woolens, calicoes, and cashmeres from Britain; and feathers and artificial flowers from France.

The modern textile industry began in England with John Kay's development of the "flying shuttle" in 1733, James Hargreaves' invention of the "spinning jenny" in 1764, Richard Arkwright's "water frame" in 1769, and Edmund Cartwright's power loom in 1785. To protect their industry, England

passed strict laws preventing textile machines, parts, blueprints, tools, and even the mechanics and inventors themselves, from leaving the country. However, clever Samuel Slater memorized every detail of Arkwright's water frame and other machinery and secretly left England. Within two years of his arrival in New England, he had a new mill built and in operation. Textile mills began to produce cloth in America, the first evidence of fashion independence to parallel its political independence. New England became America's first textile industry center.

In the late 1800s, the American textile industry began to relocate to the South, the source of cotton. Southern states offered producers incentives such as tax advantages, with the added advantage of lower labor costs. Eventually the South became the center of the textile industry in the United States.

Invention of the Sewing Machine

Democratization of fashion began with the sewing machine, which turned an art into an industry. The mass production of clothing would have been

[6] Ibid., p. 12.

The first Singer sewing machine, 1851
(Courtesy of The Singer Company)

In 1859 Isaac Singer, whose name has become a household word because of his mass production of the sewing machine, developed the foot treadle, an improvement that left the hands free to guide the fabric. Electrically powered models were not available until 1921. (Even in those days, Singer spent $1,000,000 a year on sales promotion with the result that by 1867, a thousand machines were being produced per day.[7])

MASS PRODUCTION OF CLOTHING

An early use for sewing machines was to make Civil War uniforms, but it was not long before they came to be used for the mass production of everyday men's wear. At first, manufacturing was done by the *cottage industry* process. Garments were cut in a plant and bundled to be sent out to homes for sewing. Later, to save time and the cost of delivering pieces and picking up garments, and to keep control on production, workers and machinery were brought together in factories. This caused many people in search of work to move to the cities where the factories were located.

To speed production even further, a system for the division of labor was started in England about 1880. Each worker sewed only part of a garment; after many repetitions, workers could do their jobs quickly and easily. This system, now called section work, is fully discussed in chapter 10.

[7] Ross, *Crusades and Crinolines*, p. 12.

impossible without it, and without mass production, fashion would not be available to everyone. In 1829 a French tailor named Thimmonier patented a wooden chain-stitch sewing machine, but all existing models were later destroyed by rioting tailors who feared for their jobs. Walter Hunt, an American, developed a sewing machine in 1832 but failed to patent it. Thus, the man who is usually credited with the invention of the sewing machine is Elias Howe, who patented his in 1846. All of Howe's machines were run by hand.

Women working in Levi Strauss' Valencia Street factory
(Courtesy of Levi Strauss & Co.)

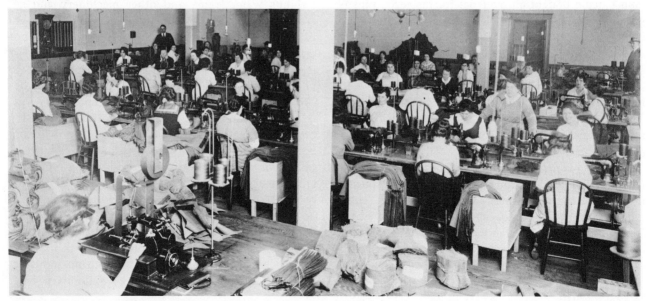

Specialized Work Clothes

In 1850, a 20-year-old Bavarian immigrant by the name of Levi Strauss arrived in San Francisco with a small stock of canvas that he intended to sell to the gold miners for tents and wagon covers. Instead, in answer to a prospector's request for pants that would last more than a few days, Strauss had a pair made by a tailor from the canvas. They filled the need for strong, long-lasting work pants, so Strauss set up a shop to manufacture and sell overalls. Soon he switched to a tough cotton fabric originally loomed in Nimes, France, and called *serge de Nimes* (later shortened to *denim*).

Levi Strauss would probably be surprised that his company has grown into the biggest apparel manufacturer in the world. Approximately 800,000,000 pairs of Levis have been sold since 1850; they are the only item of wearing apparel whose style has remained basically the same for more than 125 years. It is especially unusual to find a staple work garment that became fashionable *after* 100 years in production.

CHANGES IN WOMEN'S FASHION

Fashion conveyed the rigid differences between the roles of the sexes. Men "wore the pants," which became a symbol of dominance, while women wore constraining garments characteristic of their restricted life styles and obedience to their husbands and fathers.

With the development of practical, simple clothes for men, most fashion emphasis has since been placed on women's wear. As a result, women have often been criticized for paying too much attention to their dress. That interest seems perfectly understandable, however, considering that until recently men did not give women the right to own anything else *but* their wardrobes.[8]

Aside from the small numbers of the wealthy who bought couture, most women had basically three garments in their wardrobes: a house dress, a day dress, and a good dress for Sundays. Work dresses were old dresses. Even after the invention of the sewing machine, only hoop skirts and cloaks could be manufactured for women. Fashionable one-piece fitted dresses were impossible to mass produce because each dress had to be custom made to fit at least three sets of usually irregular measurements.

[8] Ibid., p. 99.

Mass Production of Women's Separates

The introduction of separate blouses and skirts in the 1880s made it possible to manufacture ready-to-wear clothes for women. A blouse could be made to fit the shoulder and bust measurements, the skirt to fit the hips. Waistlines and hemlines were easily adjusted and blouses were simply tucked in. This innovation made it possible for the working or middle-class woman to add variety to her wardrobe simply by mixing separates. The cost of a new "ready-made" blouse was a mere fraction of the cost of a custom-tailored dress.

The "Gibson Girl" Look

The Gibson Girl was the personification of the ideal young middle-class American woman, as sketched by popular illustrator Charles Dana Gibson in the 1890s. The Gibson Girl gave style to the basic high-necked, long-sleeved blouse-and-skirt look. It was practical yet feminine and could be worn anywhere. By 1900 the American labor force included more than 5.3 million women at all levels of the social scale, properly attired in practical blouses and skirts.

Besides some businessman's suits and the working woman's blouse and skirt, the only other manufactured clothes were uniforms or working men's gear. Both Levis and the Gibson Girl look paved the way for the simplified, functional dress that typifies American fashion.

A young woman dressed in the Gibson Girl style
(Courtesy of the National Archives, Washington, D.C.)

CHILDREN'S FASHION

The wealthy were the only ones who had money to spend on fashionable children's clothes; members of the middle and working classes made their children's clothes at home. Small children, both girls and boys, wore dresses—perhaps the first attempt at "unisex" fashion. As they grew older, children were supposed to act like adults, and they were dressed in miniature versions of adult apparel. In fact, many children wore cut-down remakes of their parents' old clothes. Mothers were particularly grateful for the advent of patterns for children's clothes.

COMMERCIAL PATTERNS FOR HOME USE

A logical development after the invention of the sewing machine was the idea of commercial patterns. Before their introduction, home-sewn garments were cut and fitted by trial and error.

The first paper patterns were displayed in 1850 in Philadelphia by Ellen and William Demorest.[9] The patterns were well received, and the Demorests brought out the first issues of "Madame Demorest's Mirror of Fashions" in 1860 in New York. One could order patterns by mail from their quarterly magazine, which showed engravings of French-inspired fashions. Finding Americans more conservative than the French, the Demorests adapted European styles to American taste.

There were also European pattern companies, but Demorest did more business than the English and French companies together. Patterns from Demorest, followed by Butterick in 1863 and McCall's in 1870, fostered fashion consciousness on all levels of society. Women on small budgets were especially happy to have patterns to make the clothes they could never afford to buy.

RETAILING DURING THE NINETEENTH CENTURY

Fairs and bazaars, regaining popularity today, were the predecessors of the retail store. The traveling merchant brought clothes to and from these markets. Expensive goods were shown only to selected wealthy customers. Prices were not marked on the merchandise, so buyer and seller usually bargained over the price.

As large numbers of people settled in towns, the first general stores were established to cater to their desire for wider assortments of merchandise. Also, craftspeople sold their handmade goods in their own shops. Regulated by the Guilds, these shops were grouped together by trade.

The Industrial Revolution triggered a self-supporting manufacturing and retailing cycle. As more goods were produced, there were more products to sell and increased business activity gave the growing middle class more money to spend which created a demand for more products. This growing demand for the variety of goods being produced was the basis for the growth of retailing. The new breed of retail stores grew up in the cities, close to production and population centers. As more people clustered in cities to work, stores opened in areas convenient to shoppers.

Two types of stores finally emerged to bring fashion to the public: the specialty store and the department store. Traditional handicraft stores evolved into specialty stores which grew in importance in the late nineteenth and early twentieth centuries. An outgrowth of the general store, the department store, that carried a wide variety of merchandise, developed as a product of the nineteenth century. Shopping in department stores became a popular activity, like going to an exhibition. For the first time, people of all incomes could at least enjoy browsing and looking at beautiful things.

The First Department Stores

In 1826, Samuel Lord and George Washington Taylor formed a partnership to open the first Lord and Taylor store in New York City. Jordan Marsh and Company, opening in Boston, claimed that they could sell, cut, sew, trim, and furnish a dress in half a day.[10] Edward Filene opened a comparable department store in Boston; John Wanamaker in Philadelphia; Joseph Hudson in Detroit; Morris Rich in Atlanta; and R. H. Macy, Nathan Straus, B. Altman, and Adam Gimbel in New York. Remarkably, all of these stores are still prospering after 100 years; Macy's Herald Square is now the largest store in the United States.

The American contribution to retailing is not only size but also customer service. In Chicago, Marshall Field admonished a store clerk who was arguing with a customer, "Give the lady what she wants." "The customer is always right" has been a principle of American retailing ever since.

9 Ibid., p. 20.

10 Ibid., p. 116.

John Wanamaker's Grand Depot store (formerly a Pennsylvania Railroad freight station) in 1877, located on the same site as today's 12-story building in Philadelphia (Courtesy of Carter Hawley Hale Stores, Inc.)

Harrod's of London, established by Henry Harrod in 1849, has become the largest department store in Europe. It began as a small grocery store and expanded until it had 100 employees by 1880. Liberty of London opened its retail store in 1875 and produced its own prints as early as 1878. In France, department stores such as the Bon Marché, Samaritaine, and Printemps opened in the nineteenth century.

Early Mail Order Merchandizing

In 1872, nearly three quarters of the American population lived in rural areas, usually served only by a few general stores with limited selection. The extension of the railroads to the West Coast and the inauguration of a free rural mail delivery provided the opportunity to start mail order services to reach these potential consumers.

While working for a wholesaling firm, traveling to country stores by horse and buggy, Aaron Montgomery Ward conceived the idea of selling directly to country people by mail. He opened his business in 1872 with a one-page list of items that cost one dollar each. People could order goods through a distributed catalog, and the store would ship the merchandise cash-on-delivery. The idea was slow to catch on because people were suspicious of a strange name. However, in 1875 Ward announced the startling policy of "satisfaction guaranteed or your money back." Contrasting with the former retailing principle of *caveat emptor* (Latin for *buyer beware*), this set off a boom in Ward's business.

In 1886 Richard Sears accidentally entered the mail order watch business. A Chicago jewelry company erroneously shipped some watches to a jeweler in Sears's home town in Minnesota. Sears offered to resell them for the jeweler, creating his own watch business. As the business grew, some earlier customers complained about watches that needed repairing. Therefore, Sears placed a newspaper ad: "WANTED: Watchmaker with reference who can furnish tools. State age, experience, and salary required. Address T39, Daily News." Alvah Roebuck answered the ad and was hired on April 1, 1887. He and Sears became business partners, and in 1893 the firm name was changed to Sears, Roebuck and Company. From a modest beginning they expanded by 1895 to a 507-page catalog including clothing and household goods, often referred to as the "dream book" or "wish book." The mail order business did more to bring a variety of up-to-date merchandise to rural consumers than any other form of retailing.

THE EFFECT OF COMMUNICATIONS ON FASHION CHANGE

The desire for fashionable clothing was fostered by its increased availability as well as by the invention of new communications media such as the mail service, magazines, newspapers, telephone, automobile, airplane, and later the radio, motion pictures, and television.

First Fashion Magazines
Magazines quickly spread the news of the latest fashion trends. During the 1800s fashion magazines began to be published in France and England. These publications spread the latest fashion ideas from Paris by means of sketches and descriptions. Dressmakers in other countries copied the styles as best they could with available fabrics.

Popular American fashion magazines included *Godey's Ladies Book* (published from 1830 to 1898) and *Leslie's Ladies Gazette* (from 1855 until 1922). Eighteen fashion magazines were being published in New York and Philadelphia in the late 1800s.[11] Two magazines that began in the nineteenth century are still published today. An outgrowth of *Harper's* and modeled after *Der Bazar* magazine of Berlin, *Harper's Bazaar* commenced publication in both New York and Paris in 1867. *Vogue* started in 1894 in New York. In London, *Queen* magazine, now merged with *Harper's*, began in 1861. Regularly featured were reports on Paris fashion worn by prominent women to smart restaurants, the theatre, the races—or just strolling down the Champs Elysees. However, French protocol dictated that the couture house could not be mentioned, as women of society did not want their names connected with advertising. For this reason, it is impossible to learn from magazines who was the most popular trend-setting couturier (creating styles that others copied), until 1910, when the fashion press was permitted to see the collections.

As more women became aware of fashion styles through magazines and other forms of mass communication, their desire to wear those fashions increased. The faster a style was adopted by the entire public, the greater the demand was for more new looks.

THE ENTERTAINMENT WORLD'S INFLUENCE ON FASHION

Around 1900 leading stage actresses such as Sarah Bernhardt had the magnetism, taste, and glamour needed to exert fashion influence. Their profession brought them before the public, providing an excellent show vehicle for designers. Realizing the value of publicity as a means of increasing their popularity, actresses were willing to be photographed for fashion magazines.

Broadway, with its vaudeville revues, musicals, comedies, and occasional drama, became the capital of live entertainment in the United States. Florenz Ziegfeld filled his stages with dramatically attired, beautiful women and spectacular productions called Follies.

In 1911 Irene and Vernon Castle, a famous American dance team, became the "rage" of Paris. Irene Castle's grace and boyish youthfulness epitomized the new era of simplicity and she had a great impact on fashion. When she "bobbed" her hair in 1913, women throughout the Western world cut their hair short, for the first time in history.

THE EFFECT OF SPORTS ON FASHION

Need for Functional Sportswear
The popularity of sports for women, such as tennis and bicycling, created a need for functional sportswear. As early as 1851 Amelia Jenks Bloomer had tried to introduce pants for women. However, they were not accepted until the 1890s, when the bicycling craze created a real functional need for them. "Bloomers," full in the leg and gathered at the ankle, were also worn under bathing dresses. Finally, after 1900, swimwear was pared down enough that people could actually swim in it.

Pants became an acceptable part of the horse riding "habit" for women about the turn of the century, when women discovered that riding sidesaddle in a skirt "often caused one to dismount before the ride was over."[12] As women became more and more involved in sports, pants gave them the mobility for a more active life. However, it was not until the 1920s that pants became fashionable as well as functional.

---

[11] Ibid., p. 220.

[12] "Women's Pants," *L'Officiel USA*, Spring Collections, 1977, p. 109.

GARMENT INDUSTRY CONDITIONS AT THE TURN OF THE CENTURY

New York as Center of the Industry

Until 1850 the garment business in the United States was concentrated in Boston, Philadelphia, and Baltimore. By the latter part of the century, however, the influx of European immigrants to New York helped lead to the establishment of New York as the center of the American garment industry. The immigrants, used to hardship and willing to work for low wages, provided the skilled labor the industry needed to grow. By 1900 the American women's clothing industry consisted of 2,701 establishments.[13] They produced mostly cloaks and suits, with some shirtwaists (blouses) and underwear.

Unionization

As more workers crowded into the industry, working conditions became appalling. Tenement workrooms were known as sweatshops because of the excessively long hours required of laborers in unsanitary surroundings for extremely low wages.

In 1900 cloakmakers, mostly immigrants living in cities in the northern United States, met to discuss working conditions. The result was the formation of the International Ladies' Garment Workers Union, to try to protect themselves against unfair employers. At first the union was not very popular, but it did make progress with a strike against the shirtwaist industry in 1909 and the cloak industry in 1910. "On March 25, 1911, the nation was stunned by the horror of the Triangle Shirtwaist Company fire in New York City."[14] The main exit door to the factory had been bolted and the lone fire escape was a death trap that ended in mid-air. The 146 deaths, mostly of young girls, aroused Americans' indignation against the plight of the sweatshop workers. Finally, action was taken on demands for regular hours, minimum wages, paid vacations, sick benefits, and better working conditions. Added labor costs naturally added to the inevitable simplification of fashion.

[13] Florence S. Richards, *The Ready to Wear Industry 1900–1950* (New York: Fairchild Publications, 1951), p. 8.

[14] *Signature of 450,000* (New York: International Ladies' Garment Workers Union, 1965), p. 24.

EFFECTS OF WORLD WAR I ON THE STATUS OF WOMEN AND ON FASHION

Women's Status Based on Their Role in Business

The status of women has hinged firmly on the working world. Without a prominent place in business, women had no authority and no rights. Male dominance was hard to overcome, and the old patterns did not begin to change until the period around World War I. In 1914 the war began in Europe; the United States finally entered the war in 1917. World War I greatly promoted women's rights, because European and American women replaced men in previously all-male jobs. Women ran trolley cars, delivered packages, drove taxis, and became mechanics. The functional working clothes worn by these women had a great impact on fashion. *Vogue* reported in 1918, "Now that women work, working clothes have acquired a new social status and a new chic."[15]

[15] Quoted in Brockman, *The Theory of Fashion Design*, p. 69.

A woman welder at a Lincoln Motor Company plant during World War I *(Courtesy of the National Archives, Washington, D.C.)*

Clothes Tailored to Suit Jobs

Clothing was making a visual assertion that women were as useful as men. There was a trend toward masculinity in women's fashion; decorative details disappeared in favor of a tailored look that imitated businessmen's suits. Corsets were discarded and the curved hourglass silhouette was replaced by the tube. Hemlines rose and skirts widened to permit freedom of movement. Colors became somber. Fashion reflected women's growing independence. Women finally won the right to vote, in 1918 in England and in 1920 in the United States. (Women's right to vote had already been recognized in New Zealand in 1893, in Australia in 1902, in Finland in 1906, and in Norway in 1913.)

Important Designers of the Early Twentieth Century

Fashion Trend Setter: Paul Poiret

While mass production was growing in the American fashion industry, the French couture still concentrated on fashion leadership among the wealthy. Couture styles were then copied by mass producers for consumers at every price level.

Often in the recent history of fashion, one designer or a few designers have reigned supreme because they were able to capture the spirit of their times and translate it into highly accepted fashion. The first Paris couturier to become such a style trend setter was Paul Poiret (Pwah-ray'). He not only designed clothes for women; he *told* his clients what to wear. His strong personality captivated his customers, who seemed to enjoy the security of having decisions made for them.

Poiret began as an apprentice to an umbrella maker. Very unhappy, he spent nights sketching clothing designs. In 1901, after working for Jacques Doucet, he found a job at the House of Worth, then under the management of Charles Worth's sons Jean and Gaston. Poiret designed there until 1904, when he opened a salon of his own with money borrowed from his mother. He married a simple country woman who developed into a showpiece for his creations. Her slim figure required no corsets under his first modern, straight-lined dress, and

Poiret proceeded to "liberate all women from their shackles of bone and steel. . . . Poiret interpreted the change in the position of women and helped them in their emergence from the strictly ornamental position they had occupied to that time. He knew where they were going and was able to lead them there."[16]

Unfortunately, at the height of his career Poiret was called into military service at the outbreak of World War I. Official army papers listed his occupation as "tailor," and he eventually designed a new army uniform and was put in charge of all uniform production. But he was very unhappy and totally unsuited to disciplined army life. When Poiret returned to his business at the end of the war, fashion had changed and his clothes were no longer sought after. Opulence had faded with World War I and the fickle public had moved on to a new favorite. Poiret's fashion ideas had been the mirror of his time. Yet, due to his strong individuality, he was unable to change or even to understand the understated look that had replaced his colorful, bold approach to fashion. By the end of the 1920s he was forced to live on the charity of family and friends, and he died penniless in 1944.

[16] Ibid., p. 36.

Paul Poiret *(Courtesy of the National Archives, Washington, D.C.)*

Fashion Innovator: Madelaine Vionnet

After serving a 15-year apprenticeship as a *midinette* (seamstress) at Callot Sisters, Madelaine Vionnet (Vee-o-nay') rose to the position of manager of the Callot Sisters' branch in London. She opened her own Paris salon in 1914; it closed during the war but reopened in 1917.

Vionnet's creative spirit inspired other designers, who admired her originality. A truly innovative designer, Vionnet made one of the greatest contributions to fashion: the bias cut. Before Vionnet, garment pieces were normally cut on the lengthwise grain of the fabric. Vionnet began cutting each piece on the diagonal, which made garments flow and drape much more softly. She also developed other unusual approaches to design: the asymmetrical neckline, the halter neckline, the cowl neckline, and the handkerchief skirt.

One of Vionnet's very successful designs featured a new fabric called *crêpe de chine* (krep de sheen', French term for silk crepe from China). The garment had no lining, depending on the cut alone to give it shape. Her cuts were so intricate and her fit so subtle that it was impossible to copy her designs without taking them apart. Vionnet's influence was apparent in other designers' collections during the 1920s and '30s. Vionnet designed for an exclusive private clientele; other designers like Gabrielle Chanel and Jean Patou, who were more stylists and publicists, reinterpreted her ideas for impact on a larger public. In later years Vionnet was so anxious to avoid being copied that even the fashion magazines had difficulty photographing her designs, making it impossible to give her the credit she deserved.

Coco Chanel photographed by Horst about 1925
(Courtesy of the House of Chanel, Paris)

Fashion Trend Setter: Gabrielle Chanel

Despite Vionnet's technical mastery, the postwar period found Gabrielle Chanel (Sha-nelle'), also known as Coco, at the forefront of French fashion. Chanel first opened a shop in Deauville, where she designed millinery. In her Paris studio established in 1914, Chanel with her small, boyish figure was the prototype of the fashionable woman in postwar Paris. The new look visually expressed women's new freedom. Chanel felt it was smart to look neither feminine nor rich; to her, clothes were not as important as personal style. Carried to the extreme, her style included even a nonchalant way of standing and walking called the slouch.

Chanel popularized the *Garçon* (gar-sohn', meaning boyish) look with sweaters and jersey dresses. The feminine ideal had always favored the mature woman, but the 1920s saw the beginning of a desire for eternal youth. Chanel herself stated, "Always dress to make yourself feel young."[17] She was also the first to make high-fashion pants, popularizing the new category of "sportswear" for informal occasions. By the late '30s, Chanel felt that she was no longer relating to the new, structured look in fashion, and she decided to retire.

[17] Ibid., p. 39.

Chanel trouser suit of 1937, photographed by Cecil Beaton
(Crown Copyright, Victoria and Albert Museum)

THE MATURING
READY-TO-WEAR INDUSTRY

The ready-to-wear apparel industry began to prosper when Poiret, Vionnet, and Chanel simplified styles and thereby construction. Because individual fitting was not so important to their straight silhouettes, mass production of dresses became practical. Chanel liked to be copied. "I am not an artist," she insisted; "I want my dresses to go out on the street." [18] As early as the 1920s, designers such as Lucien Lelong in France and Hattie Carnegie in America were adding ready-to-wear lines to their made-to-order collections.[19] By the late 1920s American ready-to-wear was firmly established.

[18] "Chanel No. 1," *Time*, January 25, 1971, p. 38.

[19] Carter, *The Changing World of Fashion*, p. 73.

THE MOOD
OF THE ROARING TWENTIES

The postwar period saw new economic prosperity and shorter working hours; everyone seemed to have money to spend and more leisure time in which to spend it. Moreover, the reaction of women to their new-found freedoms, coupled with exuberant Jazz music that expressed the optimism of the time, helped make the "Roaring Twenties" an age that catered to the young.

Makeup added to the gaiety: rouge, lipstick, mascara, and eye shadow. Skirts grew shorter and shorter until hems were above the knees. Chanel popularized costume jewelry and long strands of beads. Flapping dresses with long ropes of costume jewelry coined the name of both the young, reckless woman and the fashion of the twenties—the "Flapper."

Fashion Trend Setter: Jean Patou

Paris in the 1920s was a cultural meeting ground for artists and writers. The exchange of their ideas created the exceptional atmosphere needed for fashion innovation. In addition, the fashion world was beginning to realize the power of publicity. In 1921 Jean Patou (Gsahn Pa-too') was the first member of the haute couture to open his collection showings to the press. As a result, Patou became one of the most financially successful couturiers.

Jean Patou and his American models arriving at le Havre in 1924 *(Courtesy of the National Archives, Washington, D.C.)*

Like those of the trend setters before him, Patou's designs captured the siprit of his time. He created the famous Flapper look in 1925 by accentuating the hipline, strengthening a straight silhouette, and making shorter skirts with uneven hemlines. These changes added excitement and exaggeration to the Vionnet-inspired body-skimming dress that slipped over the head.

RETAIL EXPANSION
IN THE EARLY TWENTIETH CENTURY

Production and consumer spending were at all-time highs in the 1920s. Consumers wanted more exciting places to buy clothing. Although wealthy Europeans went directly to designer salons in Paris to shop, most Americans bought ready-to-wear copies in retail stores.

Specialty Stores for Quality Fashion

Specialty stores tried new retailing approaches and offered their customers high-fashion merchandise. Bergdorf Goodman and Saks Fifth Avenue in New York City and Neiman-Marcus in Dallas concentrated solely on the finest quality fashion and customer service. By the 1930s the first female presidents of major retail firms were installed, at Lord and Taylor and Bonwit Teller. Dorothy Shaver and Hortense Odlam, respectively, set new directions in sophisticated store images.

Expansion of Chain Stores

While great retailing establishments were growing in the big cities, chain stores selling lower-priced merchandise were taking hold elsewhere. James Cash Penney (whose middle name may have inspired his cash-and-carry policy) was such an industrious employee at a small Wyoming store that the owners offered him a partnership in their new store in 1902. Called the Golden Rule Store in honor of their belief in high business standards, it proved an immediate success, in part because of his door-to-door advertising campaign.

In 1907 the original partners sold their shares to Penney; the store's name was officially changed to J. C. Penney in 1912. When the chain store concept caught on in the '20s, Penney opened stores in all parts of the United States. By 1927 there were more than 800 Penney stores.[20]

Advent of Suburban Retail Centers

People's mobility increased as more and more of them owned cars, creating a revolution in retailing. Finding that its mail order business was dropping off, Sears, Roebuck opened stores not in the city centers but rather near the highways, where they could offer free parking. The Country Club Plaza in Kansas City was the first outdoor shopping center.

EFFECT OF THE DEPRESSION
ON ECONOMICS AND FASHION

Bursting of the Credit Bubble

The sense of economic security in the 1920s was unfortunately false. As installment buying became popular, so much credit was extended that there was no longer any real money to back it up. In the stock market a person needed to put up only 10 percent of the price to buy stock; when the price rose, the shares could be sold at a profit. So it went until September 3, 1929, when the stock market reached an unbelievable height. Then it started a steep decline. In less than a month the market value of all stocks dropped by $30 billion. Unemployment rose from 1.5 million to 12.8 million, and business profits fell from $10.3 billion to a net loss of $2 billion. Nearly half of the nation's banks had to close.[21] The slump set off a chain reaction that soon put the whole world into a depression. The carefree '20s were over.

The Industrial Slump

Industrial production fell to half of what it had been and many companies went out of business altogether. Millions of workers were jobless, and those still working suffered wage cuts. Even drastic reductions in prices failed to attract customers. Humorist Will Rogers commented that things were so bad that even the people who didn't intend to pay had stopped buying.

Eventually, the United States recovered, partly by means of its own confidence. However, although the people's mood began to improve, the Depression did not really end until World War II escalated production.

Hollywood's Influence on Fashion

Americans tried to take their minds off the Depression by means of radio and movies. Radio became the home center of entertainment, offering a wide variety of comedy, music, mysteries, westerns, and dramatic plays.

Movies were better than ever at providing an escape from reality. Film actresses became the new fashion ideals. Americans daydreamed about the glamorous life styles and wealth depicted in the movies: the expensive wardrobes and jewelry of Claudette Colbert, Rosalind Russell, Joan Crawford, Katherine Hepburn, Bette Davis, Jeannette Mac-

[20] Evelyn Grace, *Introduction to Fashion Merchandising* (Englewood Cliffs, N.J.: Prentice-Hall, Inc., 1978), p. 41.

[21] Philipp Frings, *Berichterstattung Deutscher und Amerikanischer Aktiengesellschaften im Jährlichen Geschäftsbericht* (Bonn: Rheinische Friedrich-Wilhelms-Universität, 1975), p. 130.

**Joan Crawford glances admiringly at Adrian,
Hollywood designer of the 1930s.
She is wearing one of his designs.**
(*Courtesy of the Joseph Simms Collections*)

Donald, Jean Harlow, Eleanor Powell, and Ginger Rogers; and the charm and style of their leading men like Clark Gable, Spencer Tracy, Lawrence Olivier, Cary Grant, and Fred Astaire. The 1930s were the most glamorous years in film history, a paradoxical contrast to the deprivation of real life.

The image of women in movies was very positive. Women were not only charming and appealing, but also intelligent, witty, and efficient. The smartly tailored suit, revived for women in the mid-30s and seen in the movies, was adopted by every style-conscious working woman in the country. The neighborhood movie theater brought fashion to every woman. Yet reality was often a woman in a house dress, out of work. A production number in the film *Fashions of 1934* shows her dreaming of an unattainable glamorous life.

Shirley Temple, America's sweetheart child star, had an enormous effect on the children's wear industry. Every mother wanted her daughter to look just like Shirley, in fluffy little dresses and ringlet curls.

The demand for leisure sportswear continued to grow, especially with Clark Gable popularizing the sport shirt. Slacks and shorts became popular for both men and women, as Marlene Dietrich films demonstrated.

Film costume designers had a great impact on ready-to-wear. For example, Gilbert Adrian designed a ruffled dress with puffed sleeves for Joan Crawford in 1932; her "Letty Lynton" film audience could not wait to buy a simplified version at an affordable price. Macy's alone sold half a million copies.[22]

The Joan Crawford dress was made of rayon, the new synthetic fiber created to imitate silk. Nylon, too, was introduced in the late 1930s, the first of a whole new wave of synthetics. Nylon stockings soon replaced the more fragile and expensive silk.

European Hypersophistication

The United States and Europe reacted somewhat differently to the '30s. In continental Europe it was a time of pessimism, as expressed in Salvador Dali's art and the decadent cabaret entertainment in Berlin; a sense that war was imminent combined with the economic depression. Humor was expressed sarcastically. In clothing it appeared as hypersophistication. Marlene Dietrich was the epitome of all that the '30s were in Europe. She found her ideal designer in Elsa Schiaparelli (Ska-pa-rell'-ee).[23]

[22] Carter, *The Changing World of Fashion*, p. 70.
[23] Brockman, *The Theory of Fashion Design*, p. 48.

Fashion Trend Setter: Elsa Schiaparelli

Elsa Schiaparelli, born in Rome, was the design trend setter of the 1930s. With a background in the arts, she had a natural sensitivity to fashion styling. Famous for her audacious improvisations, she truly did design the unusual.

In the mid-'20s, "Schiap" got her start in Paris by sketching a sweater and having it made by an American craftswoman. The black sweater had a large white bow motif on its front, actually knitted into the sweater. At the time it was such a novel idea that Schiaparelli immediately received an order from an American buyer. Her sweater designs fitted in perfectly with the surrealistic art of the time. One looked like an X-ray view of the chest, with white ribs outlined on a black background—the forerunner of the decorated T-shirt.

Schiaparelli's first salon opened in 1927 and called Pour le Sport, specialized in sportswear and suits. She used bold accents of color, especially "shocking pink," which she made famous.

When the Depression put an end to frivolity, it also ended the Flapper Look. The waist returned to its normal position and skirts lengthened to below the knee. In addition, Schiaparelli moved the center of interest to the shoulders, which she began to widen, accentuating them by pleats, padding, or braid—a silhouette that remained popular through World War II. Often called "hard chic," her designs were smart rather than pretty. Schiaparelli used the bias cut for dresses, giving them a sensuous, clinging look to show off the female figure. Very photogenic because of their bold statements, her designs dominated the fashion magazines.

Schiaparelli's daring nonsensical gadget accessories, like fish buttons, foxhead gloves, and newspaper print scarves, were just the right touch for the last frivolous, decadent years before World War II. Schiaparelli also had a personal interest in her clients, often trying to help them find the clothes best suited to their type. She believed that clothes should suit one's life style.

Design by Schiaparelli (Courtesy of Claudy Stolz and Maison Schiaparelli, Paris)

Elsa Schiaparelli at home with her daughter Gogo (Courtesy of Claudy Stolz and Maison Schiaparelli, Paris)

Fashion Trend Setter: James Mainbocher

James Main Bocher was born in the United States in 1891. He began his fashion career as an illustrator at *Harper's Bazaar* in Paris and then at French *Vogue*, where he moved up to become editor, a position he held for six years. In 1929 he left *Vogue* because he felt he could contribute more to fashion as a designer. First, however, he had to learn how to drape, cut, and fit.

As "Mainbocher" (Main-bow-shay', his names combined and given a French pronunciation), he opened his salon in Paris in 1930. His immediate success was due partially to American patrons, happy that an American had joined the Paris couture. Mainbocher was the first American designer to succeed in Europe. He once said, "I try to design clothes that are related to life and to the body, believing as I do that my job is to establish a liaison between designing and living." [24]

In 1937 King Edward VIII of England created the scandal of the decade by abdicating his throne to marry the divorced American Wallis Simpson. Partly due to publicity, partly because of her luxurious life style, and partly because of her fashion sensitivity, the future Duchess of Windsor became a fashion leader. Her selection of a wedding dress designed by Mainbocher, which became the most copied dress of the era, made him a trend setter.

Fashion Trend Setter: Edward Molyneaux

Another top couturier of the 1930s, Edward Molyneaux (Molly-no') opened his first salon in Paris in 1919 after serving as a captain in the British army. Best known for his understated, exquisitely tailored clothes, he also designed for the English court.

A Mainbocher jacket designed for the Duchess of Windsor in 1938, photographed by Cecil Beaton *(Crown Copyright, Victoria and Albert Museum)*

FASHION EVOLUTION INTERRUPTED BY WORLD WAR II

America Cut off from Paris Fashion

The outbreak of the Second World War in 1939 cut American communication with the fashion world of Paris. Because he was an American, Mainbocher was forced to return to New York, where he reestablished a salon.

During this period the French couture banded together under the leadership of Lucien Lelong, then president of the Paris Couture Syndicale (see chapter 8), to prevent their being sent to Berlin. Under great restrictions and privation, most barely managed to stay in business, with practically no fabrics to work with, no trimmings, no press coverage, no heat, and little food. Some were forced to close. Of course, under these circumstances little was achieved.

[24] Ibid., p. 72.

American Fashion Directions

Isolated from Paris fashion leadership during the war, Americans had to find their own style direction. The lack of imports from France was actually a boon to the development of American talent. In 1940 *Vogue* reported on the New York collection openings, and retail stores such as Lord and Taylor promoted American designers. With Mainbocher as an example of success, Americans also began to appreciate designers such as Hatti Carnegie, Vera Maxwell, Nettie Rosenstein, and Claire McCardle. McCardle, considered the top American designer, was credited with originating the "American Look" in practical separates, borrowing ideas from the work clothes of farmers, railroad engineers, soldiers, and sportsmen.

American designs reflected both the American life style and the American manufacturing style. The trend toward outdoor living called for play clothes, which were suited to mass production methods because they were easy to construct. American designers became especially skilled at and known for their sportswear, which would eventually influence the rest of the world.

Fashion remained relatively stable during the war years. Women doing war work wore uniforms or work clothes. "Rosie the Riveter" symbolized women taking over men's jobs, and functional clothes became a necessity.

Government Regulation of Fashion

The United States government's wartime regulation L-85 restricted the use of fabric to 3-½ yards per garment. This obviously limited innovation in fashion. Hems could not exceed two inches; there could be no ruffles and no cuffs on coats or suits for men and women; and only one patch pocket was permitted. Zippers were not allowed; this rule fostered the wrap-around skirt. The most practical costume for a woman was a suit that could be accessorized differently for day or evening. The suit was an exaggeration of Mainbocher's silhouette, with even more padding at the shoulders as well as a slimming down and shortening of the skirt in keeping with the L-85 yardage restriction. The result was a masculine silhouette for the women who shouldered the responsibilities of men who were away at war.

Accent on Youth

During World War II youth were again in the spotlight, this time because young men were the national heroes. Since most of those in their twenties were involved in the war, attention was also given to their younger siblings at home. The result was the creation of a new phenomenon—the teenager. Before this time there were only adolescents, in the awkward time between childhood and adulthood. There were no special clothes for them, just smaller versions of their parents' clothes. Now teenagers could earn money at odd jobs because of the labor shortage, and wherever there is a market, business caters to it. Industry produced records, cosmetics, magazines, and "junior" fashions specifically for teens. Known as "bobby-soxers" for their distinctive attire, both boys and girls wore thick white socks, loafers or saddle shoes, and oversized shirts with the tails hanging out over a pair of dungarees (now called jeans).

Wartime also saw the beginning of the biggest increase of births ever. The postwar baby boom was to have a great effect on the fashion industry in the 1960s and '70s. This increase of births reflected a return to traditional male and female roles and a longing for family life and security after the ravages of war.

REACTIONARY POSTWAR FASHION

Emphasis on Femininity

The end of World War II had the opposite effect on society from that of World War I, which had brought women position in the world. Women were so happy to see their men home alive after the devastating war, that most reverted completely to stereotypical feminine roles, leaving jobs open for the returning men. In addition, of course, women were tired of the clothes made under wartime restrictions. They were ready for change.

Feminine contours in fashion and images of the scatterbrained wife (Lucille Ball) and the dumb blond (Marilyn Monroe) prevailed throughout the 1950s. Even men's suit silhouettes flaunted the large shoulders and slim, straight figure of the ideal male.

Fashion Trend Setter: Christian Dior

It is no wonder that when Christian Dior (Chris'-tee-ahn' Dee-or'), even though still an unknown designer, opened his first collection in 1947, it revolutionized fashion. The gradual evolution of fashion had been halted by the war so that a change in silhouette was long overdue.

Although he was called into the army, poor health put Dior back into civilian life. He found work with the House of Lelong, where Pierre Balmain (Pee-air' Bal-man') was currently designing. When Balmain opened his own salon, Dior took over his position as designer at Lucien Lelong. Then in 1946, Marcel Boussac (Mar-sell' Boo-sak'), a wealthy industrialist and famous name in French fabrics, offered to back Dior in a salon. Lelong, eager to re-

Christian Dior sketching design ideas
(Courtesy of Christian Dior, New York)

establish the French couture, unselfishly encouraged him to accept the offer.

Within a few seasons Dior's name was a household word and he was doing as much business as the rest of the couture combined.[25] His collections included something to please everyone: his private made-to-order clientele, retail store buyers, and wholesalers who were buying copyrights.

Dior had an intuitive sense of what women were ready to accept in fashion. His "New Look" capitalized on everything that was the reverse of wartime styles, stressing the most feminine of silhouettes.

Paris recaptured fashion dominance—almost to the point of dictatorship in Dior's case, as women of all heights actually measured their hems 12 inches from the ground. His look infiltrated fashion for women of all ages, in every Western country. American manufacturers sold millions of bouffant petticoats in the 13 years after their popularization by Dior.

In his book, *Talking About Fashion,* Dior explained, "No one person can change fashion—a big fashion change imposes itself. It was because women longed to look like women again that they adopted the New Look, with longer fuller skirts, and smooth rounded sloping shoulders and tiny fitted waists. The change was due to a universal change of feeling, of atmosphere. Fashions are not put over on women."[26]

Dior maintained his fashion leadership for ten years, until his death of a heart attack in 1957.

Fashion Innovator: Cristobal Balenciaga

Paris recaptured its earlier position mainly because of Dior and another strong talent, Cristobal Balenciaga (Bah-lehn'-see-ah'-gah). After an apprenticeship in a Madrid couture shop, Balenciaga opened three shops of his own, called Eisa, in Madrid, Barcelona, and San Sebastian, Spain. He made regular trips to Paris for fabrics, and then in 1936, when the Spanish Civil War interrupted business in Spain, he moved to Paris to bring out his first collection in 1937. Balenciaga's life was his work. He was a perfectionist, the only member of the postwar couture who could actually make every one of his garments if necessary. He was regarded as the master of tailors.

Balenciaga wanted his clothes to be comfortable. He used as few seams as possible, even creating a unique one-seam coat. His sophisticated dresses were usually in black or earth tones, with lace or other trimmings in keeping with his Spanish heritage. His fashions were not revolutionary, yet he always seemed to be ahead of other designers. In 1945 he was already making suits that were

Dior's New Look *(Courtesy of Christian Dior, New York)*

the forerunners of Dior's New Look in 1947. He also preempted Dior's A-line silhouette and shift, perhaps a little too early for the public. Dior capitalized on Balenciaga's styling but added publicity and good timing.

Balenciaga did not stand out as the most powerful trend setter, simply because he *wanted* to stay in the background, like Vionnet. Balenciaga's reticence dictated that fashion magazines could photograph no more than two of his models per issue.

Not until the late 1950s and early '60s, when "line-for-line" copies were popular in the United States, did Balenciaga finally give in and sell some designs for export. Stores like Alexanders and Orbach's in New York made a name by purchasing rights to couturier designs and having exact copies, even to the same fabrics, manufactured in America. Balenciaga's designs were always the most popular of those that were produced.

Last Major Influence of the French Couture

The influence of the French couture continued with Hubert de Givenchy (Sh-vahn'-shee'), a disciple of Balenciaga, and Yves St. Laurent (Eave Sahn' Law-rahn'), who briefly took over for Dior before going on his own.

One of the fashion surprises of the 1950s was the comeback of Coco Chanel at age 71! Chanel felt that the time was again right for her designs. By 1960 her collarless tweed suits were being copied everywhere. She died in 1971 at age 88, still active in her business, having twice been a worldwide fashion influence.

[25] Charlotte Calasibetta, *Fairchild's Dictionary of Fashion* (New York: Fairchild Publications, 1975), p. 561.

[26] Christian Dior, *Talking About Fashion* (New York: G. P. Putnam's Sons, 1954), p. 23.

In the United States, American designers were finally being appreciated for their talent and skills.

Bonnie Cashin specialized in comfortable country and travel clothes.

Oleg Cassini, born in Italy, designed fitted dresses called sheaths and became designer for Jackie Kennedy.

Ann Fogarty, a designer of junior dresses, is remembered for her full-skirted, tiny-waisted shirt-dresses.

James Galanos, a Californian, created expensive, elegant day and evening ensembles in the couture tradition.

Charles James, born in England, created new shapes in dress forms and elaborate ball gowns, also in the couture manner.

Anne Klein, well known for her classic sportswear, designed for Jr. Sophisticates in the 1950s.

Claire McCardell, regarded as the top American designer of the 1950s, originated an American concept in separates and casual fashion.

Norman Norell, called the dean of the American fashion industry, was famous for precision tailoring, purity of line, and conservative elegance.

Mollie Parnis, in partnership with her husband, Louis Livingston, specialized in flattering feminine dresses in her ready-to-wear collections.

Fernando Sarmi, born in Italy and chief designer at Elizabeth Arden in the 1950s, was recognized for romantic evening clothes and elegant daytime combinations.

Arnold Scaasi, one of the few custom designers in America, was known for spectacular evening wear.

Adele Simpson is famous for pretty, feminine dresses and ensembles for women with conservative taste.

Jacques Tiffeau, born in France, designed uncluttered, youthful clothes for Monte Sano & Pruzan in New York.

Pauline Trigere, also originally from France, specialized in coats, capes, suits, and dresses cut intricately to flatter mature figures.

Sydney Wragge, whose clothes were status symbols in the 1950s, pioneered the concept of coordinated sportswear.

Ben Zuckerman, born in Rumania, was New York's master tailor, creator of quality suits and coats for day and evening.

Some American designers custom made fashions for the wealthy, but most built their reputation on what they did best: ready-to-wear. The French may have been the innovators and the experimenters, but the Americans developed and excelled at producing fashion looks in quantity.

The Trend to Casual Fashion

Jacqueline Kennedy, wife of the president, was a trend setter for Americans in the early 1960s much as Empress Eugenie had been for the French in the 1860s. "Jackie" practically made a uniform of her two-piece jewel-necked, A-line dresses and pillbox hats. However, the late '50s and early '60s saw the last of elegant fashion for over ten years.

In the postwar search for domestic tranquility, American families wanted to escape the deteriorating cities and find a healthy environment in which to raise their children. For many this meant a move to the suburbs. Therefore, as the era of elegant dress faded, the popularity of casual sportswear increased, for which American designers developed their own style. Summer weather brought pants of all lengths: slim ankle-length Capri pants, below-the-knee pedal pushers, above-the-knee Bermuda shorts (for both men and women), and short shorts.

Suburban life styles included prepared food mixes to help the homemaker, new easy-care, wash-and-wear man-made fabrics, and more convenient shopping centers. Another new convenience was television: entertainment without leaving the house. Television instantly spread fashion news, and America found its taste heavily influenced by advertising.

YOUTH POWER

The postwar boom babies were beginning to reach their teens in the 1950s. Television helped teenagers create unique styles in fashion and music, many of them short-lived "fads." Styles for girls included "baby doll" blouses and felt circle skirts with poodle appliques.

The biggest fashion change of the '60s also came as a result of the postwar baby boom. By now 50 percent of the United States population was under age 25. Sheer numbers brought increased buying power and encouraged a specialized youth industry, especially for rock music and junior fashions. The junior dress and sportswear markets boomed. Young people's tastes were to dominate the fashion scene through the 1970s.

England's Influence on Fashion

The youthful look of the 1960s originated in England. Young intellectuals and artists, dissatisfied with "stuffy" society, criticized and satirized it to draw attention to a need for change. Many young people felt that they could demonstrate a break from the "establishment" by dressing differently. One group of publicized young people, collectively called "Mods," put together odd separates to create an individualistic, layered look. The Mods borrowed many ideas from historical costume, but usually combined periods. Often they bought the originals on Portabello Road or at other "antique" clothes markets in London. Their style influenced the entire fashion industry; people even referred to the new young fashion as being "Mod." Mini skirts (above the knee) were characteristic of the new look, which in turn fostered a boom in the hosiery business.

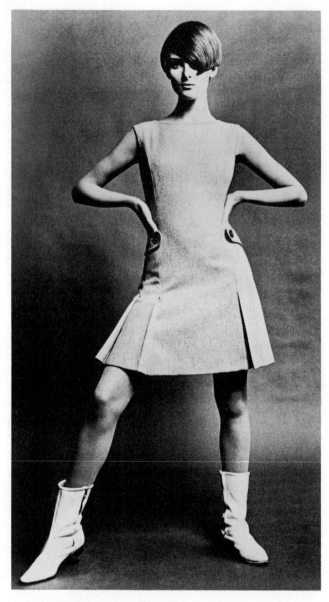

A Mary Quant mini dress from the 1966 Ginger Group
(Courtesy of Mary Quant Limited)

Boutiques

Boutiques (a French term for small shops) sprang up on the King's Road in Chelsea, a borough in southwest London. The best known of these was Bazaar, opened in 1955 by Mary Quant, Alexander Plunket Green (her husband), and Archie McNair. Because she could not find the things she wanted to stock her store, Quant herself began designing. Quant's apparel designs caught the spirit of the 1960s. By the mid-'60s her success and fame had grown so much that she was doing 22 collections a year on a royalty basis, including four lines each for Bazaar and the Ginger Group, her own mass-produced line.[27]

Another interesting 1960s boutique was Biba, owned by Barbara Hulaniki. Beginning in a tiny shop, it finally took over a large department store. Decorated in art nouveau, Biba was the perpetrator of the coordinated "total look" in which everything matched

[27] Maureen Cleave, "Mary Quant: London's Kooky Success Story," (Reprinted from *the New York Times Magazine*, March 19, 1967) *Reader's Digest*, June, 1967, pp. 109–112.

Mary Quant *(Courtesy of Mary Quant Limited)*

—coats, dresses, separates, sweaters, hats, stockings, shoes.

Advent of Young Designers

The 1960s saw the beginning of youth designing for youth. No longer did young people have to wear watered-down versions of the couture. They designed for themselves. Other young London designers included Zandra Rhodes, Bill Gibb, Caroline Charles, Gerald McCann, Sally Tuffin and Marian Foale, John Bates, Roger Nelson, Jean Muir, Angela Cash, Ozzie Clark, and Alice Pollack.

The personification of young fashion in England was Twiggy, a pencil-thin 17-year-old model. She was a female heroine in a world dominated by male pop singers. The media proclaimed Twiggy's the "face of the year" in 1966. Not only did she have the perfect look for the time, with a boyish haircut and painted-on eyelashes, but because of her working-class background teens identified with her. Twiggy was a little of both boy and girl, a mirror of her time, when one had difficulty differentiating between them.

The Unisex Look

As the distinctions between the social roles of males and females decreased, there was less need for distinction between them in dress. The mid-1960s saw the beginning of the unisex look; boys and girls dressed alike in jeans and T-shirts and wore their hair the same length. A pop song asked the question, "Are you a girl or are you a boy?"

Revival of Men's Fashion

The English Mod look affected men's wear as well as women's. John Stephen and the other Carnaby Street tailors made a brave attempt to return color and fashion to men's clothing in a "Peacock Revolution." Their supporters argued that since the male animal of each species is usually the more colorful, the human male should be also. Carnaby Street boutiques showed wide lapels, ruffled shirts, flared jackets, bell-bottom trousers, and the first coordinated look for men. Their influence became so widespread that there was hardly a manufacturer of men's apparel whose line did not include some Mod-influenced merchandise.

The initial impact of Carnaby Street did not last, but the general awareness of the need for more interesting men's clothes did. Men became more concerned with their roles outside of work and with dressing for those other sides of life. French and Italian designers became as important in men's wear as the traditional English. Pierre Cardin (Car-dahn') signed his first contract for men's shirts and ties in 1959 and opened his men's ready-to-wear department in 1961. Dior, St. Laurent, and other women's designers followed his example. The 1960s brought the first designer clothes for men and the first fashion changes since the introduction of the business suit.

Youthful Direction in International Fashion

Through British exports, the world at large, and the United States in particular, experienced and embraced the Beatles and other pop music groups, English films about James Bond, Mary Poppins, and Tom Jones with their English stars, and English fashions. As a result, the entire Western world followed England's youthful direction in fashion. In France, the designer who most accurately captured the mood for women was André Courrèges (Coor-redgé), who in

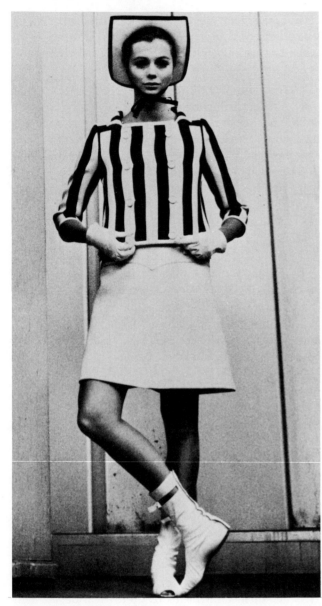

A mini by **Courrèges** *(Courtesy of André Courrèges, Paris)*

1964 anticipated the mini with his four-inches-above-the-knee skirts.[28] Other French couture designers such as Cardin and Emmanuel Ungaro followed with "sportif" looks in the early 1960s, along with the youthful "YeYe" dresses of the French *prêt-à-porter* (pret'-a-por-tay', ready-to-wear) designers like Emmanuelle Khanh.

The avant garde presentations of American Rudi Gernreich were in the same spirit of breaking from

[28] Carter, *The Changing World of Fashion*, p. 48.

tradition. Gernreich, a Californian, specialized in dramatic sport clothes with bold color combinations. His topless bathing suits and see-through blouses won him sensational publicity.

Youthful Influence on Retailing

Traditional retailing in department and large specialty stores began to suffer from the competition of small boutiques. Yves St. Laurent opened his Rive Gauche boutiques around the world. (The name refers to the left bank of the river Seine in Paris.) An Englishman, Paul Young, opened a chain of boutiques in America called Paraphernalia; Betsey Johnson was one of the star designers supplying clothes for them. To win back customers, Geraldine Stutz, the new president of Bendel's in New York, introduced an atmosphere of many boutiques within one store. This idea helped many retailers adapt to new retailing trends.

Youthful Influence on All Levels of Fashion

The well-to-do discovered that they could find many of the styles they wanted in boutiques and stores carrying ready-to-wear, without time-consuming fittings. This change and rising labor costs led to a decline in the influence of the couture. To maintain business, even the couture began following the lead of youthful designers. This was the first evidence of a reverse in the traditional fashion adoption process: styles were beginning to filter up from the inexpensive clothes of the young to the couture. Previously they had always filtered down, copy for copy, from the high prices to the low (see chapter 3).

The popularity of the youthful look in England and the United States, and the power of the large numbers of youth, made all women want to look younger. It had formerly been stylish to look mature or at least fashionably sophisticated; now it was suddenly "in" to look just plain young. American women of all ages eventually accepted some variation of the mini skirt, so much so that when European designers came out with longer skirt lengths, Americans were not ready for them.

Indecision in Fashion Direction

The late 1960s and early '70s were a time of confusion in dress, reflecting an unstable economic situation and social unrest. There were micro-mini skirts (eight to ten inches above the knee), minis (five to six inches above the knee), midis (below-the-knee lengths to mid-calf), and maxis (mid-calf to ankle and floor lengths). While many Europeans accepted the midi advocated by designers Louis Feraud and Pierre Cardin, there developed an all out mini–maxi controversy. Actually, a variety of choices provided more opportunities for self-expression, but most American women were afraid to be different from their contemporaries and the stores were afraid to take the chance on stocking potentially unsalable merchandise. Many manufacturers and stores learned the hard way, with big losses. Some even went out of business. The best alternative seemed to be pantsuits.

Pantsuits were perfect for the times. They began with both St. Laurent and Courrèges in France and Tuffin and Foale in London in the mid-'60s. They were comfortable, practical, and businesslike, which was just the image wanted by women who were struggling for equal job opportunities and equal pay for equal work. In "middle America" the polyester pantsuit became almost a uniform.

Anti-fashion

The tumultuous 1960s, a time of assassinations, riots, and civil strife, made people turn from showy displays of frivolity. It even became stylish to look poor. Workmen's Levis became an anti-fashion statement and, at least on the surface, further broke class barriers.

Some people could not cope at all with society and the economic situation. In tattered jeans, long hair, beads, and old clothes, society's dropouts tried to escape to a psychedelic world of drugs. Although they soon saw the drawbacks of their life style, the "hippies" did have an effect on fashion that eventually reached the establishment. In their desire to emulate the ordinary life, the hippies wore parts of folk costumes, adapted at first from the Indians.

The Ethnic Look

Eventually the ethnic look widened to include traditional folk costume from practically every country: India, Guatemala, Greece, Africa. Black people developed pride in their heritage, sporting Afro hairdos and the *dashiki*, traditional African garb. The resumption of United States relations with China created widespread interest in the Chinese people and Chinese costume in 1972. Designers incorporated into their collections the ethnic idea of layering and combining separates. The epitome of reverse fashion adaptation was St. Laurent's "elegant peasant" collec-

tion of 1975: ethnic looks done in silks, with higher price tags.

RETURN TO TRADITION

During the popularity of jeans, pantsuits, and the peasant look, the only high fashion looks that survived were the timeless ones that never were out of style. Jean Muir's jersey dresses from England, Missoni knits from Italy, and Anne Klein's American sportswear were the most notable examples. Designer accessories such as Gucci shoes and Louis Vuitton bags became "status symbols." The dress business in America was practically dead until Diane von Furstenberg and the Albert Nipons proved the continued existence of a market for dresses among American women.

The post peasant period saw a return to the safe, traditional look of conservative three-piece suits for both men and women. Women were now trying to make it up the corporate ladder rather than the social one.

There was also a return to natural fibers—wool, silk, and cotton, or their blends—after the polyester craze of the 1960s. The trend in life styles was back to nature and back to basics: home cooking, urban rejuvenation, and physical fitness. People turned to active sports as well as healthful eating to get themselves in shape. They began to buy special clothes for all of these athletic activities, wearing their running suits even to the grocery store.

Advancing Age of the Average Consumer

The fashions of the 1970s were again affected as the postwar babies grew older. Now in their late twenties and thirties, their tastes were changing. A "contemporary" style category was born, a more sophisticated look for this large market. Because this age group constitutes such a large market, it affects the total impact of American marketing. On *Harper's Bazaar's* list of the most beautiful American women in 1978, all were between the ages of 30 and 60. The median age of Americans was getting older; it was healthy to realize that people of all ages have wants and needs that must be satisfied.

The 1970s ended with a return to traditional values, seasoned with the knowledge of fairness and equality learned the hard way in the '60s. Fashion became more elegant; once again Americans were watching the French and Italians—the *prêt-à-porter* designers rather than the couture—for fashion direction. However, the Europeans were aware of American designers, too; they would not quickly forget the impact on the rest of the world of American jeans, ethnic looks, and sportswear.

SUMMARY

This chapter has briefly covered the growth of the fashion industry. We saw how technological advances, especially the invention of the sewing machine, changed clothing production from custom made to ready-to-wear. The Industrial Revolution also nourished the growth of a large middle class, who demanded and could afford fashion at every price level. As a result, fashion became available to everyone instead of just the wealthy few. We also saw that fashion was influenced by the changing status of women and by the changing roles of both sexes. Fashion leadership originated with and was maintained by the French, except during World War II and the youth-oriented late 1960s and early '70s. However, United States designers have challenged the French as innovators, and have surpassed them in terms of production.

CHAPTER REVIEW

CHAPTER OBJECTIVES

After reading this chapter you should be able to
A. Give evidence of having attained competence in the following areas:
1. Awareness of the major changes in American life styles since the Industrial Revolution and how they related to fashion 2. Ability to understand how fashion reflected the social, cultural, political, economic, and technological changes of the Industrial Revolution 3. Ability to outline and discuss major changes in the fashion industry 4. Knowledge of the names and contributions of major designers of the past 100 years
B. Define the following terms and concepts in relation to their discussion in the chapter:
1. Paris as fashion capital 2. Royalty as trend setters 3. Development of the couture 4. Growth of the middle class 5. Growth of the textile industry 6. Impact of the invention of the sewing machine 7. Development of mass production 8. Changes in men's or women's fashion in relation to life styles over the last 100 years 9. The Gibson

Girl 10. Commercial patterns 11. Development of retailing: department stores, specialty stores, mail order houses 12. Fashion magazines 13. Influence of the entertainment world, including films 14. Development of active sportswear 15. Garment industry development and conditions 16. Unionization 17. Influence on the change in women's status 18. Retail expansion 19. Effect of the Depression on fashion 20. Effects of World War II on fashion 21. The New Look 22. Causes of "Youth Power" 23. Effects of shifts in the age of the population 24. The Mods and English fashion influence in the 1960s 25. New York as domestic fashion capital 26. Anti-fashion 27. Ethnic look

Questions for Review

1. Discuss the change in emphasis over the years from the couture to ready-to-wear.
2. Give two examples of how fashion reflects social or political history.
3. What factors made Paris the center of world fashion?
4. Discuss the growth of mass production in the United States and the technical development that made it possible.
5. Discuss retail development and expansion in the nineteenth and twentieth centuries. How did this reflect social changes?
6. Discuss four of the most important influences on women's fashion styles between 1850 and 1920.
7. Referring to the historical chart of designers in the appendix, discuss their impact on fashion.

PROJECTS FOR ADDITIONAL LEARNING

1. Trace the fashions of one American or European designer listed in the historical chart of designers (appendix) through back issues of newspapers and magazines from the period in which he or she was best known. Trace the evolution of the designer's styles with sketches or photo copies. Discuss the characteristics that made his or her designs unique. How did the designs reflect life styles?

2. Start a costume collection. Canvass your family, friends, and neighbors for attic donations, or shop at flea markets and the Salvation Army. Label all items carefully as to donor and year made. Examine them for construction methods and design details. Design students can use these items as inspiration for future design projects.

3. Visit a local sewing machine dealer. Ask him to trace the technical advances in machines as far back as he can remember. He may have old catalogs or old machines that you can examine. Discuss the advantages of the old and the new models.

INFLUENCES ON FASHION AND CONSUMER DEMAND

2

A shopper looks for a handbag
to suit her tastes and needs
(Photograph by the author)

Because fashion reflects the way the consumer thinks and lives, it is influenced by the same social, economic, political, technological, and other environmental forces that influence all other aspects of people's lives. Executives on all levels of the fashion industry must be aware of these environmental conditions if they are to make informed decisions about styling and merchandising. This chapter examines the predominant influences on the consumer and, in turn, on fashion.

SOCIAL INFLUENCES

Changes in people's attitudes and life styles consequently change fashion and buying habits. People want fashions appropriate to their interests and activities.

Change in Women's Status

Only in this century have women been allowed to vote, to own property, and to pursue careers—and only after a long struggle. Women's new status and life styles in turn have changed the way they dress. Better educated and exposed to new ideas, women want wider fashion choice. To participate in sports, women needed more active clothing. For jobs they needed practical and businesslike clothes, such as suits.

Writer Lance Morrow comments, "What women wear has had a psychological impact upon how they thought of themselves, and what they believed to be possible. In the past, women after 25 started to dress like matrons. But the vivid costume party of the '60's taught women of all ages to wear almost anything they pleased. Fashions are more subdued now, but many women of all generations have escaped the typecasting of dress. Fashions have changed in part because women's roles are different." [1]

Change in Men's Roles

Men's roles, too, have changed, affecting their style of dress. The shortening work week and a more casual life style have increased men's participation in home life and leisure activities. Their wardrobes— formerly limited to suits, slacks, and sportshirts—have expanded along with their activities, and increased clothing choices have made them more fashion conscious.

On the other hand, despite designers attempts to revolutionize men's fashion in the '60s, their business clothing has remained basically conservative. Business dress codes have altered little, aside from a slight easing in formality in all but the financial and legal sectors.

[1] Lance Morrow, "In Praise of Older Women," *Time*, April 24, 1978, p. 99.

Equality of the Sexes

With today's emphasis on equal career opportunities for both sexes, investment dressing—wearing classic, durable clothing made of quality materials—has become important.

A major influence on fashion in the last decade, reflecting both sexes' increased awareness of physical fitness, is the popularity of active sports. Many varieties of clothing are now on the market for each sport. Increasingly, people are spending more money to look right and be comfortable for each activity.

POLITICAL INFLUENCE

International Relations

As we saw in chapter 1, even politics—including both foreign relations and domestic legislation—can affect fashion. For example, when the United States reopened trade relations with China, there was widespread interest in the Chinese people, their way of life, and their style of dress. This interest strongly influenced both European and American fashion in the mid- and late '70s. Stores were filled with quilted jackets and mandarin collars. International ethnic influences on fashion reemerged in the early '80s.

Civil Rights Legislation

New laws have brought better education and better job opportunities to minority groups, resulting in more spending power and, thus, new influential consumer groups. For instance, it became fashionable for black Americans to wear traditional African garb as a result of growing ethnic pride. Many such fashion ideas have crossed ethnic lines and influenced fashion for all Americans.

ECONOMIC INFLUENCES

Highly developed countries have the means for fashion demand and the facilities for fashion production. Where economic and industrial growth do not exist, such as in underdeveloped countries, fashion is static. The economic growth of a country is reflected in the variety of its fashion.

The Economic Situation's Effect on Fashion

When the economic situation is unstable, the fashion picture is also unstable. Not only is money in short supply, but people seem to be confused about what they really want. For example, in the late '60s and early '70s there was a confusing variety of fashion looks from which women could choose: mini, midi, and maxi skirts, as well as pants. In a recessionary period, people are likely to buy conservatively or at least buy fashions they believe to be of lasting value. Some people believe that hemlines go up when the stock market goes up. However, this theory is an oversimplification. For instance, in 1947 the stock market dropped only a few points, yet skirt lengths dropped considerably with Dior's New Look. From 1975 to 1976 the stock market rose over 100 points, but skirts stayed considerably below the knee, in keeping with the prevalent ethnic look.

Consumer Groups

Traditionally, society has been divided by income classes. The wealthiest were the most fashionable, because they could afford to buy lavish clothes. Eventually clothes themselves became status symbols (rather than just an expression of good taste); people tried to prove success by wearing expensive clothing.

Today the traditional classifications have broken down. Almost all clothing is mass produced, and almost everyone can enjoy fashion on some price and quality level. Because most people in the Western countries are in the middle income group, it has the largest spending power. Therefore, fashion (as well as other goods) is manufactured primarily for the needs of this group.

Consumer goods are directed at large groups of people who have the most money available to spend. Consumer groups can be powerful enough to have whole new categories of clothing created for them. For example, in the 1960s the members of the post–World War II baby boom were all under 25, creating a mass "junior" market. In the '70s, as this group grew older, it needed a more sophisticated look; manufacturers created the "contemporary" look. This group will continue to be a major economic force, and the market will cater to its specific needs at each advancing age level. Another potentially powerful consumer segment is being created by increasing birth rates in the late '70s and early '80s and its impact on the fashion market will be evident into the twenty-first century. Society is further segmented into more specific consumer groups by categorizing their interests, education, location, life styles, etc.

Consumer Spending

The amount of money consumers spend on fashion and other goods depends on their incomes. Income as it affects spending is measured in three ways: personal income, disposable income, and discretionary income.

> **Personal income**   is the gross amount of income from all sources, such as wages, salaries, interest, and dividends.
>
> **Disposable income**   is personal income minus taxes. This amount determines a person's purchasing power.
>
> **Discretionary income**   is the income left after food, lodging, and other necessities have been paid for. This is the money available to be spent or saved at will. The increase in discretionary income for most people in our society means that more people are able to buy fashion.

If the total personal income, disposable income, or discretionary income for an entire country is divided by its total population, the result is the average *per capita income* in each category.

Income, however, is relative to the economic situation. Although incomes in the Western world have risen in recent years, so have prices. Thus, income is meaningful only in relation to the amount of goods and services it can buy or its *purchasing power*. Inflation, recession, the international value of currency, and productivity affect purchasing power.

Inflation   In an inflationary period such as the United States experienced in the 1970s and into the 1980s, people earn more money each year, but higher prices and higher taxes result in little or no real increase in purchasing power.

Recession   A severe recession would have the opposite effect. Recession is a cycle beginning with a decrease in spending. Thus, many companies are forced to cut back production which results in unemployment and a drop in the Gross National Product

(GNP). Unemployment then furthers the cycle of reduced spending.

The International Money Market   If the dollar loses value relative to other currencies, then imports such as shoes from Italy become more expensive.

Productivity   Modern techology can make production more efficient, which results in reduced costs and cheaper prices.

Labor Costs

As people receive higher salaries and live better, the cost of making garments increases. Rising labor costs have practically forced the couture out of business. As a result, custom designers have started ready-to-wear lines to serve the general public. Now there is little style difference between the clothes of the wealthy and those of the average person; a democratization of fashion is closer to being reality. Expensive clothes are made from richer fabrics and have finer detailing, but the difference is not so obvious as it was before.

High labor costs have caused many manufacturers to search for cheaper sources of labor, in the Far East and elsewhere. This has caused a controversy between American workers, who feel that their jobs are in jeopardy, and proponents of free trade, who feel that consumers should pay the lowest possible price for quality merchandise (see chapters 10 and 12).

In the future, increased labor costs may also dictate more simply constructed clothes, barring a technical breakthrough that reduces the impact of labor costs.

TECHNOLOGICAL INFLUENCES

Mass Production

Obviously, mass production would be impossible without technological inventions like the sewing machine. The development of modern production machinery, such as power sewing machines and cutting tools, has naturally speeded up the process of fashion manufacturing. Today's power machines can run faster than a car engine, sewing over 5,000 stitches per minute. Modern cutting techniques include water jets and laser beams. Mass production makes more goods at different price levels available to more people in a shorter time.

Technological inventions in the textile industry actually triggered the Industrial Revolution. Since

Shuttleless weaving machines have helped to increase efficiency in the textile industry *(Courtesy of Burlington Industries, Inc.)*

then, advances in spinning, weaving, and knitting processes have fostered the growth of our giant textile industry. Modern agricultural developments have improved the quantity and quality of natural fibers. Technological research has made synthetic fibers possible, as well as finishes that actually change fabric characteristics.

Transportation

The speed and convenience of airplane and automobile travel have given Americans a mobile life style. Travel necessitates a light-weight, seasonless, packable wardrobe. Textile technology answered the need with easy-care, wrinkle-free fabrics.

Modern transportation has also had a positive effect on the logistics of the fashion business. Improved trucking, railroad, and air freight services quickly bring the newest fashion to the retail store and the consumer. Availability often increases demand.

Communication

Modern communications media bring different cultures into contact, making people more aware of other life styles and modes of dress. In the past it took many months for a magazine showing the latest Paris fashions to be printed and shipped to its readers. Now television and daily newspapers bring fashion from around the world into our homes almost instantaneously. As a result, the public is made aware of the existence of new styles. If the image presented

is pleasing, the public wants to have the same or similar styles themselves. Thus, one of the greatest impacts that modern communication has on fashion is to accelerate change. Communication also speeds up the process of copying, with the result that merchandise produced throughout the world tends to look similar. The sooner a fashion saturates society, the sooner people tire of it and want change.

MARKETING INFLUENCES

Since World War II there has been a major change in marketing philosophy. Because more people have more money to spend, competition for consumers' dollars has become very intense. Sophisticated marketing research methods have been developed to find out consumer wants and needs; emphasis has been put on product development to answer those needs; and, vast amounts of money are being spent by fashion firms to increase advertising and other promotional activities to "create" consumer demand.

Advertising and publicity stimulate the public's desire for new clothes. The ultimate achievement of advertising is to establish the identity of a particular brand name or store to such an extent that they will be preferred over the competition.

However, there is a limit to the ability of sales promotion to win acceptance for a fashion. If the public is not ready for something, or is tired of it, no amount of advertising or publicity can gain or hold its acceptance. In 1970, the midi skirt length was praised by the press but was rejected by most American women.

SEASONAL INFLUENCES

Changing seasons and rising or falling temperatures also promote a desire for new fashion. When fall breezes blow, light summer clothes are no longer appropriate. However, the increased use of air conditioning and central heating has created a demand for seasonless clothes (see chapter 9).

CONSUMER DEMAND

Because fashion reflects life, people are obviously important in determining what fashion will be and what the fashion industry will produce. Designer Bill Blass states, "You have to understand people to make clothes for them." [2] Mary Quant reiterates, "Good designers . . . know that to have any influence they must keep in step with public needs . . . [and] public opinion. . . . They must catch the spirit of the day and interpret it in clothes." [3]

Today fashion begins and ends with the consumer. *Consumers* are people who buy and use merchandise. *Customers*, on the other hand, is a more specific term, describing people who buy merchandise from a particular producer or retailer. As marketing strategies have become more sophisticated, manufacturers and retailers have had to take consumers' wants and needs into consideration. The ability to understand consumer preferences is a valuable asset at any level of the fashion industry.

Consumerism

The retailing visionaries of the late nineteenth century—such as Montgomery Ward, who guaranteed "satisfaction or your money back," and Marshall Field, who advised that "the customer is always right"—began the development of consumerism in the United States. *Consumerism* refers to the right of the buying public to be protected against unfair marketing practices. The economic depression of the 1930s stimulated reform legislation in many areas of

[2] Barbra Walz, *The Fashion Makers* (New York: Random House, Inc., 1978), p. 47.

[3] Mary Quant, *Quant by Quant* (London: Cassell & Company Ltd., 1965), p. 74.

business, including some laws for consumer protection. The Robinson-Patman Act of 1936 provided added security against unfair competition; the Wheeler-Lea Act of 1938 outlawed fraudulent advertising involving interstate commerce.

After the artificial economy created by World War II and the enormous growth of advertising in the 1950s, the consumer rights–conscious mood of the '60s again spurred consumer protection action and additional government regulations. Today there are many regulations, especially concerning truthful and factual labeling.

Although government regulations are well intended, sometimes all consequences are not thoroughly considered. For example, California passed a law stating that all children's sleepwear must be treated with a flame retardant finish. California sleepwear producers found it very difficult to compete with producers in other parts of the country due to the extra cost of the finish. Moreover, many consumers did not understand that a flame retardant is not a preventive treatment. The final blow came when it was discovered that the chemical used in the retardant caused cancer in test animals. Much research and testing must be done to make such legislation both fair and effective.

CONSUMER BUYING MOTIVATION

In the past, most people bought new clothes only when a need arose, for a very special occasion, or because their old clothes wore out. The average person simply could not afford to buy more than the basic necessities. In Western society today discretionary income is larger; people can buy new clothes rather frequently. Therefore buying motives have changed; we are able to buy clothes because we want or like them. Buying motives vary from consumer to consumer and from day to day. They include the desire to

be fashionable. We discard clothing that is still wearable only because it is out of fashion. This is referred to as *consumer obsolescence.*

be attractive. We want clothes that will make us look our best or show off physical attributes.

impress others. We may want to exhibit our taste level or income level through the visual means of clothing. Expensive brands of certain items have been labeled status symbols.

be accepted by friends or colleagues (peer groups). Average Americans have conservative tastes; they do not want to differ from their peers. Buying patterns suggest that they like some direction or guidance as a framework for personal choice.

fill an emotional need.   New clothes often help a person feel better psychologically. However, this motive often leads to impulse buying (buying without careful consideration).

CRITERIA CONSUMERS USE IN FASHION SELECTION

To determine the possible acceptance of fashion, criteria used by the consumer in its selection must be considered. Elements of fashion appeal draw the consumer's attention to a fashion. There are also practical considerations, including quality and price, which the consumer usually evaluates before making a purchase.

Elements of Fashion Appeal

The elements of fashion appeal are basically the same as the elements of design, viewed by the purchaser rather than the creator:

Color   Color is usually the first aspect of a garment or accessory to which consumers respond. People relate very personally to color, usually selecting or rejecting a fashion because the color does or does not appeal to them or flatter their own coloring.

Texture   Texture is the surface interest in the fabric of a garment or accessory. Consumers relate to texture because of its sensuous appeal.

Style   The elements that define a style include line, silhouette, and details. A garment's appearance is also affected by hanger appeal. Depending on the consumers' level of fashion consciousness, their judgment will be conditioned by their opinion of what is currently fashionable.

Practical Considerations

Price   Price is probably the most important practical consideration for the average consumer. The consumer evaluates the total worth of all the fashion appeal aspects of the garment or accessory and their relationship to its retail price.

Fit   The try-on is a crucial step in the consumer's selection of a garment because sizing is not a guarantee of fit. The Department of Commerce has

A customer considers fit in his selection of a jacket
(Photographed by the author)

tried to set sizing standards, but each company tends to vary somewhat. Each company experiments, trying its sample garments on models who are typical of the company's customers. However, it is difficult to set size ranges and grading rules to fit all individual figures. The fitting room try-on further enables the customer to judge if fashion appeal elements are suitable to his or her figure type or general appearance.

Appropriateness   It is important that a fashion item be suitable or acceptable for a specific occasion or to suit the needs of the consumer's life style. For example, life in a large city requires more formality in clothing than life in the country. Impulse shoppers do not consider appropriateness and therefore purchase many items that do not fit into their wardrobes.

Brand   Brands are a manufacturer's means of product identification. Some consumers buy on the basis of a particular brand's reputation, often as a result of heavy advertising.

Fabric Performance and Care   The durability and ease or difficulty of caring for a garment or accessory are often factors in selection. Most consumers prefer easy-care, wash-and-wear fabrics, although designer and contemporary customers may not mind paying for dry cleaning the more delicate fabrics they prefer. Easy care and durability are of special concern in children's wear and work clothes. Government regulations now require fiber content and care instruction labels to be sewn into apparel.

Workmanship Workmanship refers to the quality of construction, stitching, and finishing. Quality standards have fallen as labor costs rise and managements favor more profitable balance sheets. Unfortunately, many consumers cannot and do not bother to evaluate workmanship. The generation born and raised since World War II have not been exposed to fine quality workmanship and therefore do not demand it.[4] The junior customer cares little about quality; she is likely to throw away a garment before it wears out. The designer, contemporary, or missy customer, on the other hand, generally considers clothing an investment and may not mind spending more for the lasting qualities of fine detailing and workmanship.

[4] Stanley Marcus, "Who's Minding the Customer?," *The Commonwealth*, November 5, 1979, p. 1.

MEETING CONSUMER DEMAND

To meet consumer demand and changes in consumer life styles, manufacturers and retailers have developed various size and price ranges as well as categories for styling and clothing types. (See table 2-1.)

Size Ranges
Each size range caters to a different figure type.

The **junior** customer, sizes 3 to 15, has a less developed figure with a shorter back-waist length (higher waistline), compared to missy.

The **missy** figure, sizes 6 to 16 (or 4 to 14, or 8 to 18), is fully developed. In missy separates, some blouses and sweaters are sized 30 to 36 (8 to 14), or small, medium, and large.

Petite sizes come in both junior and missy. Junior petite is meant for shorter junior figures, while petite sizes in missy (2 and up) are for smaller-proportioned missy figures.

Large or **women's** sizes, used for sportswear, are 36 to 52 uppers (jackets and shirts) and 30 to 40 lowers (pants and skirts) (there is a current void of half-size sportswear).

TABLE 2-1 TYPICAL RELATIONSHIP OF STYLE, SIZE, AND PRICE RANGES IN WOMEN'S WEAR

Style Range	Styling	Age	Size Range	Figure	Price Range
Junior	Youthful styling, small space divisions, figure conscious	15–25	Juniors 3–15	Small proportions	Moderate to budget
Contemporary–junior	More sophisticated styling	15–30	Juniors 3–15	Small proportions	Better to low moderate
Contemporary–missy	Sophisticated styling, versions of *prêt-à-porter*	20–40	Missy 6–14	Missy; fully developed but slim	Better to moderate
Designer	Unique, top-name designer fashion	25–up	Missy 4–14	Missy; fully developed but slim	Better and up
Missy	More conservative adaptations of last season's designer looks	25–up	Missy 8–18	Missy; fully developed	Moderate to budget
Women's or large sizes	Same as missy plus some junior looks for younger customers	18–up	Large sizes 36–52; half sizes 12½–24½	Large size	Better to budget

Women's large size sportswear *(Courtesy of Koret of California, model Deborah Lancaster, and photographer Brent Lindstrom)*

Men's suits range in size from 36 to 44 (with additional large sizes to 50), based on chest measurements. Lengths are designated after the size number: R for regular, S for short, and L for long. European sizes are 46 to 54 (just add 10 to each American size). "Young men's," equivalent to junior sizes for women, have a narrower fit in the jacket and hip and a shorter rise in the trouser than regular men's sizes. The fashionably snug "European fit" has influenced the cut of men's suits, with the consequence that some men's clothing manufacturers have started producing a "gentlemen's" cut, which gives a more ample fit for those who need it.

Dress shirts are sized by collar measurement (inches in America and centimeters in Europe) and sleeve length. Sportshirts are sized in small, medium, and large. Trousers are sized by waist and in-seam measurements.

Children's wear is sized by age groups. Infant sizes are based on age in months, usually 3, 6, 9, 12, and 18 months. However, since development varies so much from child to child, many manufacturers are now also identifying weight ranges on their labels. In Europe, sizes are based on the overall length of the baby.

Toddler clothes, for the child who has learned to walk, are sized 1 to 3; children's sizes are 3 to 6X.

Appliqued velour toddler jumpsuit *(Courtesy of Etablissements Fra-For S. A., Troyes, France)*

Half sizes (12½ to 24½) are used for large-sized dresses. They have a shorter back-waist length and slightly larger waist than regular large sizes (there is also a void of regular large sizes for dresses).

It is difficult to compare sizes from country to country. Particularly in France, the sizing is not always standard. Table 2–2 shows how confusing a comparison of sizes can be.

TABLE 2–2 INTERNATIONAL DRESS SIZES				
American	8	10	12	14	16
British	10	12	14	16	18
French	40	42	44	46	48
German	36	38	40	42	44

At this point sizes separate for boys and girls. Girls' wear comes in sizes 7 to 14; the developing adolescent wears subteen 6 to 14; and the young teen wears young junior 3 to 13. Boys' sizes are patterned after men's and include sizes 7 to 14, cadets, and chubbies.

Price Ranges

A garment should give good value for its price. There are many price ranges, each with a different level of customer expectations. As the price goes up, the customer expects higher quality in fashion, fabric, fit, and finish.

Designer garments are becoming so expensive that the group of people who can afford them is shrinking. Therefore, many designers are adding less expensive lines such as St. Laurent's Tricot knit line and Geoffrey Beene's Beene Bag sportswear division. On the other hand, many retail stores are trading up—i.e., stores with low-end (inexpensive) merchandise are now trying to give themselves a fashionable image.

Each garment manufacturer generally specializes in one price range. The designer and merchandiser must consider the cost of every fabric trim or construction detail that goes into a garment. Costs must fit into a specific price range. In turn, each retail store has various departments, from budget to designer, again classified by price range.

Style Ranges

Both women's dresses and women's sportswear currently come in style ranges as well as size ranges. Some of the terms overlap because style ranges grew out of age groups. However, many women today cross the boundaries, dressing to fit their figure and personality rather than their age.

Designer. Formerly, *couture* would have been the classification for better, more expensive fashion. However, with the decline in the couture business, the general classification of designer clothes has arisen. Today even some of the designer ready-to-wear is as expensive as couture used to be. Examples of designer styling include clothes by the designers listed in chapter 1.

Missy. These are more conservative adaptations of proven or accepted designer looks, in less expensive fabrics and less extreme silhouettes. Examples include Rona and Leslie Fay dresses, and Koret, Evan Picone, and Jones New York sportswear.

Contemporary or **up-dated.** This is a sophisticated approach to styling based on the directions set by French, Italian, English, and American ready-to-wear. Examples include Willi Wear, Liz Claiborne, and Stephen Burrows.

Junior. Young styling generally means small proportions, higher waistlines, softness, and trimmings, but it often is also very body conscious. Some junior dress lines are Gunne Sax, Foxy Lady, and Young Edwardian by Arpeja. Junior sportswear companies include College Town and Bobbie Brooks.

There is overlapping even in these categories—for example, some stores put Diane von Furstenberg in their "better missy" dress departments, others in a "designer" department. Jones New York is found in some "contemporary" departments and elsewhere in "better missy" sportswear. Categorizing depends on the size and clientele of the store.

Designer and contemporary styling has carried over to men's wear, although designer clothes for men tend to be more classic than those for women. Sportswear or "related separates" for men have followed almost the same trends as women's sportswear in the last ten years, especially since many designers are doing both.

Small children's styling is the only styling not aimed at the consumer who will wear the garment. The consumer in this case is a parent, grandparent, or other adult. Children's clothes of the past tended to be fussy but now are more functional. Older children today have more definite opinions on what they want to wear, partly because of advertising and television exposure and peer group pressures. This development has had an effect on styling.

Clothing Classifications

There have never been so many types of clothing as we see today. Variety in dress has resulted from changes in our habits and roles. We now have clothing for all occasions, all life styles. Retail stores have separate departments for each category of clothing. And with these categories, many subclassifications based on price range and the target customer's life style.

Women's Wear Women's clothes are divided into many classifications: lingerie, dresses, evening clothes, suits, outerwear, and sportswear. There are also specialty categories, like bridal gowns and maternity clothes. In addition, there is a huge array of accessories within the general categories of wraps, head coverings, handbags, and footwear.

Lingerie includes undergarments, sleepwear, and loungewear. There is currently increased interest in designing lingerie, because women again desire pretty things and will spend the money to have them.

Dresses range from the very tailored with crisp lines for wearing on the job, to the very softest with gathers and ruffles for dressy occasions.

Evening clothes run the gamut from party pajamas through long and short cocktail dresses to opulent gowns.

Suits are jackets and skirts (or pants) sold together as units. Suits also range from the soft "dressmaker" suit to the strictly tailored.

Outerwear has primarily a protective function: it covers us and keeps us warm or dry. Outerwear includes coats, capes, and heavy jackets. Its warmth may come from traditional wool or quilting; rainwear receives a water-repellent treatment.

Sportswear is the category that has grown most over the years, as leisure time and discretionary income have increased. Sportswear can be classified as active or spectator. *Spectator sportswear* was intended for watching sports events, although the term now includes sportswear worn for day-to-day activities. *Active sportswear* is created for movement and worn for participation in sports.

Sportswear lines are organized in two different ways: in *separates* such as skirts, pants, blouses, shirts, sweaters, and tops; or as *coordinated sportswear*, pieces planned to mix and match but priced separately.

Men's Wear There are now almost as many categories available to men as to women. Stores use elaborate promotions to lure their increasingly fashion-wise male customers.

Tailored clothing for men includes suits, overcoats, topcoats, sportcoats, and separate trousers for both day and evening wear.

Furnishings include shirts, neckwear, sweaters, tops, underwear, socks, robes, and pajamas.

Lingerie designed by Charlotte Hilton *(Courtesy of Percy Savage and Casey Tolar, Fashion Promotions, London)*

Men's sportswear from Christian Dior
(Courtesy of Christian Dior, Paris)

Sportswear is made up of related separates to fill the demand for more leisure and casual wear.

Active sportswear includes windbreakers, ski jackets, jogging suits, tennis shorts, and the like.

Work clothes include overalls, work shirts, and pants required by laborers; they now are also worn by women.

SUMMARY

Outside influences, such as changing life styles, general economic conditions, labor costs, political developments, government legislation, technological advances, and advertising strongly influence fashion and consumer demand. If we learn to be observant of these influences, we can better foresee fashion developments.

The consumer is an important determinant of what fashion is and what the industry produces. The fashion industry caters to powerful consumer groups because they have the most discretionary income. Consumers buy clothes for many reasons, including the desires to be fashionable, attractive, impressive, accepted, or emotionally fulfilled. Considerations in fashion selection include color, texture, style, price, fit, appropriateness, brand name, fabric performance, and workmanship.

CHAPTER REVIEW

CHAPTER OBJECTIVES

After reading this chapter you should be able to
A. Give evidence of having attained competence in the following areas:
  1. Ability to understand how social, cultural, political, economic, and technological changes influence fashion and the fashion industry 2. Awareness of the effects of consumer demand on fashion today 3. Knowledge of influences on consumer demand. 4. Understanding of buyer motivation
B. Define the following terms and concepts in relation to their discussion in the chapter:
  1. Equality of the sexes 2. Consumer groups 3. Disposable income 4. Discretionary income 5. Inflation 6. Recession 7. International money market 8. Productivity 9. Labor costs 10. Consumer protection legislation 11. Consumerism 12. Consumer demand 13. Buyer motivation 14. Fashion selection 15. Style ranges 16. Size ranges 17. Price ranges

---

Questions for Review

---

1. How have life style changes affected dress for both men and women?
2. How have income groups influenced fashion?
3. Discuss people's motives for buying clothes.
4. How have technological advances changed fashion?
5. What should a consumer consider when buying clothes?

1. Analyze fashion styles today. Is there one that you feel is the result of a social, economic, political, or technological influence? Briefly explain in writing the reasons for your choice.

2. Interview two executive businesswomen and find out what type of clothes are in their wardrobes. How do their needs affect the fashion industry?

3. *Market research.* In a local department store, compare two dresses of similar price from different manufacturers. Try them on. Which has the better fit? Compare fabric choices in terms of quality and suitability to the design. Compare styling. Which has more innovative styling? Taking all factors into consideration, which dress is the better buy? Discuss your findings in a written report. Describe or sketch the two garments.

4. In a local department store, compare contemporary and junior departments. List the major manufacturers in each department, and explain the general styling differences.

FASHION CHANGE AND CONSUMER ACCEPTANCE

3

A new style is introduced
at Oscar de la Renta's
collection showing.

Consumers' wants and needs create a cycle of consumer demand, industry catering to that demand, and finally consumer acceptance of merchandise offered on the market. This cycle results in fashion change, discussed at the beginning of this chapter. The remainder of the chapter covers the resulting consumer acceptance or rejection of fashion.

FASHION DIMENSIONS

Fashion is the style or styles that are most popular at a given time. The term implies three components: style, acceptance, and timeliness.

Style is any particular characteristic or look in apparel or accessories. Designers interpret fashion ideas in this creative form and offer them to the public. Style may come and go in fashion, but a specific style always remains the same, whether in fashion or not. For example, the shirtwaist style will not always be in fashion, yet it will always involve the same cut and details, which make it a shirtwaist.

Acceptance implies that consumers must buy and wear a style to make it a fashion. Acceptance by a large number of people makes a fashion important. However, different groups adopt different fashions. What appeals to a junior customer would probably not appeal to a missy customer. Designers plan styles to appeal to certain consumer groups—their particular customers. It is then up to the public whether to make the offered style into a fashion by acceptance.

Timeliness indicates change: what is in fashion one year will be out the next. Many people criticize the fickleness of fashion. However, if fashion never changed, the public would not continue to buy clothing. Obviously, the senses become bored without variety. Change is what makes the fashion business exciting. Because fashion is a product of change, a sense of timing—the ability to understand the speed of acceptance and change—is an important asset for anyone involved with product development or marketing in the fashion industry.

FASHION EVOLUTION

Generally, fashion changes evolve gradually, giving consumers time to become accustomed to new combinations and looks. New fashion looks are arrived at by changing design elements such as line, shape, color, fabric, and details, and their relationship to one another. For instance, a change in skirt lengths might in turn affect the proportion of the skirt to the bodice of a dress. In men's suits, the narrowing of lapels tends to reduce the scale of other details and accessories, such as neckties.

Fashion Cycles

Consumers are exposed each season to a multitude of new styles created by designers. Some are rejected immediately—often by the buyer on the retail level—while others go through a period of acceptance, demonstrated by consumers purchasing and wearing these styles.

The way in which fashion change and acceptance occur is usually described as a *fashion cycle*, composed of the introduction, popularity, and finally, the rejection of a style. It is difficult to categorize or theorize about fashion without oversimplifying. However, the fashion cycle is usually depicted as a bell-shaped curve encompassing five stages: introduction, rise in popularity, peak of popularity, decline in popularity, and rejection. The cycle can reflect the acceptance of a single style from one designer, or of a general style such as the shirtwaist dress or the mini skirt.

Introduction A designer interprets the times in a creative form, and then a manufacturer offers the new styles to the public. When we speak of the "latest fashions" from Paris, they may not yet be accepted by anyone. Therefore, at this first stage of the cycle, fashion implies only style and newness.

Most new styles are introduced at a high price level. Designers, whose names are respected for both their creativity and their sense of timing, are often given the opportunity (with financial backing) to design with very few limitations on creativity, quality of raw materials, or amount of fine workmanship. Naturally, production costs are high and only a few people can afford these clothes. Designers such as Mary McFadden, whose clothes are works of art, do not expect to sell in quantity. Production in small quantities gives a designer more freedom, flexibility, and room for creativity.

Increase in Popularity As the new fashion is purchased, worn, and seen by more people, it begins to rise in popularity. In the case of an expensive item, the volume of sales will never be high, but the item may be the most popular style in a designer's collection or even the most popular of all high-priced new fashions.

The popularity of the style may further increase through copying and adaptation. Some manufacturers may buy the rights to produce *line-for-line* copies (exact duplicates) of the original style but to be sold at somewhat reduced prices. Other manufacturers may try to copy it with cheaper fabric and less detail, at still lower prices. Other designers or stylists may modify the original to suit the needs of their customers. Volume production requires a relative sureness of mass acceptance. "Large manufacturing firms cannot allow the creative freedom that high fashion demands because of manufacturing and marketing re-

Fashion cycle

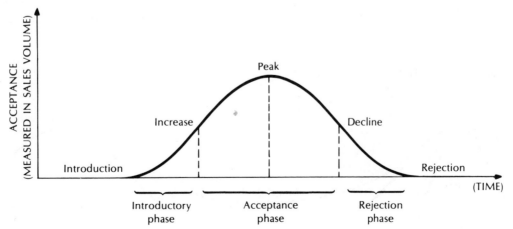

strictions. The larger firms must follow pre-established trends rather than create new ones."[1]

Peak of Popularity   When a fashion is at the height of its popularity, it may be in such demand that many manufacturers copy it or produce adaptations of it at many price levels. Styles with great appeal are produced in many variations.

Decline in Popularity   Eventually, so many copies are mass produced that fashion-conscious people tire of the style and begin to look for something new. Consumers still wear garments in the style, but they are no longer willing to buy them at regular prices. Retail stores put such declining styles on sale racks in hopes of clearing room for new merchandise.

Rejection of a Style, or Obsolescence   In the last phase of the fashion cycle, consumers have already turned to new looks, thus beginning a new cycle for another style.

Length of Cycles

Although all fashions follow the same cyclical pattern of movement, there is no measurable timetable for the duration of a fashion cycle. Some fashions take a short time to peak in popularity, others take longer; some decline slowly, others swiftly. Some last a single selling season, others last through several seasons. Some are of very short duration, others never completely disappear.

Classics   Some styles never fall completely into obsolescence, but instead remain more or less in general fashion acceptance for an extended period. A classic is characterized by simplicity of design, which keeps it from being easily dated. An example of a

[1] Thaddeous Taube, former Chairman of the Board, Koracorp Industries, as quoted by Larry Wood, "Taube Turns Over Reins After Reviving Koracorp," *Fashion Showcase*, October, 1979, p. 28E.

A classic pin-striped suit from the men's prêt-à-porter collection, House of Balenciaga, Paris.

classic is the Chanel suit, which peaked in fashion in the late 1950s and enjoyed moderate popularity again in the late '70s. In the interim, the house of Chanel in Paris, as well as other manufacturers, produced the suits for a small dedicated clientele.

Fads   Short-lived fashions, called *fads*, can come and go in a single season. They lack the design strength (character) to hold attention for very long. Fads usually affect only a narrow consumer group, begin in lower price ranges, are relatively simple and inexpensive to copy, and therefore flood the market in a very short time. Because of the market saturation, the public tires of them quickly and they die out.

Cycles for fads and classics, in relation to normal fashion cycles

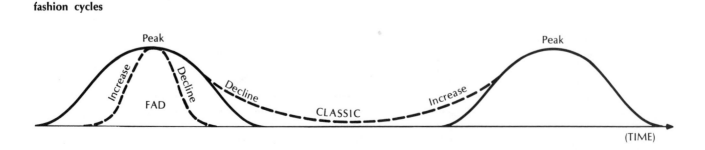

In early 1971, for example, the fashion press used the term *hot pants* to describe the leather and shiny-fabric short shorts that were the current fad.

Cycles within Cycles   One design element (such as color, texture, silhouette, or detail) of a style may change even though the predominant feature remains popular over a longer period. Jeans became a fashion item in the late 1960s and remained so throughout the '70s. Therefore, their fashion cycle was very long in duration. However, various jean silhouettes—including bell, cigarette, and baggy legs—came and went during that time.

Interrupted Cycles   Consumer buying is often halted prematurely because manufacturers and retailers no longer wish to risk producing or stocking any merchandise that will soon decline in popularity. This is obvious to consumers who try to buy summer clothes in August.

Sometimes the normal progress of a fashion cycle is interrupted or prolonged by social upheaval, economic depression, or war. For instance, the large-shouldered, wedge-shaped silhouette in women's fashion began in the 1930s. Because people were concerned with things more important than fashion during World War II, the same silhouette continued, without the normally expected decline, for the duration of the war. The New Look of 1947 was a radical change because the old cycle had been unnaturally prolonged.

Recurring Fashion Cycles   After a fashion dies, it may resurface later. Designers often borrow ideas from the past. When a style reappears years later, it is reinterpreted for the newer times. Silhouette or proportion may recur, interpreted with a change in fabric and detail. Nothing is ever exactly the same—yet nothing is totally new. In the late 1970s the wedge silhouette and the fashion suit of the '40s were reintroduced. However, the use of different fabrics, colors, and details made the look belong to the '70s.

CONSUMER IDENTIFICATION WITH FASHION CYCLES

Taste
An individual's personal preference of one style over another is referred to as *taste*. Good taste in fashion implies sensitivity to what is beautiful and appropriate.

Acceptance by the public does not prove that a design is necessarily beautiful, ony that its timing is right. Really beautiful design is often not accepted by the general public at all, either because it is too extreme or because it is too expensive. Watered-down copies often lose their original beauty.

Consumer Groups
Consumers can be categorized and identified with various stages of the fashion cycle. Fashion leaders buy and wear new styles at the beginning of their cycles; others tend to imitate. Because of differences in their tastes, what is in fashion for one group is not for another group: what is in fashion for fashion leaders is too extreme for followers, and what is finally accepted by followers is already out of fashion for leaders. Manufacturers and retailers may also be identified as fashion leaders or followers, depending on which consumer groups are their target customers.[2]

Fashion Leaders   While fashion leaders are not usually the creators, they may give impetus to a fashion by discovering and wearing a certain style. Fashion leaders are a very small percentage of the public.

Most fashion leaders are members of higher income groups, because quality high fashion is expensive. Fashion leaders constantly look for interest-

[2] Fashion leaders and followers may also be referred to as *fashion sensitives* and *insensitives*, the E. I. Dupont de Nemours & Co. National Dresswear Conference, October 3–5, 1979.

Recurring fashion cycles

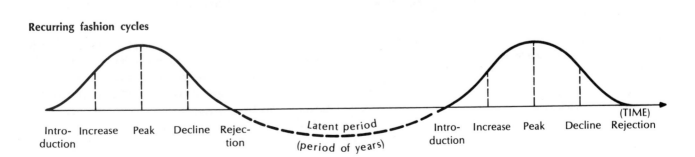

Intro- Increase   Peak   Decline   Rejec-   Latent period   Intro-   Increase   Peak   Decline   Rejection   (TIME)
duction   tion   (period of years)   duction

Diana, Princess of Wales
became an overnight fashion leader
on her engagement to Prince Charles.
Copies of her wedding gown
were in London shop windows
eight hours after the wedding.

ing new styles, colors, fabrics, and ways to accessorize their clothes. They go to great lengths to find unique fashion—to an out-of-the-way boutique, or even to another country. They often become aware of various modes of dress while traveling. They are discerning shoppers who would rather have a few beautiful things than many mediocre things.

Many fashion leaders are in prominent positions which give them exposure, notice, and influence over the way others dress. The press reports details of what they wear, and they are seen at public events, in films, or on television. Because of their support of the couture and boutique designers over the years, fashion leaders are a stimulant to designers and to the fashion industry as a whole.

Most fashion leaders are confident of their own taste and do not need others' approval. Individualists, they do not need the security and safety of standardization. They dare to be different, and their acceptance of a designer's clothes makes the clothes fashionable.

Fashion Followers Most men and women, however, seek acceptance by conformity and follow world, national, or community fashion leaders in order to feel confident in wearing a new look. Fashion followers emulate others only after they are sure of fashion trends.

Most consumers are fashion followers, for several reasons:

They lack the time, the money, and the interest to devote to fashion leadership.

They need a period of exposure to new styles before accepting them.

They are insecure about their tastes and therefore turn to what others have already approved as acceptable and appropriate.

They want to keep up with their neighbors or peer group or to be accepted by them.

They tend to imitate people they admire.

Fashion followers cause most of the fashion industry to be copyists or adapters. From a marketing point of view, fashion followers make mass production successful, because volume mass production of fashion can be profitable only when the same merchandise is sold to many consumers.

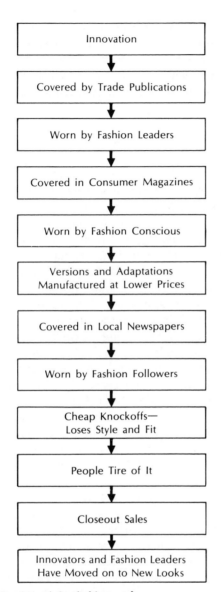

| Innovation |
| Covered by Trade Publications |
| Worn by Fashion Leaders |
| Covered in Consumer Magazines |
| Worn by Fashion Conscious |
| Versions and Adaptations Manufactured at Lower Prices |
| Covered in Local Newspapers |
| Worn by Fashion Followers |
| Cheap Knockoffs— Loses Style and Fit |
| People Tire of It |
| Closeout Sales |
| Innovators and Fashion Leaders Have Moved on to New Looks |

Inter-relationship of the fashion cycle, the traditional adoption theory, the fashion press, and manufacturing

ADOPTION OF FASHION

Basically, there are three variations of the fashion adoption process: traditional adoption, reverse adoption, and mass dissemination. It is important to understand how new fashion ideas are disseminated, or spread, and how they are adapted to fit the tastes, life styles, and budgets of various types of consumers.

Traditional Fashion Adoption
(or the Trickle-down Theory)
Innovative designers have the courage and confidence to try new looks. At first the looks seem out-

rageous to many people, until it is seen how they can be adapted to the American life style. Not every extreme design is accepted by the general public. Just because a top designer shows harem pants does not mean that everyone will be wearing them, but it does indicate a possible trend toward ankle interest. Extravagance is needed to make an impact that may swing the whole fashion pendulum only a little. To cause attention and change direction even moderately, high fashion often seeks to be extreme.

The traditional adoption theory is based on the fact that most high fashion is expensive, and therefore affordable by only a few people. As the new fashions are worn by publicized fashion leaders or shown in fashion publications, more consumers are exposed to the new look, and some will desire to have it for themselves. Manufacturers produce less expensive versions or adaptations of high fashion, to appeal to this broader group of consumers. These are copied again and again at lower prices, until they have been seen often enough to become acceptable to the most conservative buyer. Soon afterward the cheapest versions are seen at discount houses. Consumers tire of the look and its popularity fades.

The length of this process is influenced by geographical location. If the new look starts in Europe, then New York and other northeastern cities will probably be the first to accept it, followed by California. It may take a year or even two for middle Americans to fit the look into their life styles—and even then in a modified version.

Fashion implies newness and freshness. Yet, as it is copied and modified at lower and lower prices, it loses its newness, quality, and other essential design elements. Therefore, one disadvantage of traditional adoption is that the original is often modified so much that it is no longer attractive or even recognizable.

Reverse Adoption
(or the Bottom-up Theory)
Although most fashion filters down from high-priced designer clothes, fashion occasionally begins with the actual consumer. For example, in the 1960s and early '70s young people in both London and San Francisco influenced the whole fashion industry. Young people created unique combinations of old, new, and handcrafted clothes. Designers began watching the people on the streets to find ideas. Eventually, these looks reached the designer market level, as exemplified in St. Laurent's 1975 "elegant peasant" collection. Reverse adoption in the 1960s and 70s

was caused by the enormous consumer group of young people; one half of the population was under age 30. Young people rejected fashion offered by older designers. As the median age of consumers gets older, reverse adoption has less impact.

Although the trend now is back to the traditional adoption process, with the worldwide influence of many ready-to-wear designers in Paris, Milan, London, and New York, designers now pay more attention to consumer innovation.

Mass Dissemination
(or the Trickle-across Theory)

Modern communication sometimes seems to make fashion available simultaneously throughout the industry. This process of dissemination was especially evident in the 1960s when many young designers, such as Mary Quant and Betsey Johnson, mass-produced new styles for their contemporaries, at affordable prices. Manufacturers did not copy from a higher price range. Other manufacturers—also in moderate to low price ranges—quickly copied. Speed of production was of the greatest importance.

Obviously, several separate fashion markets exist. No single adoption theory is appropriate for the total fashion industry. Each market caters to a different taste, age, and price level. Missy market styling is generally adapted from designer fashion by the traditional process. Styling ideas for active sportswear and denim wear are usually inspired by the actual consumer, by the reverse process. Junior fashions might be disseminated by the mass-market method, since the original ideas are often produced precisely for this youthful market. It should also be remembered that many American consumers today are not even interested in high fashion.

INDIVIDUALITY VERSUS CONFORMITY

Most consumers seek varying amounts of both individuality and conformity in their dress. To feel a sense of belonging to their peer group, they follow fashions; to express their personality, they find ways to individualize fashion. A consumer can select from a wide variety of fashion looks on the market, combining and accessorizing them for individual expression, which is particularly important in today's mass-oriented society. Yet, many consumers find variety of choice confusing, making shopping decisions difficult. These people often gain support from knowing that others share their preferences.

The fashion industry reacts in the same way. Manufacturers and retailers try to establish a particular merchandising specialty, something their customers can identify with. Yet, few manufacturers or retailers want to be outside the mainstream of fashion.

SUMMARY

Fashion has three properties: style, acceptance, and change. Change makes the fashion world go 'round. New styles are introduced, rise to their heights of popularity, and then decline into obsolescence. Some styles remain in fashion for longer periods of time, others for shorter. Some come back into fashion after a latent period. Because fashion is a product of change, a sense of timing is an important attribute at all levels of the industry. The speed of change is influenced by modern communication, modern marketing, advances in mass production, greater discretionary incomes, and seasonal change.

Consumers can be grouped and identified with sections of the fashion cycle. Fashion leaders, a very small percentage of the population, buy and wear new styles at the beginning of the cycle; other consumers imitate. The majority of consumers are followers, which facilitates the mass marketing of fashion.

Fashions generally sift down from the original ideas of high-fashion designers to reappear in cheaper fabrics at lower price levels. Other styles are either adapted "up from the streets" or are disseminated quickly through mass marketing. Consumers can choose among a wide variety of styles, dressing to conform to peer group preferences or to be individualistic. Consumer acceptance is a main influence on styling and merchandising decisions.

CHAPTER REVIEW

CHAPTER OBJECTIVES

After reading this chapter you should be able to

A. Give evidence of having attained competence in the following areas:
   1. Understanding of the dimensions of fashion   2. Ability to identify the phases and lengths of fashion cycles and to relate them to consumer acceptance   3. Understanding of fashion adoption theories in relation to consumer acceptance

B. Define the following terms and concepts in relation to their discussion in the chapter:
1. Fashion 2. Style 3. Acceptance 4. Timeliness 5. Fashion evolution 6. Fashion cycles 7. Phases of fashion cycles 8. Classics 9. Fads 10. Interrupted cycles 11. Recurring fashion cycles 12. Taste 13. Fashion leaders 14. Fashion followers 15. Fashion adoption 16. Traditional fashion adoption 17. Reverse adoption 18. Mass-market dissemination

Questions for Review

1. Define the three components that make up fashion.
2. Discuss how fashion acceptance affects the timing of design.
3. Discuss the phases of a typical fashion acceptance cycle.
4. Discuss the relationship of consumer acceptance to the fashion cycle.
5. Relate the various types of fashion adoption to various consumer groups.

PROJECTS FOR ADDITIONAL LEARNING

1. Is there a well-known movie star or public figure (either male or female) in the news who you feel is a fashion leader? Give your reasons in a short report documented with examples of how this person influences the way others dress.

2. From current fashion magazines, collect five examples of each of the following types of fashions: a. high fashion; b. mass fashion; c. classic; d. fad.

FASHION
RESEARCH
AND
ANALYSIS

**Designer Pierre Cardin visits
a Parisian costume museum**
(Courtesy of Pierre Cardin, Paris)

4

Sophisticated marketing techniques developed in the 1950s, along with systematic approaches for evaluating consumer tastes—such as surveys—have increased the industry's awareness of the importance of pleasing the customer. It would seem a simple matter to make or sell what people want to buy. However, the textile sector of the industry must plan up to five years ahead of a finished product's arrival in the store, because the development and production processes from fiber to completed garment take that long. Therefore, good research and planning—and obviously, a little intuition—are needed for producers and retailers to make and buy what consumers will want in the future. Without proper research, or if there is an unexpected turn of events, merchandise ends up on the sale racks, causing losses for producers, manufacturers, and retailers alike.

Because the very term fashion implies a state of flux, textile producers, fashion manufacturers, and retailers all need to absorb a constant flow of information in order to anticipate future change and consumer preferences. This chapter is concerned with the information needed to forecast trends and with the sources of such information. In addition, the chapter examines influences on creativity. Research is done before any other design or merchandising activity may begin, at every level of the industry. It becomes second nature to every decision maker in the field of fashion.

FORECASTING TRENDS

Fashion *trends* are directions in which fashion styling is moving. Because most fashion producers and retailers want their merchandise to fit into the mainstream of fashion, and because they must work so far ahead of the selling season, they must learn to be fashion trend forecasters. Fashion forecasters have to identify and analyze signs indicating forthcoming change. They base their judgment on experience, awareness of trend-setting designers, fashion cycles, and economic, political, social, and technological influences on both the garment industry and the consumer. Fashion forecasters must do all of the following:

Decide which fashions are prophetic,

Estimate which segment of the market will accept a particular fashion, and

Determine at what time these fashions will be acceptable to target customers.

Identifying Prophetic Styles

Fashion forecasters analyze the designer collections for what they call *prophetic styles*, fresh ideas that capture the mood of the times. If several designers move in a similar fashion direction (that is, use similar fashion elements such as color or silhouette), this is due to their having common sources of inspiration based on current interest or events. That several designers simultaneously express similar ideas, in response to the same stimuli, may indicate a fashion trend.

Adapting to a Target Market

The adaptation of a trend depends on the particular group of people who are potential ultimate consumers. Different sources and different methods of adaptation are used according to the consumers' age, income level, life style, and fashion preferences.

For example, the junior market is heavily influenced by the French *prêt-à-porter* because of its youthful styling. Some merchandise is actually imported by retail stores for their better junior departments, to appeal to more affluent customers. Most often, however, the *prêt* serves as the fashion trend setter for American junior volume manufacturers. They interpret *prêt* fashions to suit American tastes and life styles.

French fashion tends to be extreme, either to express the creativity of the designers or to draw attention to the individual collections. American designers tend to soften the French silhouettes and modify other extremes, because our life style is more casual than the European.

How Geographical Location Affects Timing

The timing of fashion trend adoption and adaptation depends on the geographical location of potential customers. Designer fashions from Paris and Italy are quickly accepted on a worldwide level by those whose incomes and life styles afford them the opportunity to wear European fashion. Otherwise, it usually takes one or two years for the ideas put forth in Europe to be accepted by Americans. New York designer fashions are accepted more readily and widely in this country because they are specifically designed to meet our needs. However, in both cases people with high incomes, in high-level jobs, and living in a sophisticated urban environment will accept fashion change more quickly than others.

Manufacturers and retailers naturally adjust their trend predictions accordingly. They need to determine how long it takes for their target customers to accept a new fashion. They measure the length of time between fashion origin (when a fashion was first designed) and fashion acceptance (when the particular customer bought that fashion or a modification of it). Merchandisers then know if their customer will accept current fashion immediately, six months from now, or a year from now.

SOURCES OF INFORMATION

In fashion forecasting, good merchandisers and designers draw on information from every available source. They interpret the information in terms of the fashion preferences of their particular target customers.

Market Studies

It would be impossible to ask all consumers what they will want two or three years from now. Therefore, producers and manufacturers must anticipate consumer wants and needs. Before any designing, manufacturing, or retailing is done, market studies are made to determine who current or potential customers are, and what factors influence their buying decisions, and ultimately what they will want.

Manufacturers and retailers *shop the market* to see what is selling well and why. They compare styling, price, fit, and quality of lines that compete with their own. They also analyze lines at higher price levels to get a feeling for directions that may soon affect their own price levels. Market information sources include analyses of new collections, sales records, and customer surveys.

Evaluating the Collections Traditionally, both manufacturers and retailers turn first to Paris for indication of the newest fashion ideas. Twice each year, the members of both the *prêt-à-porter* and the *couture* show their spring and fall collections. From all over the world, retail buyers and fashion editors, as well as designers and manufacturers, invade Paris. Milan, London, and New York are also good places to evaluate collections.

When viewing the major collections, manufacturers, retailers, and the press try to analyze trend directions. Usually a few collections take similar directions due to common economic, technological, political, and social influences. Designers and buyers alike try to single out the styles they feel are prophetic of future directions in fashion. It is very helpful to be able to see and feel the actual garments and to examine styling details, construction techniques, and fit.

Sales Records Every manufacturer and retailer keeps records of all sales. Properly interpreted, this information indicates customer interest by proof of purchase. It also shows what fashion trends are developing (by sales on the rise) and what trends may have passed their peak (by a decline in sales). This method of research is especially necessary on the moderate and lower price levels. Manufacturers

Translate spring 80 COATS into autumn 80

HALSTON SPORT   CALVIN KLEIN   RICHARD ASSATLY   CALVIN KLEIN   THIERRY MUGLER

IM'S OWN TRANSLATION DESIGNS

IM International ideas on how to adapt fashion trends from one season to the next (Courtesy of IM International)

who produce in volume cannot afford to take risks. They need the concrete proof of sales figures to show current trends. However, since fashion is constantly evolving at a rapid pace, sales statistics alone are not reliable to evaluate trends. Also, they do not show what merchandise is *lacking*.

Consumer Surveys Methods of questioning consumers can be formal or informal. Formal surveys such as mailed questionnaires and personal interviews are made by reporting services, publications, some manufacturers, and stores. Informally, information can be obtained by asking store customers what they would like to see on the market, what styles they like that are currently on the market, and what merchandise is *lacking*.

Reporting Services

Design reporting services try to analyze the collections and design trends for both manufacturers and retailers. They act as consultants to both those who can and those who cannot attend the collections. (The collections can be so overwhelming that even those who attend may need assistance in identifying major trends.)

Design reporting services work quickly, often writing up the last collection while attending the next. For example, the staff at *IM International* write up information on the Italian collections in the evenings and weekends while attending the Paris shows a few days later. They produce approximately 75 camera-ready pages (ready for printing plates to be made) in about five days, and the finished printed report is mailed to their clients eight days later. Without traveling to Europe or New York, a designer or buyer can learn about new trends from reporting services such as the following:

Design Direction, 39 Great Windmill Street, London W. 1, England

Design Intelligence, John Michael Ltd., 19 Savile Row, London W. 1, England

Faces, 51 Great Portland Street, London W. 1, England

Here and There, 55 W. 39th Street, New York, New York 10008

IM International (abbreviation for Imaginative Minds), Lee Rudd Associates, 28 Old Church Street, London S.W. 3, England

Nigel French, 167 Oxford Street, London W. 1, England

Promostyl, 12 rue Auber, 75009 Paris, France

Both newspapers and magazines rely on advertising to pay most of their production costs. As a result, the bulk of the publication is often paid advertising, and the editorial section is often influenced by paying advertisers. To give manufacturers and retailers design information without advertising, the service reports must charge an expensive subscription rate—between $1,000 and $10,000 per year. They provide varying viewpoints of fashion trends using descriptions, sketches, photographs, fabric swatches, and color samples, usually in 12 to 16 issues a year. Some offer slides, original designs, and consulting services as well. Most offer information on both men's and women's wear.

Other services, aimed specifically at retailers, include the following:

Tobé Report, 500 5th Avenue, New York, New York 10036

Retail News Bureau, 232 Madison Ave., New York, New York 10016

RAM Report (Rome Arnold Marketing Service, actually a sampling of sales statistics), 1440 Broadway, New York, New York 10036

Fashion Calendar, 185 E. 85th Street, New York, New York 10028 (lists dates and details about upcoming collection openings, market weeks, and fashion shows)

Fashion Publications

Trend research also depends on a variety of trade and consumer publications. *Trade magazines* and *newspapers* are intended for people working in the fashion industry; *consumer publications* are created for the general public. Both manufacturers and retailers must constantly read as many publications as possible, because each fashion journalist edits fashion trends from a different perspective.

Fashion Editing Fashion editors, together with journalists, stylists, and photographers, act as the eyes and ears of the consumer, letting the nation or the community know where to find the fashions that are currently on the market, and reporting on how new fashions should be worn and accessorized. Exceptional fashion editors may be prophetic in their analysis of coming fashion trends.

Ideally, the role of the fashion editor is to educate: to provide fashion information from all phases of the industry in all parts of the world to make the industry and the consumer aware of all that is available and to help them make wise and suitable styling and buying decisions.

Fashion editors of prominent newspapers and fashion magazines attend the collections, taking notes on what they like best. They then request sketches or photographs of their favorite garments to keep on file. Editors try to sift through all the news releases that come into their offices, as well as to do their own investigating by attending the markets, and to report on what they feel is important. When they are ready to write an article on coats, for instance, they pull out the coat file, find suitable styles that would look good together, and ask to borrow samples from the manufacturers.[1] After planning a layout for both the visual and the written part of the article, they do the production. Photography is done in a studio or on location, or illustrations are sketched by an artist, depending on the mood or effect to be achieved. Finally, garment and fabric descriptions are requested from the manufacturers, as well as a list of stores that carry the merchandise described or depicted in the article.

[1] Catherine Rousso, Fashion Editor, *Elle Magazine*, Paris, personal interview, August 1978.

Fashion Ideas editor Catherine Rousso supervising copy writing at Elle Magazine in Paris *(Photographed by the author)*

Trade Publications Trade publications offer information not only on fashion trends but on textile industry, fashion industry, and retailing business developments as well. Some specialize in a particular branch of the industry.

Women's Wear Daily is a newspaper published five days a week by Fairchild Publications, 7 East 12th Street, New York, New York 10003. The Bible of the apparel industry, it covers both domestic and European women's and children's wear as well as fabrics. A biweekly condensed version called "*W*" is available to consumers.

Daily News Record is another Fairchild newspaper, covering men's wear.

California Apparel News is published weekly by California Fashion Publications, 1016 South Broadway Place, Los Angeles, California 90015. It concentrates on the California apparel industry. California Fashion Publications also publishes *Men's Apparel News*.

Fashion Showcase, 1145 Empire Central Place, Suite 100, Dallas, Texas 75247, concentrates on fashion in the Southwest.

Fabric News to the Trade, 21 East 40th Street, New York, New York 10016, is a textile industry newspaper.

American Fabrics and Fashion, published by Doric Publishing Co., Inc., 24 East 38th Street, New York, New York 10016, is a trade magazine featuring thorough coverage of fibers, fabrics, and apparel in four issues per year.

Apparel Industry Magazine, 6226 Vineland Avenue, North Hollywood, CA 91606, covers manufacturing news.

Stores, 100 W. 31st Street, New York, New York 10001, is a retailing trade magazine.

Retail Week, 380 Madison Avenue, New York, New York 10017, is another retailing trade magazine.

Style, 481 University Avenue, Toronto, Ontario M5W 1A7, is Canada's monthly trade fashion magazine.

Textile Forecast, Fabric Forecast, and **Fashion Forecast** are magazines published by Benjamin Dent, 33 Bedford Place, London W.C. 1, England.

Gap, 59 rue de Billancourt, 92100 Boulogne, France, is the French trade magazine.

Consumer Fashion Magazines Of the most helpful international fashion magazines, some come out only two or four times a year to report on the collections; others are monthly or semimonthly. It is not necessary to read the text of the foreign language magazines; the ideas come from the photographs. Some consumer fashion magazines are listed below:

L'Officiel de la Couture et de la Mode de Paris, 226 rue de Faubourg St. Honoré, 75008 Paris, France. (Referred to simply as L'Officiel, it covers the French couture collections.)

L'Officiel du Prêt-à-Porter, 265 Avenue Louise, 1050 Brussels, Belgium (covers the prêt-à-porter collections).

Femme Pratique Prêt-à-Porter, 352 rue St. Honoré, 75001 Paris, France. (Twice-yearly special issues of *Femme Pratique* with excellent presentations and analyses of *prêt-à-porter* fashion directions.)

Elégance, Publications AG, Gartenstrasse 14, 8039 Zürich, Switzerland.

Linea Italiana, 20090 Sagrate, Milano, Italy (the Italian collections).

Town and Country, 717 Fifth Avenue, New York, New York 10022. (February and August issues have comprehensive coverage of designer collections.)

L'Officiel—USA, 300 East 42nd Street, New York, New York 10017 (American designers, reports on French collections).

Vogue, 350 Madison Avenue, New York, New York 10017 (features American designers).

English Vogue, Vogue House, Hanover Square, London W. 1, England (features English designers).

Paris Vogue, 4 Place du Palais-Bourbon, 75005 Paris, France (features French couture and *prêt-à-porter*).

Italian Vogue, Piazza Castello 27, 20121 Milano, Italy (features Italian designers).

Harper's Bazaar, 717 Fifth Avenue, New York, New York 10022 (American designers).

Harper's and Queen, Chestergate House, Vauxhall Bridge Road, London S.W. 1, England (features English designers).

Harper's Bazaar Italia, Via Nino Bixio 45, 20129 Milano, Italy (features Italian designers).

CONTEMPORARY AND JUNIORS

Elle, 6 rue Ancello, 92521 Neuilly (Paris suburb), France. (Actually a "women's" magazine with other features, *Elle* is respected as one of the most outstanding interpreters of the *prêt-à-porter*.)

Brigitte, Postfach 30-20-40, 2000 Hamburg 36, West Germany (also a women's magazine, but has especially good ideas for contemporary, juniors, and children).

Designer Barbara Colvin researches ideas in trade and consumer fashion publications and costume books *(Photographed by the author)*

Depeché Mode, 3 rue de Teheran, 75008 Paris, France (features *prêt-à-porter*).

Glamour, 350 Madison Avenue, New York, New York 10017 (contemporary fashions for the young career woman).

Mademoiselle, 350 Madison Avenue, New York, New York 10017 (contemporary fashions for the college woman).

Seventeen Magazine, 850 Third Avenue, New York, New York 10022 (America's junior magazine for the high school girl).

CHILDREN'S WEAR The Italian magazines, such as *Vogue Bambini,* seem to be the best in the children's wear area. Junior fashions are also a good source for interpretation into children's wear.

MEN'S WEAR *Gentlemen's Quarterly* and Fairchild's *Men's Wear* specialize in men's fashion. *Gentlemen's Quarterly* is now published in twelve issues a year instead of four, showing the increased interest in men's fashion in America. France has a men's collection magazine called *L'Officiel Hommes* (262 rue de Faubourg St. Honoré, 75008 Paris, France), and *Vogue Homme.* Italy has many men's wear magazines, including men's wear versions of popular women's fashion magazines, such as *L'Uomo Vogue* and *Linea Italiana Uomo.* English *Vogue* often devotes a section to men's fashion.

BRIDAL Magazines specializing in bridal gowns include *Bride's* and *Modern Bride* in the United States, and *Sposa,* via Burlamacchi 11, 20135 Milano, Italy.

There is an ever growing number of magazines on the market. Designers and buyers evaluate them and determine which are most helpful for their particular specialty. Retailers also find local newspaper advertisements helpful because they indicate what other stores in their area are featuring.

CREATIVE DESIGN SOURCES

What makes a textile or fashion designer's line special is his or her unique interpretation of fashion trends. Ideas do not simply materialize out of thin air. A combination of many influences results in a designer's personal style.

A designer who develops and is recognized for a particular style attracts buyers who come back year after year. Two examples of designers who have distinctive style identification are Jean Muir, a London designer, and Jessica McClintock, of San Francisco.

A design by Jean Muir showing her use of jersey combined with suede and top-stitching details
(Photo by Charlie Gerli, courtesy of Jean Muir Fashion Designs Ltd.)

These designers appeal to two entirely different types of customers, in two vastly different price ranges.

Jean Muir achieved recognition in the mid-1960s with the popularity of her timeless, graceful dresses. She continues to specialize in jerseys, leathers, and the use of top-stitching detail.

Jessica McClintock, owner of and designer for Gunne Sax, a junior house, has kept the same romantic, country feeling in her clothes since she started her business in 1970.

Printed Design Sources

Textile and fashion designers use printed sources (magazines, trade papers, and design reports) to analyze trends because they want their designs to fit into the mainstream of fashion. But in addition to supplying trend information, these publications are good sources of ideas. Designers collect pictures showing appealing ideas for color, line, fabric, and trimmings. One idea may inspire a whole line. For example, Barbara Colvin, a talented California designer, once based a whole group on a photograph in a European fashion magazine of Persian rug factory workers in their colorful costumes.

Historic Costume

A designer often turns to the past for line and silhouette ideas that can be used in a new way for the present time. Designers must become sensitive to the combinations of colors, motifs, lines, shapes, and spaces of design in each historical period of art and costume. These elements can be revived for modern clothing. One way to adapt ideas from historic costume is within a framework of current trends.

Designers search for ideas from costumes in museums, books, and flea markets. Costume falls into two categories: *historic costume*, the fashion of a certain historical period, and *folk costume*, traditional national or regional dress (ethnic). Both are inspirational sources of design.

Costume Museums Museum costume collections offer the unique opportunity of seeing actual preserved garments displayed on mannequins. A popular exhibit can influence many designers. For example, the Metropolitan Museum's 1980 exhibit of "Fashions of the Hapsburg Era" influenced many designers who included Austrian looks in their fall 1980 collections. Outstanding collections include the following:

Costume Institute, The Metropolitan Museum of Art, 5th Avenue and 82nd Street, New York, New York 10028

The Costume Gallery, The Brooklyn Museum, 188 Eastern Parkway, Brooklyn, New York 11238

The Costume Gallery, Los Angeles County Museum of Art, 5905 Wilshire Blvd., Los Angeles, California 90036

Costume Institute, McCord Museum, 690 Sherbrooke Street West, Montreal, Canada

Musée du Costume de la Ville de Paris, 14 avenue New York, 75016 Paris, France

Victoria and Albert Museum, Brompton Road, London S.W. 7, England. (Besides a huge collection of costumes, this museum also has collections of old fabrics and embroideries, including directions on how to make the stitches.)

The Museum of Costume, Assembly Rooms, Alfred Street, Bath, England

Rijksmuseum, Stadhouderskade 42, 020 Amsterdam, Netherlands

Kostümforschungs Institut (Costume Research Institute), Kemnatenstrasse 50, 8 Munich 19, West Germany (documents)

Centro Internazionale Arti e del Costume, 3231 Palazzo Grassi, 30124 Venice, Italy

In addition, there are many regional museums with fashion collections, and almost every national museum of folklore includes ethnic costumes. Of course, studying historic costume is not limited to seeing the actual garments. Costume can be studied in historic paintings or books. Most museums have bookstores containing excellent costume references.

Books and Magazines Besides costume books, many libraries also have collections of old fashion magazines, including *Godey's Ladies Book* from the 1830s to the 1890s, *Harper's Bazaar* from 1867, and *Vogue* from 1893.

Films and Theater

Film costume designs do not set fashion trends as much today as they did in the past. However, occasional films do influence style. *Dr. Zhivago* popularized the Russian look, *Bonnie and Clyde* revived '30s fashions, *Annie Hall* popularized a look of vests and baggy pants, *Grease* created a rage for '50s clothes, and *Star Wars* inspired some designers to do futuristic coats and jackets. Both theater and films reflect people's tastes. Designers want to keep in touch with the public, and this is an enjoyable way to do it.

THE IMPORTANCE OF AWARENESS

Designers surround themselves with photographs of ideas, fabric swatches, and anything else that will stimulate creativity. They leave their studios to shop, visit museums, study nature, attend the theater, or people-watch. Designers usually carry sketch books, jotting down ideas whenever and wherever they find them. They hunger for information, letting ideas mingle and shape themselves into new forms.

Awareness is the key to developing a good design. Most of all, designers must learn to keep their eyes open, to absorb visual ideas, and to translate them into clothes their customers will like. Some people are more sensitive to good composition than others, but practice and observation make a person more aware, sensitive, and confident. Design direction comes from many sources. A designer needs to study almost constantly to capture the subtle nuances.

Merchandisers, too, should be open to everything that goes on around them, as it affects the clothing industry: economics, politics, art. Good taste and a good sense of timing are results of exposure. Constant exposure to beautiful merchandise helps a buyer distinguish real beauty and quality from fads and mediocrity.

SUMMARY

Research and observation are critically important in the fashion business. By watching for directions in designer collections, studying markets, reading the best fashion publications, and observing fashion leaders, manufacturers and retailers can predict what the majority of their customers will want in the foreseeable future. To keep up with the changing world of fashion, one must constantly read trade and consumer periodicals such as those listed in this chapter. Researching design sources such as museums should also become routine. For anyone serious about a career in design or merchandising, fashion awareness should become second nature.

CHAPTER REVIEW

CHAPTER OBJECTIVES

After reading this chapter you should be able to
A. Give evidence of having attained competence in the following areas:
1. Understanding of the importance of awareness 2. Understanding of market studies and trend or design research 3. Knowledge of informative sources for research 4. Ability to analyze fashion direction
B. Define the following terms and concepts in relation to their discussion in the chapter:
1. Market studies 2. Consumer surveys 3. Fashion editing 4. Fashion forecasting 5. Fashion trends 6. Prophetic styles 7. Target market 8. Timing 9. Evaluating collections 10. Design services 11. Examples of trade publications 12. Examples of consumer publications 13. Creative design sources 14. Awareness

Questions for Review

1. Why is awareness important for the designer and the buyer?
2. Explain fashion trends.
3. Explain the difference between trade and consumer fashion publications.
4. What role does historic or folk costume play in today's fashion?
5. Give an example of how film costumes have influenced fashion.

PROJECTS FOR ADDITIONAL LEARNING

Every student should subscribe to "W" (a less expensive, condensed version of *Women's Wear Daily*) or *California Apparel News*, and to at least one fashion magazine.

1. *Trend research.* Make a survey of fashion resources available to you. Read the fashion column in the daily newspaper. Read the latest issues of fashion magazines and compare them to fashion looks six months ago. From the information you find, try to analyze the fashion direction for the future. Organize your ideas into a few basic trend forecasts for color, fabrics, silhouette, and line.

2. *Fashion magazine evaluation.* Examine four different fashion magazines and compare their content. How many pages are devoted to paid advertisements? How many pages are devoted to editorial fashion reporting? Which magazine has the most interesting information?

3. Look through costume books for pictures of Oriental dress. Using these as inspiration, design a garment using the line, shapes, colors, and details from the Oriental garment in a new combination for our life style.

4. Visit a local art museum. Select a favorite painting—period or contemporary—and discover whether the colors, lines, shapes, or any other details of the work give you inspiration for garment design. Sketch your interpretation of that influence in a garment design.

THE
RAW MATERIALS
OF
FASHION
PART TWO

TEXTILE FIBER AND FABRIC PRODUCTION

5

Ripe cotton bolls,
a fiber provided by Mother Nature
(Courtesy of Cotton, Inc.)

Before we can even begin to think of a finished garment, we must go to the source of the raw materials from which it is made. Collectively, the producers of these raw materials are the suppliers to the apparel industry.

Primary suppliers are the producers of textiles, as well as of furs and leathers, some plastic, paper, and other nonwoven materials. Secondary suppliers provide the trimmings (decorative materials including buttons, laces, and ribbons) and findings (functional materials like zippers, elastic, interfacing, and linings) needed to complete a garment.

Since most garments are made from fabrics, the textile industry is our major concern. Textiles is a broad term referring to any materials that can be made into fabric by any method. Occasionally the term textile industry is used to cover the whole apparel industry: the production and marketing of textile merchandise from raw materials to the final product in the retail store. This production and marketing chain includes the following steps:

Fiber production

Yarn spinning

Fabric production

Dyeing, finishing, printing

Garment manufacturing

Retailing

More precisely, the textile industry encompasses the production and marketing only of fibers, yarns, and fabrics, including trimmings and findings. In this definition the textile industry represents the first steps in the fashion industry. This chapter follows the order of textile production from fiber to fabric. Production is the process of generating a product, such as a fiber, a yarn, or a fabric. Chapter 6 discusses the marketing steps that put fabrics into the hands of designers and manufacturers. Marketing refers to the entire process of planning, promoting, and selling a product.

This chapter is intended primarily for readers who lack a background in textiles. It is a short, simplified treatment of the basics; by no means can it substitute for a complete course in textiles.

The American textile industry is now the largest in the world, involving over 5,000 companies. Production is dispersed throughout the country, with a heavy concentration in the Southeast—especially in North and South Carolina. Because New York City is the nation's fashion capital, most textile companies have New York offices, as well as sales representatives all over the country.

NATURAL FIBERS

Before the textile industry can supply fabrics to the apparel manufacturers, it must first develop and produce both natural and man-made fibers. The most important natural fibers are flax, wool, cotton, and silk. Others are jute, sisal, and hemp. All of these are either animal or vegetable fibers that have been used for thousands of years and are still considered the most luxurious fibers. For beauty, nothing can compare with natural fibers. Factories processing natural fibers are located along the Atlantic and Pacific coasts, concentrating increasingly in the southern states where overall expenses, especially labor, are lower.

Flax

Flax is made from the fibrous material in the stem of the flax plant, a weedlike grass. This substance is processed and used to make a fabric called linen. Belgium, Egypt, France, Germany, Holland, Ireland, Italy, Poland, and the Soviet Union are the principal growers of flax for fabrics. Linen is the oldest known textile, dating back as far as the Stone Age. At one time linen was used extensively for bedding; this explains why we still call sheets, towels, and tablecloths collectively "linens." Flax was an important crop in the United States until the invention of the cotton gin in 1792 made cotton cheaper to produce. Today, most of the flax fiber used in textiles in the United States is imported.

The cool, light-weight qualities of linen make it especially suited for summer clothes. The popularity of no-iron fabrics made of man-made fiber blends has caused linen to lose favor with consumers because it wrinkles easily. However, renewed interest in texture and natural fibers has repopularized linen and linen blends and has promoted linen look-alikes in rayon and other fiber blends.

Wool

According to the slogan of the American Wool Council and the International Wool Bureau, wool is "the new miracle fiber just 8,000 years old." Wool fiber comes from the *fleece* of animals, most commonly sheep. Sheep are a natural and renewable re-

Shearing Merino sheep in Victoria, Australia
(Courtesy of the International Wool Secretariat, London)

source: "Shear a sheep today and a year from now the same sheep is ready again for shearing."[1] (Shearing is the removal of wool from the sheep by the use of shears or clippers.)

Raw wool is *carded* to separate short fibers from long ones. Later, long fibers are spun in a special worsted process to make smooth, compact *worsted* yarns used for fabrics such as gabardine or crepe, while short fibers make up the soft, dense *woolen* yarns used in textured tweeds.

Wool-bearing sheep are raised in almost every country of the world. Australia, New Zealand, and South Africa are the major wool-producing countries. Other countries, such as Great Britain, Argentina, Uruguay, China, India, the Soviet Union, and the United States, also have considerable production. The wool produced in the United States comes mostly from the western mountain states of Utah, Nevada, and Colorado, but the Northeast has considerable production, too. Total world wool production is about 3 billion pounds per year.[2] Major buyers and importers of wool fibers are Japan, Great Britain, and the United States.

Because the supply of new wool is not sufficient to meet the world's needs, and in order to cut costs, reclaimed woolen fibers are sometimes used. To protect the consumer, the Wool Products Labeling Act requires all wool fabrics to be labeled as "virgin" (new wool), or "recycled" (reclaimed wool from used or unused woven goods). The city of Prato near Florence, Italy, has become well known for recycling wools into fashionable fabrics.

Properties of Wool The structure of wool fiber makes fabrics that retain body heat. Because it is warm, wool has traditionally been used in fabrics for fall and winter suits and coats. Yet, wool, a versatile fiber, can be woven or knitted into light-weight fabrics such as challis. Wool fibers are firm, yet soft and elastic, helping wool fabrics to resist wrinkling. This elasticity also makes wool fabrics give with the body's movements, so that they are very comfortable to wear.

Other Wools Although wool is commonly understood to be fiber from the fleece of sheep—because most wool in clothing *is* sheep's wool—some

other animal fibers, usually called *specialty hair fibers*, are also classified as wool. They include camel's hair, cashmere, mohair, angora, alpaca, vicuna, and horse hair.

Camel's hair comes from the double-humped Bactrian camel of Asia. The hair is collected as the camels shed their coats in the spring. Its fine fibers, used alone or in blends, make fabrics that are soft, warm, and luxurious, usually for suits or coats. Because of the beauty of its color, most fabrics containing camel's hair are left undyed.

Cashmere comes from the hair of the Cashmere goat of Central Asia, China, Iran, and Afghanistan. Cashmere fabrics are soft, silky, and luxurious. The hair is removed from the goats by combing once a year by nomadic tribesmen. Each goat provides only four or five ounces of fleece a year. Because it is available only in limited quantities, it is costly. Therefore, ownership of a cashmere coat or sweater has become a status symbol.

Mohair comes from the Angora goat, originally from Angora (Ankara), Turkey. Now the United States and South Africa are also major mohair suppliers. Its light fibers add density and softness to fabrics. It is used in combination with the other wool fibers in knitted or woven fabrics, to give them airy and fluffy textures.

Angora fur from the Angora rabbit is lightweight, soft, and fluffy and is blended with other wool to give a furry texture. This special breed of rabbit is raised in China, France, Czechoslovakia, Japan, the Netherlands, Belgium, and the United States.

Alpaca, producing a fine, lustrous fiber, is a domesticated llama of Peru.

Vicuna, which has the softest and finest of the wool fibers, is a wild llama found in the Andes mountains. However, Vicuna is now rarely used as the animals must be killed to obtain the fiber.[3]

Horse hair can be made into canvas for backings in suits and coats but is now rarely used.

Cotton

Cotton has long been the world's major textile fiber. A vegetable fiber, it grows best in tropical and subtropical climates. Most cotton is grown in the United States, the Soviet Union, China, and India. Smaller but still important cotton producers are Brazil, Egypt, Mexico, Pakistan, Peru, Turkey, and the Sudan. The total world production is about 14 million

[1] *Fleece to Fabric* (Denver: American Wool Council, 1977), p. 1.

[2] Vincent Cable, "World Textile Trade and Production," *EIU Special Report*, no. 63 (London: The Economist Intelligence Unit, Ltd., 1979).

[3] Norma Hollen, Jane Saddler, and Anna Langford, *Textiles* (New York: Macmillan Publishing Co., Inc., 1979), p. 30.

tons. In the United States, 14 states in the South make up what is known as the cotton belt, with Texas having the largest acreage under production. The cotton belt stretches from the Southeast (the Carolinas, Georgia, and Alabama) through the Mississippi Delta (Arkansas, Mississippi, and Louisiana) to the Southwest (Texas and Oklahoma), and lately to the West (New Mexico, Arizona, and California). In California cotton has become a major crop, generating more income than any other crop except grapes. Cotton is a relatively inexpensive fiber to produce, but its price tends to fluctuate with cycles in the commodities market.

The cotton plant has blossoms that wither and fall off, leaving green pods called cotton bolls. Inside each boll, moist fibers push out from newly formed seeds. The boll ripens and splits apart, causing the fluffy cotton fibers to burst forth. The cotton is then picked and put through a ginning operation which separates the fiber from the seed. The fibers are further cleaned and straightened by the carding process. Cotton fiber may be processed on a combing machine

that removes short fibers and naps, resulting in a smooth, uniform yarn referred to as *combed cotton*, a very fine quality cotton. The quality of cotton depends on the length and fineness of the fiber or *staple*, long-staple cottons being the finest. In American cottons, pima ranks second to Sea Island in quality.

Cotton is washable and durable, holding up well after many launderings. Because it has little elasticity or resilience, it wrinkles easily. (However, wrinkle-resistant finishes have recently been created to make cotton easier to care for.) Cotton absorbs dyestuffs easily to produce a wide range of vivid colors. It also absorbs moisture, which makes it feel cool against the skin in hot, humid weather. For that reason cotton has traditionally been a summer fabric. Yet cotton is very versatile and can be made in both light weights for summer and heavier weights for winter. Cotton fabrics range from the light and sheer (such as voile and batiste) to the heavy and thick (corduroy, flannel, and chenille) to the strong and sturdy (denim).

Emptying cotton from the picker into trailers for transportation to the ginner where seeds and impurities will be removed *(Courtesy of the National Cotton Council of America)*

Silk

Silk is a protein filament spun by a silkworm to make its cocoon. The silkworm, the forerunner of the silk moth, makes the cocoon as a shell to protect itself during its transformation from caterpillar to moth. Silk harvesters unwind the filament from the cocoon onto silk reels. A typical cocoon will produce 1000 yards of continuous yarn. There are four kinds of silk fibers.

Cultivated silk comes from the domesticated silkworm. The filaments are almost even in size, their fineness indicated by a unit called *denier*. Cultivated silk is used for the finest silk fabrics, such as crepes, taffetas, and satins.

Wild or tussah silk comes from the wild silkworm. Less secure conditions cause the filaments to be coarser and more uneven. Therefore, fabric made from wild silk is not as smooth as that made from domesticated silk.

Douppioni silk is the filament from two or more cocoons that have grown together so that the fibers join at intervals. Yarns made from these fibers have thick, uneven nubs from the joinings. Such yarns are used in shantung.

Waste silk is composed of short fibers from damaged cocoons, not strong or long enough to be used on their own. Yarn spun from waste silk also has irregular slubs; it is used in rough-textured silks.

The patience and hand work necessary for silk production make silk fabric rather expensive. Japan is the largest producer of silk fiber, followed by China, India, Korea, and Italy. The most famous silk fabric mills are in Como, Italy, and Lyon, France. United States silk mills must import all their silk fibers. Silk fabrics represent only a small part of the United States fiber consumption.

Silk has always been used for the finest garments. Because it takes dyes with exceptional depth and clarity and has a luxurious feel, it adds elegance to any garment. Silk also has insulation properties, making the wearer feel cool in summer and warm in winter. Silk drapes exceptionally well; it is very strong yet lightweight; and it is comfortable as well as beautiful.

MAN-MADE FIBERS

Before the advent of man-made fibers, only the natural fibers existed. "Man-made" fibers are all fibers that are extruded from a viscous solution.[4] As the filaments are spun, they are coagulated or dried to form textile fibers. Their greatest attribute is that they can be created with a specific use in mind, or to fill a particular need.

Development of Man-Made Fiber Industry

Chemists began to experiment with man-made fibers as early as 1850.[5] In 1884 a Frenchman named Hilaire de Chardonnet patented a fabric he called "artificial silk," which is known today as rayon. He discovered that silkworms use cellulose from mulberry leaves to make real silk, and he reproduced the process chemically. Rayon was first produced chemically in the United States in 1910, but not until 1939 was the first completely chemical fiber, nylon, introduced by DuPont.

The phenomenal growth of the textile fiber production industry would have been impossible without the development of man-made fibers. Their growth rate far outstrips the growth in natural fiber production. In the United States, man-made fiber use is already far greater than natural fiber consumption. Worldwide, however, only about half the textile fibers used in apparel are man-made. World man-made fiber production exceeds 20 billion pounds per year.[6] The United States produces about 30 percent of the world's synthetic fibers. The European Economic Community (West Germany, France, Italy, the Netherlands, Belgium, Luxembourg, and Great Britain), Japan, and the Soviet Union follow.

Of utmost importance is the use of man-made fibers in *blends*, in combination either with each other or with natural fibers. Blends capitalize on the best qualities of each fiber, making possible fabrics with the look and feel of natural fibers but the easy-care properties of synthetics.

---

[4] Originally the term "synthetics" was used to denote all chemically produced fibers. Today, however, the textile industry has chosen the term "man made" (perhaps a poor choice linguistically) for two reasons. They feel that the word "synthetic" has a negative connotation, representing "plastic" or "fake" qualities. More importantly, on the world market, the term synthetic covers only the noncellulosic fibers. Perhaps a better term for these fibers would be "viscous fibers" or simply "chemically-made fibers."

[5] *Textiles from Start to Finish* (Charlotte, N. C.: American Textile Manufacturers Institute, 1978), p. 3.

[6] *Guide to Man-Made Fibers* (Washington, D.C.: Man Made Fiber Producers Association, Inc., 1977), p. 2.

Man-Made Fiber Classifications and Production

There are two classifications of man-made fibers: *cellulosic* and *noncellulosic*.

Cellulose is the main constituent of all plant tissues and fibers. For the fabric industry it is derived mostly from spruce pulp and other soft woods. Cellulosic fibers include rayon, acetate, and triacetate.

Noncellulosic fibers are made from chemical derivatives of petroleum, coal, and natural gas. Noncellulosic fibers include nylon, acrylic, and polyester.

Both cellulosic and noncellulosic raw materials are converted into chips, crumbs, or pellets, which are then melted into a syrupy liquid and pumped through the tiny holes of a spinneret to form continuous filaments. The filaments solidify as they pass through an air or chemical bath. Man-made fibers can be extruded in different shapes or thicknesses to create certain properties suited for special purposes. They can be left as continuous filaments or they can be cut into staple (short, uniform lengths) to be blended with other fibers.

EFFECTS OF RESOURCE AVAILABILITY ON THE FIBER INDUSTRY

The vast differences between the natural and man-made fiber industries have resulted in markedly different operational and organizational forms, even though the final goal of both groups is the same—to produce fibers that fill consumer needs.

The natural fiber industry is dependent on animals and living plants. Thus, the production of those fibers depends on climate and geography, and most often the majority of the crop is produced by thousands of small farmers.

In contrast, synthetic fiber production depends mainly on the supply of crude oil, which is subject to shortages and ever-increasing prices. Coal is a possible substitute for oil in synthetic fiber production. However, only a few countries, such as Germany, have made effective use of coal's potential in fiber production.

Also in contrast to natural fibers, man-made fibers are produced by a few chemical companies with huge facilities, making full use of the advantages of mass production. For reasons of profitability, these factories are located in areas where the combined cost of raw materials, labor, energy, and transportation is the lowest.

YARN PRODUCTION

Spinning Staple Fibers

Before being woven or knitted into cloth, fibers must first be made into yarn. Spun yarns are made from natural and man-made staple fibers. Yarn can be made as coarse as rug yarn or even finer than sewing thread.

Natural fibers such as cotton, flax, and wool must go through a long and expensive series of processes to become yarn. First, there are several processes to clean, refine, and parallel the raw fibers. Next they are drawn out into a fine strand and twisted, to keep them together and to give them strength to withstand the spinning process. Run onto spools, the strands are finally spun into tight threads. Spinning may be done by any one of five conventional systems: cotton, woolen, French, Bradford, or American. Once the fibers have been spun into yarn, they can be made into fabrics.

Man-made staple fiber is spun on the same conventional spinning system that is used for cotton or wool. For this reason the resultant yarns have characteristics similar to those of spun natural fiber. In fact, staple man-made fibers are often blended with natural fibers.

Yarn spinning (Courtesy of Springs Mills, Inc.)

Filament Yarn Processing

Filament yarns are made from long, continuous filaments. These yarns are primarily man made because, although silk is also a filament, it accounts for less than one percent of fiber and yarn production. Filament may be knit or woven as is directly from the fiber producer. In this case, individual filaments are brought together, with or without a twist, to create the yarn. Generally, however, synthetic fibers are textured to provide bulk, loft, or elasticity. *Textured* is a general term used for any continuous filament yarn whose shape and characteristics have been changed into some form of crimp, loop, curl, or coil.

Robert LaForce, Director of Fabric and Styling and Development for Celanese Fibers Marketing Company, explains that there are three basic texturing methods:

1. *Air texturizing:* In this process the filament is overfed in an air jet, which, because of turbulence, loops and bulks the yarn.
2. *A saw tooth or loop crimp:* Achieved in a stuffer box or by gear crimping.[Filament yarns are actually stuffed into one end of a heated box and are withdrawn at the other end in crimped form; or, the filament passes between the teeth of two heated gears that mesh to give the yarn a saw-tooth crimp.] Knit-de-Knit yarns are also associated with this type of textured product. In the case of Knit-de-Knit, the yarn is actually knit into a fabric, set by heat in the configuration of the knit, and then raveled for subsequent re-knitting or weaving. These processes, whether saw box crimp, gear crimp, or Knit-de-Knit, utilize heat to set a specific two-dimensional configuration permanently into the fiber.
3. *False twist method:* The third and by far the most popular means of texturizing synthetic fiber is the use of a false twist spindle. High twist is inserted in the yarn, heat is applied to set the twist, and then the twist is removed with the yarn retaining a memory for the three-dimensional helical curl.

Except for air bulked yarn which mechanically locks loops into the yarn bundle, the saw tooth, gear, or false twist crimp is set into the thermoplastic fiber with heat much in the same way a steel rod can be bent and twisted when hot.[7]

FABRIC CONSTRUCTION

Fabric is material or cloth made from natural or man-made yarns by any of the following methods: weaving, knitting, bonding, crocheting, felting, knotting, or laminating. Most textile fabrics are woven or knitted. Fashion preference for one or the other is cyclical.

Weaving

Woven fabrics are made by interlacing (at right angles) warp yarn (lengthwise) and filling yarn (crosswise—called "weft" in England and in handweaving). Weaving begins with a process called warping: yarns are wound onto a beam and hung lengthwise on the loom to create the warp. There may be as many as 15,000 warp threads on one loom (ready-to-wear manufacturers need wide fabrics for efficient pattern layout).[8]

In the conventional method of weaving, filling yarns are fed into the loom by a shuttle carrying yarn wound on a bobbin. The warp yarns separate alternately to allow the filling yarns to interlace with them as the shuttle passes through the warp shed.

An even faster method of weaving uses a shuttleless loom, which carries the filling yarns through the warp on steel bands (see photograph in chapter 2). Still other types of looms carry the filling yarns by means of tiny shuttles called darts, or by tiny jets of water or air.

Kinds of Weaves

There are three basic weaves: plain, twill, and satin.

A **plain weave** is the simplest, most common weave. The warp and filling yarns alternately pass over and under each other.

In **twill weave** the filling yarn passes over a number of warp yarns before going under one. The same pattern is repeated row after row, but each time it is moved over one step, creating a diagonal pattern. The resulting fabric is **very** durable.

A **satin weave** is achieved by one warp yarn crossing over several filling yarns, creating "floats" on the face side of the fabric. The floats give the fabric luster and smoothness. However, because the floats are caught into the fabric only

---

[7] Robert LaForce, Director, Fabric Styling and Development, Celanese Fibers Marketing Company, letter, July 31, 1979.

[8] *Textiles from Start to Finish*, p. 8.

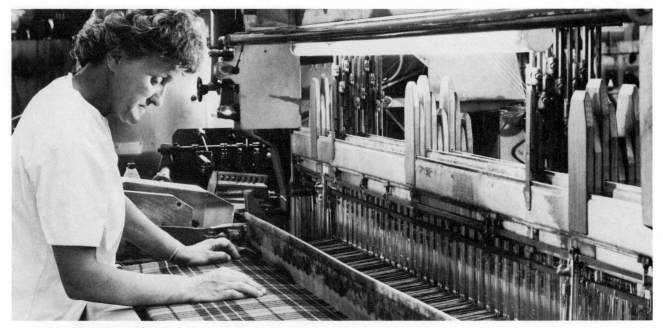

Tartan wool cloth being woven on an automatic loom
(Photograph by Maurice Broomfield, courtesy of the International Wool Secretariat, London)

at comparatively wide intervals, a satin weave does not wear as well as others.

Novelty weaves is the general category for the many variations of basic weaves used to create design or pattern in fabrics.

In the weaving process, pattern can be introduced by using yarns of different colors in the warp, the filling, or both, to create plaids, checks, or stripes. Called *yarn dye patterns*, these can be distinguished from prints because their pattern appears the same on both sides of the fabric. Woven patterns may also be produced by reversing the direction of the weave in certain areas or in alternate rows, such as in herringbones. Small figures, called *dobbies*, can be woven into the fabric by a special attachment on the loom.

Fancy woven patterns, such as brocade, damask, and tapestry, may be created on a *Jacquard* (ja-kard') loom, run by computers. The pattern is programmed on a series of computer cards, which manipulate the individual warp yarns, raising and lowering them to create the desired pattern.

Knits

Knitted fabrics are made from one continuous yarn or combination of yarns formed into a series of interlocking loops to make cloth. There are two basic ways of knitting fabrics.

When the loops run across or in a circle, the process is called *weft* or *circular knitting*. This is the least expensive method of converting yarn into fabric. Typical weft knits are ribs, interlocks, and double knits (given double thickness by a double stitch). Weft knits generally have more stretch than warp knits.

Circular knitting machines *(Courtesy of Burlington Industries, Inc.)*

In the other method, *warp knitting,* multiple yarns are used and the loops run vertically. Warp knits include jersey, tricot, and raschel.

In addition, there are novelty or patterned knits that may be produced on special machinery.

In comparing one weft knit fabric to another, people in the trade refer to the "cut," the number of needles per inch. The more needles there are, the finer and closer the knit loops are. The term "gauge" refers to the number of needles per inch used in making warp knits.

Nonwoven Fabrics

Although most fabrics are produced by weaving or knitting, there are also nonwoven (sometimes called "engineered") fabrics. These are made by either bonding or interlocking fibers, filaments, or yarns into a web or sheet by mechanical (pressure), chemical, thermal (heat), or solvent means. Examples of such fabrics include nonwoven interfacings like Pellon. Felting is another process for making matted fabrics, such as nonwoven felt. Nonwoven fabric production usually includes four elements: 1) fiber preparation; 2) web formation; 3) web bonding; and 4) post treatment. One of the fastest growing segments of the textile industry, nonwoven fabric consumption in the United States alone has grown from less than $300 million annually at the beginning of the 1970s to more than $800 million by the end of the '70s.[9]

DYEING

Dyeing can be done at any stage of fiber, yarn, or fabric production. Some of the most important methods of dyeing are listed below:

Solution dyeing, used for synthetic fibers, adds the pigment or color when the fibers are still in solution, before the filaments are formed.

Stock dyeing, used for natural fibers, is the dyeing of loose fibers before yarn processing.

Yarn dyeing is done after the yarn is spun but before weaving or knitting. Yarn dyeing is necessary for certain woven patterns, such as stripes, plaids, and checks.

[9] Roberta Maguire, "Nonwovens: Engineered Fabrics of the Future," *Apparel Industry Magazine,* vol. 40, no. 7 (July, 1979), p. 44.

Large quantities of yarn can be dyed simultaneously in dye vats *(Courtesy of the National Cotton Council of America)*

Resist dyeing involves treating the yarn or cloth before dyeing so that the treated portion resists dye.

Piece dyeing is done on fabric after weaving or knitting.

Cross dyeing achieves varied color effects in one dyebath during piece dyeing. It occurs because the cloth contains fibers with affinities to different dyes.

Special Dyeing

If apparel manufacturers want to order a fabric in a color that is not regularly available, there is a minimum yardage requirement. Yarn dyed and solution dyed fabrics require the largest orders (although the minimums are so high for solution dyed fabrics that special orders are rarely done).

PRINTING

Printing is used to apply design or pattern to fabrics. There are three basic printing techniques: engraved roller printing, screen printing, and heat transfer printing.

Engraved roller printing uses a separate roller engraving for each color in the pattern. The design is rolled onto the fabric as it passes through the printing machine.

Screen printing

Flat-bed screen printing uses a screen spread over a frame. The portions of the design to be printed are made of porous nylon that allows the color to pass through the screen. The areas that are not to be printed are covered or coated with enamel. Color is poured into the frame shell and is forced through the nylon by means of a squeegee worked back and forth. Flat-bed screen printing is versatile but expensive.

Rotary screen printing is a mechanized version of flat-bed screen printing. In this method, the roller itself is porous in the areas to be printed. Dye is forced into the roller cylinder and through its porous screen as it rolls over the cloth. This method is faster than flat-bed screen printing and continuous, leaving no breaks between screens.

In each of the methods above, dyestuffs are applied wet for optimum color penetration. In pigment printing the pigment is attached to the fabric surface with a resin. Other wet prints use dyestuffs that have a chemical affinity to the cloth fiber without the need for resin. With wet printing it is possible to achieve a soft, drapable hand (the feel, body, and fall of a fabric) as well as a crisp finish.

Heat transfer printing, the process used on polyester and some nylons and acrylics, uses rotary screens or rollers to first print dyestuffs onto paper. The paper can be kept for use at any time. To print on fabric, the paper and fabric are put through hot rollers; the dyestuffs sublimate into a gas, which moves from the paper base onto the fabric. The advantages of this method are that it gives a clean, fine line on knits, and that the paper is a smaller investment than the elaborate equipment needed for other methods. However, care must be taken that the hand of the goods does not become stiff under heat.

Flat-bed screen printing by hand (Courtesy of Marimekko, Inc., Helsinki, Finland)

Rotary screens speedily print fabric (Courtesy of Burlington Industries, Inc.)

FINISHING

Some of the most important developments in fabric treatment are finishes. *Finishing* is a general term covering all the treatments done on fibers and fabrics. Finishes can drastically alter fiber and fabric characteristics, performance, or hand. A few common finishes are described below.

Mercerizing is a process by which cotton is treated with a cold, strongly caustic chemical solution to achieve a lustrous silk-like finish.

Sanforizing preshrinks cotton cloth so that it will not shrink or stretch more than 1 percent during laundering.

Calendering (called *Ciré* in French) is a mechanical process of passing fabric between heavy rollers. By using different combinations of heat, pressure, and rollers, it is possible to produce a wide assortment of effects such as glaze, watermark, or moiré. Calendering is usually done on synthetics, because it is not permanent on fabrics made of natural fibers. A "Schreiner," one type of calendering, gives the cloth luster by pounding it with steel rollers to impress microscopic reflective lines on the surface.

Durable press (also called permanent press, although it is rarely permanent) is the application of certain resins on cotton to create fabrics that require little or no ironing.

Heat setting, done after other finishes have been applied, heats thermoplastic man-made fabrics to just below their melting point. This treatment stabilizes them so that there will be no further change in size or shape. The process can be used to permanently set in new forms such as pleats.

Other finishes can make fabrics flame retardant, water repellent, fade resistant, mildew resistant, bacteria resistant, or stain resistant.

When production is completed, fabrics are measured and rolled onto tubes. Each finished roll, called a *piece,* may have 40 to 100 yards on it, depending on the weight of the goods (heavier knits and wools have less yardage on a piece, to make it easier to handle). The rolls are shipped to manufacturers to fill production orders for multiple pieces that can amount to thousands of yards. Smaller quantities, in the form of three- to ten-yard *sample cuts,* may be ordered for designer styling; or *duplicate yardage* (perhaps 100 yards) can be ordered for sales representatives' samples.

TEXTILE PRODUCERS

Textile Mills

Each of the steps in the textile production chain is a separate unit. Some textile mills produce only yarns. Others knit and weave unfinished fabric, called *greige goods* (pronounced "gray"), from their own or purchased yarn. Most mills produce both greige goods and finished fabrics. J. P. Stevens, for example, produces 60% finished fabrics and 40% greige goods to sell to converters.[10] Small mills often specialize in one type of fabric aimed at a particular market, such as junior dresses. Large companies create divisions to do the same thing, grouping similar fabrics under one division.

[10] Chester Wolfe, Vice President, Woolen & Womenswear Division, J. P. Stevens & Co., Inc., interview, August 7, 1979.

Woven fabric travels through gigantic frames as it receives a variety of finishing treatments *(Courtesy of Burlington Industries, Inc.)*

The various stages in textile production may or may not be handled by firms under common ownership. In the past 20 years, there has been a tendency for firms to grow vertically, either forward or backward into the production and marketing chain. Fiber producers have expanded into the yarn texturing business. Some fabric producers have gone into yarn production. Large "vertical" mills like Stevens, Milliken, and Burlington extend from the yarn spinning and texturing stage directly through fiber production into dyed and finished cloth. (They are called vertical mills because they do all processes, from "top" to "bottom.") Some garment manufacturers, like Jonathan Logan, also produce fabric and yarns.[11]

Converters

The converter buys greige goods from a mill and contracts to have them dyed, printed, and finished at outside facilities in accordance with the requests of his customers, the apparel manufacturers. The converter does not own any mills; he is the middleman between the knitting and weaving mills and the apparel manufacturer.

A vertical mill is often committed to operating one certain type of machinery, and it must produce large yardage of a special design in order to stay profitable. Such a mill has more difficulty keeping up with diversified fashion trends than does the converter, who is more flexible and can supply shorter runs of selected fabrics in a shorter time. Therefore, the converter is an important supplier to small, fashion-oriented clothing manufacturers.

SUMMARY

Textile producers, the suppliers to apparel manufacturers, are an integral part of the fashion industry. Textile fibers are the basis for fabrics. They are classified as natural (cotton, flax, wool, or silk) or synthetic (cellulosic or noncellulosic). Yarns are made from fibers or filaments and are usually woven or knitted into fabrics. Then fabrics are dyed or printed and finished in preparation for shipment to manufacturers.

The phenomenal growth of the textile industry would not have been possible without the development of man-made fibers. Man-made fibers have revolutionized the industry, especially yarn and knit production and fabric printing. The textile industry is now dominated by huge conglomerates rather than by farmers and smaller companies.

[11] LaForce.

CHAPTER REVIEW

CHAPTER OBJECTIVES

Study of the chapter should enable students to
A. Give evidence of having attained competence in the following areas:
1. Awareness of the sources of fibers 2. Understanding of the processes involved in the production of fibers and fabrics 3. Knowledge of the roles of mills and converters
B. Define the following terms and concepts in relation to their discussion in the chapter:
1. Suppliers 2. Raw materials 3. Textiles 4. Natural fibers 5. Flax 6. Wool sources 7. Worsted yarns 8. Woolen yarns 9. Other wools 10. Cotton sources 11. Types of cotton 12. Silk sources 13. Types of silk 14. Man-made fiber development 15. Rayon 16. Filament yarns 17. Spun yarns 18. Chemical resources 19. Types of filament yarn processing 20. Plain weave 21. Twill weave 22. Satin weave 23. Novelty weaves 24. Circular knitting 25. Warp knitting 26. Nonwoven fabrics 27. Types of dyeing 28. Printing techniques 29. Finishing methods 30. Mills 31. Converters

---

Questions for Review

1. Why is a study of textiles important to someone working in apparel production?
2. What determines the quality of cotton?
3. What are the two basic ways of making fabric?
4. How is knit yardage made?
5. Give examples of textile dyeing methods that can be used at three different levels of fabric production.

PROJECTS FOR ADDITIONAL LEARNING

1. Examine the fabric content labels in the clothes in your wardrobe. How many garments are made from natural fibers? How many from man-made fibers? How many from blends? How does the fiber content affect the care of the garment?

2. Visit a local fabric store and find examples of a plain weave, a twill weave, a satin weave, a novelty weave, a warp knit, a circular knit, and a nonwoven fabric. Ask for tiny swatches of each or purchase the smallest amount possible to illustrate your findings.

TEXTILE
PRODUCT
DEVELOPMENT
AND
MARKETING

6

Pierre Cardin imagining how
a fabric might look made up
(Courtesy of Pierre Cardin, Paris)

The development of man-made fibers has dramatically changed textile fiber marketing. The industry now focuses on the potential for fiber and fabric development to fill the wants and needs of the consumer.

This chapter discusses the textile marketing chain, including product development and sales promotion of both fibers and fabrics.

FIBER PRODUCT DEVELOPMENT AND MARKETING

In the past, the marketing role of the natural fiber producer was relatively simple. The crop was raised, harvested, and sold at local markets to wholesalers who, in turn, sold the fibers at central markets. Sheep farmers and cotton growers did not have to be concerned with fabric and garment production.

The development of man-made fibers changed all that. Now producers can create whatever kind of fiber the consumer needs or desires. Especially in the United States, huge research and development efforts have been initiated to meet consumer demand. Because new fibers mean potential new markets, synthetic fiber producers search for new uses for their fibers and educate the public accordingly. For example, if trend forecasters predict that designers will be featuring silk crêpe de chine, textile producers may try to develop a less expensive man-made copy for the mass market in anticipation of its coming popularity.

Textile companies must have their fabrics on the market at the time of peak demand, not too early or too late. The companies that foresaw the demand for double knits in the early 1970s and had them ready for delivery at the peak of demand, made a fortune. The companies that reacted too late lost money, because they were stuck with the double knit fabric after the demand was gone.

New product development begins at the fiber level. The industry needs up to *five years* before a target selling season to develop new fibers or fiber variants (see table 6-1). When a company invests years of development into a new product, it follows that they will also devote time and money to promote it, in order to *create* consumer demand. In other words, development of a new product can actually cause a new fashion.

Research and Experimentation

The chemical companies that produce man-made fibers invest a great deal of time and money in research. Consumer or industry demand for certain fiber or fabric properties may cause several textile companies to research the same problem simultaneously. As a result, several companies may develop similar, competitive fibers.

Experimental new or modified man-made fibers are usually produced on a limited basis at first. Natural fiber producers, because of their generally small size, often work together in group research. If evaluation studies show potential acceptance of the new product by both the industry and the general public, then additional facilities are devoted to its production, new uses for it are explored, and industry is encouraged to use it.

Generic and Brand Identification

When a completely new fiber is developed, the United States Federal Trade Commission assigns it a generic name. Today there are 21 generic names; however, not all of them are used in clothing nor are all of them produced in the United States.

It is possible to work within the basic generic composition and modify it, both chemically and physically, to produce a great variety of fibers called *variants*. Each has different characteristics, but falls under the generic fiber family name. To identify the generic fibers or variants, and to promote them independently, fiber manufacturers give them brand names or trademarks (identifiable symbols). A brand name or trademark is owned by the manufacturer and becomes well known through advertising. Consumers often confuse brand names with generic names. For example, Qiana (the trademark name) is a variant of nylon (the generic name) produced by E. I. duPont de Nemours and Co., Inc.; Enkalure, also a variant of nylon, is produced by American Enka Co. It is important to understand clearly the difference between a *brand name* and a *generic name*. The Textile Fibers Products Identification Act of 1960 requires that end products carry labels with fiber content, listing generic name and percentage used.

SALES PROMOTION

To foster sales, any producer must make its product known to potential customers. Of course, the giant chemical companies that produce man-made fibers have more money to spend on promotion than do the natural fiber producers. The man-made fiber industry has concentrated on brand name advertising, creating a competitive atmosphere and stimulating natural fiber producers to do more promotion in order to retain their market share.

TABLE 6–1   TIMING OF PRODUCT DEVELOPMENT IN THE TEXTILE AND APPAREL INDUSTRIES

Activity	Length of Time before Selling Season
Development of new fiber variants	4 to 5 years
Fabric development (fiber associations and companies work in conjunction with mills to research and develop new fabrics)	2 years
Color predictions (fiber level)	2 years
Presentation of new fabric lines by fabric producers (Interstoff, Ideacomo, etc.)	1 year
Designer and/or merchandiser shops fabric lines	10 months to 1 year
Design development (manufacturer)	7 to 9 months
Lines released/collection openings (market weeks, lines shown to buyers; orders taken)	6 months average
Production (manufacturer)	2 to 5 months
Shipping (delivery)	1 month
Selling season (retail store)	Selling season (before and at beginning of actual wearing season)

Cooperative advertisement between Hoechst, the fiber producer
(Trevira is the fiber brand name); Dynamic Trends, the fabric
producer; and L. F. Petites, the garment manufacturer.
*(Illustration by Thea Kliros, courtesy of Hoechst Fibers Industries,
producers of the Trevira Trademark) Registered TM of Hoechst AG.*

Because of their average small size, natural fiber producers usually work together on group promotion. To do this, natural fiber producers have formed trade associations, each representing the producers of a particular fiber. The International Institute for Cotton (Cotton Incorporated in the United States), the National Cotton Council of America, the International Wool Secretariat (the Wool Bureau in the United States), the American Wool Council, the Silk Institute, and the International Linen Promotion are among them. The natural fiber industry focuses its promotional efforts on product recognition. Natural fiber associations use trademarks or logos for identification purposes, such as the Wool Bureau's ball-of-yarn symbol.

Advertising and Publicity

Fiber producers advertise (a *paid* promotional activity) on both the trade level in trade publications and the consumer level in consumer newspapers and magazines and on television. In fact, fiber producers offer "cooperative advertising dollars" (sharing the cost of advertising their product) to manufacturers who use substantial quantities of their fibers and to stores that buy volume quantities of merchandise made from their fibers. "Co-op" allowances are based on percentage of net fiber sales as used in fabrics sold to the manufacturer or in garments sold to the retailer. In addition, fiber firms often provide ad materials, such as glossy photographs.

Publicity is another form of sending a message to the consumer. In this case there is no cost for media coverage; however, a great deal of time and effort must be spent to communicate information. Fiber producers and trade associations continually provide the press with newsworthy material in the hope of a mention.

Consumer Services

In addition to offering advertising money and materials, fiber producers' sales promotional efforts also include providing many services to their customers on both the manufacturing and the retailing levels.

Distribution of Fiber Information Man-made fiber producers and natural fiber trade associations continually provide information on their products to the fashion industry, to schools, and to the general public. This consumer education takes various forms such as pamphlets, exhibits, lectures, audio-visual aids, and films. The information covers every aspect of fibers and fabrics, including their history, production, use, and care.

Technical Advice Fiber producers offer advice to yarn and textile mills as well as to garment manufacturers. For example, European fiber producers commission fabric designers to work up new ideas for them. Samples of these ideas are woven or knitted, and swatches are sent to the mills. Many producers follow through by having designers create new styles and sample garments from the sample fabrics to show at Interstoff (the international fabric market), giving manufacturers ideas on how to use the fabrics.

American producers look for interesting new textile developments in Europe and Japan. They purchase fabric or the actual garments in shops and try to copy them in their experimental laboratories. Domestic fiber producers can then offer mills production advice based on their experiments.

Fashion Presentations Based on their European research, fiber producers make styling direction information available to mills, manufacturers, and sometimes to retailers, usually on a semiannual basis. A stylist representing the fiber producer makes a presentation showing garments, European fabrics, experimental fabrics, and color prediction charts. Some fiber associations and companies also produce fashion styling reports, such as the Wool Secretariat's *Wool Flash*, as an aid to manufacturers and retailers.

Alison Webb, color coordinator for Celanese Fibers Marketing Company, presents a color and fabric forecast to designers and merchandisers. *(Photograph by the author)*

Color Predictions   About two years in advance of the selling season, fiber companies start planning color lines (about the same time that they work with mills to develop fabrics). Because it is very difficult to know what consumers will want so far in advance, the textile and fashion industries are anxious for accurate predictions. Color predictions are researched at the fiber level and made available to fabric producers, manufacturers, and retailers to help them plan ahead. Some color predictions are the results of group efforts.

Twice a year in Paris there is a meeting of *Inter-Color,* an association of representatives from the worldwide fashion industry. (The Color Association of New York is represented, for example.) Participants analyze color direction two years in advance of the target selling season. In July 1980 for instance, representatives at the Inter-Color meeting discussed colors that they predicted would be worn in spring and summer 1982. They try to analyze color cycles and the natural evolution of color preferences. For example, if pale neutrals are predicted for spring, it might be reasonable to assume that dark versions of neutrals would evolve for the following fall. The Inter-Color representatives take the results back to their countries, where they are reinterpreted for national tastes.

The *International Color Authority* (ICA) is a color-prediction service offered to textile producers, apparel manufacturers, and retailers by subscription. The ICA too meets twice yearly with international representatives to determine the new color story. For example, in June 1979 they decided on their color story for spring–summer 1981. By September 1979 they had compiled and printed complete color charts to send to subscribing fiber, yarn, and fabric producers. In March 1980 they sent a modified version of that report to member apparel manufacturers (who need the information only 14 months ahead of selling season), and in September 1980 to member retailers (8 months before their 1980 spring–summer selling season).

Fabric Libraries   Another important service of the fiber producers is their fabric libraries, located in major fashion centers such as Paris, London, New York, and Los Angeles. Fabric libraries keep samples of fabrics from every mill or converter using their fibers. A designer can visit the library for an overall picture of what is available. The library affords an impartial view of new developments from many mills. If a designer is looking for a specific kind of fabric, the library can help locate a mill or converter who has it.

Colorists meet at the International Colour Authority to determine forecasts *(Courtesy of the International Colour Authority, Benjamin Dent, London)*

Nancy Richards points out collages of new fabric swatches and idea sketches to a designer, while Caroline Scudamore prepares additional visual material, at the International Wool Secretariat, London *(Photograph by the author)*

FIBER DISTRIBUTION

Natural Fibers

Fibers are sold to mills for yarn spinning and weaving or knitting. The small farmers who produce natural fibers sell their goods at the markets organized by their various trade associations. The major central markets in the United States are Dallas, Houston, Memphis, and New Orleans for cotton, and Boston for wool. Farmers have no control over prices, which are set in the marketplace by supply and demand.

Man-Made Fibers

On the other hand, the large chemical companies that produce man-made fibers have their own sales forces and set prices based on their costs. In some cases, when fiber producers and mills are vertically integrated into one large company, the producing company becomes its own market.

Fibers are often sold with certain obligations to control standards of quality. After spending a great deal on advertising to build a good reputation for a fiber's performance, the producer wants to preserve that good name. Restrictions on standards are imposed when the fiber is sold under a brand name or a licensing agreement. There are no restrictions if the fiber is sold without the use of a brand name.

FABRIC PRODUCT DEVELOPMENT AND MARKETING

Fabric producers try to anticipate consumers' needs by doing intensive market research; this helps them compete for the business of the apparel manufacturers, their direct customers. The textile industry must develop fabrics several seasons ahead of the actual manufacturing season so that designers have enough time to find and test suitable goods. Fabric producers study fashion and fabric trends in Europe and Japan and work along with fiber producers and associations to develop fashionable products with desirable fiber blends, finishes, and other properties. In turn, they offer their expertise to apparel manufacturers and give them sample cuts of fabrics for test garments.

Sometimes a company may want the exclusivity of a "confined" fabric or print for one season. *Confinement* means that only one manufacturer is allowed to use the fabric, giving a unique look to its line. The textile firm also benefits: confinement becomes a testing period at the consumer level before the fabric is offered to the general market the following season. When Ultrasuede was first available in the United States, Halston had it confined for a season, just long enough to create a sensation with his Ultrasuede shirtwaist dresses.

Textile Design

Textile designers create print designs for fabrics or suggest styling ideas for a weave or knit to the textile engineer. Their ideas come from many of the same sources used by apparel designers, but especially from historic motifs, wallpapers, old fabrics, and nature. They must consider the essential elements of color, texture, line, shape, and space. Textile designers are concerned primarily with a two-dimensional surface, the flat fabric, rather than with the three-dimensional human form. Yet they must keep the end use of the fabric in mind to create practical designs.

Most fabric designs originate in Europe or Japan; independent design studios or converters from elsewhere buy them to copy. The converter may buy a piece of the original fabric or may buy designs from an art studio. The converter pays around $100 to $250 for a fabric design *croquis* (painting) or for an actual piece of fabric. European fabrics are often too sophisticated and must be modified for the American market. Variations, repeat work, restyling, and coloring may be done by the converter's studio or by an independent design studio.

Print Design The motifs for a print should have interesting shapes, a pleasing rhythmic pattern, and a harmonious relationship to one another. No single part of the overall pattern should stand out or claim too much attention. Print design is a continuous repetition of motifs, and the fabric designer must consider how cutting will affect the pattern. Different types of prints may be designed for particular segments of the apparel industry. For example, florals and feminine motifs may be aimed at women's apparel; traditional geometrics intended for men's wear; and small, whimsical prints planned for children's wear. However, the use of prints is also a matter of fashion: some kinds of prints are more popular than others at a given time.

Coloring A manufacturer may find an attractive print but may need it in a different color combination to fit into a particular fabric line or group. For a new color combination, a *croquis* is made by the textile firm's design department. If that is approved, a *strike-off* is run on a short piece of fabric. Minimum yardage requirements vary according to the printing method.

Painting a croquis of a fabric design at Kuttner-NAK Prints, New York City (*Photograph by the author*)

Sales Promotion

Fabric producers compete for the business of apparel manufacturers and for retail-level acceptance of products made of their goods.

Advertising   Large fabric producers advertise on a grand scale, emphasizing the brand names of their products. Like the fiber producers—and often in cooperation with them—they use television, newspapers, and magazines to reach national audiences. They also join with apparel manufacturers and retail stores in co-op advertising on a national or local level. Co-op ads must contain the brand names or trademarks of all participants.

Publicity   Many fabric producers also provide educational materials to consumer groups, schools and colleges, and the general public. They also supply information on fabric fashions and developments to the press in expectation of editorial coverage.

Customer Service   Some fabric producers provide apparel manufacturers with printed hang tags listing care instructions, as a form of publicity. Federal regulations require fabric producers to supply manufacturers with care instructions that must be listed on labels sewn into the garments.

Large fabric producers also employ merchandising and marketing experts who analyze trends and pass the information on to manufacturers and retailers. They provide printed or visual materials and presentations to manufacturers and give in-store fashion shows and sales training sessions for retailers.

Fabric Markets

Twice a year important fabric shows are held in Europe to exhibit fabrics to apparel manufacturers. Textile producers from all over the world display their lines. American textile producers visit the European shows to see the latest directions in fabrics. Manufacturers and their designers visit the shows to buy fabrics and gather ideas on how to use them.

Interstoff ("Inter-Fabric" in German), with more than 800 exhibitors from 24 countries, is the world's largest fabric fair for clothing manufacturers. Approximately 25,000 trade visitors attend Interstoff's four-day market each fall and spring in Frankfurt.[1]

Premiere-vision is the French fabric fair also presented each fall and spring in Paris.

[1] Interstoff press release, Frankfurt am Main, 1978.

Fabric buyers and designers look through headers of new fabrics offered by one of Interstoff's exhibitors
(Courtesy of the Messe und Ausstellungsgesellschaft m. b. H., Frankfurt, Germany)

Ideacomo is presented by Italian fabric producers each fall and spring in Como, Italy, and is followed by exhibits in New York.

Beginning in 1981, a new fabric fair, organized by the English, will take place each fall and spring in Geneva.

TALA, a fabric show presented by the Textile Association of Los Angeles, is of particular interest to California and other West Coast manufacturers.

The Sales Representative

In addition to attending the textile shows, fabric producers maintain showrooms in major fashion centers to display their new lines of fabrics. Each fabric company also has sales representatives who periodically visit manufacturers and their designers, showing them suitcases full of "headers" (head ends of fabrics).

Most salespersons in the textile industry, especially for large companies, are salaried employees of the firms they represent. Independent sales agents or representatives (usually for converters) handle several textile lines and are paid by commission (usually 2 percent of the price of fabrics sold *and shipped*). Salespeople are assigned specific manufacturers to call on. They try to make contacts to gain new accounts, as well as to show and sell fabrics to regular customers.

The Role of the Jobber

Another independent agent who deals in fabrics is the *jobber.* A jobber is essentially a middleman who purchases fabrics and resells them. He may buy from several sources and put together his own "line," or he may speculate and buy up goods in hopes of selling them later at a good markup during a period of peak demand. This clears warehouse space and gives operating cash to the textile producer and makes these fabrics available to a manufacturer late in the season. Another role of the jobber is to buy up unsold goods at great reductions, for resale to discount stores or other outlets. As compensation for the financial risks jobbers take, they are able to buy the fabric at considerable discounts, which enables them to make a profit on resale.

Importing and Exporting

In addition to large domestic production, an ever-increasing amount of textile products is being imported into the United States. Because of rising costs of both labor and raw materials, competition from foreign companies has increased. On the other hand, American textile products, especially fibers, are becoming very competitive in the international market. While Europe excels in producing small runs of expensive fabrics, the United States does well at producing large quantities. The three major factors cited for the new strong competitive position of American fiber producers are:
— the declining value of the dollar in recent years,
— greater efficiency and superior technology of large-scale production, and
— the lower cost of raw materials.[2]

The textile industry views exporting as the key to growth in the coming years. Increasing exports may help United States textile mills to compensate for fluctuation in the domestic market.

SUMMARY

Accurate forecasting and planning are very important to textile product development. Fiber and fabric technology is highly advanced by research at United States textile firms, while most design ideas originate in Europe or Japan and are adapted to American needs. Both fiber and fabric firms concentrate advertising efforts on brand identification and offer many customer services to manufacturers and retailers to promote sales. Manufacturers can preview fabrics at markets such as Interstoff or at fabric libraries and order sample cuts to test garment designs.

CHAPTER REVIEW

CHAPTER OBJECTIVES

After reading this chapter you should be able to
A. Give evidence of having attained competence in the following areas:
1. Understanding of the role of the textile industry as supplier to the fashion industry 2. Understanding of product development timing in the textile and apparel industries 3. Knowledge of marketing tools of the textile industry
B. Define the following terms and concepts in relation to their discussion in the chapter:
1. Product development timing 2. Fiber research 3. Generic names 4. Brand names 5. Trade associations 6. Cooperative advertising 7. Consumer services 8. Color predictions 9. Fabric libraries 10. Distribution 11. *Croquis* 12. Types of print design 13. Strike-off 14. Interstoff 15. Headers 16. Role of sales representative 17. Role of jobber 18. Imports

[2] "AFF Surveys the World's Fabric Market," *American Fabrics and Fashions,* no. 117 (Fall, 1979), p. 5.

Questions for Review

1. Why must textile color predictions be made two years in advance of a selling season?
2. Describe the services of a fabric library.
3. How has the development of man-made fibers influenced the textile industry in relation to consumer demand?
4. How does modern marketing differ from marketing in the past, when only natural fabrics were available?
5. How do trade associations use modern marketing methods?

PROJECTS FOR ADDITIONAL LEARNING

1. Select a print that you like from a historical costume or art book. Trace (or modify the print to update it, if necessary) and recolor it in the current season's fashion colors.

2. Shop a local department store to compare fabrics used in designer or contemporary fashions.

   What fabrics look the freshest and most exciting?

   What kinds of fabrics are used the most?

   What are the predominant colors?

   Are prints fashionable? If so, what kind? Geometric? Spaced florals? Small? Large?

   What fabric characteristics are emphasized?

   Examine hang tags and labels for fiber content. What kind of fiber is used more in the department—natural or man-made?

   Can you identify fiber brand names and generic names on the labels?

   Can you identify fabric producers by information on the labels?

   Summarize your findings in a written report.

TRIMMINGS, LEATHER, AND FUR

7

Lace and button details on a Caroline Charles design. *(Photograph by Peter Smith, courtesy of Carmal Enterprises Ltd.)*

To complete our discussion of the raw materials of fashion, it is important to include fur, leather, and trimmings.

Trimmings, *covered in the first half of the chapter, are necessary additions to any fabrication in order to complete a garment. The category of trimmings is very diversified, comprising both textile and non-textile areas. Thread, interfacing, and narrow fabric manufacturing are extensions of the textile industry with similar production and marketing procedures. Zipper and button manufacturing are entirely separate industries with their own resources and production methods.*

The second part of the chapter is devoted to the sources of and treatment to leather and fur. *Leather and fur were used for clothing long before textiles were developed. Even today leather and fur are important materials for the fashion industry. Leather's essential use is in the fashion accessories area—for shoes, handbags, gloves, and belts—while fur is mainly a garment material.*

Although much older than the textile fiber industry, the processing of leather and fur is not as sophisticated as fiber and fabric production–and it takes much longer. Lately, however, improved production methods have been developed, greatly increasing the supply and variety of leather and fur and bringing new vitality to the industry.

TRIMMINGS

Trimmings are necessary supplies used to finish and adorn both garments and accessories. *Trimmings* are decorative materials including buttons, belts, braids, ribbons, and laces. Sometimes functional trimmings such as elastic, tapes, interfacings, threads, and zippers are referred to as *findings*.

Thread

Thread is another product of the textile industry, supplied by the yarn producers. Formed by spinning and twisting textile fibers or filaments together into a continuous strand, thread is vital in determining the quality of workmanship in a garment.

Until recent years, cotton and other natural fiber threads continued to meet requirements of durability, appearance, and sewability because the majority of fabrics available were also made of natural fibers. However, the advent of man-made fibers brought about the development of many new fabrics including knits. With their new characteristics, these fabrics demanded a thread with increased elasticity and strength. To meet these specifications, polyester threads were developed.

There are three types of polyester threads available on the market today:

— a polyester core wrapped in cotton,
— a 3-ply 100 percent spun polyester, and
— long staple polyester.

The long staple thread is relatively new in the United States, introduced by Swedish and Swiss firms.

Threads are wound on cones in 1,200 to 24,000 yard lengths for factory use. The Thread Institute has suggested metric conversions that approximate current yard lengths. For example, the 6,000 yard cones will be converted to 5,500 meters (actually 6,010 yards).

Manufacturers use various thread sizes—the thickness or thinness of threads—according to fabric and quality needs. A metric system called "tex" has been suggested to measure thread size. Based on the weight of the raw material, the tex number increases as the size increases, average thread sizes ranging from 10 to 500.

Interfacings

Reinforcement is needed to give a garment support and to keep it in shape longer. The most essential kind of inner construction is the use of interfacing—a layer of fabric placed between the garment fabric and its facing. Interfacings have always been an important part of garment production, especially for structuring and support in tailored jackets and coats. They are also used to reinforce details such as collars, lapels, cuffs, pocket flaps, buttoning areas, and waistbands.

Formerly, linen, burlap, and horsehair were primarily used for interfacings. Today, there are many new developments using natural fibers, man-made fibers, and blends.

Types of Interfacings *Stable* interfacings have no give and are designed to add stability to heavier tailored garments. Stable interfacings can be either woven or nonwoven textiles. As with other textiles, wovens are made by interweaving yarns at right angles. Nonwoven interfacings have no grain and therefore can be cut in any direction. *Stretch* interfacings for use in knitted fabrics may have one-way stretch or stretch in all directions. Stable and stretch interfacings are available in both fusible and sew-in forms. Fusable interfacings have become important in saving labor and time.

Weights of Interfacings Basically, interfacings are available in three weight categories: light weight, middle weight, and heavy weight, which are used in relationship to the weight of the garment fabric as well as for the support and affect desired. However, interfacing should never be heavier than the actual garment fabric. Heavy-weight fleece and thermo interlinings are also used in jackets and coats to give additional support and warmth.

Narrow Fabrics

Woven, knit, and braid trims are produced by narrow fabric manufacturers. Narrow fabrics include narrow laces, ribbons, braids, other woven and knit decorative bands, pipings, and cordings. Until about 1960, 80 percent of the trims sold in the United States were imported from Europe. Now, although fine laces, velvet ribbon, and beadwork are still imported, the situation has reversed and imports account for only 20 percent.

Narrow fabrics are either functional (such as tapes for inner construction) or decorative. The decorative trims industry is a fashion-oriented business although there are really no seasonal lines. The fashion for trims is cyclical like any other fashion. When the ethnic look was popular, trims were in great demand. When a tailored look is popular, trims are less in demand. Most trims are used on children's wear and juniors and less on women's and men's wear.

Trim Types There is a great variety of trim types especially made for different uses and methods of application:

Appliqué is an individual motif that can be used singly or in multiples as a top trim. (It is also a technique whereby the edges of a motif are attached to fabric.)

Banding is narrow fabric having two straight or decorative edges that make it interchangeable for various top trims such as borders, edging, insertion, or accenting of a design-line.

Beading is openwork trimming, usually lace or embroidery, through which a ribbon may be threaded. (Not to be confused with beads used to create banding or edging for evening wear.)

Binding is a prefolded trim meant to enclose a raw edge, finishing and decorating it at the same time.

Edging is a trim having one decorative edge, generally used at a garment edge.

Galloon is lace, embroidery or braid having two scalloped edges. It can be used as a banding, border, or design-line accent or can be applied the same as insertion for a see-through effect.

Insertion is trim with two straight edges. (It is also a method of applying trim, inserting and sewing it between two cut edges of fabrics.)

Medallions are a chain of trims with individual motifs that can be used continuously as banding, edging, or galloons, or clipped apart and used as appliqués.[1]

Laces and Embroidery   The popularity of handmade laces led to the invention of lace-making machines. Although narrow textile manufacturers primarily produce bands of lace, the same methods can be applied to produce lace fabric. Today, there are basically four types of machine-made lace.[2]

Barmen lace has its roots in Germany and France. A Jacquard system governs the movements of the Barmen machine. Threads on bobbins are plaited together to resemble heavy, crocheted lace.

Leaver lace is sheer bobbin lace named after John Leaver, an Englishman, who developed the machine. Also Jacquard programmed, threads are twisted into a giant web that can have up to 180 bands, each connected by auxiliary threads. To separate the bands, one of two methods is used. Auxiliary trends can be hand pulled (as is usually done in Europe) or certain threads can be dissolved in an acetone chemical solution.

Raschel knitted lace is less expensive than Leaver due to the high speeds at which it can be produced. Also made in a giant web form, bands are separated by pulling draw strings.

Venice lace is made on Schiffli embroidery machines. The needles are controlled by a Jacquard system. Embroidery machines are also used on fabric to make embroidered *eyelet*.

---

[1] "Trims," *Sew Business*, October 1974, p. 38.

[2] Nick Messina, America Fabrics, interview, February, 1980.

Major types of machine-made laces and eyelet (bottom to top): Raschel, Leaver, Barmen, Venice, and eyelet. *(Photograph by the author)*

Ribbons   Ribbons are another category of narrow fabrics. Many ribbons are woven at one time on 2, 4, 6, 8, 16, 24, or 48 space looms. The width of the ribbon and the volume of production determine the size of machine to be used. Satin and velvet ribbons are made in much the same manner as their fabric counterparts. Grograin is woven on a belting or Dobby loom.

Ribbons can be yarn dyed or solid colors can be dyed after weaving to match manufacturers' color specifications. However, patterns such as stripes are woven with pre-dyed yarns. For intricate patterns, Jacquard looms are used. Some motifs, such as polka dots, are printed on the woven ribbons.

Many quality ribbons are imported from Europe: velvet from France, Germany, and Switzerland and plaids from England.

"Throw away" or "craft" ribbon is woven on a broad loom and cut with hot knives. This type of ribbon can be used on budget apparel or accessories but is usually reserved for the gift wrapping market.

Braids   The category of braids includes not only braided trims but also woven and knitted flat decorative trims that are heavier than ribbons.

Braided trims are made by interlacing three or more yarns to form a flat narrow fabric. They include soutache, middy braid, braided cord edging, and rickrack. Knitted braids, made by a few needles on a warpknitting machine, include both flat and fold-over braids. Woven braids made on textile looms, include flat and fold-over braid and piping made with bias strips. Patterned braids, like ribbons, are produced on Jacquard looms.

Automatic braiding machines making rickrack.
*(Courtesy of Trimtex, a division of the
William E. Wright Co.)*

Zippers

Whitcomb Judson, a Chicago inventor, first introduced a metal "slide fastener" in 1891. However, it went through several developmental stages until a practical fastener could be made on a tape. In 1923, B.F. Goodrich Co. first used the term "zipper" to describe the fastener and manufacturers began to use them in fashionable garments.[3] In 1960, the nylon zipper was introduced, which provided the industry with an alternative light-weight zipper that could be dyed to match any garment fabric.

Zippers are not only functional but can be decorative as well. Fashion sometimes calls for zippers to show on purpose. The popularity of active sportswear has resulted in the increased use of separating zippers, some which open from either end.

Talon is the biggest domestic zipper producer while YKK, a Japanese Company, is the biggest worldwide. There are several methods of zipper production, depending on the materials used. Zippers made from interlocking metal scoops (teeth) are either clamped or hot molded onto pre-sewn tapes. For coil zippers, a continuous filament of nylon is first molded into a coil. Then the tape is either woven around the

coil or the coil is sewn onto the tape.[4] The chain of scoops or coil ranges from a very fine size one to a bulky size nine. After zipper lengths are cut to various size specifications (at present the 7-, 9-, and 22-inch fasteners outsell most other sizes for uses in skirts, pants, and dresses), a lock is stapled at the bottom and "stops" to the top. Finally, a slider is attached which opens and closes the zipper.

Buttons

Buttons are an important aspect of a garment both for functional purposes and fashion interest. When fashion emphasizes detailing, the market becomes stronger for buttons. Most button lines follow fashion trends in both color and styling.

Buttons are both imported and domestically produced. New York City was originally the center of button production in the United States. Now, although the markets remain there, much of the production has moved in search of lower costs for labor and facilities. Large volume manufacturers of buttons include Blumenthal (La Mode) and Rochester.

Traditionally, buttons were made from natural materials like wood, metal, pearl, porcelain, and bone. Today, due to technological advances and the wide

[3] "Focus Report: Zippers: Will Slide Be Reversed?" *Sew Business*, April, 1979, p. 49.

[4] Patricia Cornelius, Marketing Manager, Donahue Sales, Talon Division of Textron Inc., interview, February, 1980.

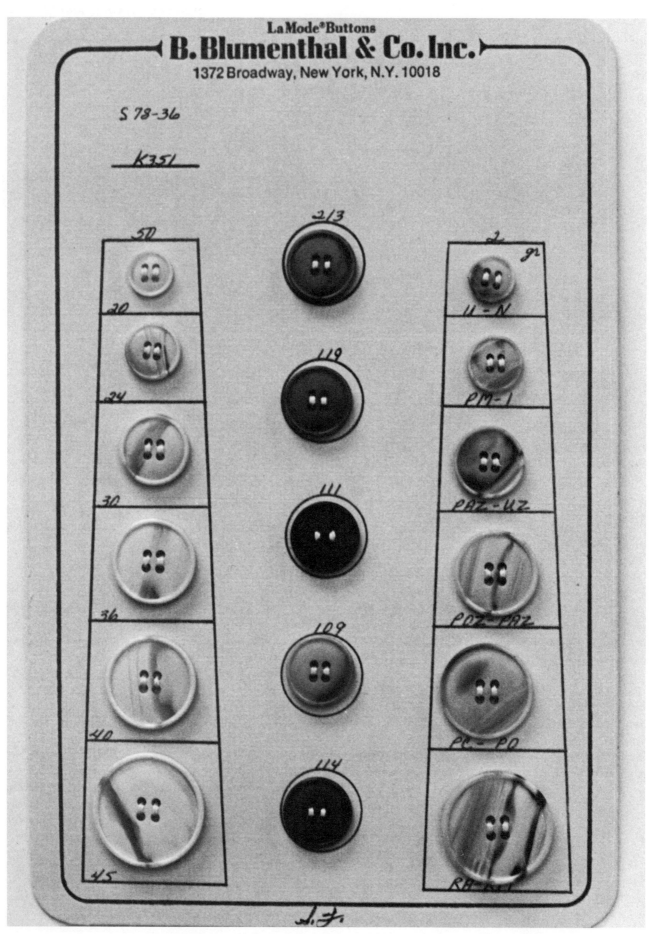

Button size chart. *(Courtesy of B. Blumenthal & Co., Inc.)*

use of synthetics, less than 10 percent of all buttons sold in the United States are constructed of natural materials. Today, most buttons are made of polyester or nylon because of their versatility and because they can be dyed to match fabric. Polyester is produced in sheet form and the button shapes are cut out of the sheet. Liquid nylon is poured into button molds.

Most metal buttons are made from brass; a stamped-out face is put together with a stamped-out back. There are also some pewter buttons, which are cast. Metalized buttons are made with a core of acetate, covered by a coat of copper and finally a gold- or silver-look metal finish. Most of these buttons are produced in Connecticut. (Other metal garment and accessory trimmings products include buckles, eyelets, and rings, used as fastenings.)

Mother-of-pearl buttons are made from natural shells found in the waters around Japan, the Philippines, and Australia. Relatively expensive, they are often copied in plastic. Other materials used for buttons, such as leather, wood, and bone, are expensive and are also copied in plastic.

There are basically two types of buttons: sew-through (cheapest to apply to garments) and shank (with a loop on the back). Buttons are purchased by the gross (144) and all sizes are expressed as lignes (one ligne = .025 inch or .635 mm). For example, a one inch button is a 40 ligne button. Self-covered buttons are made to order for apparel manufacturers by contractors.

Belts

There are two types of belt manufacturers: the "rack" trade, who sell to retailers and the "cut-up" trade, who sell less expensive belts to apparel manufacturers to be used on dresses, jackets, skirts, or pants.

Garment belts are usually made of inexpensive materials such as vinyl (a leather look-alike) and ribbon. The belt material is either glued or sewn onto a stiff interfacing or backing. Stitched belts hold up longer than glued ones. Novelty belts are made of braid, elastic, chain, or rope.

Belts can also be made "in house" by the garment manufacturer with buckles from the button supplier. Most of these belts are made from garment fabrics. Self-belts can also be made to order by a contractor.

THE LEATHER INDUSTRY

Leather is preserved animal hides and skins, supplied mainly by the meat packing industry. The world's largest producers of cattle hides are the Soviet Union, the United States, and India; most goatskins come from India and China and most sheepskins from the Soviet Union, Australia, and New Zealand. Although the developing nations of Asia, Africa, and Latin America raise 60 percent of the world's cattle, 50 percent of its goats, and 33 percent

Leather fashions by Gianni Versace. *(Courtesy of Gianni Versace, Milan, Italy)*

of its sheep, they still have not realized the full potential of the sale of hides and skins. If their methods are modernized, the leather industry may shift from Western nations to the developing countries.

In the United States the leather industry is located mainly in the northern and northeastern states, where plants are close to their major customers—the shoe, glove, and handbag manufacturers. The domestic industry is composed of about 500 small firms and a few giants. Companies usually specialize because processing methods depend on the nature of the skins treated and the end use of the leather.

*Organization and Operation
of the Leather Industry*

Three major types of producers make up the leather industry in the United States. These are tanneries, contract tanneries, and converters.

Tanneries purchase and process skins and hides and sell the leather as their finished product.

Contract tanneries process the hides and skins to the specifications of other firms (mainly converters), but are not involved in the final sale of the leather.

Converters buy the hides and skins, commission the tanning to the contract tanneries, and then sell the finished leather.

Types of Leather

The many varieties of leather produced throughout the world are used in hundreds of different ways. The list below groups the important leather types and their uses in fashion apparel and accessories.

Cattle This group includes steer, cow, and bull hides, as well as calfskin and kipskin (large calves or small breeds of cattle). They are used for boot and shoe soles, heels, and uppers; handbags; belts; gloves; and garments.

Sheep Sheep and lambskins are used for shoes, slippers, gloves, coats, hats, and handbags. Sheepskins are also the source of chamois, an especially soft leather.

Goat Goat and kidskins are used for shoe uppers, handbags, gloves, and garments.

Equine Included in this group are horse, colt, ass, mule, and zebra hides for shoes, belts, gloves, and garments.

Buffalo Domestic land and water buffalo hides provide leather for shoe soles and uppers and for handbags.

Pig This group includes pig, hog, and boar leathers, which are used for gloves and shoe uppers.

Reptile This group includes alligator, crocodile, lizard, and snake, which are used for shoes, belts, and handbags.

Leather Processing

Differentiation between hides and skins is based on weight. *Skins* come from small animals, such as goats, deer, pigs, and calves, and weigh less than 25 pounds. *Hides* come from large animals such as steers, cows, buffaloes, and horses, and weigh over 25 pounds each.

The process by which hides and skins are made into leather can take up to six months and requires extensive equipment and skilled labor. There are three basic steps in leather processing: pretanning, tanning, and finishing.

Pretanning Operations Pretanning is basically a cleaning process. The cured hides are soaked in water to rehydrate them and to remove dirt, salt, and some proteins. Hides and skins must also have hair and fat removed by additional treatments that differ with each type of hide or skin. A cleaned hide is referred to as a *pelt*.

The Tanning Process Tanning protects the hide or skin against decomposition, by means of treatment by various agents. Treatment methods include soaking and dry powder. The choice of agents depends largely on the planned end use of the leather. Tanning agents include vegetable products, oils, minerals, and chemicals. The roots, bark, wood, leaves, or fruits of various trees and shrubs provide the vegetable tannins, which produce a firm, heavy leather. Oil tannages, especially codfish oil, produce relatively soft and pliable leathers such as chamois. Mineral tannages, such as alum and especially chrome, are common, as are the newer chemical tans such as sulfonic acid. Each tanning agent imparts special characteristics to leather. A combination of agents usually produces the best results.

Finishing The last step produces the desired thickness, moisture, and aesthetic appeal. After excess water and wrinkles are removed from the tanned leather, it is shaved or split into uniform thickness and then dyed. Color is applied to leather by brushing, or by tray, drum, spray, solvent, vacuum, or tank dyeing. Special effects may be created by dabbing color with a sponge, padding color on through stencils, sprinkling, spraying, or tie-dyeing. Next, dyed leathers are treated with oils and fats to provide lubrication, softness, strength, and waterproofing. Oiled leathers are then dried to fix the dyes and oils permanently. Dried leather is conditioned with damp sawdust to obtain uniform moisture content and then stretched for softness. Finally, leathers are coated with a seasoning or finish to improve their properties or character. For example, urethanes are used to add shine for patent leather. Leathers may even be further treated with buffers, rollers, or presses to achieve glazed, matte, and embossed effects.

Leather Promotion and Marketing

Like fiber and fabric producers, the leather industry promotes its products to apparel manufacturers, fashion editors, retailers, and the consumer. Promotion is done on an individual company basis or through trade associations like the Tanners Council. Yet, unlike fiber producers, individual tanners are not known by the public. Retail advertising for leather products may mention the type of leather and the designer, but not the leather producer.

Leather markets are concentrated in Western countries. The major exporters of finished leathers are France, the United Kingdom, Germany, the United States, and Italy. International trade in leather is approximately $1 billion per year.

Rising world population and incomes, along with new fashions for leather, have contributed to an ever-increasing demand for leather. However, the use of synthetics as leather substitutes is growing. In Western countries man-made products have supplanted 50 percent of goods formerly made of leather. To protect and expand their markets, leather producers must be innovative, constantly striving to develop new leather types and colors.

THE FUR INDUSTRY

The fur industry is another important supplier of raw material for the fashion industry.

Fur is the hairy coat of a mammal. From prehistoric times, people have used animal fur for both its warmth and its attractive appearance. Because fur has long been associated with wealth and prestige, the demand for luxury has played a major role in the development of the fur industry.

This section discusses the characteristics of various animals furs, the processes involved in preparing fur pelts for their use in the manufacture of fur garments, and the marketing of furs to these manufacturers.

Prospective buyer examines leather hides and skins. *(Courtesy of Salamander AG, West Germany)*

Inspection of fur pelts. *(Courtesy of the Informationsbüro Pelz, Bad Homburg, West Germany)*

The fur industry consists of three major groups: pelt producers or trappers, fur processors, and companies that produce fur garments for consumers. (We shall discuss fur garment producers in chapter 11.)

Fur Sources

In the first step of production, the industry must obtain the pelt or skin of the fur-bearing animal. The supply of furs comes from both wild animals and, more often, fur farms or ranches.

The major animals raised or trapped for the United States fur business are the following (in descending order of importance):

Mink, which is mostly bred

Fox, trapped and bred

Raccoon, trapped only

Sable, imported from the Soviet Union and Canada, where it is trapped

Other furs, used in smaller quantities include muskrat, skunk, opossum, lamb, and rabbit.

Wild Furs Wild furs for commercial use come from over 80 countries on all six continents, but mainly from North America, which has the greatest variety (40 different types). In the late 1960s individuals, international organizations, and governments became concerned about the possible extinction of endangered species. As a result, some countries enacted legislation restricting or prohibiting the commercial use of particular animals, including certain monkeys, seals, and leopards.

Wild fur-bearing animals are usually caught in baited traps. There is public concern about the agony animals suffer in this slow, painful death. In many areas seals are brutally clubbed to death, a practice that has caused great protests and efforts to prohibit the commercial use of wild seal fur. In fact, any use of animal skins to beautify our bodies, when they are no longer necessary for warmth, is a conscience-raising issue.

Fur Farming Fur farming has greatly increased the supply of fur for the fashion industry. General livestock methods are adapted to the keeping and breeding of animals for their pelts. Research in management, feeding, and breeding techniques has resulted in production of quality furs in thousands of mutations. The mutation of the silver fox from the red fox generated a great fashion demand in the 1930s and '40s. Mink has since become a more popular fur, accounting for approximately 60 to 70 percent of today's fur trade. Much of mink's increased popularity, too, has resulted from the development of a variety of mutant colors. Chinchilla, Persian lamb, and nutria are now also raised mainly on farms.

Pelt Characteristics

Fur pelts are animal skins with the hairy body covering remaining intact. Pelts consist of a soft, dense undercoat called ground hair, underhair, or underwool, and a longer protective covering called guard hair or top hair. Persian lamb, although sold as a fur, has only underwool. Mink, however, is a true fur, with both layers of hair. Fur-bearing animals in northern regions produce their fullest, glossiest coats as a protection against approaching cold weather.

Furs have different wearing qualities. The most expensive will not necessarily wear the best. The following list categorizes furs by durability—an important concern to the consumer when making such a major clothing investment.

Very durable:	Otter
	Raccoon
	Mountain lamb
	Mink
	Beaver
Durable:	Persian lamb
	Sable
	Dyed muskrat
	Alaska fur seal
Semidurable:	Fox
	Opossum
	Nutria
	Marten
Semiperishable:	Caracul
	Squirrel
	Rabbit
	Broadtail
	Ermine
	Mole
	Chinchilla

Marketing

Trappers normally sell their catches to collecting agents, who in turn sell them at auctions or to wholesale merchants. These merchants maintain stocks of furs, selling them to manufacturers as they are needed.

The auctioneer closes a bid at a fur auction.
(Courtesy of Hudson's Bay and Annings Ltd., London)

Fur farmers and ranchers, however, sell their pelts at public auction directly to the wholesale pelt merchants, manufacturers, or commission brokers (who buy for merchants or manufacturers). The Hudson Bay Company of Canada is the world's dominant fur marketing agent. Major fur auction centers are New York City, London, Leningrad, and Montreal. Other domestic fur auctions are held in Minneapolis, St. Louis, and Seattle. Pelt prices can fluctuate sharply, because price is dictated by supply and demand. The fashion for a particular fur can drastically drive up the price for those pelts.

When the manufacturers have purchased pelts at auctions or from wholesale pelt merchants, they contract with fur dressing and dyeing firms to process the pelts.

Fur Processing

Dressing   New York is the largest fur processing center in the United States. Fur skins are dressed to make them soft and pliable and to preserve their natural luster. Dressing processes vary with the nature and condition of the skin treated, but there are usually at least four distinct steps in the operation: preliminary cleaning and softening of the pelt; "fleshing" (cleaning) and stretching; "leathering," a tanning process using oils or other solutions; and finishing.

Dyeing   After dressing, the pelts may be sent out to a dyer. The modern use of chemical compounds known as fur bases has enabled fur dyers to produce a wider variety of colors. Although not all furs are dyed, dyeing has led to the use of many skins that were unattractive in their natural colors. New colors are an important selling point among fur retailers. Dyers often keep their techniques secret from competitors to maintain a market edge. The chief international dyeing centers are in France, Belgium, London, Frankfurt, and New York.

The pelts are now ready for garment production, a process covered in chapter 11.

SUMMARY

Leather and fur are the oldest body covering. Although leather and fur are no longer as important as textiles, face competition from vinyls and fake furs, and fluctuate in popularity, they are still an important part of the fashion industry.

Sources for both leather and fur are animals, either wild or raised on farms. The treatments of tanning (for leather) and dressing (for fur) are similar; they clean, preserve, and bring out the natural beauty of the skins, hides, or pelts. Although modern technology has speeded processing and made it some-

what easier, leather and fur production are still basically craft industries.

Trimmings *are necessary materials used to finish and decorate both garments and accessories. The decorative materials include buttons, ribbons, laces, braids, and belts. The functional materials include thread, interfacing, zippers, tapes, and elastic and are often classified as findings. Thread, interfacing, and narrow fabrics are an extension of the textile industry.*

Thread is the necessary element that holds garments together. Woven and nonwoven interfacings are needed to give support and shape to garments. Both come in a variety of weights appropriate for their use. Narrow fabrics, which can be woven, knitted, or braided include lace, ribbon, braid, piping, cording, tapes, and banding. The primary types of machine-made lace today are Barmen, Leaver, Raschel, and Venice. Venice is made on embroidery machines as is eyelet.

Zippers, buttons, and belt buckles represent the hardware used in garment and accessory manufacture. There are two basic kinds of zipper construction: either metal scoops are clamped onto tapes or tapes are woven around nylon coil. Buttons, formerly made out of natural materials like wood, metal, pearl, porcelain, and bone, are now primarily made from nylon or polyester for commercial use. Fabric belts for the cut-up trade can be sewn or glued onto stiff backings and finished with buckles or they may be made from braid, elastic, chain, or rope.

Each area in trimmings is a separate industry with its own resources and markets and a study in itself.

CHAPTER REVIEW

CHAPTER OBJECTIVES

After reading this chapter you should be able to
  A. Give evidence of having attained competence in the following areas:
    1. The ability to explain the basic types of threads and interfacings and their uses 2. The ability to list the various kinds of narrow fabrics and their functions 3. The ability to explain the basics of how narrow fabrics, zippers, buttons, and belts are produced 4. Knowledge of animal sources for fur and leather and of their major countries of origin 5. Understanding of the pretanning, tanning, and finishing processes for leather 6. Understanding of the dressing processes for furs

  B. Define the following terms and concepts in relation to their discussion in the chapter:
    1. Long staple thread 2. Stable interfacings 3. Stretch interfacings 4. Narrow fabrics 5. Barmen or Cluny lace 6. Leaver lace 7. Raschel lace 8. Venice lace 9. Braids 10. Zipper scoops 11. Coil zippers 12. Button materials 13. "Cut-up" belt trade 14. Leather sources 15. Tanneries 16. Leather types 17. Skins 18. Hides 19. Steps in processing leather 20. Fur sources 21. Wild furs 22. Fur farming 23. Pelts 24. Pelt characteristics 25. Fur auctions 26. Hudson Bay Company 27. Fur dressing. 28. Fur dyeing

---

Questions for Review

1. Briefly explain the three types of thread.
2. Discuss the various types of interfacings and their uses.
3. Describe how the four basic kinds of machine lace are produced.
4. What various categories are included as narrow fabrics?
5. Describe the two basic types of zippers and how they are made.
6. Discuss the various natural and man-made materials used to make buttons.
7. Explain how belts are produced for the "cut-up" trade.
8. Discuss briefly the three basic steps in leather processing.
9. Discuss how recent legislation concerning animal furs might affect the industry.
10. Discuss the four dressing processes for the treatment of furs.

PROJECTS FOR ADDITIONAL LEARNING

1. Select one category of trim (i.e., laces) and find a variety of examples at fabric stores. Describe their pattern or construction. Show examples (photos or actual garments) of their end use.

2. At the library trace the origin and development of a specific trim. Explain the differences between how they were made by hand originally and how they are mass produced today.

3. Visit a local department or specialty store and find five garments which use decorative and functional trimmings. Make a list of every trim on each garment. Discuss how the trims affect the total design of the garment. How do you think the manufacturers balanced the added cost of the trimmings with fabric and labor costs?

4. Write to a national animal protection agency such as Greenpeace. Find out what its members are doing to help protect endangered species and to prevent clubbing and other brutal methods of killing animals.

5. Visit a furrier. Learn to identify various furs by their characteristics.

THE MANUFACTURING OF FASHION

PART THREE

INTERNATIONAL AND DOMESTIC FASHION CENTERS

8

The Christian Dior salon
on the corner of rue François 1er and avenue Montaigne
in Paris. *(Courtesy of the French Government
Tourist Office)*

Now we are ready to examine the current international fashion manufacturing picture. This chapter covers the major fashion capitals of the world, as well as important domestic fashion centers. You will read about the specialties of each and about the creators who have made their cities into fashion centers.

The impact of international fashion has created what most experts consider to be four major fashion capitals: Paris, Milan, London, and New York. However, Paris still has the edge on the other three. The fashion industry is becoming a worldwide exchange of ideas, talent, material, and products. Americans still borrow ideas from Europe, but now Europe is often influenced by American fashion as well. Ideas come from all over the world; nearly every country contributes in some way.

Fashion centers develop because of concentrations of resources, supplies, skilled labor, and creative inspiration. All designers are influenced by what other designers and artists are creating. Excitement about a new idea acts as a catalyst for more creativity. That is the reason why many creative people gravitate to major creative centers.

PARIS

Paris became the capital of fashion for all the reasons above and more. Paris has the necessary resources and a creative atmosphere, but in addition, the French government has always supported and encouraged *les mains de France* (the hands of France), giving the needle trades much-deserved respect. There is also tremendous cooperation among the design firms, the fabric mills, and the auxiliary shoe, hat, fur, trimmings, findings, and embroidery industries. A designer who needs special fabrics finds the mills willing to weave or print just a few meters as a test run.[1] Shoe manufacturers plan designs to complement designer garments, and button and trim manufacturers will create items for the exclusive use of one designer. In such an atmosphere, it is no wonder that we have looked to Paris for fashion leadership.

For years there has been debate over whether Paris remains the fashion capital of the world, whether the couture is "dead." In the 1960s the fashion world experienced a strong trend toward youthful, more casual styling that practically forced the couture out of business. However, the emergence of a strong *prêt-à-porter*, (pret-a-por-tay, French for "ready-to-wear"), along with economic and social stability, have reasserted the traditional fashion leadership of France to some degree. Recognizing Paris as a center, many fiber and fabric associations, promotion agencies, and information sources have established their main fashion offices there.

The Couture

As we learned in chapter 1, *couture* is simply the French word for fine custom dressmaking, made to measure for a particular customer. However, the modern use of the term also implies originality, rather than the process of following an existing pattern with someone else's choice of fabric.

A *couturier* is a male couture designer, a *couturiere* his female counterpart. The business is called a "house" (*maison* in French). The private

[1] Bertrand Djian, President-Directeur-General, Per Spook, Paris, personal interview, August 1978.

112

client comes to the *salon*, an elegant showroom in the same building as the design studio, to see sample garments in the collection. When a client orders a dress or suit, it is made up in her exact measurements, with two or sometimes three fittings. Construction usually takes several weeks.

Haute Couture *Haute couture* translates literally as high dressmaking, or as we use it, high fashion. In the United States, promoters tend to overuse the expression; whereas it should be reserved for the very highest quality of fabrics and workmanship.

In France, only members on the selective "Couture-Creation" list of the official Federation Française de la Couture are considered members of the haute couture; membership is based on high standards of excellence and special requirements. The Federation includes three branches:

The Chambre Syndicale de la Couture Parisienne is an association to promote and protect the couture.

The Chambre Syndicale de Prêt-à-Porter is an association of the ready-to-wear branches of the couture, plus the best of the other French *prêt-à-porter*, currently Karl Lagerfeld for Chloe, Sonia Rykiel, and Kenzo Takada for Jungle Jap.

The Chambre Syndicale de la Mode Masculine is an association of the men's wear industries of the couture.

In addition, there are associations of artisans and manufacturers.

CHAMBRE SYNDICALE DE LA COUTURE OF THE
FEDERATION FRANCAISE DE LA COUTURE
"COUTURE-CREATION" LIST [2]

Couturiers are chosen for this category by a special commission of the Department of Industry. In the cases where the original couturier is no longer living, former assistants or other designers have taken over design responsibilities.

[2] Sylvie Zawadzki, Secretaire Generale, Federation Française de la Couture, du Prêt-à-Porter des Couturiers et des Createurs de Mode, Paris, personal interview.

André Courrèges (Coor-redge'), 40, rue François 1er, 75008 Paris

Carven (Car-van'), 6, rond-point des Champs-Elysees, 75008 Paris (Mme. Carmen Mallet)

Chanel (Shah-nell') 31, rue Cambon, 75001 Paris (now designed by Jean Cazaubon and Yvonne Dudel; *prêt-à-porter* designed by Philippe Guibourge)

Christian Dior (Dee-or') 30, avenue Montaigne, 75008 Paris (now designed by Marc Bohan)

Emanuel Ungaro (Un-gah'-row), 2, avenue Montaigne, 75008 Paris

Gilbert Feruch (Fa-rusch') 35, rue François 1er, 75008 Paris

Givenchy (Gsh-vahn-shee'), 3, avenue George V, 75008 Paris (Hubert de Givenchy)

Grès (Gray), 1, rue de la Paix, 75002 Paris (Alix Gres)

Guy Laroche (La-rosh'), 29, avenue Montaigne, 75008 Paris

Hanae Mori (More'-ee), 17–19, avenue Montaigne, 75008 Paris

Jean Patou (Pah-too'), 7, rue Saint-Florentin, 75008 Paris (now designed by Roy Gonzales)

Jean-Louis Scherrer (Scher-rare'), 51, avenue Montaigne, 75008 Paris

Lanvin (Lahn-vahn'), 22, rue de Faubourg Saint-Honoré, 75008 Paris (now designed by Jules-François Crahay)

Louis Feraud (Fair-oh'), 88, rue de Faubourg Saint-Honoré, 75008 Paris

Nina Ricci (Ree'-chee), 20, rue des Capucines, 75002 Paris (now designed by Gerard Pipart)

Per Spook (Norwegian name, rhymes with book), 5, rue de l'Université, 75007 Paris

Pierre Balmain (Bal-mahn'), 44, rue François 1er, 75008 Paris

Pierre Cardin fitting a toile. *(Courtesy of Pierre Cardin, Paris)*

Yves St. Laurent *(Courtesy of Yves St. Laurent)*

Pierre Cardin (Car-dan'), 27, avenue de Marigny, 75008 Paris

Serge Lepage (Le-pahgsh'), 29, rue Cambon, 75001 Paris

Ted Lapidus (Lap'-i-dus), 37, avenue Pierre 1er de Serbie, 75008 Paris

Torrenté (Tor-en'tay), 9, rue de Faubourg Saint-Honoré, 75008 Paris

Yves St. Laurent (Sahn-Law-rahn'), 5, avenue Marceau, 75016 Paris

Ateliers The couture salons (couture showrooms), boutiques (retail shops for ready-to-wear and accessories), and ateliers (workshops) center around the Avenue Montaigne and the Faubourg Saint-Honoré in Paris. To qualify for the Chambre Syndicale de la Couture list "Couture-Creation," a house is required to have at least one atelier in Paris with a minimum technical staff of 15, not including the director. A couturier may have anywhere from 15 to 400 employees in one or a combination of several ateliers. Ateliers are separated into *flou* for dressmaking and *tailleur* for making tailored suits and coats.

In large houses, where there is much work to be done, *modelistes* work under the head designer, executing the individual designs. They are the liaison with the ateliers, where they supervise construction of the *toile* or sample garment. The head designer makes all final decisions on what designs will appear in the collection. Some designers have several workshops while others have only one, depending on the size of their collections and the amount of business they do. Each atelier is headed by a production manager or chief technician called the *premier d'atelier* (pre-me-air' dah-tel-yay'). Under the manager are the shop assistant, fitters, *midinettes* (seamstresses, classified as "first" hands or "second" hands), and apprentices.

Government Support of the Couture The French government gives much support to the couture in order to promote exports. Government-owned French television gives the couture, as the prestigious segment of the industry, free television exposure. The government also pays the costs involved in sending shows of couture clothing all over the world. The cost of this kind of advertising is enormous; that the government pays the expenses certainly helps to compensate for the costs of producing a collection. The publicity is especially important because it generates both exports (the couture exports 55 percent of everything it produces) and licensing businesses, helping to keep the couture alive.

Licensing

Under licensing agreements, designers give manufacturers permission to use their names and/or designs, for which the designer is paid a percentage of sales. For example, perfume companies often give a new perfume the name of a well-known designer.

Licenses provide a means of diversification and cover nearly every product imaginable. Pierre Cardin, probably the most financially successful of the couture, has 390 licenses.[3] His manufacturing licenses include women's wear, men's wear, and children's wear, from underwear to coats, hats to shoes, swim suits to ski wear; accessories; jewelry; eyeglasses; sheets and towels; ceramics; furniture; and even bicycles! Licensing is geographically separated. A Pierre Cardin suit purchased in the United States is made in the United States; Cardin does no exporting. However, all designs are done in his studio, and representative agents control quality at the various manufacturers around the world.

Licensing has become popular with both couture and ready-to-wear designers worldwide. It promotes their names without exposing the designers to any financial risk associated with the product.

The Future of Couture   With today's economic priorities shifted to other areas, very few people want or can afford to pay couture prices for dresses that may be in fashion for only one year. Today the couture shares only 4,000 private clients worldwide, hardly enough for each house to stay in business if they were doing only couture.[4] Most Americans find it difficult to understand why the couture continues to exist when it no longer makes a profit—and in fact usually loses money. It costs between $250,000 and $1,000,000 to produce one couture collection; some houses lose up to $1,000,000 a year.[5] However, these losses are more than made up by the publicity the couture collections bring to the houses' other businesses, such as licensing and *prêt-à-porter* lines.

For the French, the couture still means prestige. Yves St. Laurent, probably the most successful couturier, says that the couture "provides the standards, the craftsmanship that makes fashion possible."[6] "The couture is the showpiece of French fashion and still serves an important function even though the *prêt-à-porter* is the money maker,"[7] according to Bertrand Djian, President-Directeur-General of Per Spook Couture. He compares the couture to Le Mans, the race that is the showpiece for experimental designs in the automotive industry.

Prêt-à-Porter

The couture tends to be classic and conservative, but elegant. When a client spends so much money on one garment, she wants it to be timeless. *Prêt-à-porter*, on the other hand, is more avant-garde (the French term meaning ahead of the rest). The "*Prêt*" collection openings are scheduled earlier than the couture because mass production takes longer. Because the *Prêt* shows are earlier, and because the *Prêt* have become the innovators, much of the excitement and glamour have been taken away from the couture.

Except for a few couture designers such as St. Laurent and Givenchy, the ready-to-wear collections receive most of the publicity now, and *Prêt* designers set most of the trends. Each of the outstanding French ready-to-wear designers has a distinctive style. Top names of the French *prêt-à-porter* include those listed below.

Yves St. Laurent   (Eve Sahn-Law-rahn'). Often referred to as Y.S.L., he is also a member of the couture. He is a steady, major influence in the fashion world, setting trends in a restrained, sophisticated way with a good sense of timing. St. Laurent has a series of boutiques called Rive Gauche (reev gosh, meaning Left Bank) in major cities that carry his elegant, sophisticated clothes.

Kenzo Takada   (Ken'-zo Ta-ka'-da) for Jungle Jap. Usually called Kenzo, he came to Paris from Japan in 1965 and became one of the most innovative designers, setting color, fabric, and styling trends. He is noted for his smocks, popular in the early 70s, and the Chinese look of the middle '70s.

Karl Lagerfeld (Karl La'-ger-feld).   The designer for Chloe, he is originally from Germany. His designs are bold, dramatic statements that have an important impact on fashion direction.

---

[3] Bernard Danillon de Cazella, Pierre Cardin, Paris, personal interview, August 1978.

[4] Zawadzki.

[5] Djian.

[6] Patrick McCarthy and Edwina LaFarge, "Paris Opens: Still Elite, Extravagant," *Women's Wear Daily*, July 23, 1979, p. 1.

[7] Djian.

Karl Lagerfeld sketching a design. *(Courtesy of Karl Lagerfeld for Chloé, Paris)*

116

Sonia Rykiel (Rick'-ee-el). Her soft, subtle, body-conscious clothes and long, fluid looks, based on the sweater, have already become *prêt-à-porter* classics. She has experimented with new, simple construction methods, such as seams that show on the outside of the garment.

Emmanuelle Khanh (Kan). Khanh's last name comes from her Vietnamese husband. She is consistently one of the best-selling designers of young looks. Known for interesting embroidered treatments, she now also does knitwear.

Jean Cacharel (Cash-a-rel'). He began as a men's shirt manufacturer until women started wearing his shirts in the 1960s. Now the firm's youthful print separates and charming school-girl dresses, designed by his sister-in-law Corinne Grandval, have become neoclassics.

Dorothy Bis (Dor'-a-tay Beec). Owned and operated by Jacqueline and Elie Jacobson, this house has been a trend-setting boutique (carrying their own clothes) since the early 1960s. The firm is known especially for knits.

Other important names in French *prêt-à-porter* are Christian Aujard (Michaele Aujard), Anne-Marie Beretta, Corinne Bricaire, Jean-Charles de Castlebajac, Jean-Claude de Luca, Daniel Hechter, Claude Montana, Thierry Mugler, Chantal Thomass, and Kansai Yamamoto. Although all these designers do ready-to-wear, their clothes are still too expensive for the average person and often too experimental for volume production. Along with the old-line couture and other prominent international "name" designers, they form the new "upper class" of fashion. Their clothes are modified and adapted for mass production at lower prices.

Prêt-à-porter manufacturing is centered in the Sentier district of Paris. Identical garments are made up in quantity in various sizes and colors. The customer needs only to try one on in a store to see if it fits, purchase it, and take it home immediately.

Mass production makes garments much less expensive. For example, a single couture dress or suit might cost between $1,000 and $2,000, an evening gown from $2,500 to $4,000. A *prêt-à-porter* dress designed by the same couturier would cost $100 to $1,000. However, a *prêt-à-porter* garment brings no exclusivity with it.

Actually, it is still very expensive to create the original sample garments that will be included in the ready-to-wear collection. There is as much experimentation involved in pattern making and style development for that initial sample (although construction is based on mass-production methods) as for a couture garment. Only the final mass production of those samples makes it a profitable business.

ITALY

It is difficult to confine discussion of Italian fashion to one city. Although Milan has become the most important fashion center for Italian ready-to-wear, Florence and Rome are fashion cities as well. The fashion industry in Italy is smaller than that of Paris, but its impact on international fashion has grown. The rich, beautiful fabrics manufactured in Italy must be a major inspiration. As in Paris, the *alta moda* (Italian couture) has branched into *moda pronta* (ready-to-wear). Unlike the French, the Italian government does not directly support the *alta moda*, but it does sponsor showings in the Pitti and Strozzi Palaces in Florence.[8]

The Camera Nazionale dell'Alta Moda, the Italian couture association, has divisions for men's wear, women's wear, ready-to-wear, accessories, furs, and knitwear. Famous members include Count Emilio Pucci di Barsento (Poo-chee) of Florence, Valentino

[8] "Italian Fashion, Twenty-Five Years After," Camera Nazionale Dell'Alta Moda Italiana, press release, 1977.

Emilio Pucci. *(Courtesy of Emilio Pucci, Florence, Italy)*

and Galitzine (Gal'-it-zeen) of Rome, and Mila Schoen (Shone) of Milan. About 80 percent of the *alta moda* now have ready-to-wear and licensing.[9] Emilio Pucci, for example, designs lingerie for Formfit Rogers of New York.

The Italians have become particularly well known for their high-quality leather goods, silks, and knitwear. We are familiar with Italian fashion names such as Pucci's prints, Fendi furs, Gucci shoes, and Missoni knitwear because their products are exported to the United States.

It is difficult for the consumer to separate the names of firms from those of designers. For example, Walter Albini, Giorgio Armani, and Gianni Versace are talented designers in both men's and women's wear who work for famous manufacturers such as Complice, Genny, Trell, or Callaghan. However, Mariuccia Mandelli and Aldo Ferrante are both designers and the owners of their respective firms, Krizia and Basile.

LONDON

Men's Wear

London has long been the respected world center for classic men's fashion because of its famous Savile Row tailors (although some "Savile Row" tailors are not on Savile Row at all). Prince Charles still has his suits made at Gieves and Hawkes at Number 1 Savile Row, where his father ordered suits as a young man. Other famous tailors include H. Huntsman & Sons, Kilgour Weatherill, Anderson & Sheppard, and Henry Poole, the oldest Savile Row–area firm.

Savile Row offers three variations of the basic suit silhouette. The first is very traditional and somewhat form-fitting; the second is squarer for the more conservative man "who wants to give an impression of solidity," and the third has the slim, trendy, Continental fit. A custom tailored suit, completed in three or four weeks, usually costs between $350 and $900.[10]

Gieves & Hawkes at No. 1 Savile Row.
(Courtesy of Charlie Gerli, the photographer)

Women's Wear

As for women's wear, London is a combination of "establishment, tradition, eccentricity, and rising new talent."[11] English women have traditionally followed royal leadership, which since Queen Victoria has been rather dowdy. Again, the wish to give an impression of stability has led to conservatism in dress for women. Also, London's damp weather naturally favors tweeds and layering for warmth, with a partiality toward pastel garden-party dresses at the first sign of spring. The modern young designers changed that image in the 1960s, at least for young people; but designers have had a hard time maintaining their image since the fading of the "swinging London" of the '60s.

[9] Massimo Ludovisi, Deputy Italian Trade Commissioner, Los Angeles, personal interview, October 1978.

[10] Pearson Phillips, "From Suits to Snuffboxes, T & C Shops London," *Town & Country*, April 1978, p. 81.

[11] Casey Tolar, Fashion Promotions, London, personal interview, August 1978.

**Designer Zandra Rhodes with Percy Savage,
director of the London Collections.**
*(Courtesy of Percy Savage and Casey Tolar, Fashion
Promotions, London)*

The couture in London (the English and Americans have adopted even French terminology) was very strong after World War II but has since nearly died out. Norman Hartnell and Hardy Amies are the only couturiers left from the former Incorporated Society of London Fashion Designers.[12] The new breed of couture designers, such as Zandra Rhodes, John Bates, Yuki, Roland Klein, and Belleville-Sassoon, must finance their custom operations with their ready-to-wear collections.

Ready-to-Wear

North of Oxford Street in London, in the area around Margaret Street, lies the West End "rag trade" district, supporting a conglomeration of fashion suppliers, studios, and showrooms. This area of approximately one square mile can be likened to New York's Seventh Avenue, although the London buildings are older and smaller and most even lack elevators. Actual manufacturing is done in London's East End and is now spreading to neighboring parts of North London.[13]

Many young designers have come from all over the world to study at London's famous art colleges, staying on to open businesses, unfortunately with little financial backing. Consequently, with so many different cultural backgrounds influencing design, there is no single London fashion direction. Moreover, since most designers are undercapitalized, individual promotions are financially impossible, and only exhibitions abroad are supported by the government.

[12] R. C. Whiteman, Licencee Director, Hardy Amies, London, personal interview, August 1978.

[13] Tricia Whitehead, Director, *Faces* Consultant Service, London, September 4, 1979.

Efforts to promote London fashion in the 1970s involved groups of designers whose work could be promoted collectively. One such group is the London Collections, run by Percy Savage and Casey Tolar's Fashion Promotions; the other is the London Designer Collections (the newer designers), organized by Annette Worsley-Taylor. Only some of the established designers can afford separate showings of their collections. For example, Jean Muir, noted for her timeless jerseys and leathers with fine attention to details, Zandra Rhodes and Bill Gibb, known for eccentric designs and extraordinary fantasy creations, have their own showings. Other well-known London designers include Gordon Clarke, John Bates, Bruce Oldfield, Adrian Cartmell, Jeff Banks, Ann Buck, Jane Cattlin, Gina Fratini, Caroline Charles, Janice Wainwright, and Sheilagh Brown & Sheridan Barnett.

OTHER INTERNATIONAL FASHION CENTERS

Europe

Germany Germany's fashion industry is decentralized: Berlin, Munich, Krefeld, and Düsseldorf are major production centers, and fashion publications emanate from Hamburg. Germany is known for accurate and dependable technical production. Only in the past few years, however, has German styling been known internationally, primarily through the exports of companies such as Mondi. Continuing Germany's historic role as the crossroads of European trade, fashion fairs in Düsseldorf, Munich, and Cologne bring fashion from many nations together, creating an international market of great dimensions (see chapter 12).

Spain Spain still has a government-subsidized *alta costura* (haute couture), centered in Madrid. There are 14 members, including Pertegaz, Berhanyer, and Mitzou. Also in Madrid is the headquarters of Spain's women's and children's ready-to-wear association, Camara de la Moda Española, with member firms scattered throughout the country. Spain is an important producer of leather products, particularly shoes, and also of moderately priced knitwear. Spanish companies also mass produce for some manufacturers in France.

Scandinavia The four Scandinavian countries have different fashion specialties. Denmark tends to produce more conservative apparel, while Sweden, Finland, and Norway concentrate on more youthful styling. Together all four countries form the Scandinavian Clothing Council, headquartered in Copenhagen. Internationally known Scandinavian fashion creators include Margit Brandt of Denmark and the late Armi Ratia of Finland, founder of Marimekko (which means "country women's dress").

Eastern Europe Factories in Poland, Yugoslavia, Hungary, and Romania produce apparel for manufacturers in Germany, France, and England on a contract basis. Yugoslavia, however, is the only Eastern European country that has tried to promote its own fashion products internationally.

The Soviet Union has a large potential fashion market, yet its entire apparel industry is highly structured and directed by a central bureau, the Dom Modele. As a result, the consumer has little fashion choice. Economic and political conditions in Western countries are more conducive to fashion innovation: individuals can go into business for themselves, with opportunities to express new ideas.

Israel

There are approximately 200 clothing and textile plants spread throughout Israel, concentrating in and around Tel Aviv. The textile and fashion industry produces about 12 percent of the nation's industrial output, providing employment for more than 60,000 people.

The Israeli textile and fashion industry exports approximately $300 million annually.[14] Exports are chiefly to Great Britain, Germany, France, and Denmark, in part because as an associate member of the Common Market, Israel pays no import duties to these countries.

Due to its exports, Israel has become internationally well known for its leather wear (from companies such as Beged Or, Carnit, and Alaska), swim wear (Gottex and Diva), sportswear (Sportlife and Rikma), children's wear (Tip Top and Dorit), and knitwear (Barbour).

14 *Israel Textile and Clothing Directory*, Manufacturers' Association of Israel, Textile Department, 1979, p. 3.

Latin America

Many Latin American countries, with important raw materials and a large supply of low-cost labor, can offer low-cost production to North American manufacturers. Apparel and accessory production industries are encouraged by their governments, because additional exports help their balance of payments and increase their gross national product (see chapter 10).

The Orient

Traditionally known for fine textiles and craftsmanship, Japan has recently developed a large and skillful ready-to-wear industry. Although they are potential fashion innovators, Japanese manufacturers concentrate on translating European trends—perhaps because Japanese consumers would generally rather buy fashion from Europe. Talented young Japanese designers like Kenzo Takada often leave Japan to study and work in Europe. Currently, Japan's acclaimed designers, both at home and abroad, include Kenzo Takada, Hanae Mori, Issei Miyake, Jun Ashida, Yuki Torri, Junko Koshino, and Kansai Yamamoto.

Hong Kong has long been known for fast, low-cost, made-to-measure dressmaking and tailoring. Today, along with Taiwan, Korea, the Philippines, and India, Hong Kong can produce finely made apparel at much lower cost than Europe or the United States, because wages are still so much lower in the Orient. Many Western manufacturers either have factories of their own in the Orient, or at least supervise production to ensure that standards and time schedules are met (see chapter 10). It will be interesting to see what fashion industry develops in the People's Republic of China, now that trade with the West is being promoted.

Canada

With an estimated 2000 apparel firms, the fashion industry is the fourth largest employer of labor in Canada.[15] Montreal is the center for approximately 65 percent of the garment industry. Toronto is second in importance with some 22 percent of the apparel manufacturing activity. Winnipeg has about 8 percent, and the rest have another 5 percent, chiefly

in Vancouver. In Montreal, the garment district was originally located in the area between Bleury Street, Peel Street, St. Catherine Street, and de Maisonneuve. In search of reasonable rents, more room and modern facilities, it has since spread out especially to the north end of the city, close to the work force. In Toronto, the garment industry has also spread out from the Spadina Avenue area where it originated.

Canada's apparel industry is quite diversified due to its infinite variety of cultural influences, climates, and lifestyles, resulting in a vast array of fashion styles and tastes. Therefore, Canada produces a full range of products, from better-priced designer apparel to inexpensive mass-appeal clothing. In terms of exports, the strength is, by descending order of importance, in outerwear, furs, leather goods, and children's wear.[16] Although it is difficult to pinpoint area specialties, the Montreal area is particularly noted for fur, children's wear, and skiwear manufacturing. In Toronto, men's clothing is especially notable. Winnipeg is prominent for its outerwear and Vancouver for sportswear and leathers.

Some of the better-known designers in Canada are Léo Chevalier (Brodkin, Van Essa, Natural Furs, etc.), Michel Robichaud (Burtmar, Canadian Beach Wear, etc.), Harry Parnass and Nicola Pellai (Parachute; also with shops in Montreal, Toronto, and New York), Margaret Godfrey (Bagatelle), Marielle Fleury (Sport Togs), François Guénet (Malanson, Aline Marelle, etc.), Jean-Claude Poitras (Beverini), Robert Chernin (Champs Elysée, etc.), Marilyn Brooks (Marilyn Brooks, etc.), John Warden (Molyclaire, Canadian Children's Wear, etc.), and Serge et Réal (Trois, Inc.).

The Canadian fashion industry is supported by several organizations. Fashion Canada is a private corporation, funded by the Department of Industry, Trade & Commerce, to promote the development of fashion design potential and increase Canada's international fashion image. It is directed by a board of 25 representatives of all branches of the fashion business. The Fashion Designers Association of Canada (FDAC) was also created to promote Canadian fashion and designers. It sponsors a Trend Show each season which is held before the French *prêt-à-porter* collection openings to prove Canadian designers' originality.

---

[15] Neil Peacock, Director, Fashion Canada, interview, April 1980.

[16] Chantal Tittley-Moreault, the Fashion Group, Montreal, April 1980.

A few of Canada's well-known designers (left to right): Leo Chevalier, Marielle Fleury, with the design coordinator for the Montreal Olympics Georges Huel, Michel Robichaud, and John Warden. *(Courtesy of Chantal Tittley-Moreault)*

DOMESTIC FASHION CENTERS

New York

Although Paris is still the most innovative fashion center, the American ready-to-wear industry is the largest and most competitive and has the most innovative marketing methods. New York remains the American garment center, mainly because supplies and skilled labor are concentrated there.

The Seventh Avenue Garment District Most fashion originates in the vicinity of Seventh Avenue on Manhattan Island in New York City. Seventh Avenue gives its name to the whole garment district bounded by 34th and 40th Streets and Sixth and Ninth Avenues. Into this area are crowded over 6,000 garment firms. Two-thirds of all American-made women's and children's clothes and nearly half of all men's and boy's wear are either designed or made there.

The streets are jammed with trucks, taxies, and people pushing racks of fabrics or clothes from supplier to manufacturer to contractor. Design studios, showrooms, and offices crowd each building, on every block. There is a sharp contrast between the plush showroom in front, for the outside world to see, and the cluttered design rooms in back.

Nearly all manufacturers formerly had their production facilities in this area as well. However, the need to keep costs down has caused many apparel producers to move production from New York to other areas, especially the South, where rents and labor are less expensive. To revitalize New York's largest industry, a task force has been created to clean up the district, locate easier bank credit, and create work space. A new mart has been proposed for 42nd Street, but controversy has stalled the plan.

Company Size   In the modern world of large corporations, most fashion businesses have been small, often family owned and operated. Small size allows flexibility in both designing and production. Styling can quickly follow fashion trends because fewer people are involved in decision making. Production is flexible because outside contractors are used almost exclusively (see chapter 10). Today, however, successful small businesses are often purchased by large conglomerates or holding companies, which generally allow the companies they own to continue functioning with an independent identity as long as profit goals are realized. The sizable advertising and marketing budgets of large companies make it difficult for small companies to compete. Therefore, although there has been a decrease in the total number of apparel firms, production has increased due to the growth of larger companies.

Designers   Especially in companies that produce moderate or lower priced women's, men's, and children's wear, the designer's name is unknown to the public. The name of the company is either fictitious, such as Jones New York and Bobbie Brooks, or the name of the business head or founder, such as Jerry Silverman. In high priced clothing it is a different matter. Designers have become a part of the world of show business. They get to the top of their field by means of talent and promotion of their names through advertising. The public becomes aware of a name and often buys only because the name is well known. But the fashion public is as fickle as the film-going public. A designer is often in today and out tomorrow; the picture changes every season. Reading fashion publications regularly is the only way to keep informed about current designer favorites and best-selling styles. However, it is best to judge designs and designers by quality and talent rather than by persuasive advertising. As Geoffrey Beene said, "The public . . . knows too little about design and too much about designers." [17]

The list below includes the best-known United States designers, as seen on designer labels:

Adolfo.   Born in Cuba, Adolfo Sandini originally designed millinery but added clothes to his line in the late '60s. Now Adolfo designs both ready-to-wear and made-to-order day and evening dresses and suits.

John Anthony.   Born Giantonio Iorio in New York, John Anthony developed an excellent background in suits and coats at Devonbrook and Adolph Zelinka before opening his own business in 1971 and moving on to softer looks. He presents a small, concise collection each season. He won the Coty Fashion Critics Award in 1972 (see chapter 12).

Geoffrey Beene.   Beene, who studied art in Paris, is one of America's most internationally well-known designers, with an office in Milan. He was one of the first designers to set up his own business, in 1963, adding Beene Bag, his sportswear line, soon after. Beene won the Coty Award in both 1964 and 1966.

Bill Blass.   Beginning as a sketcher at David Crystal in the 1940s, Blass became a partner at Maurice Rentner and then bought out the business. To his women's day and evening wear he has added Blassport sportswear, men's wear, and other licenses. One of the most stable names in fashion design, he won the Coty Award in 1961, 1970, and 1971.

---

[17] Christopher Petkanas, "The Fashion Makers," *Gentlemen's Quarterly*, May 1978, p. 128.

Bill Blass at work in his office at 550 Seventh Avenue.
(Courtesy of Bill Blass; photograph by the author)

Halston. Born Roy Halston Frowick in the Midwest, he began his career as a millinery designer in Chicago. Now Halston has a boutique and a custom salon, as well as his ready-to-wear business established on 7th Avenue in 1972. He won the Coty Award in 1972.

Bill Kaiserman. Kaiserman made his reputation designing men's wear but now does women's wear in addition. Under the label "Rafael," his clothes are produced in Europe.

Donna Karan and Louis Dell'Olio for Anne Klein. After attending school together, Karan and Dell'Olio took over as head designers after Anne Klein's death in 1974. (Karan had been Klein's assistant.) Together they won the 1977 Coty Award for their sportswear.

Kasper. A three-time Coty Award winner, Kasper studied in New York and Paris before starting in millinery. Since 1964 he has been at Joan Leslie, specializing in dresses, to which he added the J. L. Sport line.

Calvin Klein. With a good understanding of timing and consumer needs, Klein first established himself as a coat designer. In 1967 he added sportswear. He won the Coty Award in 1975 for the third time.

Ralph Lauren. Known for his classic sportswear for both sexes, Lauren actually began in men's wear with neckties in the 1960s. He later opened his own company, Polo.

Mary McFadden. McFadden's designs are works of art—fabric as sculpture. With a very individual look, her simple shapes are a background for her fabric designs. Her fabrics are also adapted for upholstery, wallpaper, and table coverings.

Oscar de la Renta. Born in Santo Domingo, he studied in Spain and under couturier Castillo in Paris before coming to New York. He opened his own women's wear business in 1965; he now also licenses designs for men's wear, shoes, furs, sheets, umbrellas, and eyeglasses. He won the Coty Award in 1967, 1968, and 1973.

Diane von Furstenberg. As Princess von Furstenberg, she used her name to promote the comeback of dresses, which she had produced in Italy. Now, having closed her manufacturing business, she licenses everything: dresses, cosmetics, jewelry, furs, shoes, and accessories.

Other well-known designers include Gil Aimbez, Bill Atkinson, Scott Barrie, Donald Brooks, Stephen Burrows, Albert Capraro, Perry Ellis, Bill Haire, Cathy Hardwick, Stan Herman, Carol Horn, Julio,

Mary McFadden fitting a sleeve to one of her pleated gowns. *(Courtesy of Mary McFadden; photograph by the author)*

Ronald Kolodzie, Anthony Muto, Clovis Ruffin, Giorgio Sant'Angelo, Willie Smith, Charles Suppon, Koos van den Akker, and Chester Weinberg.

Although some designers, such as Adolfo and Halston, do made-to-order fashions, the mainstay of American fashion is ready-to-wear. Internationally, the United States is known especially for its sportswear.

REGIONAL CENTERS

Although the state of New York remains the largest fashion center in the United States, with 6,500 apparel manufacturers producing goods worth more than $7.5 billion each year, there is a trend toward decentralization. Some manufacturers have moved from New York City in search of a cheaper labor supply and more space, although they may have to pay more for delivery of raw materials from East Coast supply sources. Other companies have started locally, fostered by available credit and support from retailers. The result is growth in regional fashion centers.

California is the second largest apparel manufacturing state with 3,150 firms, followed by Pennsylvania, New Jersey, and Massachusetts.[18] The largest apparel cities, in descending order, are New York, Los Angeles, Chicago, Philadelphia, Boston, and Dallas.[19] It should be pointed out, however, that some of this production is owned by or contracted for manufacturers whose headquarters and design facilities are in New York City.

California

The apparel manufacturing growth rate is currently 120% as compared to a 48% growth rate for the entire United States.[20] At least two-thirds of California's fashion companies are headquartered in Los Angeles County, even though the state's largest—Levi Strauss & Co. (incorporating Koracorp, formerly the second largest company)—is based in San Francisco. Much of the California companies' success is based on the ability to promote a certain life style approach to fashion. Because of a mild climate and a casual life style, California designers have been most innovative in sportswear and swim wear. Sales of the "California Look" keep booming as Americans become more leisure conscious and as population shifts toward the sun belt. Ready-to-wear designers such as Carlos Arias, Holly Harp, Bonnie Strauss, Chance Wayne, Dennis Goldsmith, Norma Fink, Phyllis Sues, Barbara Colvin, Jeanne Allen and Marc Foster Grant, Karen Alexander, and Jessica McClintock have lately received increasing nationwide recognition. James Galanos represents the old couture tradition in California, and, of course, the film industry's costume designers have long influenced American fashion.

Other Regional Centers

Chicago and Rochester have long been known as centers for men's wear. Philadelphia has a concentration of children's wear and women's dress firms. Dallas is growing, especially in moderately priced

sportswear. St. Louis is recognized for junior dresses, Miami for resort wear, and Boston for outerwear. However, as regional fashion manufacturing develops, it becomes less and less specialized. The spreading out of fashion centers throughout the United States and the world is helping to balance fashion influence, resulting in diversified styling and wide consumer choice.

SUMMARY

Paris remains at the summit of fashion but now shares the spotlight with New York, Milan, and London. The French couture is still prestigious but must support itself by licensing and prêt-à-porter. As long as the French government continues its support of the industry, the couture will probably go on. It will be interesting, however, to note the government's reaction as prêt-à-porter designers grow in importance, increasing their contribution to exports and licensing.

Internationally, ready-to-wear has become the focal point and money maker for the fashion industry. The United States leads the world in ready-to-wear manufacturing. Innovative designer fashions from the top creators in each fashion center are translated, modified, adapted, or even copied at lower prices to fit the life styles and budgets of all types of people.

CHAPTER REVIEW

CHAPTER OBJECTIVES

After reading this chapter you should be able to
A. Give evidence of having attained competence in the following areas:
1. Ability to recognize and pronounce the names of well-known international fashion creators 2. Knowledge of the design and manufacturing specialties of four international fashion centers 3. Ability to explain the reasons for French fashion leadership 4. Ability to explain the role of the Federation Française de la Couture in the French fashion industry 5. Ability to describe the growth in importance of the *prêt-à-porter* 6. Knowledge of the reasons for the importance of New York as a fashion center 7. Ability to outline the role of other international and domestic fashion centers.
B. Define the following terms and concepts in relation to their discussion in the chapter:
1. Paris 2. Couture 3. *Prêt-à-porter* 4. Haute couture 5. Federation Française de la Couture 6. "Couture-Creation" list membership requirements 7. Atelier 8. Flou 9. Tailleur 10. Toile 11. *Premier* 12. Boutique 13. Salon 14. Licensing 15. Milan 16. *Alta moda* 17. *Moda pronta* 18. London 19. Savile Row 20. Seventh Avenue 21. Los Angeles

[18] "Fashion's New Regional Look," *Business Week*, November 6, 1978, p. 188.

[19] Research Division, International Ladies' Garment Workers' Union.

[20] "Fashion's New Regional Look," p. 188.

1. Why does the couture continue to have prestige in the fashion world even though it suffers losses?
2. What are the functions of the Federation Française de la Couture?
3. Name and explain the two classifications of ateliers and discuss the organization of a typical atelier.
4. Explain the meaning of *licensing*.
5. What are the differences between the couture and the *prêt-à-porter?*
6. Discuss decentralization of fashion centers in Germany and Italy versus centralization in England and France. Why do you think this occurred?
7. What name is used to refer to New York's garment district? Explain why the name is used.
8. Discuss the growth of regional fashion centers in the United States.

PROJECTS FOR ADDITIONAL LEARNING

Each student should have a subscription to "W" (Women's Wear Daily is rather expensive) or to *California Apparel News.*

1. In a fashion magazine, find a photograph of a garment you particularly like. Find the name of the designer in the description. Trace that designer's name through older issues of fashion magazines until you have found ten examples (in ten separate issues) of his or her work. Analyze the unique characteristics of the designer's style.

2. Shop a store that carries Italian or French fashions. Find on garment labels five of the names mentioned in this chapter. Discuss the style characteristics of each garment in a written report. If possible, illustrate with sketches. If a store is unavailable, find your examples in magazines.

3. Shop an exclusive specialty store and ask to see their most expensive evening dress ($500 and up). You may be able to try it on in your size. Then go to a department store and try on an evening dress in the $100–$200 range. Next, go to a discount store and try on an evening dress in the $30–$50 range. (Male students should try on suits in the same price ranges.) Make a written comparison of the quality of fabric, construction, and styling. Document your report with descriptions or sketches.

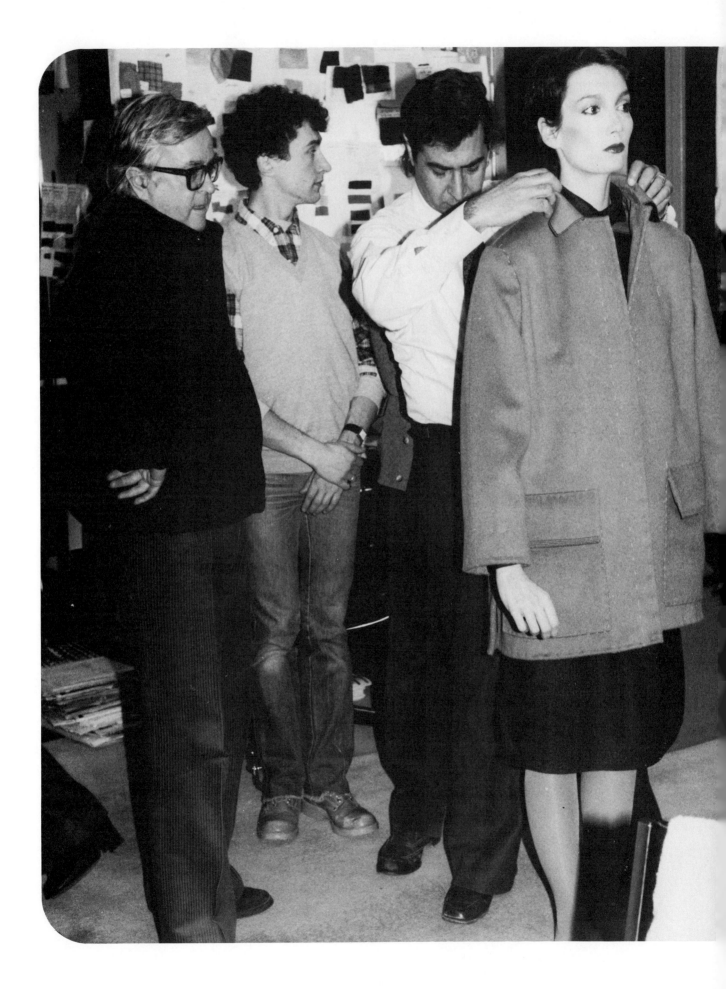

DESIGN DEVELOPMENT

Geoffrey Beene (left) supervises
a fitting in his Seventh Avenue studio.
(Courtesy of Geoffrey Beene; photograph by the author)

Manufacturers are the companies that produce fashion. Each firm is defined by its customers and identified by its particular style.

The three major divisions of a clothing company are design, production, and sales. Each is interrelated with and dependent upon the others. The design department *creates the new styles, within the company's image or identity; the* sales department *markets each line, acting as a liaison between the manufacturer and the retailer; and, the* production department *produces the line in all required sizes and fabrics, filling retail store orders. The next three chapters cover each of these functions. This chapter explains how a manufacturer's line is developed, and discusses fashion design elements and principles including color and fabrication. Finally, the chapter describes the development of the sample line and analyzes line selection. The major portion of the chapter is devoted to women's wear because it is the focus of the industry, having more seasonal styling changes.*

LINE DEVELOPMENT

Traditionally, manufacturers specialized in a particular styling category, price range, and size of clothes. Today, however, there is a trend towards expansion through the addition of diversified lines. Many manufacturers have broadened their product lines to include other style categories, or size and price ranges, but they have separate divisions and/or label names for each. For example, a missy dress manufacturer might add large or petite sizes; a shirt house might add coordinating sportswear. As manufacturers diversify, they need to keep their identity oriented toward the customers they hope to please.

Pearl Nipon, designer and partner of her husband, Albert Nipon, in dress manufacturing, might consider herself her own typical customer. "I used myself as the criterion" for starting our dress business. "The reason we have been a success is because the need was there. Other women felt exactly as I did. . . . I'm our model. When I put something on, if it feels good, I know it's a winner. If it doesn't feel good, it doesn't make the line." [1] However, although it is easier for a designer to be his or her own typical customer, the situation rarely exists. One of the hardest things for a designer to do is to *judge fashion apart from personal preference.*

Seasons

Each season, the design department is responsible for creating a new "line," or the seasonal "collection" that the manufacturer will sell to retail store buyers. The terms are synonymous; *collection* is used primarily in Europe and for high priced lines in the United States, while *line* is used more often in the United States for moderately and popularly priced fashion. Designers and merchandisers work on two or more lines at once, designing a future line while solving problems of the line that is about to be shipped. Work on a new line begins approximately eight months before the selling season. Companies that produce high volume and depend on less innovative styling plan even further ahead. Designers

[1] "Off the Cuff: Pearl Nipon," *Ambience*, January 1979, p. 93.

must think ahead to the season when the garment will be sold and worn. For example, a velvet dress to be worn in December must be designed in May.

Most companies produce four or five seasonal lines a year: spring, summer, transitional, fall, and holiday or possibly resort. Even these divisions are becoming less distinct; many manufacturers constantly fill in their lines with new items, shipping to stores almost monthly. Manufacturers that conform to a structured number of lines per year, may add additional items they call *sweeteners* in order to respond quickly to customer needs.

The Merchandising Function

Merchandising is planning to have the right merchandise at the right time, in the right quantity and at the right price to meet the needs of the company's target consumers. Each company has financial goals, set by company executives, which allow for the cost of producing and marketing fashion, operating costs, and a profit.

The first step in line development is to decide how many groups are needed per season to meet both the demands of retailers and the financial goals of the manufacturer. A "dollar merchandising plan" is established for each line per season. Last year's actual sales are used as a basis for figuring projected sales goals. Next, company executives, the merchandiser, and/or the designer develop a merchandising plan to determine the line concept and the approximate number of styles and fabrics required to meet sales goals.

The Design Function

In a small company the design and merchandising functions may be headed by one person, a designer or stylist. Or, in some cases, the owner/business head might assume some of the merchandising responsibilities. In a large company, product development duties may be a team effort involving a designer, a merchandiser, and their assistants. The merchandiser may concentrate on the planning, organizational, and sales aspects of the business, while the designer creates the styles, giving form to fashion ideas. The designer must also supervise pattern making and sample making, seeing the line through to a successful completion. The designer is concerned with and/or responsible for all the areas discussed in the rest of this chapter.

Women's Wear

Items Some manufacturers produce single *items* that do not relate to each other. In this case, coordination of a group or of a line is not required. However, each garment must be strong enough to stand alone, not depending on the strength of other garments in the group. Such garments are usually produced by a "knock-off" house.

A *knock-off* is a copy of someone else's design, usually a garment that is already a best seller for another manufacturer. For that reason, knock-off houses can safely invest in large-volume production. They simply buy a particular garment, make a pattern from it, order large quantities of the same fabric, and have the garment manufactured in large volume. The knock-off, however, often misses the fine points of fit and construction and may substitute a cheaper fabric or trim. Production and fabric costs are lower because of the huge quantities produced. Moreover, the knock-off house has no expense for design development.

Three essentials for the knock-off firm are an acute *awareness* of what garments are selling well at the retail level; *speed* of production (timing is crucial if the firm is to capitalize on the success of a style); and large *volume* sales. A retail buyer, after seeing a small quantity of a high priced garment selling well in the store, may choose to have it copied by an item house exclusively for that particular store. The whole system seems very unfair to the creative designer. There have been attempts to patent clothing designs, but it is nearly impossible because of the fast pace of the industry and the time involved in patent application. By the time a design is granted a patent, the garment is no longer in fashion.

Groups In many cases, a line is subdivided into groups of garments. Each group has a specific theme based on fabric, color, or a particular fashion direction. Ideas for the theme come from trend research and other design sources, color, or fabrics.

A group of silk crepe de chine and organza dresses in the same floral print. *(Courtesy of Bill Blass, Ltd.)*

Sometimes the design for one garment may inspire a whole group. The styling within each group should have variety yet carry out the central theme.

To present a visually pleasing group of *dresses,* the line need have only a few elements in common, such as a fabric or color story. Often a manufacturer emphasizes only a few silhouettes (called *bodies* in the trade), interpreting each of them in several prints; or it will feature one print in a variety of styles. Within the group, the dresses must offer a variety of silhouettes, sleeve treatments, necklines, and other details.

In *coordinated sportswear,* the objective is to have the individual pieces mix and match interchangeably. Fabric combinations are carefully thought out. There should be a good variety of coordinating skirts, pants, jackets, shirts or blouses, and other tops in each group. Variety aside, however, there should still be consistency of theme, with color, fabric, and line or detail to tie the whole group together. To round out the group, basic styles are needed as well as fashion pieces. The number of pieces or styles in the group is determined by the statement the designer wishes to make, the importance of the fabric, and the group's importance in the total line.

In a *separates sportswear* group, pieces do not have to coordinate, and there must be a variety of styles and fabrics (solids and prints) to please various consumer tastes. The main difference between coordinated sportswear and separates is the way they are sold. Both are visually pleasing; however, coordinates are sold as a package while separates are sold individually.

Men's Wear

Compared to women's wear, men's clothing is still basically conservative, with very little fashion innovation each season. Only recently has there been any designer men's wear, and it constitutes only a small percentage of the men's apparel business. Methods of styling men's suits vary greatly from the styling of men's sportswear.

Men's *suits* are treated as individual units. Although not called items, their appeal cannot depend on the strength of a group theme. The manufacturer's objective is to include a variety of colors and suitings in the line, providing wide choice for both the retail buyer and consumer. The three main styling factors in men's suits are fit, fabric, and silhouette. Therefore, there is generally little detail change from season to season; the ideal is a timeless classic. (We shall discuss the quality of men's suits in chapter 10.)

Sportswear from Guy Laroche Monsieur.
(Courtesy of Guy Laroche, Paris)

Men's *sportswear* is still in the experimental stage. Attempts have been made at coordinated groups, but most men are not accustomed to sportswear pieces that match. Generally, a men's sportswear group consists of *related separates,* pieces that go together but without obvious visual effect. A group may include pants, jackets, vests, shirts, and sweaters. It is important that a group have a central color theme carried out in a variety of related fabrics.

ELEMENTS OF DESIGN

Keeping the theme of the group in mind, a designer must incorporate all the elements of good design into each garment in a pleasing combination. These elements are color, fabrication, line, shape, and detail. One of them usually predominates in each design. These same ingredients are essential to every art form, but they alone are not a recipe for success and cannot substitute for experience. Fashion changes continually; there are no hard and fast rules.

Color

Color is the first element to which consumers respond. People relate personally to color, usually either selecting or rejecting a garment because of its color appeal. Therefore, designers must consider their customers and provide colors that are both appealing and flattering.

The reason people relate so personally to color is because it causes emotional responses, some of them based on events in our lives and on our culture. People whose roots are deep in folk traditions, as in many agricultural countries, have been exposed to different uses of color than have people who live in business-oriented Western countries.

People connect certain colors with holidays and seasons of the year. They expect to see the colors of autumn leaves in fall clothing, reds and greens for the winter holidays, the pastels of flowers in the spring, and refreshing white for the summer. All manufacturers include some of these colors in their lines.

Color Dimensions Color has three different dimensions: hue, value, and intensity.

Hue enables us to tell one color from another, such as red from blue or green.

Value refers to the use of darks and lights; it is the variation of light strength in a color. The value scale runs from white to black. White is pure light, and black is the total absence of light; adding white lightens a color and adding black darkens it. The lighter values are called *tints* and the darker ones *shades*. Every garment has value contrasts, even if only those created by normal gathers and folds. Strong value contrasts (pure black against pure white is the strongest) achieve a dramatic effect. Close value contrasts lend a more conservative, refined impression that is easier for the average person to wear.

Intensity refers to the brightness or paleness of a color or the distinction between a strong and a weak color. Bright colors are considered high-intensity, pale ones low-intensity. For instance, when paint is paled by adding water, the intensity of its color is lowered. Within the blue hue, marine blue is of high intensity and soft pastel blue is low.

Generally, vivid colors should be combined with others of the same intensity for balance. However, balance is also achieved when large amounts of pale or dark color are used in combination with a touch of bright color in a trim, top stitching, or embroidery.

Warm Colors We classify red, yellow, and orange as warm colors because of their association with fire and the sun. Warm colors are stimulating, aggressive, and lively.

Red has come to denote valentines, love, and romance; it is also exciting, fiery, and dangerous. A popular color for sportswear and evening wear, it is one of the few colors used in high intensities for clothing in every season.

Yellow is bright, sunny, cheerful, friendly, and optimistic. It is often a difficult color to wear because it conflicts with many skin tones.

Orange combines the sunniness of yellow and the warmth of red, but it can also be a difficult color to wear. Intense orange can be irritating and overpowering and is best toned to a softer peach or apricot or limited to use in active wear.

Cool Colors Cool colors, as the word implies, are refreshing in contrast to warm colors. Blue, green, and purple remind us of the sky and the sea.

Blue is quiet, restful, and reserved. It is usually found in very high (pale blue) or very low (navy blue) values in clothing. Navy blue is one of the most popular clothing colors. For that reason most manufacturers include it in at least their spring or summer lines.

Wool Flash

Old Masters

F_1
F_2
F_3
F_4
F_5

Antiquity

F_6
F_7
F_8
F_9
F_{10}
F_{11}

Primitives

F_{12}
F_{13}
F_{14}
F_{15}
F_{16}

Modern Art

F_{17}
F_{18}
F_{19}
F_{20}
F_{21}

Fall/Winter 1979/80 is a blending, mixing and culling-out of the colors from the past few seasons. What is left is a color story as refined as the Old Masters and, at the same time, as free-thinking as Modern Art. It's made for mixing and blending for each to achieve his or her own color statement.

Judy McIlvaine

PURE WOOL

The Wool Bureau
360 Lexington Ave · New York
N.Y. · 10017 · 212-986-6222

Wool Flash color forecast *(Courtesy of the Wool Bureau)*

An analogous color scheme: grape, cinnamon, and magenta.
(Model Donna Monti; photograph by the author)

A triad color scheme: emerald, tangerine, and lilac.
(Model Diane Anderson; photograph by the author)

Fabric and color story for a coordinated sportswear group. *(Courtesy of Koret of California)*

The resulting coordinated sportswear group.
(Courtesy of Koret of California)

Green is the most refreshing color, suggesting peace, rest, calm, and quiet. Although popular for interior design, it is inexplicably the least popular color for dresses. It is used primarily in a dark value in fall sportswear lines or mixed with neutrals to create earthy olive or loden.

Purple, historically associated with royalty, has come to represent wealth, dignity, and drama. Because it can be melancholy when dark and intense, it is more often used as a paler violet.

Neutrals In clothing, neutrals such as beige, tan, brown, white, gray, and black, are even more popular than the colors we have mentioned above. The reason is probably that they present a pleasing background for the wearer without competing for attention. Neutrals are part of every season's fashion picture, as either a strong fashion statement or to round out a color story.

White is associated with purity and cleanliness, which is why doctors and nurses have traditionally worn it. Because it reflects light, it feels cool in the summer.

In Western culture black has been connected with villains and death. However, it has come to be regarded as sophisticated and as an important fashion "color."

Color Naming An exciting color name can be important in promoting a fashion look. Fashion colors sometimes reappear with new names to make them seem fresh. Plum of one year might return as aubergine in another. Oil paint color lists, as well as books featuring the names of flowers, trees, wood, fruit, vegetables, spices, wines, gems, and animals, can provide color name ideas. To spark interest, colorists and fashion journalists even use double names such as emblem green or spellbinding blue.

Color Selection Every line should include a range of colors that will appeal to a variety of customers. Within the line, each group is usually formulated around a color plan consisting of as few as two colors or many colors. Color choices must consider season, climate, and type of garment. Active sportswear, for example, employs much more vivid colors than spectator sportswear.

The line's "color story" should include some fashion colors selected from research provided by trade associations, fiber companies, or design report predictions. By basing a color story on these predic-tions, the designer is assured that the group will be in the mainstream of fashion. Sometimes the designer selects one or two colors from the predictions and then adds his or her own color choices to balance them. The group is then rounded out with staple colors such as neutrals, darks, white, or black. In any case, the color story must be meaningful, not just a group of unrelated colors. It might be all brights, or all muted, or a balance of darks and lights.

Color Relationships within a Garment There are several systems using measured scales to guide in selection of color combinations. Primary and secondary colors differ from one system to another, but looking at a rainbow will show you the basic order of colors' relationship to one another.

The Brewster and Prang theories define red, yellow, and blue to be the three *primaries* from which all other colors are derived. Mixing yellow and red paints creates orange; red and blue creates purple; and blue and yellow creates green—the three *secondary* colors. Mixtures of primary and secondary colors create every color in between. The entire spectrum is often arranged into a color wheel to demonstrate the concept more clearly. However, the working fashion industry pays little attention to theories and systematic color relationships, basing selections instead on intuition and researched color forecasts.

There are no hard and fast rules for the use of colors. *Colors are harmonious if they are used so that one color enhances the beauty of the other.* Colors are now combined in many more unusual ways than ever before. Colors that in the past were appropriate only for evening are now used also in sportswear. Ethnic influences on fashion have changed our view of color combinations, making us more receptive to new ideas. In addition, colors run in fashion cycles just as styles do. Color combinations that look right to us now will not work with the looks that are new a few years hence.

Guides to color combinations are not rules for success, but simply aids to the designer for new ways to experiment with color. There is no limit to the kinds and varieties of color combinations.

Guidelines for Possible Color Combinations *Monochromatic* or *tonal* color schemes employ varying values and intensities of one hue. (*Mono* means one and *chroma* means hue or color.) The resulting look is very refined; however, textural variety is needed to create interest.

Analogous colors lie next to each other on the color wheel and are related in hue. Used together, they present a rhythmic, exciting effect. An example is a combination of royal blue and turquoise (blue-green), blue being the common hue.

Complementary colors are opposite each other on the color wheel. The contrast makes both colors more intense. They may be used in equal amounts or with one color merely accenting the other. A traditional complementary color scheme is the Christmas theme of red and green.

A *triad* is a combination of three colors equally distant on the color wheel, such as green, purple, and orange. This is a much more unusual color combination and is more difficult to achieve successfully.

Illusions Created by Color   Color can also create illusions. For example, a garment in one color adds to the illusion of height. Warm, light, or bright colors advance visually, making a design seem larger; cool or dark colors recede, causing the figure to look small or slender. Both intensity and value contrasts are frequently used to disguise figure problems.

Fabrication

Fabrication is the selection or creation of an appropriate style for a fabric—or the reverse, the selection of the right fabric for a design. Fabrics are the designer's artistic medium, as fashion design is essentially sculpture in fabric in relation to the body.

Fabrics themselves often inspire garment design. For example, the softness and drapability of a jersey might inspire gathers in a dress. Christian Dior wrote, "Many a dress of mine is born of the fabric alone." [2] Other designers work the other way around, first getting an idea, perhaps developing it in a sketch, and then finding the appropriate fabric for it.

However the designer works, he or she must ultimately decide on which fabric will work best with a design. Designers must develop the ability to picture a design already made up in the fabric. This ability comes through observation and experience. *Next to understanding the needs of the customer, choosing a fabric suitable for a particular style is probably the most important aspect of designing.* The designer chooses fabrics on the basis of fashion trends, quality, performance, price, and suitability.

[2] Christian Dior, *Talking About Fashion* (New York: G.P. Putnam's Sons, 1954), p. 35.

Fabric Characteristics   Fabric suitability is determined by characteristics such as fiber, weave, texture, performance, hand, pattern, and color.

Texture is the sensuous element of design. It is the surface interest of a fabric, created by the weave and by light reflection because of its smoothness, or light absorption because of roughness. We appreciate with our eyes the play of light on smooth or rough surfaces; we feel the surface with our hands; and we can even hear the texture, such as the rustle of taffeta. Combinations of textures, such as suede with jersey (rough with smooth), create interest in a garment.

Mary McFadden creates a beautiful texture combination of macramé and finely pleated silk. *(Courtesy of Mary McFadden)*

Performance of a fabric refers to its wearing and cleaning properties based on fiber content, weave, and finish.

Weight and *hand* dictate the silhouette of a garment. Weight is the heaviness or lightness, thinness or thickness of a fabric. Hand is the feel, body, and fall of a fabric. A designer must know how a fabric will behave and whether it will carry out an idea. A garment must be styled in a fabric that is compatible with the desired silhouette.

Firm fabrics, such as worsted wools, gabardines, and linen, are needed to carry out a tailored look. These fabrics have both the crisp look and the fall necessary to achieve the desired effect. Interfacing, a fabric sewn or ironed into the garment's inner construction, is used to give additional stiffness to finished edges such as necklines, collars, cuffs, and buttoning areas. The weight of the interfacing must be compatible with the weight of the garment fabric. At times fashion has dictated that fabrics assume a structured look, so stiff linings are used; at other times, fabrics are used in their natural state.

Soft fabrics, such as crepe, jersey, chiffon, and challis, are ideal for draped designs that delineate body shape. Additional fluidity can be achieved by cutting fabric on the bias grain, so that the diagonal of the fabric falls vertically in the garment. However, bias is difficult to lay out on a marker (pattern layout), making it expensive to produce. Softness may be increased by the additional use of gathers, shirring, smocking, and unpressed pleats.

Fabric weight should vary with the type of garment. For example, blouse weights are lighter than bottom (skirt or pant) weights. Manufacturers often buy fabrics in specific weights, such as a 5-ounce shirting or an 11-ounce denim. The weight is determined by the square yard for wovens and by the linear yard for knits.

Fabric weight must also be appropriate for the season. Heavier, warmer fabrics are wanted for winter and light, cooler ones for summer. As we saw in chapter 5, specific natural fibers have traditionally been considered appropriate for certain seasons. Wool is used for fall and winter because it is heavy, bulky, and warm. Linen and cotton are used as warm-weather fabrics because they are light, cool, and washable. However, there are now more seasonless fabrics and fashions. Many fabrics, such as jerseys, can be worn year-round. Cotton, traditionally a summer fiber, can be woven into warmer, bulkier weights such as corduroy for fall and winter garments. Wools can be woven into light-weight voile for spring. The popularity of the layered look, starting in London in the mid-1960s and seen again in the mid-'70s, made warmth fashionable.

Pattern Scale in Relation to the Whole Garment
The scale of a pattern must complement the design. A large print would dominate a design. To show a large print to its best advantage, it should not be cut up with seams and details; the fabric print should be allowed to be the most important element of the garment, keeping construction simple. On the other hand, if a design idea begins with dominating lines and details, then the fabric must be plain and of secondary importance.

Technical Considerations   The *repeat* of a print is the amount of fabric necessary for a floral or geometric pattern to duplicate itself totally. Large repeats are not suitable for trims or for children's wear. In addition, garments to be made in border prints must be carefully thought out so that fabric is not wasted in production cutting.

The designer must recognize patterns that require special matching because they increase the fabric used and therefore the cost. Bold plaids and irregular stripes must match when sewn together.

One-way prints and pile fabrics also use more yardage because all the pattern pieces must be cut in the same direction. Most prints are two-way (that is, they have a motif that faces both directions), which makes cutting simpler and more economical.

Reviewing Fabrics   The designer's involvement in fabric selection for a manufacturer varies. Sometimes designers have the entire responsibility for fabric selection; sometimes they work with a fabric merchandiser.

Before a new season, a designer should develop a feeling for fabric trends by reviewing the fabric market. There are several ways to research fabrics. First, the designer may visit one of the fabric trade fairs or fabric libraries for an overall picture of the season's textile offerings. Designers and merchandisers frequently travel to New York, where most textile mills and converters have headquarters. This is the best way for them to keep abreast of the newest fiber or fabric developments that might be the source of ideas for garments. Moreover, in New York the designers can discuss their ideas directly with textile designers and technicians. Designers also regularly read fabric trade publications to learn how to use new fabrics.

Fabric mills or converter sales representatives also call on the designer at work. Each season de-

The author and merchandiser Judye Marino review Wullschleger prints with sales rep Harvey Browne.

signers try to see as many fabric representatives as possible, to become aware of the variety of fabric available. It is also important to establish a working rapport with sales representatives because they can furnish a great deal of fabric information. For example, a designer should be careful not to use a print that is being used by another manufacturer in a lower priced garment. The reliable fabric sales "rep" will help the designer avoid this and other mistakes.

Price Considerations   The designer must not exceed the limitations set by the line's price range. Fabric quality, and therefore price, must be consistent with the price of the line. An expensive designer line uses the finest fabrics while a moderately priced line requires the use of less expensive materials. A general rule is that fabric and trimming costs must balance labor costs. More expensive fabrics go into understated, simple garments whose construction is less complicated. Garments requiring more yardage may also be cut from less expensive goods, so that no garment will exceed the price range of the line. On the other hand, if the designer saves money by using a less expensive fabric, he or she can afford to put more money into labor or trimmings.

Sample Cuts   The designer or merchandiser must be sure to include a variety of weights, textures, and prints in a line, and a balance of fashion and classic fabrics.

Color or swatch cards sent by textile companies help designers and merchandisers to make fabrication decisions. However, swatch cards are not large enough to give the total idea of a print or a texture. Therefore, the designer orders a three- to five-yard cut of a fabric to make a test garment. In some companies, if the design department is very enthusiastic about a fabric, they may initially order enough for samples and duplicates—perhaps up to one hundred yards.

Once fabrics have been selected, the designer can begin to create styles for the new line. The basis of a line is often a "body" that sold well the previous season carried over to the next, in a new fabrication appropriate for the new season. An unexpected use of fabric can create a fresh look. For example, in one collection Marc Bohan did a khaki anorak (hooded jacket), but made it of silk taffeta for evening wear.

Line Direction in a Garment

After selecting the fabric, the designer must consider the rest of the design elements: line, shape, and detail.

Vertical line interest is created in this silk ensemble by the neck tie, tunic, and trousers. *(Courtesy of Emilio Pucci)*

Line, an important element of structure, determines the direction of visual interest in an entire garment. (This term should not be confused with a "line" or collection of garments that is shown each season.) Details such as seams, openings, pleats, gathers, tucks, topstitching, and trims contribute toward the line direction for the whole garment. Line should flow from one part of the garment to another and should not be meaninglessly cut up.

Straight lines suggest crispness, such as that of tailored garments; *full* curved lines imply buoyancy. However, a garment designed with only straight lines is too severe, while all curves are too restless. Curves need the steadying influence of straight lines. For optimum beauty, they should work together. Straight lines are softened by the curves of the body, and full curves must be restrained to be compatible with the human form.

Lines have the power to create moods and feelings. *Vertical* lines remind us of upright, majestic figures and suggest stability. *Horizontal* lines are like lines at rest; they suggest repose, quiet, and calm. Soft, *curving* lines express grace, while *diagonal* lines imply powerful movement and vitality. *Zig-zag* lines create excitement but are often disconcerting.

Optical Illusions   Optical illusions are lines that fool the eye, making things seem to be what they are not. Garment lines can create optical illusions such as slimness, an ability especially important in designing for large sizes. Because the eye unconsciously follows line, it is possible by means of line to draw the eye to flattering areas, away from less attractive ones. Clothing can alter a person's appearance, helping to make up for discrepancies between the average body and the fashion ideal. The current ideal is youthful and slim. The most successful clothing uses optical illusions to make the wearer seem taller and more slender than he or she truly is.

Design elements should be interpreted for each figure type. Long, unbroken vertical lines are most effective in adding height; the longer and stronger the line, the more effective it is. An example is a center front closing running from neckline to hemline. Vertical lines can be further strengthened by accentuating them with contrasting trimmings or buttons. (This makes the popularity over the years of the shirtwaist dress in women's and half sizes understandable.)

Probably the most slimming vertical lines of all are princess seams, which create a vertical panel down the front of a dress. The viewer is most aware of the area between the lines, while the side panels seem to recede.

The eye judges any measurement of length or width in relation to other measurements in the same composition. Longer skirts make the wearer appear taller and slimmer simply because the length is greater compared to the width.

Horizontal lines widen the figure, sometimes beneficially and sometimes not. A contrasting belt on a dress cuts the average figure in two, creating two chunky portions instead of one long, thin one. A self-belt can partially avoid this problem.

The use of illusion is also important in men's wear. Generally, men want to look taller and stronger. Therefore, throughout history men's apparel has tended to increase their stature with vertical lines in jacket closings and trousers and with built-up shoulders.

Shape

Another function of line is to create shape. We use the term *silhouette* to describe the outline of the whole garment. Because the silhouette is what we see from a distance, it is responsible for first impressions. Silhouettes tend to repeat themselves in cycles throughout history. Sometimes a more body conscious, natural silhouette is popular for women, one that follows the curves of the body and accentuates the smallness of the waist. This look was especially prominent in the 1950s.

At other times a rectangular or tubular shape such as the tunic has been the prevailing style. Rectangular shapes generally conceal some parts of the body, creating their own proportions. Rectangular silhouettes for women were prevalent in the 1920s and the 1960s.

There have been many variations of basic silhouettes; generally the shape reflects the mood of the times. For example, the wedge shape, a masculine silhouette with padded shoulders, characterized the early '40s, when women took over the responsibilities of the men who were away at war.

A silhouette should be related to body structure, but some variation is needed to add interest. Sometimes one part of the silhouette, such as a large sleeve, predominates.

Lines also divide total areas into smaller shapes and spaces by means of seams, openings, pleats, and tucks. A good silhouette is composed of parts that in themselves have interesting shapes. There are square shapes and round, oval, rectangular, triangular, and more. The minute a waistline is added, the garment is divided into two new shapes: a bodice and a skirt. The sleeve becomes another shape. These parts create new spaces for smaller details, such as collars and pockets. Fabric pattern can create even smaller shapes.

A dramatic silhouette accenting natural body proportions, by Capucci. *(Courtesy of the Camera Nazionale dell' Alta Moda Italiana)*

PRINCIPLES OF DESIGN

The successful use of design elements depends on their relationship to one another within the garment. Principles of design serve as guidelines for combining elements. Designers may not consciously think of these principles as they work, but when something is wrong with a design, they are able to analyze the problem in terms of proportion, balance, repetition, emphasis, or harmony (the first four principles work together to create the ultimate goal of harmony). They are flexible, always interpreted within the context of current fashion.

Proportion

Proportion is simply the pleasing interrelationship of the size of all parts of the garment. When conceiving a style, it is important to consider how the silhouette is to be divided with lines of construction or detail. These lines create new spaces and they must relate in a pleasing way. Generally, unequal proportion is more interesting than equal. Many mathematical formulas have been proposed as guidelines, but the best results come from practice in observing and analyzing good design as standards for proportion change with fashion cycles.

Height and width of all parts of a design must be compared. Individual sections of a garment, such as sleeves, pockets, and collar, must all relate in size to each other as well as to the total silhouette. A jacket length and shape must work with the length and shape of the skirt or pants.

Background space is just as important as the detail or shapes within it. A large, bold shape against a plain background is dramatic. Areas broken into small shapes suggest daintiness. Therefore, smaller space divisions are used for teens and juniors and fewer divisions for dramatic evening wear. Each detail or shape within the silhouette should complement the whole.

The spacing of trimmings, pleats, and tucks must have meaning in relation to the total design. Trimmings must not be too heavy or too light, too large or too small to harmonize with the space around them as well as with the feeling of the total garment. Ideally, the trim on a smaller space should be narrower than the trim on a larger area. Every line, detail, or trim changes the proportion because it breaks up the space even more.

The designer continually experiments with subtle variations in proportion, line placement, hem length, and size and placement of trim. Proportion sometimes follows natural body divisions and some-times creates its own. Concepts of proportion vary with each new fashion direction, changing with the evolution in silhouette and line.

Balance

Vertical Balance Proportion may also be discussed in terms of perpendicular or vertical balance—the impact or "visual weight" relationship between top and bottom, shirt and skirt, jacket and pants. We might refer to a poorly balanced outfit as being top-heavy. In this sense, often the terms *balance* and *proportion* are used interchangeably.

Symmetrical Balance In the context of design principles, the term *balance* is most often used in reference to horizontal relationships, or the relationship of one side of the garment to the other. A garment should look stable and not lopsided. Imagine a line down the center of a garment. If the design composition is the same on both sides of this line, then the design is considered *bisymmetrical* or formally balanced, following the natural bisymmetry of the body. Just as we have two eyes, two arms, and two legs, a symmetrical garment must have exactly the same details in just the same place on both sides. Formal balance is the easiest, most logical way to achieve stability because it takes no experimentation. Used in most apparel, it gives a conservative feeling. Even slight deviations, when minor details such as pockets are not exactly alike on both sides, are considered *approximate symmetry*. A sensitive use of fabric, rhythm, and space relationships is needed to keep a design from being boring.

Asymmetrical Balance To achieve a more exciting, dramatic effect, *asymmetrical* or informal balance can be used. Examples are side closings, or one-shouldered evening dresses. While asymmetrical design composition is not identical on both sides of a garment, it still must be stable. It is not a matter of actual weight but one of visual attraction. A small, unusual, eye-catching shape or concentrated detail on one side can balance a larger, less imposing area on the other side. Striking line, color, or texture can appear to balance larger masses of less significance. The means of achieving informal balance are infinite and subtle, giving the designer more freedom of expression but requiring imagination, experimentation, and sensitivity. Technically, asymmetrical designs require separate pattern shapes for the right and left sides that cannot be reversed when cutting. Because of the design and technical skill required, fewer asymmetrical than symmetrical garments are produced.

Another Mary McFadden design showing a combination of pleasing proportions, asymmetrical balance, rhythm in repeating pleats, and emphasis at the hip.
(Courtesy of Mary McFadden)

Repetition

Rhythm *Rhythm,* or a sense of movement, is necessary to create interest in a design. Interesting rhythm can be achieved by the repetition of lines, shapes, and colors to give direction. We can see rhythm of lines and shapes in the repetition of pleats, gathers, and tiers, and in rows of trim, banding, or buttons. The dominant color, line, shape, or detail of the garment should be repeated elsewhere with variation. Sometimes it is implied or subtle, but the sense of movement must be felt. There are varying ways to use rhythm.

Uniform rhythm is the regular repetition of equal space divisions—for example, even spacing of pleats or stripes in fabric. It may be so soothing that it is monotonous. It becomes more interesting if the repeated lines or shapes are alternated or broken.

Unequal rhythm is also repetition of color, line, shapes, or detail, but not in a regular order. It is one of the most interesting ways to create movement.

Progression or graduation is another means of creating organized movement, by gradually increasing or decreasing space divisions (sometimes seen in the spacing of tiers). A focal point is often created as the series comes closer and closer together.

Continuous line movement is often used in draped garments, when soft fabrics hang in gathers or folds. The folds and the shadows they create make the rhythmic lines. They should flow from one to another without a distracting break.

In *radiation,* the least used manner of developing a rhythmic pattern, all the lines originate from a central point. This creates movement around the center, which attracts attention and becomes the focal point.

Other Uses of Repetition The use of repetition is one of the most helpful guidelines in designing. A design line, shape, or detail repeated in another area of the garment helps to carry the theme throughout the whole design. In dress design, for example, a V neck might be repeated upside down in bodice seaming or in an inverted pleat in the skirt. Soft gathers at the neck could be repeated at the hip so that all parts work together harmoniously.

Emphasis

Emphasis, or a center of interest, draws attention to the focal point of a costume. This point is the central theme; the rest of the garment is of secondary importance. "A center of interest must have more eye-pulling power than any other design element in the garment, and all other elements must support it by echoing its design message with weakened impact."[3] The point of emphasis should be related to the total structure of the garment. Such a focal point can be achieved by accenting it with color, significant shapes or details, lines coming together, groups of detail, or contrast. A combination of these methods gives the focal point added strength, as does placing the decorative emphasis at a structural point.

Garments with no focal point are weak and boring. On the other hand, there should never be more than one main center of interest. Two or more would compete confusingly with each other. Spotty use of details—especially those of equal importance, such as pockets—is distracting. Such distractions should be removed and the dominant design feature strengthened. Care should be taken not to emphasize awkward parts of the body.

Above all, the wearer should be the primary center of attraction. Lines leading to the face are particularly effective. Light colors around the face also help direct interest to the wearer. This is one reason why contrasting collars are common.

Harmony

Harmony is simply the condition in which all the elements and principles work successfully together, following the theme of the garment, with nothing overdone and nothing forgotten.

A sample garment is a good test of whether a design is successful. The designer must analyze objectively whether all the elements work together to create a harmonious, consistent visual effect.

The best way to gain experience in the use of design elements and principles is by experimentation. A designer on the job is always learning. Most often, the designer tries many variations of a design before creating one that has the perfect combination of fabric, color, line, and silhouette and the correct use of balance, proportion, emphasis, and repetition.

A beautiful design results from a well-developed idea or theme. "The fabrics, trimmings, every line, shape, and detail must be a part of the idea itself."[4] For example, if the theme of a design or group is dramatic, the design should have a bold statement of line, an exaggerated silhouette, large space divi-

[3] Helen L. Brockman, *The Theory of Fashion Design* (New York: John Wiley & Sons, Inc., 1965), p. 108.

[4] Grace Margaret Morton, *The Arts of Costume and Personal Appearance,* 3rd Ed. (New York: John Wiley & Sons, Inc., 1964), p. 100.

sions, bright or dark colors and strong contrast, or large prints and extreme textures. Of course, there are many ways to develop an infinite number of ideas; however, the use of any design elements or combination of them must be thought out in relation to the theme.

Economy of Design   Every line and detail of a garment should be essential to the completeness of the design. "The strength of a design is weakened by extraneous elements that do not contribute to its central, unified theme." [5] When any part of the trimmings or details can be removed without being missed, or when any of the structural style lines can be simplified or eliminated without detriment to the design, those elements should be removed.

DEVELOPING A SAMPLE GARMENT

Sketching

Ideas sometimes originate on the drawing board. Starting with an idea for a silhouette or a neckline, the designer may experiment, sketching alternate ways to complete the design. On paper, the designer can see two-dimensionally which design elements might enhance one another. (The designer must also be able to imagine how the garment will look three-dimensionally, when made up in a fabric.)

The first rough sketch, a working sketch, is very simple. However, it must be accurate so that the pattern maker can interpret it correctly. The designer must think out the garment's construction in relation to the sketch, which must be drawn in proportion to the body, showing exact details of seam line and trimmings. The working sketch usually includes notes on construction and measurements.

Designers often develop a unique sketching style that reflects the type of apparel they design. A couture design sketch would probably reflect the sophisticated, elegant image of the company; a sportswear designer might use a crisp, carefree style.

The First Pattern

The next step in the design procedure is the development of the first pattern, the pattern used to cut and sew the sample garment. The pattern is made in a "sample size," the one used for testing and selling purposes. Examples are size 7 for juniors, 10 for

[5] Brockman, *The Theory of Fashion Design*, p. 104.

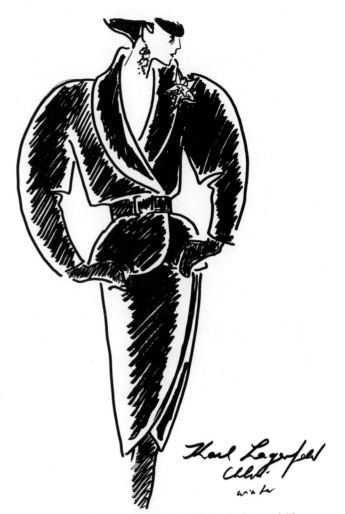

A stylized, sophisticated design sketch by Karl Lagerfeld for Chloé. *(Courtesy of Karl Lagerfeld)*

missy, 34 for men's trousers, 38 for men's suits. The pattern maker can use either of two methods for making patterns: draping or flat pattern.

The *draping method* (working with muslin on the dress form) is like fabric sculpture; it is ideal for soft, flowing designs. The pattern maker (sometimes the assistant designer) cuts and shapes the fabric to a dress form. This enables the designer to see the proportions and lines of the design exactly as they will look three-dimensionally, on the wearer. The design is often altered as it develops on the form.

Everything must be carefully marked: center front, shoulder line, seams, armholes, buttonholes, and so on. When the designer is satisfied with the look and fit, the muslin is taken off the form and "trued up"; the sketched lines are corrected using

Using the draping method to create a pattern.
(Photograph by the author at Christian Dior Lingerie, New York)

Truing up a curve in flat pattern making.
(Photograph by the author at Koret of California)

drafting curves, angles, and rulers; and the pattern is redrawn on heavy paper.

The *flat pattern method* is necessary for areas like sleeves and pant legs, which would be difficult to drape on a figure. Basic shapes, such as bodices, sleeves, pants, or skirts, are draped or drafted. *Drafting* is blocking out on pattern paper a set of prescribed measurements for each piece. These patterns, after being tested for accuracy, become "blocks" or "slopers" that can be changed or adapted to each new style by moving darts and seams.

Most pattern makers combine the two methods, depending on the dictates of the design, as well as on their technical training and preference.

The Sample Garment

After the pattern is made in Manila paper or tag board, it is laid out on the fabric, traced, and cut out by the assistant designer or the sample cutter to be sewn into the first sample or prototype.

The prototype is made by a sample maker, the best of the factory sewers. He or she must not only know factory sewing methods but also know how to put an entire garment together. The design staff works closely with the sample maker to solve construction problems. Factory construction methods must be tested as the garment is sewn.

The next step is to test the sample for fit and total effect. It is very important to see how the garment fits not only on a dress form but also on a model in motion. The model walks in the garment to learn whether it is comfortable and looks good. The designer, as his or her own best critic, must be objective in judging the design. Often the design must be altered as it is translated from a two-dimensional sketch into a three-dimensional garment. A designer must develop an unbiased, critical eye—a difficult accomplishment when judging a personal creation. Adrienne Vittadini, a New York knitwear designer feels that the hardest lesson she had to learn was "detaching myself from the emotional tie—that each garment is your baby." [6]

[6] Quoted by Lesley Nonkin, "Vittadini al dente," *Women's Wear Daily*, April 9, 1980, p. 6.

Design development

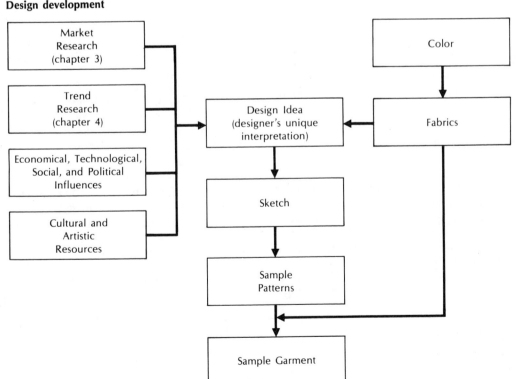

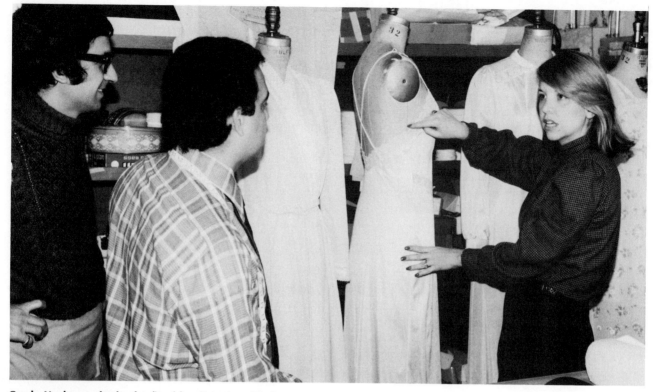

Carole Hockman checks the fit of her lingerie collection with patternmakers. *(Courtesy of Carole Hockman; photograph by the author)*

The Designer Work Sheet

Records are kept on all styles as they develop. Each designer fills out a work sheet with information to guide the production department in figuring costs and in ordering *piece goods* (the factory term for fabrics) and trimmings. The work sheet becomes an adoption sheet when the final line is selected.

The work sheet includes the following information:

1. The *date* the garment was designed.
2. The selling *season* for which the garment is designed.
3. The *sizes* in which the design will be made.
4. The *style number* assigned to the design. Each manufacturer has a code system with numbers representing season, fabric, and pattern. For example, in a series of four numbers the first number usually stands for the selling season or release date, the second number for the fabric group, and the last two numbers for the pattern or pattern type.
5. A short *description* of the garment.
6. A *working sketch* of the design, to make it easy to identify the garment.
7. The *colors* or color combinations in which the design is offered.
8. *Fabric swatches* of what is used in the garment.

9. *Material descriptions*, including each fabric type and source, width, and price per yard. Ten percent is usually added to the price to cover freight charges for delivery of the piece goods. Linings and interlinings are included as well.
10. *Marker width*, usually one inch narrower than the fabric.
11. *Trimmings* information: the kinds, sources, sizes, and prices of buttons, zippers, braids, lace, belts, elastic, and so on. Special fabric treatments done by outside contractors, such as pleating, spaghetti straps, and ties, are also included.
12. *Labor costs* for grading, marking, cutting, and sewing. They may be listed either on the designer work sheet or on a separate cost sheet, figured by the costing department (see chapter 10).

Style Board

To chart the development of the line as a whole, the designer arranges working sketches of all the garments in fabric and color groups on a large board, which is essentially a master plan. The board is posted on the wall of the design room. Styles are added and subtracted until the line is finalized. Later, the company may make notes on the plan to help keep track of production schedules.

DESCRIPTION:	FLORAL PRINT DRESS				STYLE # 1025
					PRICE: $48.00

SIZE RANGE:	FIBER CONTENT:	SEASON:
CARE:	COLORS:	DESIGN #:

MATERIAL	DUPE. YDGE.	ACT. YDGE.	PRICE	AMOUNT	RECAP	SKETCH & SWATCHES
BODY: Print	4.75		2.48	11.78		
TRIM:						
	TOTAL FABRIC COST			11.78		

TRIMMINGS	QUAN.	PRICE	AMOUNT	
BUTTONS-LINE #: 20 (covered)	6	.03	.18	
ZIPPER:				
BELTLOOPS:			.02	
HANGER LOOPS:				
THREAD:				
PELON: white woven	.15	1.05	.16	
1½" satin ribbon	1.7	.25	.43	
¼" elastic	.7	.05	.04	
OUTSIDE: Fuse			.50	

					PRODUCTION SAMPLE:
Packing			.08		GRADED MEASUREMENTS:
LABEL:			.12		

SURCHARGE/QUALITY CONTROL:					SIZE			
SHIPPING:					P 6	21		
TOTAL TRIM COST			1.53		S 8	22		
LABOR					M 8	23		
CUTTING:			2.00		L 10	24½		
SEWING: $84.00 per doz.			7.00		12			
PRESSING:			.75					
BONUS/INSURANCE			.46		REMARKS:			
GRADING & MARKING:			.50					
TOTAL LABOR COST			10.71					
TOTAL DIRECT COST			24.02					

A designer work sheet

LINE SELECTION

Designers develop many designs for each line, often two or three times as many as needed. From all of these samples, management and the designer choose the best for the line.

Often, the designer or merchandiser must actually present the line to management for approval. Many styles are weeded out, leaving only the most successful combinations of fabric, style, and price. Even a good style may be discarded if it does not fit into one of the firm's price lines. Successful buyers are often asked for their opinions because of their familiarity with customer acceptance.

At this point, the merchandising plan we discussed at the beginning of this chapter can be revised to state the exact number of styles adopted, the actual price of fabrics chosen, and the yardage estimates for each style.

Just before prescheduled line release or collection opening dates, the line is presented to the sales force. The designer or merchandiser must explain the line for the sales representatives, who can use this background information when showing the line to retail buyers.

Consistent visual image created by a well developed theme is a good selling tool on both the wholesale and the retail levels. Visual impact helps the line make a good impression compared with the competition in a store. The designer cannot be there to explain each style idea to the customer, so the garment design must speak for itself.

Duplicates

Duplicates are copies of the original sample garments, sent to salespeople on the road and in showrooms across the country to show to buyers. Duplicates are also used as guides in production at the factory. Because they are often made in the factory, they offer a good test of production and quality control.

SUMMARY

Design development is a challenge. Not only must a designer be creative; he or she must also know what sells. The ultimate blame for a bad season (economic conditions and sales force remaining the same) falls on the designer.

A styling meeting: the designer and merchandiser present the fall line to officers, operations manager, and assistants of the large size division at Koret of California

In this chapter we saw how the design department prepares a seasonal line of items or groups. The elements (color, fabric, line, shape, and detail) and principles (proportion, balance, rhythm, emphasis, and harmony) of design must be taken into consideration to develop a pleasing garment. After a sketch and first pattern are complete, the sample garment is made as a test of the design and fabric. Finally, the line is selected and duplicates are made for the sales force to take into the wholesale apparel market.

CHAPTER REVIEW

CHAPTER OBJECTIVES

After reading this chapter you should be able to
A. Give evidence of having attained competence in the following areas:
   1. Understanding of line development by item or by group   2. Understanding of the important elements and principles of design and their application to line development   3. Ability to describe the process of creating a sample garment
B. Define the following terms and concepts in relation to their discussion in the chapter:
   1. Collection or line   2. Seasons   3. Sweeteners   4. Merchandising   5. Merchandising dollar plan   6. Designer   7. Items   8. Knock-offs   9. Planning groups   10. Theme   11. Elements of design   12. Hue   13. Value   14. Intensity   15. Warm colors   16. Cool colors   17. Neutrals   18. Color story   19. Fabrication   20. Texture   21. Performance   22. Fabric weight   23. Fabric hand   24. Pattern scale   25. Sample cuts   26. Color cards   27. Line direction   28. Optical illusion   29. Silhouette   30. Proportion   31. Symmetrical balance   32. Asymmetrical balance   33. Rhythm and repetition   34. Emphasis   35. Harmony   36. Economy of design   37. Working sketch   38. First pattern   39. Draping   40. Flat pattern   41. Sample garment   42. Designer work sheet   43. Style board   44. Duplicates

Questions for Review

1. Name the three major divisions of a clothing company, and discuss the design department's relationship to the other two.
2. Discuss the merchandising function in relation to the design function.
3. Discuss the basic conceptual differences between merchandising coordinated sportswear and merchandising separates.
4. Name the elements of design. Discuss briefly why it is important for these elements to be thoroughly thought out in a design.
5. What are the principles of design? How do they help a designer analyze the effectiveness of a design?
6. Explain briefly the developing of a sample garment.

PROJECTS FOR ADDITIONAL LEARNING

1. Write a short description of an imaginary or real person. Include the person's age, build, job, place of residence, interests, and life style. This person will be the typical customer for your new sportswear line for the season six months from now. Determine the price range and style range according to your customer's life style. Design a group of 20 coordinating pieces or related separates. Develop a color story and suggest fabrications. (Merchandising students may cut pictures of sportswear items from magazines and display them on a board.)

2. Find examples of ten successful designs in European and American fashion magazines. Describe the beauty of each in terms of line, silhouette, shapes and spaces, color, and texture (fabric, pattern, and trims) as well as balance, proportion, rhythm, and emphasis. Do all elements and principles work together harmoniously? What elements dominate? Find two garments that you feel are unsuccessful. Analyze them in the same way to discover what element or principle has not been properly used.

APPAREL PRODUCTION

A factory interior.
(Courtesy of Levi Strauss
& Co., San Francisco)

Production is one of the three integral phases of the fashion manufacturing process. Without design, there would be nothing to sell; without sales, there would be no reason to produce. Conversely, sales will not continue if orders are not filled properly and delivered on time.

After the collection or line is shown at a market, orders are sent to the factory. Styles that receive insufficient orders are dropped from the line. This chapter focuses on apparel production, from pattern making to quality control.

FINANCING FOR THE MANUFACTURER

Most retailers buy from manufacturers on credit allowances; that is, they need not pay for the merchandise for 30 to 60 days. This creates a financial problem for the manufacturer, who must buy fabric and trims and pay for labor and overhead. Thus, apparel manufacturers turn to banks, finance companies, and "factoring" firms for financing.

Bank loans are either "unsecured," for well-capitalized companies with a history of good performance, or "secured," which means that they must be backed by collateral in the form of equipment or property.

A manufacturer could also sell its accounts receivable (unpaid orders) to a *factor* (a certain type of finance company) for a cash loan or for credit protection. If a customer fails to pay, the factor absorbs the loss. Factors charge a commission to cover collection services and to protect against credit losses. They also charge interest on cash advances.

In *accounts receivable financing,* manufacturers are loaned funds regularly, also based on open accounts receivable. However, in this case the manufacturer handles the collections and takes the credit risk.

All three methods of financing give the manufacturer cash to continue production.

COSTING A GARMENT

The production cost per dozen garments must be determined so that the *wholesale price* can be set—the price that retailers pay for goods they purchase from manufacturers. Each manufacturer tries to maintain a consistent price structure and quality of styling and construction, to keep its retail customers.

Wholesale Price Structure
Women's apparel is produced and marketed in a wide range of prices based on quality of construction and quality of materials used. The price ranges cover three main categories:

Better apparel is usually high priced and includes designer clothes.

Moderate apparel is medium priced for the average consumer.

Budget apparel is a low-priced, high-volume market.

Costing Methods

There are two separate costing functions: precost and final cost.

Precost is an estimate made before the garment is adopted in the line. From the outset, the designer must keep fabric and labor costs for each garment within the limits set by the company lines' price range. The designer keeps a record of all material costs on a designer work sheet. Then, either the designer or the costing department can roughly estimate the wholesale cost to determine whether the garment fits into the line's price structure.

Final costing is an exact calculation done by the costing department with final figures for materials and labor. The costing department uses the designer's work sheet, an actual sample, and the production pattern to analyze the garment's materials and construction step by step. They may consult the designer for information or to recommend more practical or cheaper ways to make the garment. A detailed cost analysis is made for each garment including expenses for fabric, trims, cutting, labor, overhead, sales commission, and manufacturer's profit.

The Cost Sheet

1. *Materials.* First, the total amount of yardage of each fabric needed for the garment is estimated and multiplied by its cost per yard. These figures are added to obtain the total material cost per garment.
2. *Trimmings.* Unit costs are multiplied by the amount of trimmings needed for each garment; these figures are added to obtain the total trimmings cost per garment.
3. *Labor.* Production directors decide which operations can be done better and cheaper "in house" and which can be contracted out (sent out to a specialized factory to be done). It may be that the whole garment will be made by a contractor.

4. *Production pattern, grading, and marking.* Most companies allow for these costs in the general overhead that also covers the design department. However, if these functions are performed outside by a pattern service, the cost is divided by the total number of units they estimate will be cut: total cost ÷ units to be made = cost per unit. If the garment is later recut (because of reorders), there will be no new cost for patterns, grading, and marking.
5. *Cutting.* If the cutting is done by a contractor, the total negotiated cutting cost is figured on the number of garments to be cut. The contractor adds his fee to this amount. The cost for cutting done in house is based on the cutter's hourly wage multiplied by the number of hours it takes to cut the style. Cutting cost per dozen is figured by calculating how many dozen garments will be made, and dividing that number into total cutting cost.
6. *Construction.* Construction labor includes not only sewing but finishing and hemming as well. Some companies break down labor costs by each individual operation. Information for such a costing structure is gathered through time-and-motion efficiency studies. The cost for each operation, such as the closing of a shoulder seam, is determined. To figure the total costs for a whole garment, the individual operation costs are added together.

   Other firms calculate the average time it takes to sew the whole garment and multiply that by the worker's hourly rate. Both methods can be figured per unit or per dozen (multiplying unit cost by 12).
7. *Trucking.* The cost of shipping completed garments to the retail store is generally called trucking. This cost is usually paid by the retail store (the receiver), but manufacturers must pay air freight if they are late with their delivery.
8. *Wholesale pricing.* The wholesale price is determined by adding the cost of labor, materials, and a markup. The markup covers sales commission (usually 7 to 10 percent), "terms" (an 8 percent discount to the retail stores if they pay their bills on time), overhead, and a profit, which is necessary to stay in business. Overhead includes all the daily costs of running the business, such as rent, cost of machinery, main-

tenance, heat, lights, staff salaries, administration, bookkeeping, advertising, markdowns of leftover fabrics and garments, and losses due to fire and theft.

Most companies add a markup between 75 and 100 percent of the cost (that is, they nearly double the cost). This is between 40 and 50 percent if figured *off* the wholesale price. For example, a blouse costing the manufacturer $10.00 to produce might have a $7.50 markup, and would therefore sell at $17.50 wholesale. This means a 42.9 percent markup based on the wholesale price (a markup of 75 percent of the cost).

Many companies figure an average markup so that their garments fit into a price line. For example, the consumer is usually willing to pay more for skirts and pants than for shirts. Yet, shirts often cost out higher because of expensive fabrications and labor. Therefore, the shirt price may be lowered to be more acceptable (called low-balling), while the skirt and pant prices may be raised (high-balling). In this way the *average* markup is within an acceptable range.

Cost Merchandising

Another important aspect of costing is whether the garment *looks* worth the price. Each garment has to compete on the market with other, similar garments. If two garments are very much alike, the less expensive one is more likely to sell on the retail level. Therefore, both styling and quality of a garment must be better than that of the competition.

The price of a garment may be adjusted slightly higher or lower to try to affect its sales potential. Occasionally a manufacturer uses a *loss leader* (a garment with a low markup) to attract buyers.

PURCHASING OF PIECE GOODS

Ordering the materials necessary to produce garments is usually done by the manufacturer's fabric or piece goods buyer. (*Piece goods* is the factory term for fabrics.) The fabric buyer may simply order goods, or may also have the responsibility with the designer for their selection. The fabric buyer acts as a liaison between the mill or converter and the manufacturer, who must have a good credit rating in order to purchase fabrics.

Generally, large-volume manufacturers purchase goods from large textile companies that can handle big orders. Ordering in quantity may give the manufacturer a lower price per yard. The goal of a volume manufacturer is to obtain the lowest-priced goods at the widest width. In addition, the volume manufacturer has the opportunity to recolor prints or order special dyes. Conversely, small manufacturers usually deal with smaller textile firms, which can do shorter runs. The buyer must know all the properties of fabrics and information on prices, availability, and delivery. For example, manufacturers on the west coast pay more than others for delivery of raw materials, and deliveries to them take longer.

The buyer must figure the amounts of yardage needed, first to cut duplicates and later for stock. Orders for stock yardage must be based on past sales or on expectations of future sales percentages. Textile sales people encourage manufacturers to make a commitment early in the season to buy a specific amount of yardage. Ordering in advance ensures the availability and on-time delivery of a popular fabric before there is a shortage of it. Large-volume orders usually require a seven- to eight-week lead time for delivery. Popular fashion fabrics and yarn dyes can require as much as a six-month lead time.

TABLE 10-1   MANUFACTURER'S COST

Wholesale Unit Pricing for a Typical Dress

Direct Cost	Amount	Average Percentages
Fabric		
4.75 yards at $2.48	$11.78	25%
Trimmings	1.53	3
Labor	10.71	22
Total Direct Cost	24.02	50
Indirect Cost		
Design and Merchandising:		
Design Staff salaries, Sample		
fabrics, Cost of samples	4.30	9 (8–10)
General Administrative Overhead:		
Office salaries, rent, insurance,		
utilities	5.28	11 (8–15)
Sales Commission	3.84	8 (7–10)
Trade Discount	3.84	8
Markdown allowance, promotion,		
or other retail services	2.40	5
Shortages	.96	2
Total Indirect Cost	20.62	43
Total Cost	44.64	93
Taxes	1.68	3.5
Profit	1.68	3.5
Wholesale Price of Dress	$48.00	100%

(refer back to design chapter for work sheet on same dress)

(see retailing chapter for retail price of the same dress)

The manufacturer must also consider how much fabric may be needed for possible reorders. There is not enough time after reorders are in to wait for fabric shipment. However, the manufacturer takes a great risk by stocking up for anticipated orders.

To eliminate some of this risk, manufacturers often commit for greige goods only, to be dyed later. Then, as sales information becomes more precise, colors can be "assorted." In other words, greige goods can be dyed in colors according to sales percentage for each color.

Trimmings

Sometimes the fabric buyer buys trimmings and findings, or there may be a separate buyer for them. Findings and trimmings are other materials used to finish garments or fashion accessories. Findings are functional and include linings, zippers, thread, and seam tape. Trimmings are decorative, such as buttons, braids, laces, and belts. Trimmings must have the same care properties as the fabrics used in the garment; that is, if the fabric can be safely washed, so must the trimmings. As trimmings and findings arrive at the plant, they must be sorted and inspected, along with fabrics. Other sundries purchased by the trimmings buyer include labels, hang tags, hangers, and plastic bags.

Piece Goods Inspection

As fabric is received in the factory, it must be carefully counted to make sure that the total amount ordered has been received. First, special equipment automatically counts the fabric yardage as it rolls from one bolt to another. Second, the fabric is pulled by rollers over large viewing tables so that it can be checked for flaws. Flaws are marked with colored threads or "flags" at the side of the fabric so that they can be avoided in cutting. If there are too many defects, such as holes or shading, the fabric is returned to the mill for a refund. (The manufacturer may pay a premium to have the mill do this inspection.)

Some companies build a strong reputation on the reliability of their product. They do washing, dry cleaning, steaming, and pressing tests to check tensile strength, durability, color cracking, color fastness, and shrinkage. Tests also determine how the fabric holds up during sewing—if needles pull it or if edges fray excessively. Colors in coordinates must match. Coordinating tops and bottoms should be cut from the same dye lot, or shipments to one store must be within acceptable variations of color from different dye lots.

Inspecting piece goods for flaws.
(Courtesy of Klopman Mills)

PRODUCTION SCHEDULING

The head of production makes up a production schedule or "issue plan" to ensure that delivery dates are met. This schedule is planned as a reverse timetable, usually on a six-month basis. The first date considered is the shipping date desired to meet the retail store's order requirements. The schedule progresses backward to include completion dates, cutting dates, etc., as far back as fabric delivery dates. This schedule in turn affects line development dates, discussed in chapter 9.

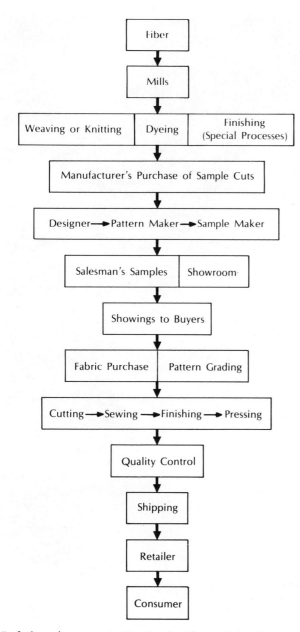

Evolution of a garment. *(Reprinted with permission from Bank of America, NT&SA, "Apparel Manufacturing," Volume 10, No. 3, Small Business Reporter, Copyright 1971.*

Orders for each style must be compiled to determine how many garments of each size to produce. The introduction of computerized inventory control to most large and some smaller firms has made planning more accurate. Computer printouts provide current information on the number of units—by size, style, and color—that are on hand, in work, and on order by retailers. With this data, manufacturers can update fabric commitments and production plans to correspond with demand.

There are two philosophies of production planning: cut to order and cut to stock. The safest method of production is to *cut to order*; that is, cut and pro-

duce only against orders. This method is used especially by producers of better-quality, lower-volume fashion.

The method with the greater risk involves cutting against estimates of projected sales *(cut to stock)*, based on sales histories of similar garments. If the manufacturer is confident of a style, or if preliminary orders indicate a big seller, the manufacturer cuts and produces that style to have stock available for fast shipment on future orders or reorders.

The cut to stock method is especially necessary for a large company that produces moderately and popularly priced fashion in volume and that has its own plant facilities. With this method, work can be started in slack months on items with the highest projected sales. This provides continuous work for permanent employees and continuous use of plant facilities. During peak production months, the manufacturer seeks additional facilities provided by outside contractors.

Plant capacity and construction difficulties must be considered in planning the schedule. For example, some styles are more difficult to produce than others and, therefore, take more time in the schedule. Operators are slower at their work when it is new to them; plant capacity builds as the sewers become accustomed to the operation and therefore work faster. A little like cooking, the production process must add each ingredient to the recipe and have it ready to serve at the right time.

When the schedule is set, the production department must follow it. If merchandise is not delivered on time, orders may be canceled.

CONTRACTING

Manufacturers do not always do all the production on a garment in their own factories. They are responsible for all phases of manufacturing, from design and fabric purchase to selling and shipping, but they may contract out some of the work. Just as a manufacturer can purchase designs from a design service or freelancer, it can also contract out pattern making, cutting, and sewing. Many small manufacturers contract out all sewing. Almost all manufacturers use contractors at least for specialized work such as sewing knits, pleating, quilting, embroidery, or piping that requires special machinery. Even manufacturers who have their own factories require the additional help of contractors at peak production periods to make entire garments. The manufacturer's own factory is referred to as an *inside shop*, the contractor's factory as an *outside shop*.

Inside Shop

The advantages and disadvantages to the manufacturer of using an inside shop include the following:

1. Advantages

   There is greater control over the construction quality of the product.

   Less physical movement of goods and personnel is necessary.

   Tax benefits accrue on the depreciation of equipment and facilities.

2. Disadvantages

   Plant facilities and machinery require large capital investment, possible only for large firms.

   Unnecessary capital outlay is unavoidable for wages during slack seasons, because assembly workers are on permanent payroll.

   Time must be devoted to union and employee demands.

Outside Shop

The advantages and disadvantages to the manufacturer of using a contractor or outside shop include the following:

1. Advantages

   There is greater production flexibility. A contractor is hired only as production is needed, to speed production during peak periods.

   The manufacturer is not concerned with hiring, training, or wage demands of personnel. (The contractor, in turn, does not have to generate sales.)

   There is no weight of overhead in a slow period.

   No capital investment in machinery (or at least in special machinery) is necessary.

2. Disadvantages

   The manufacturer has less control over quality.

   There may be communication problems.

   Extra movement of goods is necessary, resulting in extra costs and some losses.

   There is a possibility of late deliveries.

The manufacturer's production director selects the contractor most reliable and most suited for a particular job. Some contractors may arrange to work exclusively with one or more manufacturers. A contractor agrees to maintain a certain standard of workmanship and to finish work by a specific date. The contractor is given cut work, a sample duplicate, and specifications to follow. It is very important that the production head work closely with the contractor to make sure that standards and time schedules are met. Finished garments are returned to the manufacturer for shipping to retail stores.

Contractors can be located anywhere in the world where labor is abundant, wages are reasonable, and facilities, machinery, and transportation are available.

Overseas Production

Although garment workers in the United States are paid relatively low wages compared to other skilled craftspeople, manufacturers are turning to even cheaper sources of labor in Hong Kong, Taiwan, Korea, and India. For example, according to the International Ladies' Garment Workers' Union, typical wages in the United States in the women's dress industry are $3.34 per hour, compared to $.46 per hour in Colombia, $.62 in Hong Kong, $.21 in India, and $.34 in Taiwan.[1]

There are three alternative methods of producing clothing overseas:

Production package. A manufacturer purchases a production "package" through an agent. In this case, everything comes from the Orient, including raw materials, production, finishing, labeling, packaging, and shipping. Using an agent is the most expensive method, but it is advantageous because the agent takes responsibility for production, quality control, and the delivery time schedule. (A manufacturer may also have its own representative abroad to find raw materials, work with agents and contractors, and oversee production, quality control, quotas, duties, and shipping.)

Cut, make, and trim. A manufacturer may buy fabric from one country (silk from Japan, for example) and then send it elsewhere (to Hong Kong, for example) to be cut and sewn.

Offshore assembly. Fabric is purchased and cut in the United States and then sent abroad (to Mexico or Colombia) for sewing. Because

[1] Lazare Teper, "Women's and Children's Apparel and the Multi Fiber Textile Arrangement" (New York: International Ladies' Garment Workers' Union, April 12, 1977).

of freight charges, this method is used only for garments to be made of light-weight fabrics but requiring a great amount of labor. Otherwise, it may be just as inexpensive to produce in the United States.

Middlemen Involved in Importing Importing involves numerous negotiations, many done through middlemen: an agent to represent the manufacturer in the country where production is done; a customs broker who represents the manufacturer to obtain permission from the U.S. government to bring the goods into the United States; and a freight forwarding agent to handle shipping.

To produce overseas, manufacturers must send patterns, specifications, and samples as guidelines. All details must be exact and clear. Precise records and open lines of communication are a necessity.

Risks Involved Despite cost benefits of overseas production, there are many risk factors.

It is difficult to keep control over quality.

Long lead time is needed, because shipping takes eight weeks from Asia to the United States.

Late deliveries are a problem.

It is difficult to negotiate prices because of fluctuations in international currency exchange rates.

Raw materials are often unavailable.

Difficulties in communications are caused by language differences.

Goods are often stolen.

Weather conditions in the Orient can be disastrous. A monsoon can wipe out a shipment or even an entire factory.

Import Duties All categories of overseas production are classified as imports (along with merchandise that is totally designed and produced in another country, as we shall see in chapter 11). Duty is imposed on imports to try to protect domestic industry. For example, textile firms in the United States produce a large volume of acrylics. Because of higher wages in the United States, it costs more to produce acrylics here than in some other countries. To make U.S. acrylics competitive with those produced elsewhere, a duty is charged on the imports. The duty varies according to fiber content, whether the fabric is woven or knitted, and whether the item is decorated or nondecorated. (Decorations are nonfunctional. For example, a removable bow tie is con-

sidered decorative; an attached bow tie is considered functional. Buttons and buttonholes are functional, but embroidery is decorative.)

Quota Allocations The United States government also regulates overseas production by means of *quotas*, or limits on imports from each country. Before even considering manufacturing overseas, a manufacturer must be sure that goods are covered by the quota allocations. Frequently, all the allocations are already "held" by other manufacturers or by governments in a given country. Governments may charge for the use of the quota or try to regulate the amount of capital investiture made in their country in exchange for the quota allocation.

Countries fall under differing classifications for quota allocations. Classifications are heavily influenced by politics, especially concern over trade imbalances. For example, the United States formerly imposed few restraints on imports from India, classified as an underdeveloped country. As a result, India exported a great deal to the United States and yet imported very little, creating a trade imbalance. Therefore, India's classification has been changed to impose new quotas on imports from India. The United States recently did away with the "underdeveloped" classification entirely.

The main advantage of manufacturing overseas is that it keeps production costs down. Even with customs duties and freight costs, total production costs are usually less than for comparable garments made domestically. For example, a man's suit made in the United States might cost twice as much as the same suit made in Hong Kong.

Understandably, unions are fighting overseas production because it takes jobs away from American laborers. The future of foreign contracting is uncertain. As developing countries slowly catch up industrially with the West and as wages in those countries go up, this inexpensive source of labor may disappear.

PATTERNING AND CUTTING PROCEDURES

Making the Production Pattern

There are two methods of making a production pattern: a production pattern maker may choose to perfect the sample pattern to meet company specifications, or he or she may start over, making a totally new pattern from the corrected sample.

The production pattern maker relies on the same methods used in the sample room to make patterns:

draping, drafting, or flat patterning from standardized basic blocks. In fact, in many small companies the same person does both the sample and production pattern making. In production, strict attention must be paid to company size specifications, which are standardized measurements (including ease) for each size. Also, the edges of each pattern piece must exactly match the piece to which it will be sewn, with notches marked perfectly for operators to follow. It is extremely important to maintain accuracy throughout production.

Metric Conversion   Conversion to the metric system will have its greatest impact on sizing, pattern making, and grading because they all involve working with linear measurements. Designers and pattern makers will have to think in centimeters and millimeters instead of inches, relating body dimensions to garment patterns in metric terms. Although an adjustment period will be required to get used to working with the new measurements, it will actually be easier to work in subdivisions of 100 than in fractions of an inch.

The most critical area of adjustment will be in sizing. Trade associations and individual manufacturers will have to work closely with designers and market researchers to establish proper new size specifications that meet consumer needs. Once new sizes have been formulated, the biggest difficulty will be in educating the public.

Grading Sizes   Patterns, like garments, must provide for different sizes. Grading is the method used to increase or decrease the sample-size production pattern to make up a complete size range. For example, a size 10 is made larger to a 12, a 14, and a 16, and smaller to an 8 and a 6. Each company sets predetermined grade specifications or "rules."

The sample-size pattern is held in place over tag or Manila board by a grading machine. The operator turns one knob of the machine to move the pattern forward and backward and the other knob to move the pattern sideways to mark points of size change. The pattern is moved for each point of increase or decrease. For example, a missy manufacturer's grade rules might call for increments of 1½ inches in width

Using a sample size 7 block as the master, the grader increases pattern dimensions to make a larger size.
(Photograph by the author at Gunne Sax, San Francisco)

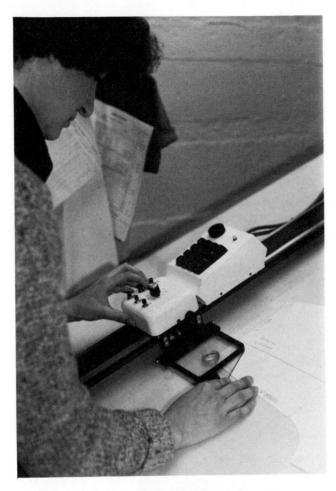

A digitizer is used to record a pattern's grade points in a computer. *(Photograph by the author)*

and ¼ inch in length for each size. But the machine does *not* do the figuring; the increases and decreases still must be figured by the operator. For example, if the waist must be increased by 1 inch to the next size, then ½ inch must be added to the front and ½ inch to the back. Additional seams would make the dimensions more complicated. In addition to knowing basic mathematics, the grader (like the pattern maker) must have good visual judgment to redraw the curve of an armhole or neckline, to decide on height and width relationships for pockets, and so on. Each size may be made on a different colored patterned board, for easy recognition.

The easiest but most expensive way to grade patterns is by computer. The operator guides a digitizer around the edges of the sample pattern. At each of the key points, he pushes a button to record a grade point. Each point is cross-referenced by the computer to a grade rule, which enlarges or reduces the pattern automatically according to predetermined increments and in a predetermined direction. The computer then prints out the pattern in each new size. Because of the high initial costs, only a company that produces a very large volume of a particular style can afford to use a computer in its operations.

Making the Marker

From all the pattern pieces of varying sizes, a master *marker* is made. The marker is the cutting guide or pattern layout, made on a sheet of paper the same width as the fabric. The purposes of the marker are these:

Tracing around patterns to make a marker.
(Courtesy of the ILGWU Justice *newspaper)*

(1) to place pattern pieces close together to avoid fabric waste. The desired economical use of space is called a "tight" marker.

(2) to accommodate the cutting order, or to lay out the patterns so that each size and color are cut as needed.

The Manila patterns, already graded, are traced onto the paper. Grain direction, one-way prints, and naps must be considered in making the marker. Copies of the marker are made to use in each cut.

A computer can also make a marker. Miniatures of the graded pattern pieces are displayed graphically on a "scope" (like a television screen). The operator can electronically position the pattern pieces into the most efficient arrangement. Once the arrangement is completed, the computer causes the plotter to print out a full-scale marker on a long sheet of paper.

Cutting Procedures

Laying up the Cut The next step in the production process is "laying up" the cut, or spreading the fabric with one layer on top of another. The spreader machine is guided up and down a table, folding back one layer of fabric over another. The length of each layer is determined by the marker. More than 300 layers may be cut at one time, depending on the fabric thickness.

Problems arise in handling stretch fabrics, such as jerseys, which can easily be stretched too much in spreading. To avoid this, they are usually left overnight to "relax."

Cutting Techniques The marker is put on top of the layers of fabric. The cutter follows the pattern outlined on the marker, using a straight knife machine with a long, thin blade that vibrates vertically as it is pushed through many layers of fabric. A vertical knife can cut to a depth of 10 inches or more. For only a few layers, a cutting machine with a rotating circular knife may be used. Its cutting edge is closer to the table, but it is not as accurate on curves. Cutters must be aware of how fabric finish, pile, stripes, floral designs, and other factors affect their work. The cutter must select the correct speed and blade for each type of fabric. For example, a coarse blade edge is used for tightly woven fabrics, a smooth edge for softer fabrics.

Die cutting may be used for garments or parts of garments that do not change from season to season. A die, on the order of a cookie cutter, is made for each piece to be cut. The sharp edges of the die

Using a spreader to lay up the cut.
(Courtesy of Klopman Mills)

are pressed against the layers of fabric to cut it. This is a faster, more accurate method of cutting. A "gang die" can be made by connecting several dies together.

For mass production, entirely new cutting methods are in the experimental stage. Laser beam cutting is already used for men's suits. The laser, a concentrated light beam, can be directed by a computer. Water jet cutting is also being used to cut some fabrics and leathers, especially in the shoe industry. A thin stream of water, also computer directed, is fired under high pressure through a tiny nozzle to cut the leather.

Notwithstanding modern technology, it is quite a contrast to find that in better suit and coat houses all cutting is done one layer at a time. Quantity is not necessary in this case, and single-layer cutting makes possible absolute accuracy. The cutter uses weights to keep the pattern in place on the fabric and cuts around the edge with shears.

Bundling The process of sorting cut pieces and tying them together is referred to as bundling. Parts of garments and necessary findings must be grouped for the sewing machine operators. Identification tickets are attached for piecework control. The style number, bundle quantity, individual piecework rate, and operation to be performed are printed on these tickets. Bundled work is distributed to machine operators in the factory or sent out to contractors to be sewn.

GARMENT ASSEMBLY

Sewing Operations

The many steps involved in sewing a garment are called *operations*. A man's suit can have as many as 200 different sewing operations. No two manufacturers use all of the same methods, but all of them follow the same basic order.

As part of production scheduling, a supervisor analyzes a garment's construction to determine the best and fastest way to sew the garment. A list or "operation sheet" is drawn up, including all necessary operations in sequential order. Sewing operations are periodically reassigned, because certain machines needed for one style may not be needed for another. Often new techniques are introduced which require specialized machinery. The introduction of specialized operations or new machinery requires additional training for operators that results in higher production costs during the training period. The purchase of new equipment, either to replace old machinery or to speed production, is considered a long-term investment. Equipment costs are balanced by savings from more efficient production.

Rate of Pay Most sewing machine operators, finishers, and pressers are paid on a *piecework* rate. That is, they are paid a set amount for each operation that they complete, rather than by the hour. Rates vary with the difficulty of the operation. As proof of work completed, the operator signs the identification ticket or removes one segment of it. Actually, most companies pay a "guaranteed wage," with piecework acting as an incentive for operators to work faster and, therefore, earn more.

Assembly Systems Each different sewing operation must be performed in sequence. There are two general methods of construction: the progressive bundle system and the tailor or whole garment system.

In the *progressive bundle system* (usually used for sportswear) each operator repeats one assembly task, such as closing a shoulder seam or stitching on a pocket. Usually, machine operators are grouped to follow the order of production; they pass the garments in units of 40 or 50 from one section to the next as each operation is completed.

In the *whole garment system* (usually used for dresses) one operator sews together nearly a whole garment. This system is similar to the one used for sewing sample garments. Even in this case, however, hems and buttonholes are usually done by another operator who specializes in these finishing tasks.

Types of Power Sewing Machines

Three main types of power sewing machines are used in factories: the lock-stitch, the chain-stitch, and the overlock.

The *lock-stitch machine* sews a straight seam on the same principle as a home sewing machine. This machine makes it possible for the top thread to go under the bottom thread by slipping it around a bobbin, creating a lock. This is the most secure stitch possible, but it leaves an unfinished seam, undesirable

The lock-stitch machine is the backbone of the industry. *(Photograph by the author)*

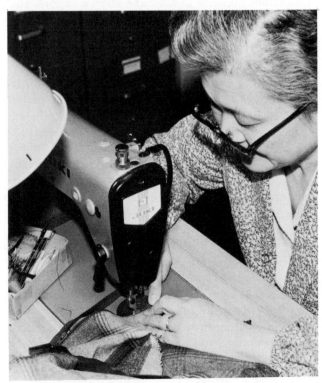

in fabrics that ravel easily. Also, of course, operations must be stopped frequently to rewind the bobbin. The lock-stitch machine, the backbone of the industry, is used for assembly work in the sample room and in most better-quality garments. In the factory the lock-stitch machine is used for finishing operations such as stitching on facings, setting front stands on shirts, setting waistbands, setting zippers and pockets, making collars, and topstitching trim.

The *chain-stitch machine* works on a principle similar to crocheting: it makes a series of loops pulled through one another. The top needle goes in and out of the fabric, making loops underneath that catch into one another. This machine could be used to do many of the operations that are done on a lock-stitch machine, although the chain-stitch is not as secure and the chain can be seen on the underside of the fabric. However, because the chain-stitch machine does not have a bobbin, the operator does not need to stop in mid-operation to rewind it.

The *overlock machine* is based on the same principle as the chain-stitch machine. The overlock machine was created to make an edge finish as well as to sew seams. In one operation it sews the fabric together, cuts off the fabric to make a smooth edge,

The overlock machine creates a finished edge as it makes a seam. (Photograph by the author)

and wraps thread around the edge. A simple overlock machine has one needle and two loopers (which look like thick, bent needles), and works with three spools or cones of thread. The machine often runs at 5,500 or more revolutions per minute (faster than a standard car engine). The needle and loopers work together in a reciprocating pattern, the loopers moving back and forth from the needle to the fabric edge. This stitch is ideal for knits because it gives with the stretch of the fabric.

The *safety overlock machine* is a combination of the chain-stitch and the overlock. The safety factor is that in case one row of stitching comes out, the other still holds the garment together. With a total of two needles, three loopers, and five cones of thread, it functions as two machines in one. It provides a straight chain-stitch needed for factory assembling plus an edge finish.

The *blind-stitch hemming machine* is also based on the chain-stitch. The hem is folded back and caught by the needle at even intervals.

Button machines sew buttons onto a garment. Button placement is marked by tiny holes punched into the fabric. A sew-through button is placed in a holder, which moves the button back and forth while the needle sews it onto the fabric underneath. A shank button is held in position sideways so that the needle can go through the shank on its back. Some machines have feeding devices that automatically position the button.

The *buttonhole machine* is essentially a zig-zag lock-stitch machine with automatic devices to control the width and length of the buttonhole and to cut it open. The operator must be careful to insert the fabric in exactly the right position each time, because the machine makes the buttonhole in about six seconds.

Modern technology has introduced more effective automation into the apparel industry. Machines can be set up to do combinations of operations. Certain machines, such as those used for embroidery, can be programmed to stitch particular patterns without an operator.

Labeling

Along the production line, various labels are attached to the garment. A union label is sewn into a seam if the garment is produced in a union shop. Another label, listing fiber content, is required by federal law. The garment also carries labels with cleaning or washing instructions. There are also, of course, the labels that identify the manufacturer and/or designer and state the size. In addition, there may be a hang tag to further promote the manufacturer or the fiber or fabric producer's name.

Many apparel firms are commissioned to manufacture clothes for large department and chain stores that wish to sell garments under their own brand name or private label. They may use the store name as the label for everything, or they may use different names for each line (see "private brands" in chapter 12).

Finishing

Tailoring, the unseen quality handwork formerly done inside collars and lapels to form and hold their shape, has virtually disappeared due to the high cost of skilled labor. Most "tailoring" today is done simply by fusing interfacings into the garment to give it shape.

In "better" garments, some hand finishing is necessary, such as sewing in linings or sewing on buttons; but this, too, is becoming rare. In moderate- and lower-priced garments, all finishing is done by machine.

PRODUCTION OF MEN'S SUITS

Traditionally, the men's clothing industry has been divided into firms that produce *tailored* suits and coats, and *furnishing* producers that make shirts, slacks, ties, underwear, and sleepwear. Tailored garment production has dominated the industry, but recently, with the trend toward casual dress for men, there has been a growing demand for sportswear. The production of men's sportswear is similar to that of women's. However, tailoring a man's suit requires a great deal more time and work. A coat and suit producer must start a collection early because of both the length of time needed for advance commitment to piece goods and the detailed steps in production. This tends to delay styling change; however, by the same token, that very lack of style and pattern change enables the manufacturer to plan far ahead.

A traditional system rated the tailoring quality of men's suits on a scale from 1 for machine-made to 6 for hand-tailored suits. Today this rating is no longer used because hand tailoring has virtually disappeared. Modern technology has introduced automation into an industry that was traditionally oriented toward hand work. Fusible interfacing replaces hand work in the collar, lapels, and buttoning areas to give them body and shape.

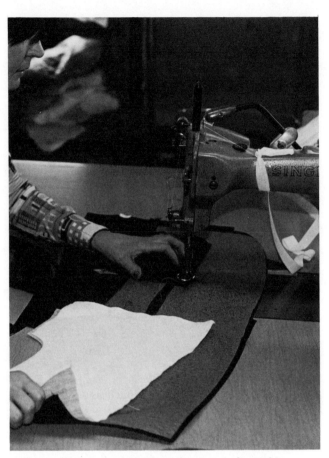

Modern tailoring: machine jump basting a chest piece into a jacket front. *(Photograph by the author at Marman, San Francisco)*

Steps in Production

The basic steps in the production of a man's suit are listed below: [2]

1. Fuse interfacings and jump baste chest pieces and "bridal" tape on lapel crease for support.
2. Press, line, and stitch on pockets.
3. "Sew around" edges or "bagging" operation. (Men's suits traditionally use a "bluff" edge, which means no finished undercollar.)
4. Join main pieces together.
5. Set in sleeves.
6. Set in linings by machine (sleeve linings may be hand felled). It may seem that a lined jacket would be more expensive than an unlined one. However(an easy, unlined sportsjacket may be costlier because the inside is visible. Binding is required to cover seam edges, and a "French facing" (which goes into the shoulder area) is needed to cover the interfacing.
7. Sew buttons and buttonholes.

[2] Stanley Orlick, Executive Vice-President, Marman of San Francisco, personal interview, February 1979.

KNITWEAR PRODUCTION

There are two commercial methods of knitwear production: cut-and-sew and full-fashioned. *Cut-and-sew* refers to the method by which garments are made from knitted yardage. This type of knitted garment requires the same patterning as that used for woven fabrics, except that no darts are needed because knits move and conform to body curves depending on the amount of stretch in the fabric. Stretchability is the key to knitted garments; therefore, an overlock stitch is used because it is flexible and gives with the fabric. Knitted braids and bands must be used as trims and finishes because all components must have the same stretchability.

Full-fashioned knits, mostly sweaters, are knitted on special machinery. The specifications for each piece are programmed into the knitting machine, which builds the shape into each piece as it is knit. Then the pieces are seamed together with sweater yarn.

Most full-fashioned production is done in the Orient because manufacturers saw the potential of cheaper labor there and invested in specialized machinery. Factories in the Orient provide both affordable prices and variety of production.

Some sweaters are also hand knitted or crocheted. Hand knits have the greatest variety of stitches and detailing. However, because of the time needed to make them, they are very expensive. Hand-knit garments for commercial marketing are made abroad, where labor is cheaper and more readily available.

PREPARATION FOR SHIPPING

Pressing

Pressing vastly improves the look of a garment. It can hide a multitude of imperfections, such as puckered seams and collars that do not lie flat. Higher-priced garments are pressed during the course of construction. However, in the production of less expensive garments, no pressing is done until the garment is completed. Pressing equipment is sometimes used to preshape pieces before sewing—for example, to fold under pocket edges.

Steam irons are used for areas not easily accessible. Various "buck" pressing machines (like those seen at a dry cleaner) are used on tailored garments to flatten jacket edges, to crease trousers, and so on. Occasionally, a "steam-air form finisher," which looks like a puffy dress form, is used to steam dresses into shape.

Full-fashioned mohair and wool sweater-jacket.
(Courtesy of Bill Kaiserman, Rafael Fashions Ltd.)

The tough job of operating a buck press.
(Courtesy of the ILGWU Justice *newspaper)*

167

Quality Control

A sample maker can make one garment neatly and accurately, but in mass production of 500 or 1,000 dozen garments it is harder to control quality. To make sure production has been done correctly and to prevent returns, finished garments are inspected either totally or by random sampling. Quality controllers not only check for uncut threads but also spot check measurements against a list of specifications. If there are mistakes in first stock, the production manager tries to correct them at the sewing or cutting source.

Production standards are very important and must equal the manufacturer's reputation and warrant the garment's price. It means nothing to have a beautifully designed garment if it is not produced well. If a total shipment of garments is sent to a store without having had threads trimmed or construction checked, the garments could be rejected by the store and returned to the manufacturer, or they would look so unappealing on the hanger that the customers would not buy them. Either event would mean loss of reputation and future sales.

Garments that are returned to the manufacturer are analyzed to find the reasons for their return. Numbers on each garment's label identify the factory or contractor where the garment was made, enabling construction mistakes to be traced to their source. Besides construction mistakes, other reasons for returns include poor quality fabric, fabric shading, and late deliveries. The manufacturer tries to prevent these mistakes in future shipments.

Filling Orders

If production work has been done by contractors, the completed garments are returned to the manufacturer for shipment to retail stores. At a central shipping point, garments are checked for quality and then divided into groups according to style, size, and color and put into "stock," a storage area where they hang on racks.

A store orders a certain quantity of units on a form that includes entries for style number, color number, and price per unit. First, the order is analyzed by the credit department for volume credibility and account payment history. The next step is to see what is available in stock or what needs to be manufactured to fill the order. In large companies, much of this checking is now done by computer. Large orders and orders from important regular customers are filled first. Shipping clerks pull merchandise from stock to fill orders in the correct style, size, and color to be packaged and shipped.

Garments are carefully folded into shipping boxes and marked with the means of transportation specified by the retailer. A packing slip (an invoice without prices) is enclosed in the box; the actual invoice is mailed separately for payment. The boxes are labeled and are moved by trolley or conveyor belt to be loaded on the delivery truck and sent to the retailer.

Weighing shipment to find freight cost. *(Photograph by the author at Gunne Sax, San Francisco)*

SUMMARY

In this chapter we have seen how garments are manufactured, tracing production through fabric purchasing, patterning, cutting, sewing, and finishing to quality control. There are manufacturer-owned production facilities, called inside shops, and outside shops or contractors. Many manufacturers use foreign contractors or offshore production to reduce labor costs.

It is not enough to design fashionable garments. They must be produced according to size specifications and they must meet quality control standards. On the basis of reliable production and delivery standards, a manufacturer builds and keeps a reputation for dependability that accompanies its reputation for innovative styling.

CHAPTER REVIEW

CHAPTER OBJECTIVES

After reading this chapter you should be able to

A. Give evidence of having attained competence in the following areas:

1. Ability to explain the costing of a garment 2. Ability to describe in sequential order the steps in garment production 3. Understanding of the various types of contracting 4. Understanding of the technical developments in production, especially the use of computers 5. Ability to explain the differences between men's tailoring and men's sportswear production 6. Ability to describe the various types of knitwear production 7. Understanding of the importance of quality control

B. Define the following terms and concepts in relation to their discussion in the chapter:

1. Factoring 2. Wholesale pricing 3. Precost 4. Cost sheet 5. Cost merchandising 6. Loss leader 7. Production schedule 8. Cut to order 9. Cut to stock 10. Piece goods 11. Trimmings 12. Fabric inspection 13. Contracting or outside shop 14. Inside shop 15. Overseas production package 16. Overseas cut, make, and trim 17. Offshore assembly 18. Import duties 19. Quotas 20. Production pattern 21. Basic block 22. Grading 23. Grade rules 24. Computer grading and marking 25. Marker 26. Laying up the cut 27. Dye cutting 28. Water jet and laser beam cutting 29. Bundling 30. Piecework 31. Progressive bundle system 32. Whole garment system 33. Lockstitch machine 34. Chain-stitch machine 35. Overlock machine 36. Finishing 37. Tailoring 38. Cut-and-sew knits 39. Full-fashioned knits 40. Quality control 41. Stock 42. Shipping

Questions for Review

1. Discuss the differences between the cut-to-order and cut-to-stock philosophies.
2. What is the difference between a first pattern and a production pattern?
3. Explain the two systems of garment assembly.
4. What are the advantages of an outside shop? Of an inside shop?
5. Discuss the three major methods of overseas production.
6. How has the construction of men's suits changed over the years?
7. Why is quality control so important?

PROJECTS FOR ADDITIONAL LEARNING

1. If there is an apparel manufacturer or contractor in your area, try to make an appointment for a factory tour. Describe production methods. Do operators do section work or does one person sew one whole garment together? What production methods are unique to the product? Is any hand work done on the garment? Compare the wholesale price range of the garments being produced to the quality of production.

2. Visit a local store and compare imported ready-to-wear with domestically produced items that retail at the same price. Consider fit, styling, and workmanship. Which are better? Why? What conclusions can you draw from this comparison?

3. Investigate a major apparel manufacturer by interviewing managers, reading the company's annual report, reading trade newspaper articles about the company, or writing to the company for information. Write a profile of the company, including ownership (see appendix), type of garments produced by each division, type of customer to which they appeal, type of production, price line, where products are sold.

FUR AND ACCESSORY MANUFACTURING

11

A funnel-collared raccoon coat shown
at the Montreal International Fur Fair
*(Courtesy of the Fur Trade Association
of Canada, Quebec)*

Furs and accessories are very much a part of the fashion scene. Furs, handbags, shoes, belts, and gloves have in common the traditional use of animal skins as a raw material.

Although fur coats and jackets are wearing apparel, we discuss them separately from other garments because of the specialized methods used in their manufacture and because of their luxurious nature. This chapter has separate sections covering fur manufacturing and the styling and production of millinery, handbags, belts, gloves, shoes, hosiery, and jewelry.

FUR MANUFACTURING

In chapter 7 we discussed the processing of furs. Some manufacturers buy furs directly at auctions and contract out the processing operations. Other manufacturers buy processed furs from merchants. Once the pelts have been processed, the actual production of fur garments can begin. Fashion influences the design of fur garments and the popularity of specific furs.

Fur manufacturing is essentially a handcraft industry carried on by small, independent, owner-operated shops. The reasons for this lie in the nature of the raw material, the pelts. No two pelts are totally alike; the furrier must match pelts according to quality and color to achieve uniform texture and color in the finished garment. Also, the sewing of furs requires much skill and does not lend itself to mass production techniques.

The two basic methods of fur manufacturing are the skin-on-skin technique and the letting-out technique.

Skin-on-Skin Method

In the less costly skin-on-skin method, one full skin is sewed adjacent to another in a uniform alignment. This method is often used to sew together the leftovers of expensive furs, such as paws and flanks, into less expensive garments.

Letting-Out Method

More luxurious furs, such as mink, are often manufactured by the letting-out method, which accentuates length, reduces width, and enhances draping. This technique involves splitting each skin in half lengthwise and then slicing every half-pelt into diagonal strips one-eighth to one-quarter inch wide. The strips are then rematched and sewn together to form a narrower, longer skin that can run the full length of the garment. The result is a slimmer, longer pelt that is often more beautiful than the original.

The strips are sewn into sections according to the coat or jacket pattern. They are dampened, stretched, stapled onto the pattern on a wooden board, and dried into shape. Afterward the dried sections are sewn together.

The next operation is called glazing. The fur is again dampened and the hairs are combed in the desired direction. Gums and other materials, which often increase the luster of the fur, are applied to hold the hair in the desired position. Then the fur is slowly dried and the label put on. Afterward the lining is sewn in. In expensive coats, a supportive backing is sometimes sewn in before the lining.

Fur Labeling

Fur garment manufacturers often alter the appearance of various furs to resemble those that are currently more stylish or more expensive. Many countries have introduced labeling requirements to make consumers aware of this practice. The United States Fur Labeling Act of 1951 (amended in 1961) requires that the label (as well as related advertising) contain the following information: animal name, country of origin, type of processing and dyeing, whether furs have been reused, and whether the garment contains paws or tails. If the garment resembles

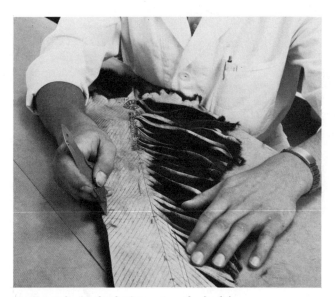

Cutting pelts in the letting-out method of fur manufacturing. *(Courtesy of the Informationsbüro Pelz, West Germany)*

Stapling damp sections of a coat into shape.
(Courtesy of the Informationsbüro Pelz, West Germany)

A fashion show at the International Fur Fair in Frankfurt.
(Courtesy of the Informationsbüro Pelz, West Germany)

another fur, it must be labeled with the name of the actual pelt used.

Fur manufacturing centers include Milan, Frankfurt, Paris, London, Leningrad, Montreal, and New York. The most famous names in fashion furs include the Fendi sisters of Milan, known for their unique styling; Dior, Ciganer, Revillon, and Alexandre of Paris; Grosvenor of Canada; and Maximilian and Ben Kahn of New York. Many well-known designers create styles for these manufacturers.

FASHION ACCESSORIES

To achieve a total fashion look, accessories such as hats, handbags, belts, shoes, and jewelry are needed to coordinate with apparel. The design, production, and marketing of each type of accessory is actually a separate industry.

Certain types of accessories tend to be more functional than others. Examples include men's belts, sport shoes for both men and women, and knit caps for warmth in winter. Other accessories are part of fashion and change with style trends. For instance, the emphasis on fashion belts for women comes and goes with waist interest. Therefore, designers and producers of such accessories must be aware of fashion trends, to make accessories that successfully complement apparel.

There are no rules for combining accessories with apparel. When the midi was popular in Europe in the early 1970s, the longer skirt was worn with a chunky shoe. In the late '70s the longer skirt was combined with a delicately proportioned shoe. A fashion statement depends on accessories sometimes more, sometimes less.

Millinery

In the past, the most "necessary" of accessories was a hat. A woman bought a new hat to add a bright spot to her wardrobe; a businessman was never seen on the street without one. The trend toward a more casual life style and bouffant hairdos for women in the '60s changed that, and the millinery industry suffered a severe setback. The return to more elegant and traditional fashion in the late 1970s brought some renewed interest in millinery.

Production The millinery industry has essentially two products: *hats* and fine *millinery*. Hats tend to be more functional and are less complicated to produce. Hats include caps that can be knitted on machines or by hand, felt hats that are stamped out by steel molds, and fabric hats that may be sewn using goods cut from patterns over buckram forms. In contrast, fine millinery is made by hand. Straw is first dipped in sizing for body; felt is wet down. Then the goods are molded by hand over wooden forms created in Paris or New York. (Only one such form maker remains in New York.) After drying in an oven, the new shapes may be decorated with ribbons, flowers, feathers, or other trims. The handcraft involved in millinery production tends to keep the industry composed of small firms. There are only about 200 hat manufacturers remaining in the United States, located for the most part in New York City, followed by Dallas and St. Louis. World centers include Germany, England, and Australia.

Blocking a felt hat at Sonni of California.
(Photograph by the author)

Handbags

A handbag must be both decorative and functional—able to store money and other necessities as well as to fit into the overall fashion picture. Large bags such as totes and attaché cases tend to be more functional, while smaller bags such as the envelope and clutch are more decorative. Handbag styles range from classic constructed types to soft, unconstructed types. Leather, leather imitations, all types of fabric, metallics, and straw are used to make women's handbags.

Production Handbag design is very much like apparel design. The elements of color, line, shape, fabrication, and detail as well as the principles of emphasis and proportion must be considered. To test a design, a "dummy" is made in flannel from a sample pattern. Ornaments, closures, and/or handles must be chosen to complete the design successfully. When fabrication is selected, a final sample is made up with supportive interlinings that differ with each type of bag and each fabrication. When the final line is chosen, cutting dies are made from the pattern and used to stamp out leather on a "clicker" machine. Fabrics may be cut by methods similar to those used in the apparel industry. Both fabrics and leathers may be stitched by machine, but much of the assembly of linings, ornaments, handles, and closures must be done by hand.

About two-thirds of the approximately 500 small companies that make up the United States handbag industry are located around New York City. Most of the hardware used on the bags is produced in the Northeast or imported from Europe. Approximately one-quarter of the fashion handbags on the market in the United States are imported from Italy, Spain, and South America.

Rising prices and reduced availability of leather in recent years have had a great impact on the styling and production of handbags, belts, gloves, and shoes.

Belts

Belts are divided between the functional—mostly for men—and fashion belts for women. Because functional belts must withstand everyday wear, therefore, they are traditionally made of heavier leather (five or six ounces). Fashion for belts in women's wear is cyclical, corresponding to waist interest in apparel styling. Fashion belts are made of various materials including lighter-weight leather and suedes, leather look-alikes, plastics, elastic, and fabrics.

Production Leather and imitation leather materials are cut on "strap cutting" machines. Comparable to a noodle maker, these machines cut the material into long, straight lengths of any desired width. Shaped belts are made either by die cutting or from plexiglass patterns. In die cutting, the pattern is made into a die like a cookie cutter. A "clicker" machine presses the sharp edges of the die through the leather. Plexiglass patterns are used like the paper patterns for single-layer cutting in the apparel industry. The cutter must carefully cut around the patterns, only on flawless pieces of leather.

The cut leather is next sewn to a backing with a "walking foot" machine. Belt buckles, made from metal, wood, or plastic, come mostly from New England and Italy. Also, buckles may be covered in self-fabric. Holes are made in the opposite end of the belt by a "foot press" machine. The holes, the slit for the buckle, and the shape of the tip may also be cut by a die. In addition, a die can emboss a pattern onto the leather. Belts are finished with trims such as stitchery, cording, nail heads, or rhinestones and may have an edge finish made by an "edge die."

The industry is centered around New York City because of its close proximity to suppliers. Belt manufacturers tend to be small firms. A large investment in various equipment is needed to finish leather well, but some of the operations can be contracted out.

Gloves

Gloves have tended lately to be more functional than decorative. Because their main function is to give warmth, they are often lined with fur or knit fabric. Glove fabrications include leather and knit or woven fabrics. Knits, which stretch, have made production simpler because only one size is needed.

Most gloves are still produced by a painstaking process that requires many hand operations. Because of this, leather glove producers tend to specialize in a single step of production, such as cutting, stitching, or finishing. However, fabric glove production is becoming more mechanized.

Glove firms have remained small due to their specialized, handcrafted operations. Gloversville, in upstate New York, is the production center for the glove industry.

Footwear

Footwear, including shoes, sandals, and boots, is the area of largest volume in accessory production. Both functional and fashionable, shoes come in assorted materials including calf, kid, suede, reptile, and—because of the rising cost of natural products—

an increasing number of imitations. Dressy and casual shoes for women are also made of fabric. Sport shoes can be made in combinations of leather and nylon. The fashion for ethnic styles helped to contribute to this variety in shoe styling and fabrication.

Design Shoe design also takes years of research and development. Shoe designers and manufacturers work with fiber producers on color projections so that their shoes will coordinate with apparel fashions.

Italy has been the original source of shoe fashions for approximately two thousand years.[1] Shoe designers, called *modelistas*, must also have skills in shoe construction and knowledge of manufacturing techniques. The modelista creates a model shoe, called a "pull-over" because it is sewn and tacked onto a wooden, foot-shaped block. Modelistas usually specialize in a particular style category such as dress shoes, sandals, or boots. The modelistas offer their collections to the trade from their own studios or at international shoe fairs.

Manufacturers may buy 50 to 100 of these models a year. A *line builder* or product manager selects the models for his company to produce and sell.

Production Shoe production is complex, involving sizes for length, width, and width combinations. The full range of women's shoe sizes includes 103 width and length combinations between sizes 5 and 10. Other factors contributing to the complexity of shoe production are the skilled labor needed and the number of operations performed. Two to three hundred operations can go into the production of a finely made fashion shoe. Whether a shoe is hand made or mass produced, there are usually ten basic steps involved:

1. *Making the last*, a foot-shaped form, is the first step in shoe production. The original last is made of wood, requiring as many as 35 different measurements to make one size. A shoe factory needs thousands of lasts as a separate one is needed for each size, width, heel height, and basic style. Duplicate polyethylene lasts are made from the master.
2. *Pattern making* is based on measurements taken from the last and from the original pull-over

---

[1] *All About Shoes*, the Footwear Council, 1979, p. 29.

Dye cutting leather soles for shoes.
(Courtesy of Salamander AG, West Germany)

model or designer's sketch. From the pattern, a "trial" shoe is made. The line builder further assesses and refines style selections at this time and the final line is closed and "frozen." Trials are duplicated for sales representative's samples.

3. *Cutting:* Paper patterns are converted into steel dies that cut the leather. A shoemaker uses a curved knife to hand cut leather. Manufacturers use cutting machines, with some ultramodern factories using laser beams.

4. *Stitching* or *fitting* the "upper" portion of the shoe includes buttonholes, top stitching, all other upper design details, and linings.

5. *Lasting* is the process of attaching the upper to the last to give it support and shape.

6. *Stock fitting* is the preparation of the sole section.

7. *Bottoming* is the process of attaching the sole to the upper by sewing, cementing, nailing, or molding.

8. *Heeling* is attaching and shaping the heel.

9. *Finishing* includes polishing, extracting the lasts, and branding.

10. *Treeing* includes attachment of decoration as well as final cleaning and inspection.

Some producers or contractors specialize in one part of production, such as the making of lasts or heels. If a shoe is factory made, 80 different types of machines would be involved in its production. It is possible for small companies to lease machinery; however, larger companies have a competitive edge because they have the capital necessary to invest in

**As part of the lasting process, the upper press will shape
the back of this shoe.** *(Courtesy of Salamander AG,
West Germany)*

the most advanced machinery. Water jet cutters and automatically controlled stitchers enable these firms to speed production and keep labor costs down.

Industry Organization Although there are about 550 shoe firms operating approximately 1,000 factories in the United States, a few large firms dominate the market. The Brown Group in St. Louis and the U.S. Shoe Company in Cincinnati are the largest producers of women's shoes. The Northeast, especially Massachusetts and Pennsylvania, has the heaviest concentration of shoe producers, followed by the Great Lakes states and the St. Louis area.

Some companies buy production time in overseas factories. Others own facilities in Italy, Spain, or South America. For example, the fashion shoe firm Joan and David uses the Martini factories, among the oldest and finest in Italy. Brand names have become important in the shoe industry through the national advertising done by large companies.

Hosiery

Pantyhose, stockings, and socks serve the practical function of keeping legs and feet warm. Women's hose in flesh tones also make legs look attractive. The fashion for pattern or color on the legs is cyclical and does not necessarily coincide with skirt lengths. Decorative legs were fashionable with the mini of the mid-1960s as well as with the longer skirt lengths of the late '70s. The popularity of fashion socks as a sportswear accessory was an interesting feature of the '70s. The development of pantyhose in the 1960s substantially added to the growth of the hosiery industry.

Production Hosiery is produced in knitting mills whose machines run 24 hours a day. Most hosiery mills perform all steps in production, although some smaller mills contract out the finishing processes. Full-fashioned hosiery is shaped as it is knitted, fulfilling size and length specifications. Pantyhose are knit on circular knitting machines; stockings are flat-knit and then seamed. The steps involved in hosiery production are knitting, dyeing, boarding (a heat-setting process), pairing (for stockings), brand stamping or labeling, and packaging.

There are aproximately 800 hosiery mills in the United States, located primarily in North Carolina, other southern states, and Pennsylvania. This second largest accessories industry, like the footwear industry, is dominated by huge firms. These firms, also part of the textile industry, include Burlington, Cannon, and J. P. Stevens.

Jewelry

There are basically two types of jewelry: fine and costume.

Fine Jewelry Fine jewelry is costly because of the precious materials and craftsmanship that go into it. Because fine jewelry is often a lifetime investment, its design tends to be classic. Walter Hoving, chairman of Tiffany's says, "There is no fashion in jewelry . . . only style." [2] Only precious metals such as gold, platinum, and some silver are used to make fine jewelry. Recent fluctuations of metal costs have made pricing difficult for the jewelry industry. Since precious metals in their pure state are too soft to retain shape or to hold stones securely, they are combined with other metals. Gold content is expressed in *karats*; 24 karats is pure gold; 14 karats is 58.3 percent gold. New York, Italy, and France are international centers for the creation of fine gold work. Goldsmiths use these precious metals to create jewelry and make settings for precious gems.

Precious gems are hard natural stones selected for their beauty. Gemstones (a category formerly divided into precious and semiprecious) include diamonds, rubies, emeralds, sapphires, alexandrites, aquamarines, topazes, tourmalines, garnets, jade, opals, lapis lazuli, coral, turquoise, and natural pearls. Their cost depends on their clarity, color, rarity, and size. The weight of gemstones is measured in *carats*, a standard unit of 200 milligrams (the term *carat* comes from the seeds of the carob tree that were once used to balance the scales weighing gems).

Diamonds have traditionally been the most valuable and coveted of gems, as Lorelei Lee sang in "Diamonds are a Girl's Best Friend." Diamonds are the strongest natural element known to man; a diamond can be cut only with another diamond. Eighty-five percent of the world's diamond production is controlled by DeBeers, a huge South African conglomerate.

Transparent stones such as diamonds and aquamarines are cut by a *lapidary* (stonecutter) into symmetrical facets to show off their beauty. At least fifty percent of a rough gem is wasted in cutting! [3] *Cabachon* stones—the unclear stones such as jade, opal, and coral—are domed, carved, or left in their natural state. Cabachon rubies and sapphires are also treated this way, a process that results in star rubies

[2] "Jewels and Gems," *W*, May 9–16, p. 34.

[3] Ibid., p. 38.

and sapphires. Although computers have recently been developed to cut gemstones, it is by and large still a craftsman's field. Major stonecutting centers are in Antwerp, Belgium; Tel Aviv, Israel; London; New York City; and Idar-Oberstein, Germany.

Costume Jewelry There are two types of costume jewelry: traditional and fashion jewelry. Traditional costume jewelry simulates fine jewelry, using base metals such as brass, aluminum, copper, tin, lead, or chromium, coated or bonded with gold or silver. Fashion jewelry also utilizes materials such as wood, plastics, leather, beads, glass, or clay. Fashion jewelry is often colorful and styles change seasonally.

Bridge jewelry is a category of better costume jewelry to bridge the gap between the cost of fine jewelry and less expensive costume jewelry. This group includes "vermeil," a process of electroplating gold over silver (a new meaning given to the name of an old hand-rubbing process).[4]

"Gold" costume jewelry is either gold filled or gold electroplated. *Gold-filled* jewelry is made from a thin metal sheet (usually brass) that is mechanically bonded with a very thin film of gold on either side (a sandwich). When shapes are cut or stamped out of the sheet, the edges must be covered with gold. *Electroplating* utilizes an electric deposition method to coat the metal piece with gold.

There are approximately 750 costume jewelry

[4] Steffan Aletti, Editor, *American Jewelry Manufacturer*, interview, March, 1980.

firms in the United States. Production is predominately in New England (especially around Providence, Rhode Island) and the Middle Atlantic States.

Jewelry Production There are as many techniques of making jewelry as there are jewelry types. Craftsmen use various methods including carving, grinding, drilling, filing, and hammering metal into desired shapes and perhaps welding parts together. There are also many ways to mass produce jewelry using metal sheet, metal cast in molds, and wire.

Flat shapes are usually stamped out of *metal sheet* and may be decorated with embossing or engraving.

In *casting*, rubber molds are used for low temperature metals, such as tin alloys, and *lost wax casting* is used on high temperature metals, such as gold, silver, and brass (for both fine and costume jewelry). In the latter method, wax is first formed in the rubber mold and a new plaster mold is made over the wax forms. The wax is then burned out and molten metal is forced into the plaster mold. Finally, the plaster mold can be broken open to expose the shaped pieces of metal, which are then snipped off of a supporting tree structure and polished.

Wire is used to make chains and various necklaces and bracelets. Band rings may also be made by slicing tubes of metal. Various components are usually welded together. Designs may be applied with enamel. Enamel work is distinguished by the way it is applied, such as cloisonné, champlevé, basse taille, or painted.

A Tiffany jeweler solders a platinum ring in the firm's jewelry workshop. *(Courtesy of Tiffany & Co.)*

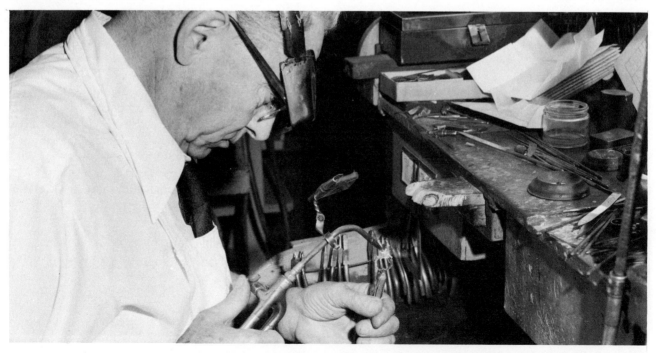

SUMMARY

Fur and accessory manufacturing were discussed separately due to the specialized production methods used in these areas.

There are two methods of fur production: skin-on-skin and letting-out. Because the latter is especially tedious and time consuming, coats and other fur garments made by the letting-out method are more expensive.

The following are the steps in production of a luxury fur coat:

1. *Buy furs in Scandinavia, the Soviet Union, Canada, the United States, or elsewhere.*
2. *Process the pelts by dressing and sometimes by dyeing for use in a few garments.*
3. *Create or buy the desired designs.*
4. *Cut skins, often using the letting-out method.*
5. *Sew skins together in strips.*
6. *Sew strips into sections.*
7. *Dampen the skins, stretch them, nail them to a wooden board to fit the pattern, and let them dry.*
8. *Sew the sections together to form a garment.*
9. *Glaze the furs to increase luster; comb to arrange all the hairs in the desired direction.*
10. *Sew in the lining and labels; apply final touches.*

Fashion accessories too are an important part of the total fashion picture. The design, production, and marketing of each category of accessory constitute a separate industry. Fashion in accessories is cyclical, usually related to apparel styling. Most of the manufacturers are small firms because of the craftsmanship involved in production. However, the shoe and hosiery industries are dominated by large companies.

CHAPTER REVIEW

CHAPTER OBJECTIVES

After reading this chapter you should be able to

A. Give evidence of having attained competence in the following areas:
   1. Ability to explain the differences between the skin-on-skin method and the letting-out method of fur garment production 2. Ability to give examples of functional aspects and fashion aspects of accessories 3. Ability to describe production methods used in each type of accessory 4. Knowledge of production centers

B. Define the following terms and concepts in relation to their discussion in the chapter:
   1. Skin-on-skin method 2. Letting-out method 3. Fur labeling 4. Accessories 5. Hats 6. Millinery 7. Handbags 8. Dummy handbag 9. Clicker machine 10. Belts 11. Gloves 12. Footwear 13. Lasts 14. Hosiery mills 15. Full-fashioned hosiery 16. Pantyhose 17. Goldsmith 18. Fine jewelry 19. Costume jewelry 20. Lapidary 21. Gemstones 22. Cabachon stones

Questions for Review

1. Why has fur manufacturing remained free of mass production techniques?
2. Discuss the differences between the two main fur manufacturing methods.
3. Why must an accessory manufacturer pay close attention to fashion forecasts?
4. Explain the complexities involved in shoe production.
5. Explain the importance of changing fashion on the costume jewelry market. Why does it have a smaller effect on the fine jewelry market?

PROJECTS FOR ADDITIONAL LEARNING

1. Arrange to visit a local furrier or the fur salon in a department or specialty store. A furrier may be able to demonstrate the letting-out process. Ask to see and feel a variety of furs. Note the fashion styling of today's furs.

2. Visit the hat department of a local specialty store. Note the differences between *hats* and *millinery*, and the variations between functional and fashion styling. How do the millinery looks tie in with the apparel trends in the store?

3. Look for shoe advertisements or editorial photos in a fashion magazine. Collect pictures of five popular dressy styles and five popular casual or sport styles, How has function affected styling?

WHOLESALE FASHION MARKETS AND DISTRIBUTION

12

Salon International
du Prêt-à-Porter Féminin.
*(Courtesy of the French
Apparel Center, New York)*

Wholesale markets are the means of distributing
the manufacturer's finished products to retailers.
A market can be any of several things: a potential
demand, a place, an area, or even a period of time.

A market is people, or a potential demand for a
product. In earlier chapters we discussed consumer
demand and market research. Manufacturers must
know whether there is a market for their product.
Conversely, they must develop a product to
answer demand.

A market is a place where sellers and buyers
meet to transact business. In this chapter we refer
specifically to the wholesale fashion market,
where the sellers represent fashion manufacturers
and the buyers are fashion retailers. For convenience,
fashion markets have located close to suppliers
and manufacturers; therefore, most market
centers are also production centers.

A market is also an area. We refer to the
domestic market (the United States), to the regional
markets within it, and to the international market.
This chapter discusses international fashion
centers and their role in buying and selling on the
wholesale level.

A market can even be a time. Although it is
usually possible to buy year round, specific
weeks are scheduled for openings or for the purpose
of bringing buyers and sellers together. For this
reason, a market calendar is also included in this
chapter.

All four definitions of the term market are
included in the concept of fashion marketing.
Marketing refers to the entire process of selling and
buying, including the research, planning, promotion,
and distribution of goods. Earlier, we covered the
demand aspect of fashion marketing in the
consumer demand chapter, market research in the
fashion research and analysis chapter, and product
development in the design chapter. An
understanding of marketing helps to explain the
interrelationship and the interdependence of one
phase of manufacturing with another and of each
level of the industry with the others.

INTERNATIONAL MARKETS

After each manufacturer's collection or line is
designed and duplicated, it must be presented to retail
buyers so that they can buy it for their stores. This
presentation can be accomplished by various means,
including fashion shows, market weeks, and contacts with sales representatives. The terms *collection
opening* and *line release* are nearly synonymous: both
signal the first opportunity for buyers to see fashion
merchandise for a new season. Collection openings
are held by important fashion houses, especially
those in Europe, and involve gala showings. The term
line release is used by other fashion manufacturers
to indicate that their new seasonal lines are ready.

European Collection Openings

In Europe, collection openings are held twice a
year; deliveries are staggered so that new merchandise arrives periodically in the stores, to capture customer interest. Internationally, the most well-known
collections are the French *prêt-à-porter*, shown in
Paris in April and October. France's biggest export
markets are Belgium and West Germany, followed
by the United States.[1] Buyers of better merchandise
and journalists from all over the world flock to see
the individual showings of designers such as Karl
Lagerfeld and Sonia Rykiel. These fashion shows are
by invitation only and have become very theatrical,
creating high excitement. Most buyers see ten shows
a day, from early morning until late at night. Buyers
interested in more moderately priced fashion, and
those who want to look for new sources, also attend
the *Salon du Prêt-à-Porter Féminin*, a market at the
Porte de Versailles, with 1,500 exhibitors of women's
apparel and accessories.

The Paris shows are generally preceded by
shows in Milan and followed by collection openings
in London. A buyer would need two to three weeks
to see the shows in all three cities. After analyzing
the collections from the point of view of their stores'
needs, buyers place orders, usually through commissionaires (representatives).

[1] "Prêt à Porter Féminin," a brochure published by the Federation Française du Prêt à Porter Feminin, Paris, 1979, p. 2.

Couture Collection Showings The French couture, the Italian *alta moda*, and the Spanish *alta costura* show spring–summer collections in January and fall–winter collections in July, although the couture showings no longer have their former impact on world fashion. In France, the haute couture (members of the Federation Française de la Couture who qualify for the Couture-Creation designation) are required to show a minimum of 75 models, or sample styles. After the openings, each house must have 45 showings a year for its private clients, which means an average of two or three showings per week.

The Federation registers all models to protect against copying, but it is difficult to control copying, especially of clothes made outside France. To see the collections, buyers pay a *caution fee* of several hundred to several thousand dollars, which is deducted from the cost of any purchases they make. The rights to copy couture designs include the original sample, a sketch, a photograph, and a pattern and cost two to five times the price charged a private customer for a single garment.

Market Weeks

After the collection openings are held in their respective fashion centers, market weeks are held in other cities. Market weeks were created to bring together manufacturers' sales forces and retail buyers. Market weeks are an excellent opportunity for the manufacturer to reach new stores and establish new accounts. They help retailers who want to shop the lines, looking for new resources. They are a convenient way for buyers to see a variety of merchandise. Market weeks are held in hotels or in specially built market buildings. The market week can last from three days to two weeks. During this time many promotional activities such as fashion shows take place.

There are collection openings, fashion fairs, or market weeks going on somewhere the year around. The German fashion fairs—Igedo in Düsseldorf, *Mode-Woche* (Fashion Week) in Munich, and Interchic in Berlin—have developed into important markets because they represent international manufacturers, presenting a cross section of European and even worldwide fashion merchandise. Shows of im-

TABLE 12–1 IMPORTANT INTERNATIONAL FASHION MARKETS

A calendar of the approximate dates of the world's most important apparel fairs and market weeks (dates vary somewhat each year)

JANUARY

MIPEL (leather goods)	Milan
Iberpiel (leather goods)	Madrid
Hellenic Fashion Fair (R-T-W)	Athens
Tokyo Fashion Week	Tokyo
Hong Kong Fashion Week	Hong Kong
New York R-T-W collections (summer)	New York
Los Angeles R-T-W collections (summer)	Los Angeles
Alta Moda presentations (spring)	Rome
Couture collections (spring)	Paris
Pitti Bimbo (children's wear)	Florence

FEBRUARY

European Men's Wear Show (SEHM)	Paris
Salon de la Maille (knitwear)	Paris
Salon de la Mode Enfantine (children's wear)	Paris
Pitti Uomo (men's wear)	Florence
Mait (knitwear)	Florence
Modamaglia (Italian knitwear)	Bologna
Scandinavian Men's Wear Fair	Copenhagen
International Men's Fashion Week	Cologne
Israel Fashion Week	Tel Aviv
International Men's and Boys' Wear Exhibition (IMBEX)	London
MESH (footwear)	Naples

MARCH

New York R-T-W collections (early fall)	New York
Los Angeles R-T-W collections (early fall)	Los Angeles
IGEDO (R-T-W)	Düsseldorf
Scandinavian Fashion Week (women's R-T-W, fall)	Copenhagen
International Fashion Fair	Stockholm

MARCH OR APRIL

Alta Moda R-T-W, knitwear, and fur collections	Milan

MARCH OR APRIL (*Continued*)

Pitti Donna (women's R-T-W for fall–winter)	Florence
Prêt-à-Porter (women's R-T-W collections for fall–winter)	Paris
Salon de la Fourrure (furs)	Paris
London Fashion Week, Collections, and Exhibition (women's R-T-W collections for fall–winter)	London
Mode-Woche (International Fashion Week)	Munich

APRIL

Premier Vision (fabrics)	Paris
International Fur Fair	Frankfurt
IGEDO (women's R-T-W)	Düsseldorf
Interchic	Berlin

APRIL OR MAY

New York R-T-W collections (fall)	New York
Los Angeles R-T-W collections (fall)	Los Angeles

MAY

Ideacomo (clothing fabrics)	Como
British Fabric Federation Exhibition	London
Interstoff	Frankfurt

JUNE

International Leathergoods Exhibition	Brussels
MIPEL (leather goods)	Milan
ESMA-Eurotricot (European Knitwear Exhibition)	Milan
Hellenic Fashion Fair	Athens

JULY

MESH (footwear)	Naples
Tokyo Fashion Fair	Tokyo
Hong Kong Fashion Week	Hong Kong
Couture collections (fall–winter)	Paris
Alta Moda presentations (fall–winter)	Rome

AUGUST

New York R-T-W collections (holiday)	New York
Los Angeles R-T-W collections (holiday)	Los Angeles
Scandinavian Men's Wear Fair	Copenhagen
International Men's Fashion Week	Cologne
Israel Fashion Week	Tel Aviv
Pitti Bimbo (children's wear)	Florence

SEPTEMBER

European Men's Wear Show (SEHM)	Paris
Salon de la Maille (knitwear)	Paris
Salon de la Mode Enfantine (children's wear)	Paris
Modamaglia (knitwear)	Bologna
IGEDO (women's R-T-W)	Düsseldorf
Scandinavian Fashion Week (women's R-T-W)	Copenhagen
Pitti Uomo (men's wear)	Florence
International Fashion Fair	Stockholm

OCTOBER

Mode-Woche (International Fashion Week)	Munich
Alta Moda R-T-W collections (for spring)	Milan
Pitti Donna (women's R-T-W for spring)	Florence
Prêt-à-Porter (women's R-T-W for spring–summer)	Paris
Salon de la Fourrure (furs)	Paris
IGEDO (women's R-T-W, four times a year)	Düsseldorf
London Fashion Week, Collections, and Exhibition	London
Interchic	Berlin
Premiere Vision (fabrics)	Paris

NOVEMBER

New York R-T-W collections (spring)	New York
Los Angeles R-T-W collections (spring)	Los Angeles
Ideacomo (fabrics)	Como
Interstoff (fabrics)	Frankfurt

ported men's clothing are held in Paris, Florence, London, Cologne, and Copenhagen in February and again in August or September. Fur fairs are held only once a year, in March or April, in Milan, Paris, and Frankfurt. Most accessory shows are held twice a year, in January and June.

The Showroom

A *showroom* is a room where manufacturers' sales representatives show samples to prospective buyers. In France it is called a *salon des presentations* (presentation room). In high fashion salons, fashions are shown on models; in medium- to lower-priced apparel showrooms, clothes are displayed on hangers. The showroom is outfitted with display racks, sometimes mounted on the walls for greater visibility, and with tables and chairs for the clients' comfort. The showroom receptionist often doubles as a model to show the buyer how garments might look on a customer. Showrooms provide continual exposure for the line. The showroom can be located on the same premises as the factory or in a mart (an office building designated as a fashion-selling center). It can also be "created" in a hotel room or market week pavilion.

A showroom at the Salon du Prêt-à-Porter.
(Courtesy of the French Apparel Center, New York)

SEHM Menswear Market *(Courtesy of the French Apparel Center, New York)*

IMPORTS AND EXPORTS

Imports

Many marketing experts and proponents of free trade (trade without restrictions) believe that in the long run it would be best if world trade were based on specialization. That is, each nation would contribute to the world market what it produces best at the most reasonable cost. In this way consumers would obtain the most value for their money as well as a wide choice of merchandise from around the world. Today's consumers demand choice because they are more widely traveled and have therefore been exposed to a variety of merchandise.

The United States has long imported fashion from Paris, woolens from the British Isles, sweaters from Scandinavia, and leather goods from Italy. The American Textile Manufacturers Institute reports that approximately 30 percent of the apparel sold in the United States is imported. However, in recent years there has been a great deal of controversy regarding imports.

By way of background, we should explain that there are two kinds of imports. The first type, referred to above, is the *importation of fashion merchandise* designed and produced by foreign manufacturers and purchased by retailers at international markets. The second type of imports is *overseas production* contracted by American manufacturers mainly to reduce costs. (We discussed this type of production in chapter 10.) The controversy revolves around two key points: the balance of trade and the loss of jobs in the United States.

Balance of Trade The balance of trade is how much a country exports compared to how much it imports. Ideally, the two figures should be about equal. Lately, however, the United States has been importing much more than it exports, sending American dollars abroad to pay for these goods. To try to offset this imbalance, duties (taxes) are levied on imports. However, even with the duty, many imports can still be purchased for less than the same merchandise produced domestically.

Labor Versus Free Trade The second controversy, between labor and proponents of free trade, concerns the second type of imports—various methods of offshore or overseas production. Labor unions complain that overseas production steals from their members thousands of jobs in apparel production. Conversely, retailers argue that workers overseas produce quality merchandise at lower prices, offering American consumers a wider choice. Because both arguments have validity, a solution to the problem will not be easy.

Exports

Some American manufacturers sell their merchandise to foreign retailers either through direct export or by licensing arrangements. Import and export duties have kept this business small in the past, but as the United States dollar loses value relative to other currencies, exporting becomes profitable. In some cases the government offers incentives such as tax breaks, tax deferral, and low-interest credit rates, to make exports even more attractive. For these reasons American fashions are beginning to be seen abroad.

DOMESTIC MARKETS

American Line Releases

American women's better fashion line releases usually occur five times a year: in January for summer, in March for transitional (early fall), in April or May for fall, in August or September for holiday, and in October or November for spring. Children's wear, formerly shown only twice a year, has now become so fashion oriented that it is shown five times a year, often at the same time as women's wear.

Men's wear is traditionally shown twice a year, for fall and spring. However, releases are becoming less structured as men's fashion becomes more style oriented. The Clothing Manufacturers Association holds its tailored suit and coat market week for fall in late January or February and for spring in late August or early September. The National Association of Men's Sportswear Buyers shows fall lines in March or early April and spring lines in October. The American fur shows are held in New York during June. Most accessory market weeks are held twice a year, for spring and fall.

Name designer collection openings in the United States are accompanied by shows, as they are in Europe, and are covered by the press. Better and updated fashion firms hold their line releases closer to the selling season than do firms that produce volume merchandise. Some knock-off producers, on the other hand, may have no official line release at all, waiting to copy other manufacturers' styles and sell to stores very close to the retail selling season.

New York

New York remains the fashion market capital of the United States. The showrooms of some of the Seventh Avenue manufacturers are located in the same buildings as their design workrooms. Showrooms are generally housed in buildings in the garment district, according to merchandise classification and price range. For example, the prestigious addresses of

530 and 550 Seventh Avenue have traditionally housed high fashion companies. The specialty at 512 Seventh Avenue has traditionally been women's coats and suits. Broadway houses showrooms for moderately priced women's wear. Many sportswear showrooms are located at 1407, 1410, and 1411 Broadway. Medium-priced missy and junior dresses are found at 1400 Broadway. Lingerie and intimate apparel are centered around Madison Avenue. Children's wear showrooms are grouped around 34th Street and Sixth Avenue. The men's suit market is divided, with one group between 23rd and 28th Streets and another in the Forties and Fifties. One large building at 1290 Avenue of the Americas has showrooms representing approximately 75 percent of domestically produced men's clothing. The Empire State Building houses showrooms of men's furnishings.

The grouping by apparel type was organized for the convenience of the buyer who has no time to travel all over town, yet must see everything offered in a particular category and price range. As part of New York City's revitalization efforts, a new apparel mart on 42nd Street has been proposed.

Regional Market Centers

In many newer fashion market centers, such as Dallas, Chicago, and Los Angeles, marts have been built to house nearly all fashion manufacturers' showrooms under one roof. Companies throughout the United States and from some foreign countries are represented in thousands of showrooms. Within these marts too, showrooms are grouped according to category for the buyers' convenience. For example, men's and boys' wear showrooms may be grouped together on one floor, women's lingerie on another, and so on.

Although buyers from major fashion stores travel regularly to the New York market, regional centers such as Los Angeles, Chicago, Dallas, and Atlanta have become increasingly important because small store owners have neither the time nor the money to travel to the major markets in New York. Regional markets are also known for local specialties, attuned to their market area. However, many national and a few international manufacturers, as well as local ones, are represented at the regional markets. Regional markets are known more for moderate and budget apparel because of the needs of the stores that buy there.

Los Angeles. Los Angeles has become the nation's second largest fashion market center. The California Mart's first building opened in 1964. Now, with additions, the complex houses 2,000 permanent showrooms of domestic and international manufacturers of women's, men's, and children's apparel and accessories, as well as textiles.

Dallas. The Dallas Apparel Mart is part of the Dallas Market Center Complex. Opened in

The Great Hall of the Dallas Apparel Mart, especially designed for fashion shows. (Courtesy of the Dallas Apparel Mart)

1964, the apparel mart now has 1,650 permanent showrooms and 300 transient showrooms. These showrooms carry 10,000 lines of apparel and accessories representing manufacturers from the Southwest, California, New York, and Europe.

Chicago. The Chicago Mart, owned by the Kennedy family, has approximately 800 permanent showrooms, exhibiting 4,000 lines of women's and children's apparel and accessory lines from the Midwest, New York, and Europe.

Atlanta. The Atlanta Apparel Mart houses 1,000 permanent showrooms representing manufacturers from the South, East, New York, and Europe in men's, women's, and children's apparel and accessories.

Other regional marts are the Denver Merchandise Mart, Colorado; the Carolina Trade Mart, Charlotte, North Carolina; the Miami Merchandise Mart, Florida; the Northeast Trade Center, Woburn, Massachusetts; the San Francisco Mart, California; Radisson Center, Minneapolis, Minnesota; and the Trade Center, Kansas City, Missouri.

All the regional fashion marts offer year-round market weeks, fashion shows, and buyer seminars on subjects such as visual merchandising, management workshops, and fashion show production. Other facilities include restaurants, auditoriums, hotels, hair salons, health clubs, printing services, and parking. The Chicago Apparel Mart even advertises its own gas pump for the buyers' use.

The Dallas Market Center brochure describes the value of a fashion mart:

> Over 435,000 professional buyers come to the Dallas Market Center each year. They come to:
> Buy merchandise
> Look for new sources of supply
> Compare a wide variety of merchandise
> Study market conditions
> Observe changes in style
> See what other buyers are doing
> Get display ideas from showroom displays
> Obtain promotion and advertising ideas
> Seek special terms and purchases
> Consult with manufacturers
In short, they come to compete.

SELLING

The Sales Representative's Role

The actual selling of manufactured goods to retail buyers is done by sales representatives. A line may be wonderfully merchandised and designed, but the sales rep still must communicate its concept to the buyer. Some large companies, such as Levi Strauss, employ a salaried sales staff. Most, however, use independent sales representatives who may carry one or more noncompeting lines. They are paid on commission ranging from 5 percent to 10 percent and averaging 7 percent. Commission is usually paid on orders actually shipped to and accepted by the stores. (Some orders are taken that cannot be filled or that are canceled or returned.) Most commissioned sales representatives pay all their expenses, including part of showroom or market costs, which can run as high as one-third of their income. Sales reps work out of New York or within the geographical territory they cover. Independent sales reps belong to sales representatives' associations that, among other services, hold market weeks.

After a line release, sales reps receive duplicate samples and sketches of the line. First they show these to a few key buyers who have a reputation for picking styles that sell well, to obtain their reactions. Then they show the line to major stores and to the manufacturer's major customers. This is often done even before official collection showings, in the hope of reaching buyers before their budgets are spent. Then the rep takes the line on the road to market weeks around the country and to towns and cities within the salesperson's territory. The rep usually sets up a presentation in a centrally located hotel room, where buyers from the area can come to see the line. Manufacturers' representatives rarely have time to visit each store personally, but they may do it to win a new account.

Apparel salespersons must understand their product, the entire industry, marketing, the economy, and the needs of retail stores. Salespeople try to establish contacts and a customer following. A good salesperson can give the manufacturer valuable information about retail needs and line evaluation for the purpose of production control.

Distribution Policy

Prices and quality must be at the proper level to attract target customers and, therefore, certain types of retail stores. For example, manufacturers of better clothing—those garments made with expensive fabrics and detailed workmanship—sell to better department stores and fine specialty shops. Boutiques may even be created within the stores to carry one line exclusively. Moderate-priced manufacturers sell to a wider variety of department and specialty stores. Popular and budget line manufacturers sell to mail-order, discount, and low-priced specialty stores and chains and to the budget sections of the department stores.

The manufacturer must plan distribution so that the proper stores buy the merchandise, so that the merchandise is represented in desired geographical areas, so that one store does not create unfair competition for another, and so that the estimated business volume is obtained. The manufacturer can decide on an *open distribution* policy (selling to anyone who can pay for the goods), or on a *selected distribution* policy (limiting the number of stores in an area that may buy). Retailers often compete to be allowed to buy designer lines.

Brand Names Manufacturers with national distribution strive for brand name status. The ultimate goal of the manufacturer is to establish the identity of a particular brand to such an extent that consumers prefer their product over all others, sometimes referred to as "consumer franchising." Thus brand name recognition and the resulting consumer demand almost dictate retail buying choices. This practice makes it difficult for other manufacturers in the same product area to compete, because retail budgets are already allocated to the popular producers.

Private Brands Many stores create a form of exclusivity by the use of private brands. The stores commission manufacturers to produce special merchandise just for them. This method fosters customer loyalty because no other store carries the same brand of merchandise, and the customer does not know the manufacturing source. The store puts its label on the merchandise or gives each category of merchandise its brand name. Private brands are used by specialty chain stores, mail-order chains, and department stores, especially for hosiery. Most hosiery producers manufacture both their own brand and unbranded hosiery for a retailer in one mill. Therefore, hosiery manufacturers are often their own competitors.

Vertical Companies One distribution method that requires no selling occurs in vertical companies—companies that both manufacture and retail merchandise. They may even produce the fabric.

Vertical operation is fairly common in the men's wear field but rare in women's wear. Examples in men's wear include Brooks Brothers, Hart Schaffner and Marx, and Richmond Brothers. Several well-known women's couturiers, such as Yves St. Laurent and Ted Lapidus, sell their ready-to-wear lines in their own shops around the world. Laura Ashley, a Welsh firm, produces fabrics, wallpapers, and dresses and sells them in company-owned retail stores around the world. Many shoe manufacturing firms are also

Laura and Bernard Ashley surrounded by their prints.
(Courtesy of Laura Ashley Ltd., Wales, United Kingdom)

vertical. I. Miller and Johnston & Murphy operate chain stores in which they sell their own merchandise.

Factory Outlets In most cases, the only actual retailing done by a manufacturer is in factory outlet stores where the public can buy directly from the company at wholesale prices. However, most of these garments are *overruns* (garments not purchased by a store) or *seconds* (garments with flaws).

Leased Departments Manufacturers often lease space in stores to sell their merchandise. This arrangement, too, requires no selling to a buyer. Leasing space is especially useful in retailing types of apparel whose salespersons need particular expertise. For example, fur and shoe manufacturers often lease departments because their salespersons must have special knowledge of fur origin, processing, and care, or of how to fit shoes.

Franchising In a franchising agreement, a manufacturer sells the rights to retail a product or product line within an area. Manufacturers benefit from this arrangement because the product must be sold under the brand name and merchandised according to their specifications, which protect the manufacturer's image. Retailers benefit because they are guaranteed availability of stock and the right to use the brand name in advertising (supported by the manufacturer's national advertising campaign). However, the store has no rights to selection from the line but must carry the entire range of merchandise, wanted or not.

The Gap stores have a Levi franchise and Estee Lauder cosmetics are franchised to retail stores. In many cases the whole store is franchised, as in the case of the Lady Madonna maternity shops.

Consignment Furs can also be sold on consignment. In this case, the retailer provides only floor space and personnel. The merchandise is lent to the store and the store pays only when the merchandise is sold. The producer takes back any unsold portion and tries to sell it elsewhere. Consignment arrangements are also used by second-hand stores.

The Role of Jobbers In the fashion industry, merchandise is usually sold directly from manufacturers to retailers. The exception is the jobber, a middleman who buys goods from many manufacturers and resells them. These goods can be overruns or markdowns, bought at the end of a season at a large discount to clear the manufacturer's warehouse, or the jobber may speculate, buying goods early in the season and storing them for resale later at a period of peak demand. Some jobbers are also producers in the sense that they have contractors make goods to their specifications.

Aids to Selling
Retailers look for manufacturers whose quality and dependability they can trust. They also look to a manufacturer for a particular identity: each season, retailers expect the same type of clothing or performance from that manufacturer. To establish identity, at least one feature of a manufacturer's product must be better than or different from everyone else's. The fashion industry is one of the most competitive in the Western world. Manufacturers constantly strive to be the best in styling and the best in quality for the price, and to have on-time deliveries.

A Fashion Sell Designer clothes can be sold primarily on the basis of styling.

A Business Sell A manufacturer in the moderate or budget range, however, has to offer even more than styling. Today's moderate or budget line buyer is more a business person than a fashion person. He or she has to make a profit. The manufacturer's sales representative tries to *prove* how his or her line can make a profit for the store. The manufacturer may try to offer the retailer one or more of the following:

Styling and fabrication that the customer will buy

Consistent quality

Continuity of styles (a guarantee that all the styles in the sample line will actually be produced)

Timely deliveries

Reorder performance (there is a trend to less availability of reorders because most manufacturers do not want to take risks on ordering piece goods in advance of orders)

Artificial aids to profit

Off-price or promotional goods (special buys at low prices, either on regular goods after initial orders are in at regular prices, or on goods made at lower cost). Promotional goods are often sold by "directional selling." Since the manufacturer offers goods at lower than regular prices, risks in fabric purchase and cutting must be avoided. Therefore, the manufacturer offers a pre-selected "package" of coordinated sportswear or dresses to the retailer. The buyer must buy the entire package (or multiples of that package) and not make selections from the line as usual.

Credit

Markdown allowances (credit on goods that had to be marked down in the store)

Exchange or return privileges called a "guaranteed sales agreement" (A retailer can return any unsold garments for credit or refund. Only a large manufacturer can afford to do this, and only on the understanding that the retailer buys from that manufacturer again.)

Discount of 8 percent if bills are paid on time

Co-op advertising allowances

Promotional aids such as in-store clinics, designer's trunk shows, and brochures

SALES PROMOTION

Manufacturers use sales promotion as a means of making their merchandise known to prospective retail buyers and to the public. Effective sales promotion can often mean the difference between success and failure. Promotional efforts can take the form of publicity, advertising, and other aids that manufacturers make available to retailers who buy their products.

Publicizing
the New Collection

Publicity spreads fashion information by means of various communication media, yet with no media costs to the manufacturer. Fashion editors of publications and television choose the material they wish to write about from information and photographs sent to them by the manufacturers. Public relations consultants or firms may be hired to plan and carry out publicity.

The Press is anxious to take photographs at the Yves St. Laurent collection opening.

In addition to publicity efforts of individual firms, press weeks are held in conjunction with collection or market week openings. The extensive arrangements for these events are handled by a press attaché, by public relations consultants, or by trade associations. For major collections, invitations must be sent to some 900 journalists the world over, and to the company's good customers.[2] A dossier or press kit must be prepared for each journalist. The kit includes a numbered list of models to be shown, photographs and sketches of a few pieces from the collection, and a press release or analysis of the collection. The analysis must be general, to entice the journalist to come without revealing all the ideas. Of course, the attaché arranges for the photographs to be taken and for the details of the show itself. Public relations is very important in assuring pleasant contacts with the press and with buyers.

Promotional Gimmicks   With so many lines for buyers to remember, manufacturers often use gimmicks to obtain attention for their product. A souvenir may help the buyer remember a certain collection better than all the others. One Paris designer had invitations to the collection opening hand delivered in red satin bags.[3] Other promotional gimmicks include articles that serve as advertisements when worn or carried. The simplest are shopping bags with the manufacturer's name on them. T-shirts with brand names serve the same purpose—joggers in Adidas T-shirts are mobile advertisements.

Advertising
Advertising is the planning, writing, producing, and scheduling of paid announcements to attract potential customers' attention to the manufacturer's merchandise. Many manufacturers advertise in trade publications, such as *Women's Wear Daily, Daily News Record, California Apparel News*, or *Retail Week*, because they wish to reach the retailers who read those publications.

Brand Name Advertising   Large apparel, hosiery, and shoe manufacturers, the biggest fashion advertisers, advertise their names nationally. They use national television and both trade and consumer publications, thereby reaching both consumers and retailers. Advertisements are repeated for brand name

saturation. As a result, consumers learn to buy particular brands. One example is the Jordache jean, riding the waves in a sea of jean manufacturers. Jordache used expensive, sexy advertisements to compete in a market dominated by designer labels and within a few years was shipping 200,000 pairs of jeans a month, at a wholesale cost of $3.5 million.[4]

Co-op Advertising   Many manufacturers cooperate financially with retailers on advertisements, to make the public more aware of brand names. The manufacturers offer money to retailers who advertise their styles. Manufacturers' co-op allocations may provide the retailer with 50 percent of its media advertising costs. Co-op allowances are based on the percentage of net sales to the retailer. Fiber producers are often involved, offering co-op dollars directly to certain retailers. The co-op ads must carry the names and logos (brand or store symbols) of each contributing firm.

Other Promotional Aids to Retailers
Manufacturers often provide retailers with aids they can use in their advertising, publicity, and public relations. A manufacturer may offer one or more of the following to stores that purchase its merchandise:

In-store clinics.   Many manufacturers have discovered that their merchandise sells better if it is thoroughly explained to both salespeople and store customers. Therefore, apparel manufacturers often make an effort to go into stores to train and educate the salespeople and/or the customers with demonstrations, slides, or a talk by a representative of the manufacturer.

Designer trunk shows.   The term originated with the idea of the designer traveling from store to store with a trunk full of clothes. Stores can place special orders on the designer's merchandise for their customers.

Display ideas and fixtures   to enhance visual merchandising.

Statement enclosures   or other mailing pieces for stores to send to customers.

Special retail promotions   to tie in with the manufacturer's advertising campaign.

Glossy photographs   of merchandise to use for publicity or in advertisements.

[2] Claudy Stolz, press attaché, Paris, personal interview, August 1978.

[3] Ibid.

[4] "Topless Jeans Make the Scene," *Time*, September 10, 1979, p. 74.

Educational booklets for salespeople and customers.

Radio scripts and TV commercials that stores can "tag" with their own name and run in their local area.

Reorder forms and even electronic data processing terminals for direct manufacturer contact.

Associations that Promote Fashion

Trade and other associations support manufacturers in many ways as well as promoting their segment of the fashion industry. Important manufacturer trade associations include the American Apparel Manufacturers Association, Inc.; the Men's Fashion Association of America, Inc.; and California Fashion Creators.

The Fashion Group, founded in 1931, fosters the careers of women in the industry. Primarily promotional and educational in purpose, it now has over 5,000 members with regional chapters in 24 American cities and five foreign countries.

Fashion Awards

Fashion awards presented by various organizations generate interest in fashion because of the publicity they create.

In 1942 Eleanor Lambert—America's best-known fashion promoter—organized the Coty Fashion Critics Awards as a means of giving recognition to American designers and of making the public aware of their names.

Neiman-Marcus, an internationally known Texas retailing firm, also gives an annual award based on contribution to fashion, by designing, publicizing, or wearing it in such a way as to influence the public. The awards were instituted in 1938, although none were presented between 1969 and 1972 or 1974 and 1979.

The Council of Fashion Designers of America (CFDA) plans to present annual American Fashion Awards on television. Two committees, of twelve retailers and journalists each, will choose nominees and winners in men's and women's fashion design categories.

ORDERS

Success in the market is measured by both buyer and journalist reaction. The real proof of success, however, comes only with actual written orders, or "paper."

Working between sales and production, the order department processes orders from the sales division, compiling totals for the production department so that it can set up a schedule to meet completion and delivery dates.

When some key orders are in, it becomes evident in only a few weeks which garments will be the best sellers. Every manufacturer hopes for a few "hot" items or best sellers. Profitability is partially a result of volume, especially for moderate- and popular-priced manufacturers. Volume results from large initial orders or reorders. However, not all companies are equipped to handle reorders. High fashion houses do not accept reorders because it would defeat one of their objectives, that of exclusivity.

A style that is not bought in sufficient quantity to make it profitable is dropped from the line. In these cases, fill-in styles may be added to a customer's order. Occasionally the style substitution may be the suggestion—or even the invention—of a buyer or sales representative.

> At Dallas not long ago, a buyer much respected by Peter Goodman [an executive of the family-owned Sportwhirl apparel firm] admired a velveteen blazer. He wished only that it came in a floral print which was on a pair of slacks elsewhere in the line. "We do have it," shot back Goodman. "Number 2023 at $24.75." The buyer wrote his order.
>
> As soon as he was gone, Goodman called his father in New York to say that he had just added a new item, 2023, and that his mother should be sure to order more of the velveteen floral fabric that had been meant only for pants.[5]

Garment industry firms can be very flexible to please their customers.

SUMMARY

The retailer and the manufacturer, two separate businesses, communicate via wholesale markets. Wholesale markets end the manufacturing cycle. Trends and information initially come from these markets, new merchandise is produced, and the merchandise is again presented for sale on the wholesale market.

5 Peter Hellman, "Anatomy of a Garment-Center Firm," *New York Times Magazine*, September 14, 1975, p. 92.

Buyers and the press are interested to see many manufacturers' newest seasonal offerings. Fashion showings and market weeks are held in market centers (most often the same as production centers) all year long, around the world.

Manufacturers have various distribution policies to ensure that their goods are merchandised properly. Working through sales representatives, many offer incentives to retailers to buy their merchandise. They also use public relations, publicity, advertising, and other promotional aids to foster sales.

The final test for fashion merchandise is whether the consumer buys it at the retail level. Each season brings a new chance for success or failure. No wonder the apparel industry is such a challenging, and often nerve-racking, business.

CHAPTER REVIEW

CHAPTER OBJECTIVES

After reading this chapter you should be able to
A. Give evidence of having attained competence in the following areas:
1. Knowledge of the approximate dates and places of at least ten major international markets of apparel, furs, and accessories 2. Understanding of the concept of marketing 3. Ability to explain the importance of markets and market weeks 4. Ability to explain the types of open and selected distribution policies 5. Ability to describe the difference between a fashion sell and a business sell, including aids to selling 6. Ability to discuss the various forms of sales promotion
B. Define the following terms and concepts in relation to their discussion in the chapter:
1. Markets 2. Collection opening or line release 3. Salon du Prêt-à-Porter Feminin 4. Igedo, Interchic, and the Munich Fashion Week 5. Imports 6. Balance of trade 7. Labor versus free trade 8. Market weeks 9. Showroom 10. Mart 11. 530 and 550 Seventh Avenue 12. Sales representative 13. Open distribution policy 14. Selected distribution policy 15. Private brands 16. Vertical companies 17. Factory outlets 18. Leased departments 19. Consignment 20. Jobbers 21. Fashion sell 22. Business sell 23. Continuity of styles 24. Artificial aids to profit 25. Off-price or promotional goods 26. Guarantee sales agreement 27. Dossier or press kit 28. Publicity 29. Advertising 30. Cooperative advertising 31. Brand name advertising 32. In-store clinics 33. Designer trunk shows 34. Coty Fashion Critics Awards 35. "Paper"

Questions for Review

1. Define the terms *market* and *marketing*.
2. What does a retailer look for from a manufacturer?
3. Why did regional fashion markets develop?
4. How does a market week help manufacturers and retailers?
5. How does presentation differ between a high-priced line or collection and moderately or lower-priced lines?

PROJECTS FOR ADDITIONAL LEARNING

1. Analyze the imported fashion merchandise and accessories at a large retail store. Make a list of the countries represented and the merchandise each country specializes in.

2. Interview a local store's fashion buyer. Ask how and when he or she buys fashion merchandise: at a market? From a sales representative? Through a buying office? From a catalog? What type of merchandise is purchased in what way? What is the buyer's favorite method and why? How often does the buyer go to a market center? Which one? Summarize the answers in a written report.

3. Ask a buyer to let you sit in when a sales representative is showing a line. Evaluate the merchandise in terms of the store's needs. Note the buyer's reactions to the line and whether he or she actually writes an order. Summarize your findings in a written report.

4. "Sell" the line you designed in chapter 9 to your class, explaining its features.

THE RETAILING OF FASHION

PART FOUR

RETAIL
STORES

A view of Fifth Avenue,
New York's most famous
shopping street.
(Courtesy of Saks Fifth Avenue)

13

Retailing is the link between the manufacturer and the consumer. Retailers buy fashion merchandise from suppliers and manufacturers all over the world and bring it to their stores for convenient selling to ultimate consumers. Final success in the fashion business is achieved only on the retail level, by consumer acceptance measured in purchases.

Many factors go into the making of a successful retail store: good management, a convenient location, a pleasant atmosphere, exciting stock, buyers with the feel for customer needs, helpful salespeople, and customer service. The first half of this chapter examines the location and types of fashion retail stores, and discusses the organization of single- and multiple-unit stores. The second part of the chapter covers the establishment of a retailer's fashion image and the role of the fashion director in maintaining that image.

LOCATION OF RETAIL STORES

There are nearly 2,000,000 retail firms throughout the United States alone, contributing approximately 40 percent of the total gross national product (the total selling price of services and goods produced). About 110,000 of these retailers specialize in fashion apparel and accessories; another 70,000 include some apparel and accessories among their merchandise. No matter where a person lives, there is at least one retail store nearby. The location of a store is very important in relation to its potential customers. Demographic research is done to determine what location would best attract customers who relate to the store's image and merchandise or, conversely, what image and merchandise would be best to present in a particular area.

Suburban Shopping Centers

The shopping center developed along with suburban living, situated near the highways. Shopping centers account for nearly half the retail sales in the United States. Shopping centers are much the same the world over. The United States has the most, followed by Canada, Australia, England, France, Germany, Sweden, Switzerland, Africa, Japan, and Denmark.[1] The development of the enclosed shopping center has created a kind of department store of independent merchants, giving many more small retailers an opportunity to be successful.[2]

City Stores

With the increasing energy crisis posing a threat to suburban living and shopping, there has been renewed interest in redeveloping the retail potential of cities. Many large cities are conducting vast revitalization projects, including the refurbishing of older department stores and the building of new downtown shopping malls such as the Gallery in Philadelphia. In Europe, cities have continued to be the

[1] Evelyn Grace, *Introduction to Fashion Merchandising* (Englewood Cliffs, N.J.: Prentice-Hall, Inc., 1978), p. 285.

[2] "The Future of Retailing," *Stores Magazine*, January, 1970, p. 7.

Country Club Plaza in Kansas City decorated with lights for the holidays. *(Courtesy of J. C. Nichols Company)*

South Molton Street in London, which has been closed off to motor traffic. *(Photograph by the author)*

centers of fashion retailing. To further encourage successful retailing, many streets have been closed to automobile traffic, creating pleasant walkways between shops.

Around the world certain city streets or city areas have become famous for shopping: Fifth Avenue in New York City, Rodeo Drive in Beverly Hills, Sherbrooke Street and Crescent Street in Montreal, the Faubourg St. Honoré on the Right Bank and the St. Germain district on the Left Bank in Paris, the Via Condotti in Rome, and the Mayfair and Knightsbridge areas of London.

TYPES OF RETAIL OPERATIONS

It would be very difficult for a store to be all things to all people. One store could not afford to carry a broad enough assortment of merchandise in all categories and at all price points. Therefore, there are basically four kinds of fashion retail businesses: department or general merchandise stores, specialty stores, discount stores, and mail-order firms. These range from small stores with one or two employees to giant retail chains with numerous branches and thousands of employees. Ownership of retail stores is discussed in the appendix because the same principles apply to all levels of the industry.

Liberty of London. *(With permission of Liberty and Company, Ltd., Regent Street, London; photograph by the author)*

Department Stores

Stores that carry general merchandise for the home as well as fashion are commonly called department stores. The term "Department Store" comes from the practice of presenting many different kinds of merchandise, each in a separate section or department. Apparel and accessories for men, women, and children are sold along with household goods such as furniture, lamps, linens, cookware, appliances, and televisions. The government defines a department store as one that employs at least 25 people and sells three categories of general merchandise: apparel and accessories, home furnishings, and household linens.

In most cases, a wide selection of merchandise at different price ranges is available. However, department stores are generally strongest at medium price points. Profit structure is geared towards a balance between departments. For example, a designer dress department demands more customer service and, therefore, costs more to run. A store expects less profits from such a department; in fact it is often happy if the department breaks even. Such a department may exist primarily to attract a certain group of customers. On the other hand, a "meat and potatoes" department, such as medium-priced missy sportswear, might be expected to bring in 14 percent profit to balance the lack of profit in the designer department.

Department stores dominate the retail market more in the United States than in Europe, where the traditional small specialty shop still claims the fashion-

Galeries Lafayette, Paris. *(Courtesy of Galeries Lafayette)*

conscious customer. This is especially true in Italy, France, Germany, and Spain. However, London has Harrod's, the largest department store in Europe, as well as Liberty's and Selfridges. Besides their specialty shops, Paris has Galeries Lafayette and Printemps, while Germany has Karstadt, Horten, Kaufhof, and many more. Japan, too, has many department stores, including the world's largest—called Matsuzokaya—and the highly respected Mitsukoshi and Isetan.

New York City has a significant share of the most outstanding department stores in the United States. Bloomingdale's has the most fashionable reputation because of its innovative, contemporary approach to retailing. The fashion concept reaches into every department, from designer apparel boutiques to designer furniture.

Fashion for everyone has been Macy's philosophy as America's largest department store for over half a century. Macy's therefore carries a variety of fashion in a wide range of prices. Other big names in retailing include Abraham and Straus and Gimbel's in New York; Filene's in Boston; John Wanamaker and Strawbridge and Clothier in Philadelphia; J. L. Hudson in Detroit; Marshall Field's in Chicago; Rich's in Atlanta; and Bullocks, the May Company, and The Broadway in California. Canada's largest and best-known department store is Eaton's.

Specialty Stores

Stores that carry one category or related categories of fashion merchandise (often referred to as *single-line* or *limited-line* stores) are commonly called specialty stores or boutiques. *Boutique* is a term adopted from France for the small specialty shop. Henri Bendel is an example of a specialty store in New York City. Bendel's specializes in fashion, eliminating household goods carried by department stores.

Specialty stores generally cater to a particular kind of customer, providing personalized service and unique merchandise specifically for that customer's tastes. The store may cater only to men, women, teens, or children, or just to the professional woman or the sports enthusiast or only to large sizes—there is an unlimited number of possibilities. The specialty may even be as narrow as shirts, shoes, uniforms, or neckties. Most specialty shops buy merchandise within a certain price range as well as in a specific category. A recent market study found that "specialization will increase as retailers target their marketing efforts to capitalize on consumer life style segmentation."[3]

[3] "Emerging Consumer Apparel Trends of the Early 1980s," a Celanese Fibers Marketing Co. study, as quoted by Marvin Klapper, "Imprints," *Women's Wear Daily*, March 27, 1979, p. 57.

Main floor of Saks Fifth Avenue, New York.
(Courtesy of Saks Fifth Avenue)

New York City, because it is the largest city in the United States and the center of the apparel industry, continues to have the most exciting array of fashion specialty stores. Fifth Avenue is synonymous with fashion retailing; Henri Bendel, Bonwit Teller, Saks Fifth Avenue, Bergdorf Goodman, and Lord and Taylor are some of the nation's best-known large specialty stores. Many of these stores also have branches in other parts of the United States.

Other leading fashion specialty stores across the country include Ann Taylor, originally of Boston; Nan Duskin of Philadelphia; Garfinkel's of Washington, D.C.; Halls of Kansas City; Sakowitz of Houston; Neiman-Marcus of Dallas; I. Magnin and Joseph Magnin of San Francisco; Bullocks Wilshire of Los Angeles; and Holt Renfrew of Canada. Large specialty stores have profit structures similar to that of department stores, whereby higher profits of one department balance lower profits of another. In addition, thousands of small specialty shops and boutiques cater only to the clientele in their locality. The small specialty store is important in the overall retailing picture because it offers the customer unique merchandise and personal service.

Discount Stores

A discount store is a limited-service, mass-merchandised retail firm that sells goods below usual prices. The term *discount store* developed after World War II, when certain retail stores claimed they could sell merchandise for less than other retailers because they had *lower overhead* (a term meaning lower operating costs: low rent, less advertising, fewer salespeople, and few customer services). However, today the so-called discount stores have become as complex as some department stores, with just as many sales personnel and at least as much advertising. Discount stores are highly promotional, emphasizing low prices in their advertising. Their major selling point is pricing below the market average, thus making price the motivation for consumer purchases.

Discount store policies and fashion images have become more sophisticated. They buy specially produced, inexpensive lines in very large quantities to keep prices down, or they buy manufacturers' overruns or leftovers at reduced prices. Loehmann's is an example of a well-known fashion discount store.

Mail-Order Retailing

The major mail-order retailers—Sears, Penney's, and Wards—are in a different position from other merchants. Although they do not own their own manufacturing plants, they do work directly with manufacturers in developing the kinds of merchandise they want for their stores. The mail-order giants are able to do this because their size allows them to order in huge quantities. However, this special arrangement demands that they make large inventory commitments way in advance. Because catalogues must be planned almost a year in advance, the mail-order chains are often the first into the piece goods market. Since they are first with the largest orders, their choices can have a big impact on fashion direction for other manufacturers, although their own customers do not see the merchandise until much later.

Years ago, it was feared that as transportation improved and shopping centers sprang up in suburban and rural areas, the mail-order business would dwindle considerably. This is one of the reasons why mail-order firms built retail stores. However, the mail-order business has boomed over the past decade. The fastest growing segment of retailing in the United States, mail orders now account for over 18 percent of all general merchandise sold.[4] Many people dislike the inconvenience of fighting traffic and going from store to store in search of a coordinating wardrobe or the perfect gift. The increasing numbers of working women find that they do not have time to shop—it is easier to order from catalogs at home and to have the merchandise delivered. Sears, Roebuck is the largest retail mail-order firm in the United States, followed by J. C. Penney and Montgomery Ward. Quelle (Kwell-a, meaning source) is the largest mail-order business in Europe.

The increasing popularity of shopping by mail or by phone has spawned a number of new mail-order firms. Roger Horchow, formerly a mail-order executive at Neiman-Marcus, started his own very profitable luxury item catalog business in 1972. In fact, all retailers are finding that mail and phone orders bring them increased business. Bloomingdale's used to put out catalogs just to draw customers into its stores; now mail and phone orders account for a substantial part of its business. Catalogs can be expensive to prepare and distribute, but it costs even more to maintain stores and sales staff. Mail-order firms generally enjoy a profit of 6 percent on sales, whereas conventional retailers make only 3.5 percent.[5] Once on a single mailing list, a consumer is likely to receive dozens of catalogs in the mail.

In Columbus, Ohio, a company called Warner Communications has established a cable TV hookup that, among other things, lets shoppers examine merchandise for sale at home. By means of a special attachment on the set, a viewer can order a product

directly. Warner is so pleased with the results of current hookups that it plans to expand.

Breakdown of Retail Category Distinctions

Distinctions among different kinds of retail stores are breaking down. For instance, mail-order businesses now operate department stores, and vice versa; many department stores have set up boutiques or specialty shops within their establishments; some discount stores have tried trading up. An overlap of price points exists between them. Thus, categorizing retail stores has become complex. Loss of distinction can be dangerous if a store moves out of its price or merchandise assortment niche in the retail market.

CUSTOMER SERVICES

American retailers were pioneers in offering customer services. Years ago, Montgomery Ward and John Wanamaker instituted guaranteed refund policies. Today, some stores offer an increasing number of customer services, such as fashion consulting, no-question return privileges, no-interest credit plans, national credit card acceptance, gift wrapping, free local delivery, and free parking. However, customer service seems to be deteriorating in many stores. Sales people are often unavailable or ignorant of stock; stores do not mail gifts overseas (as they do in Europe); and there are long waiting lines for boxes or gift wrapping. Stores should consider developing a more personal approach toward customer services and perhaps offer multilingual aids for foreigners who visit or live in the United States.

Over the years retail stores, especially those close to suburban residential areas, have been staying open longer in the evenings and on weekends, including Sundays, for the convenience of their customers. Obviously, shopping has become a leisure time activity; Sunday store openings allow the whole family to shop together. On the other hand, some retail employees would rather be home with their families during the evenings and on weekends. European stores are not open on Sundays or in the evenings, and often open only for a half day on Saturdays. This situation and the fact that European vacations are longer than ours reflect a different approach to life.

Leased Departments

To provide additional services for their customers, many stores lease certain departments to an outside organization better able to handle a particular

---

[4] "Is the Store Becoming Obsolete?" *Time*, November 27, 1978, p. 94.

[5] Ibid.

specialty. Leased departments in retail stores are merchandised, owned, and operated by an outside firm rather than by the store itself. The public is not aware of this, however, because the leased department fits the store's overall image. Services commonly leased are restaurants, hair dressing salons, shoe repair, and jewelry repair. In addition, some merchandise departments are leased, especially furs, millinery, shoes, and fine jewelry. For example, the French shoe firm of Charles Jordan leases departments in several American specialty and department stores.

SINGLE- AND MULTIPLE-UNIT STORES

Retail stores can be classified as *single-unit* (one store only) or *multiple-unit* (more than one store) operations. Department, specialty, discount, and variety stores may be found at either level.

Single-Unit Stores

Single-unit stores comprise over 84 percent of retail establishments and do nearly 53 percent of all retail business.[6] There are many thousands of single-unit stores; a notable example is Henri Bendel in New York. Many other stores, like Bendel's, prefer to be the one and only.

Multiple-Unit Stores

A natural outgrowth of the successful single-unit stores; a notable example is Henri Bendel in New only 13 percent of the 2,000,000 American retailers have more than one store, those multiple-unit stores are responsible for more than 40 percent of all retail business in the United States.[7]

There are two types of multiple-unit retail organizations: chain stores and department store groups. The fine differentiations between them have to do with organizational and operational policies.

Chain Store Organization The image of each store in chain organization is basically uniform with that of the others. All are merchandised from a central office, either in the flagship store (the largest and most representative store in the chain) or in a separate office building such as the Sears Tower in Chicago.

Many national and regional specialty stores such as Saks and I. Magnin, and mail-order retailers such as Sears, Wards, and J. C. Penney, have chain organizations. Because the term *chain* has been associated with low-priced merchandise, many specialty stores simply call themselves national specialty stores, even though they are structured as chains.

Department Store Groups Many department stores are members of group organizations consisting of a parent store with multiple satellite branches. Most of these are major department stores that originated many years ago in downtown areas of various cities, and later opened branches in outlying suburbs to serve customers who enjoy the convenience of shopping closer to home.

Department store groups are also centrally merchandised, usually from the parent store. The parent or flagship store is usually the focal point of the group, carrying a wider assortment of merchandise than the branch stores. Examples include Macy's (the east and west coast stores are in separate divisions) and John Wanamaker.[8]

The success of the multiple-unit store is based on its ability to buy in large quantities and to distribute the basic operating costs throughout the organization. Although buying is done from a central headquarters, allowances are made for regional differences. A store in Connecticut, for example, would need more heavy outerwear in winter than would a store in Pasadena, California. Centrally purchased merchandise is distributed to all stores from a central or regional distribution center.

ORGANIZATION WITHIN A STORE

Retailing functions are generally divided into five areas of responsibility:

Merchandising has the responsibility for planning, buying, and selling merchandise.

Store operations maintains the retailer's building, protects the store and merchandise, provides customer services, and coordinates the movement of goods and people within the building.

Sales promotion informs customers about the goods and services available through advertisements, displays, publicity, special events, and public relations (see chapter 15).

[6] "Firm Size in the United States," *Retail Trade, 1972 Special Report* (Washington, D.C.: U.S. Government Printing Office, 1976), p. xxv.

[7] Ibid.

[8] Philip Schlein, President, Macy's California, interview, September 12, 1979.

Finance and control keeps records of money spent and received: accounts payable (goods received but not yet paid for), payroll, taxes, credit (customers' charge accounts), and inventory.

Personnel staffs the store with qualified and trained people to handle all the work that needs to be done.

The Small Store

In a small store, all the retailing functions may be carried out by a manager and a few assistants. Small stores can offer their customers very personalized service such as wardrobe and figure problem advice, alterations, personally selected fashions, and special orders from the manufacturer. Small store owners have the unique opportunity of being so close to their customers that they are able to change their merchandise or image quickly, as the need arises. Because the small store has less inventory, it is more easily altered to keep abreast of the times. Its displays can also be changed in a short time, creating new and interesting looks for customers.

The typical small store is often run by one person, usually the owner, who assumes many roles in the store's operation—such as manager, buyer, salesperson, stockperson, bookkeeper, and even janitor. Not a glamorous job, it takes an enormous amount of ingenuity, hard work, and long hours. However, building a successful business can be very rewarding.

In some cases, several people jointly run a store, each assuming the responsibility for the jobs he or she is most capable of doing. Problems occur, however, when the people involved have different goals or inadequate experience. As a result, there are many failures among small stores.

The Large Store

In larger stores, the retailing functions are divided among people who become specialized in the performance of their respective jobs. The function of the management team is to make sure the store runs smoothly. There may be a board of directors and/or a president, depending on the ownership (see appendix).

Owner Sydney Burstein works alongside buyers and sales people at Brown's, a well-known designer shop in London. *(Photograph by the author)*

Several vice-presidents or top-level executives are usually in charge of the various functional responsibilities, such as merchandising, operations, sales promotion, personnel, and finances. The larger the store or chain of stores, the more complex the organizational structure becomes. However, each function relates to the others, and communication is the key to keeping all facets of the business running smoothly.

Usually, merchandising responsibilities are divided between two chains of command. The buying line of management has the responsibility for merchandise content and assortment while the store line is responsible for sales as well as operations. Although the individuals who buy merchandise (the buying line) are concerned with sales, the individuals who are responsible for sales (the store line) have nothing to do with their purchase.

THE STORE LINE

The director of stores (a vice president or general manager) has the responsibility for the store line. He or she oversees individual store managers in multiple-unit organizations. The main responsibility of these people is to merchandise their respective stores (to make sure that the buyer is ordering the right goods in the proper quantities for their store) and to produce positive sales results. Everything and everyone in the operation of the store must be organized to achieve this goal. Store managers delegate responsibilities to group sales managers (floor or area managers) who in turn supervise department managers. Department managers and their assistants run the department and supervise sales people.

THE BUYING LINE

Merchandise is segmented into divisions such as women's better sportswear or men's furnishings. Several divisions are grouped together under the direction of a general merchandise manager (GMM). In some cases, related areas are grouped together, sometimes not. A GMM for women's ready-to-wear, for instance, might direct several divisional merchandise managers who are in charge of missy dresses, missy sportswear, junior dresses, junior sportswear, and so on. Or merchandise divisions may simply be grouped together by floor; all of the merchandise on one floor of the store may be under one divisional merchandise manager.

Each division is composed of departments. For example, accessories is subdivided into handbags, hosiery, hats, jewelry, and so on. Each department is further segmented into classifications. Missy dresses might be divided into better, moderate, and budget price groupings. The buyer is responsible for the success, measured in profits, of a classification or department, depending on their volume. Responsibility for sales differs between specialty, chain, and department stores. The buying line must do all the planning and activities necessary to bring the right merchandise into the store at the right time to satisfy the store's customers.

THE STORE IMAGE

Each store must decide on which potential customers it wants to reach and how it wants to reach them. Whether setting up a new store or reevaluating an existing one, management must study the type of people who live in the community, their life styles, and ultimately their shopping wants and needs. Then management must determine how to fill these wants and needs.

Target Customers

The first step in reaching potential customers is to define exactly who they should be. No retail store can be all things to all people; it must select one or a few groups of people to serve. *Target customers* is the term for the group of consumers the store wishes to attract. A group of target customers is within a general age range, has similar life styles, and therefore has similar tastes. Their tastes can also be identified with the acceptance stages of a fashion cycle—whether they are fashion leaders or fashion followers.

If a store wishes to cater to the tastes of several groups, it will direct the merchandising of particular departments to appeal to each group. For example, the women's wear styling categories (designer, missy, contemporary, and junior) appeal to different customer groups and are separated by store departments.

Defining the Store Image

A clear definition of a store's character is of prime importance. Each store tries to establish an *image*, the personality or character that it presents to the public. Its particular *fashion image* is the degree of fashion leadership it endeavors to provide. The store's merchandising, interior decoration, promotion, and customer services develop, maintain, and reflect that image.

In keeping with their image, retailers strive for a store atmosphere that is both a complementary background for their merchandise and a warm, inviting environment for the customer. Architects, in-

A boutique in Paris? No, Belle Paris is a department designed to create that image at Bel Commons, a store in Japan! *(Courtesy of Bel Commons/Suzuya, Japan)*

terior designers, and display personnel work to achieve an image or personality for the store with which the customers can identify, and which also generates excitement about the merchandise and creates a desire to buy.

Boutiques or small shops have the easiest job creating a warm, inviting atmosphere. Their very smallness creates coziness. Large stores, to compete with the popularity of boutiques, often use the store-within-a-store or boutique concept. Each department is treated as an individual shop, with decor and atmosphere appropriate to its unique merchandise.

Degree of Fashion Leadership

Along with suiting merchandising policy to store image and target customers, the store must determine what role it wishes to play in fashion leadership. Naturally, the store's role is directly linked to the customers' concept of what is fashionable.

Store fashion leadership tends to fall into three loosely defined categories, no matter what the store size:

1. Stores with a strong fashion image, such as Henri Bendel's, Saks Fifth Avenue, Bloomingdale's, and I. Magnin, seek leadership by carrying the newest fashions. Most of their customers, too, are fashion leaders who accept the latest styles at the beginning of their cycles. There are fewer of these stores than of other types because the percentage of customers who can afford or have an interest in high fashion and high quality is small. Saks defines its average customer as having an income between $25,000 and $50,000 a year—a group that makes up only 10 percent of the total United States population, but has 20 percent of its buying power.[9]

2. Retailers whose fashion images fall midway between the leaders and the followers are the most numerous because they cater to the largest segment of the population. They identify with

[9] Alan Johnson, "Department Stores in Transition," Drexel Burnham Lambert Seminar, May 19, 1977.

consumers who accept fashion as its popularity grows. Therefore, fashion adaptations are available to them at moderate prices. Stores like Macy's, Gimbels, and Abraham and Straus of New York; John Wanamaker of Philadelphia; Rich's of Atlanta; Foley's of Houston; and The Broadway in Los Angeles fall into this category. However, a wide range of fashion can be found in this group. For example, Macy's also caters to fashion leaders with departments of designer clothes. Others try to compete with promotional stores on prices in some areas.

3. "Mass merchants" restrict their fashion offerings to proven styles because they appeal to fashion followers, who purchase only styles they are used to seeing on others. Fashion looks reach these stores later than the others due to the time it takes for mass producers to copy them at low prices. As fashion reaches this level, it all begins to look alike; everyone is copying everyone else. Examples of mass merchants include Sears, Wards, and Korvette.

FASHION DIRECTION

Fashion direction is needed in all stores, regardless of size or type, to maintain a consistent fashion reputation for the store. In large stores fashion direction is given by the *fashion director*. Generally, he or she gives fashion direction in three major areas: merchandising, promotion, and sales training.

The fashion director attends worldwide collection openings to study fashion trends, applies them to the store's image, and passes this information on to buyers as a guide to merchandise planning. The fashion director can also assist buyers in selecting appropriate merchandise or in coordinating their buys with other departments. However, buyers also do their own research, and final decisions are up to them.

A fashion director may also prepare seasonal fashion presentations for salespeople and give advice on promotional activities that will enhance the fashion image of the store (see chapter 15).

In large stores, a fashion office staff assists the fashion director. Related promotional activities may be handled in this office or by a special events department. In a smaller store, a merchandise manager or buyer may give the needed fashion direction. In the very smallest shops, the manager (usually the owner) performs all functions, including analyzing how fashion trends relate to store image. In every size or type of store, fashion direction is important in order to project a clear store image and, ultimately, to sell merchandise.

SUMMARY

This chapter examined various types of retailing—including department stores, specialty stores, discount and variety stores, and mail-order firms—and found that many of these classifications now overlap. There are both single- and multiple-unit stores, the latter generally being chain stores or department store groups. Organization within a store is usually divided into merchandising, store operations, sales promotion, finance, and personnel. In small stores all of these jobs are handled by only a few people; in large stores, executives specialize to direct each function.

A store's image is determined by its target customers and by a clear policy on merchandising, decor, promotion, and services in relation to those customers. The fashion director helps maintain a consistent image by studying fashion markets and guiding buyers, sales personnel, and sales promotion activities.

CHAPTER REVIEW

CHAPTER OBJECTIVES

After reading this chapter you should be able to
A. Give evidence of having attained competence in the following areas:
1. Understanding of various types of retail stores
2. Knowledge of the organizational differences between single-unit and multiple-unit stores 3. Ability to identify at least ten major international stores and three famous shopping areas 4. Ability to explain the organizational structure of a small store as compared to a large store 5. Awareness of how a store's fashion image relates to consumer groups, and of how that image is manifested in store policies
B. Define the following terms and concepts in relation to their discussion in the chapter:
1. Retailing 2. Shopping centers 3. Fifth Avenue 4. Rodeo Drive 5. Faubourg St. Honoré 6. St. Germain district 7. Via Condotti 8. Mayfair and Knightsbridge 9. Department stores 10. Harrod's 11. Liberty of London 12. Galeries Lafayette 13. Bloomingdale's 14. Macy's 15. Specialty stores 16. Henri Bendel 17. Saks Fifth Avenue 18. Bergdorf Goodman 19. Lord and Taylor 20. Discount stores 21. Variety stores 22. Mail-order retailing 23. Leased departments 24. Single-unit stores 25. Multiple-unit stores 26. Chain stores 27. Department store groups 28. Store organization 29. Store line 30. Buying line 31. Buyer 32. Store image 33. Target customers 34. Fashion direction

Questions for Review

1. What is the purpose of retailing?
2. How does a department store differ from a specialty store?
3. Why has mail-order retailing increased over the last few years?
4. Explain the differences in organization of a small store and a large store.
5. Why is the store's image important?

PROJECTS FOR ADDITIONAL LEARNING

1. Find out whether one of the department or specialty stores in your community is owned by a retail corporation such as Federated or Allied. To what corporation does it belong? Find out what other stores are part of the same corporation.

2. Research the history and growth of a large store in your area. Contact the store's publicity department for information and check your school or local library.

RETAIL FASHION MERCHANDISING

14

The handbag buying office
at I. Magnin:
the buyer writes an order
while assistant buyers
communicate with
a department manager and
study a computer printout
of sales histories.
(Photograph by the author)

Merchandise *denotes articles for sale; the word comes from* merchant, *the actual seller or retailer. Fashion merchandising includes all the planning and activities necessary to supply the fashion wants and needs of target cutomers.*

In the past, fashion merchandising was usually associated only with women's apparel and accessories. Today, however, fashion is important to both men and women. Fashion influence has also spread to other areas of retailing, from home furnishings to cookware.

This chapter will cover the planning and carrying out of buying and selling, following the flow of merchandise from arrival in the store to purchase by the consumer.

THE MERCHANDISE PLAN

When the target customer has been defined and the store's fashion image established, management determines a policy on how to develop or carry out that image. A fashion merchandising policy is a long-range standard for fashion buying and selling, including guidelines for related activities such as promotion.

Seasonally, merchandising policy is expressed in a *dollar merchandise plan,* a budget allocating specific amounts of money to each department or division or to the entire store, to buy an appropriate assortment of fashion merchandise to meet consumer demand and thus achieve predetermined sales goals during a given time period. The budget includes projected income and expenditures during a particular period. The only source of income for most retail stores comes from the sale of merchandise. This income must cover not only the cost of wholesale merchandise but also all other expenses, as follows:

Gross margin is the amount of money left after deducting the cost of merchandise sold from sales income. The gross margin must pay for all operating expenses and taxes, as well as provide for a required profit.

Operating expenses are the costs of running the department and the store. *Direct expenses* are those incurred by the operation of a department, such as buyers' and salespersons' salaries, buying trip expenses, and advertising costs. *Indirect expenses* are the costs of running the entire store and are shared by all departments. They include management salaries, rent, maintenance, utilities, insurance, receiving, and marking costs.

Planning is needed to provide for the financial needs of the store and to reduce the risks involved in stocking large merchandise assortments in advance of consumer demand. The dollar merchandise plan guides merchandising executives in their efforts to secure desired sales and profits. Later it is used as a standard by which to measure executives' performance.

Preparation of the Plan

Merchandise plans are determined several months before the selling season. The budget usually

Buyer René Carrillo works on his merchandise plan at Macy's. *(Photograph by the author)*

covers a six-month period: the spring season (February through July) or the fall season (August through January). The buyer makes up the merchandise plan within the framework of policy and goals set by management. The buyer uses actual sales figures from the corresponding season of the previous year as a basis for making up the new plan. The budget includes anticipated sales, stock, markdowns, and purchase plans for the coming six-month season.

Estimating Sales   To make a realistic estimate of prospective sales, a buyer must consider shifts in population, local retail competition, physical expansion or alterations in the store, planned promotional efforts, market and trend analyses, seasonal consumer demand, and economic conditions. For instance, buyers tend to buy short in anticipation of a recession. In a good year, they buy more in hopes of an increase in business.

Seasonal and monthly variations in consumer demand must be considered in planning sales goals. Consumer demand and purchasing create the fashion cycle; therefore, they are instrumental in planning the buying and selling cycle. There are far fewer sales at the beginning and end of the cycle, and more sales at periods of peak demand.

Planning Stock   The next step in planning is to estimate the amount of stock, in terms of dollar investment, necessary to meet consumer demand and thereby support planned sales. The same influences that affect sales also affect the planning of stock. Naturally, stock must be brought to a peak just before the expected time of peak sales.

A high stock turnover rate is the desired result of stock planning. *Stock turnover* is the number of times that inventory (stock merchandise) has been sold during a given period. The turnover rate directly affects retail profits; that is, no income is realized unless merchandise is sold.

Planning Purchases   The amount of merchandise, in terms of dollars, that may be purchased during a given period without exceeding planned inventory must be determined. Considering stock on hand at the beginning of any given month, the buyer has to calculate the retail value of the purchases that can be made that month if stock and sales are to be kept in balance. The difference between actual stock and planned stock equals *open-to-buy*, the value of planned purchases.

ASSORTMENT PLANNING

By stating sales objectives and controlling expenses, the dollar plan provides the foundation for assortment planning. A *merchandise assortment* is a collection of various types, quantities, and price lines of related merchandise, usually grouped together as one classification within a department. To be well balanced, an assortment must also be consistent enough to appeal to a particular group of target customers.

In planning assortments, buyers consider the following factors:

The store's fashion image and merchandising policies

Market and fashion trends

The effect of economic conditions on demand for certain types and prices of merchandise

Basic stock, merchandise that is in consistent demand throughout the year or the same season each year

The competitors' merchandise offerings

The extent of visual merchandising that can be accomplished in the store

The type of promotional activities planned in relation to target customer preferences

The main objectives of assortment planning are these:

To buy a suitable assortment of styles, colors, sizes, and prices to satisfy consumer demand, yet remain within a consistent style and price range to appeal to the department's target customer and within the individual department's ability to house the merchandise effectively

To time deliveries so that sufficient quantities of merchandise are in the store to meet various peaks in the consumer demand cycle

To display and promote the merchandise so as to attract customers

THE BUYING FUNCTION

The Buying Plan

Assortment planning is expressed in the form of a *buying plan*, a description of the types, quantities, prices, and sizes of merchandise that a buyer expects to purchase within a specific period of time. The totals state exactly how much may be spent on how many garments in each category in line with sales goals and the dollar merchandise plan.

The more detailed the buying plan, the less confusing buying decisions will be, allowing the buyer to concentrate on the fashion aspects of the merchandise during the seasonal market. The plan must be flexible enough, however, to allow for revision if conditions change. For example, buyers may not find what they want in the market.

The Buying-Selling Cycle

A buyer's responsibilities include both buying and selling aspects of retailing. The job involves a complete cycle: planning what to buy; searching the markets and selecting the right merchandise; working with advertising, display, and special events to promote merchandise and motivate consumers to buy; organizing and arranging the merchandise in the departments; and training personnel in sales—only to begin again evaluating those sales to plan for the next season.

Thus, the buyer works in two time zones, one anticipating future needs and one evaluating current sales. In fact, because consumer tastes change constantly, the buyer's job of identifying and interpreting consumer demand is a continuing process.

The buying and selling cycle is related to the fashion cycle of consumer acceptance (see chapter 3). The buyer adapts buying and selling to the introduction, acceptance, and declining stages of the cycle. At the beginning of a season, the buyer is likely to buy a broad but shallow assortment of merchandise (buying in breadth) to test consumer reaction. As certain styles emerge as best sellers, the buyer increases stock of those goods in depth—in complete size and color ranges. As the peak selling period passes, leftover merchandise is marked down for clearance and buying begins again for a new season. The buying-selling cycle is constantly overlapping: as new goods come into the store while other goods reach their peak in sales or decline in sales and are marked down.

The Buyer as Editor It is crucial that the buyer select items that the store's customers either want or expect to find in that store: the right styles, size range, color assortment, and fabrics, all at acceptable prices. Individual preferences must be forgotten in favor of the buyer's knowledge of customer preferences. Buyers need to keep in touch with their particular customers' life styles in order to buy merchandise to fit their needs. One San Francisco–based buyer for long formals and evening dresses spent a late spring evening sitting in the lobby of a downtown hotel to see what young people's preferences were in prom dresses. Although retailers are not fashion creators, they can influence consumer buying to some degree by their preselection of merchandise, which narrows the choice for the ultimate consumer. In this sense, then, the buyer is a fashion editor.

A buyer's knowledge of merchandise stems from both education and experience. The ability to evaluate merchandise and judge whether it is suitable for a customer develops over years of examining all types of merchandise for their quality, styling, and price. Market and trend research become second nature and part of the buyer's subconscious.

Shopping the Market

After the buying plan has been established, fashion buyers shop the market to view the merchandise available for the coming season. At this point the buyer meets the manufacturer's representative (as discussed in chapter 12). For the retailer, the manufacturer is the *supplier, vendor,* or *resource* of fashion goods.

Buying trips are generally timed to cover markets that are important for a particular category of merchandise. Buyers visit different market centers for different needs. Many people imagine a buyer's job to be a glamorous one with many trips to Europe. However, only designer department buyers, merchandise managers, and fashion directors of large stores attend the European collections. Even then, with packed appointment schedules leaving little time to eat or relax, business travel does not remain glamorous for long.

Designer and contemporary buyers go often to New York to make sure they are not missing new talent or a new look on the rise. Swim wear buyers may attend the California and/or Miami markets, where many new directions in resort wear originate. To find moderate- and budget-priced apparel, most buyers go to manufacturers' showrooms at regional markets. Merchandise can also be bought from manufacturers' representatives who call on stores.

Line Buying Versus Trend Buying The buyer shops for new fashion from both key resources and new ones. *Key resources* are vendors who have maintained a reputation for dependability and whose merchandise sells well because of appropriate styling, quality, and price. The buyer regularly buys a good portion of these manufacturers' lines, a practice called *line buying.* However, the buyer is also always on the lookout for new resources and new talent. Finding an exciting, unique resource can mean an important merchandising statement for a fashion store. Buying merchandise for its innovative styling is referred to as *trend buying.* Generally, a combination of the two methods is used.

Shopping Procedures

Each buyer develops individual ways of shopping the market based on the purpose of the trip, the length of the trip, and the number of resources to be seen. However, certain basic procedures are generally followed, including planning what lines to see and in what order.

Most buyers visit several showrooms in the same building on one trip—to save energy—concentrating on the specific types and price lines of merchandise they need. As the entire line is shown to them by a sales representative, they take the numbers of the styles they like most, along with careful descriptions and notes on available size and color ranges, fabrication, and wholesale price. At the same time, they must evaluate whether styling and quality compare favorably with other merchandise they have seen in the same price line. They must also consider the possible sales potential of each style for their store. Sales representatives try to be helpful, pointing out successes in the line based on initial orders. At the end of the market trip, a buyer compares his or

Buyers from all over the world arrive at the Salon de Prêt-à-Porter in Paris. *(Courtesy of the French Apparel Center, New York)*

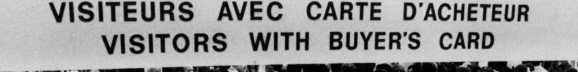

her notes on merchandise seen, eliminates the less desirable styles and any duplications, and makes decisions on which styles to purchase.

Exclusivity

Exclusivity has long been an important aspect of a fashion store's image. Buyers seek unique fashion looks from out-of-the-way sources in foreign markets or from little-known, aspiring young designers, to give their customers something that no other store has.

Private Labels Many retailers find exclusivity on a special-order basis. Buyers can request special merchandise to be made to their specifications by guaranteeing a quantity order. This merchandise carries the store's "private" label and ensures its having something different from the competition.

National Brands However, exclusivity does not seem to be as important to retailing as it once was. In the United States the consumer is more interested in availability. Stores across the country try to provide their customers with a wide selection of popular national brands. As stores stock more and more national brands, exclusivity tends to decrease. National brands, produced by known manufacturers, help the customer identify with a consistent standard of styling, philosophy, and quality from season to season. However, the growth of national brands has diluted the importance of the retail buyer because consumer demand may predetermine wholesale selection.

Buying Offices

Many stores are affiliated with resident buying offices located in international and domestic market centers. The word *resident* simply designates that they are located at the market. Buying offices are not a substitute for buyers. However, because they are in the market daily, they can provide information and representation to stores, saving them time, money, and bother.

There are primarily two types of buying offices: independent and store owned. These offices may be domestic or foreign.

Independent Resident Buying Offices Independently owned and operated, these buying offices charge fees to noncompeting stores to provide them with market services. One example is Mutual Buying Syndicate, Inc. which services Gimbels and many other stores nationwide.

Store-Owned Resident Buying Offices There are basically two types of store-owned buying offices: associated and corporate. An *associated buying office* is jointly owned and operated by a group of privately owned stores. Member stores usually have similar sales volume, store policies, and target customers. Operating expenses are allocated to each member store on the basis of the store's sales volume and amount of services rendered. An example is Associated Merchandising Corporation (AMC) which is owned by Abraham & Straus, Bloomingdale's, Bullock's, Filene's, Foley's, Rich's, Strawbridge & Clothier, Woodward & Lothrop, and others.

A *corporate buying office* is owned and operated by the parent organization of a group or chain of stores. An example is Allied Stores Marketing Corporation, owned by Allied Stores Corporation.

Foreign Buying Offices Many large retail stores have their own buying division abroad or use foreign commissionaries.

Store-owned foreign buying offices, staffed by company personnel in foreign market centers, aid visiting buyers or do the actual buying themselves. Macy's, for example, has its own buying offices all over the world.

Commissionaires are agents representing stores in foreign market centers. A commissionaire is the foreign equivalent of an American buying office. Commissionaires take care of the business end of the buying transactions: they establish a rapport with designers and manufacturers in their own language, check quality control, figure currency exchange rates, provide a consolidated center for shipping, and wade through customs red tape. Although the term *commissionaire* is French, these representatives exist wherever there is interest in buying: for leather goods in Spain and Italy, for children's wear in Sweden and Germany, and so on.

Buying Office Services The buying office is organized along the same lines as a retail store. There are merchandise managers who supervise groups of market representatives. Market representatives, like buyers, are specialists who cover a narrow segment of the market. However, unlike buyers, they do not make final decisions as to purchases and do not place orders unless specifically asked by the buyer.

For member stores, market representatives see the lines of new as well as established resources, saving the store buyer trips to the market; send out bulletins reporting on exciting new fashions, best sell-

mutual/new item

Bulletin #9224-SW-EM-February 7, 1980

DEPT: Moderate Young Career (Updated) Dresses

#3423

#3703

#3056

mutual buying syndicate, inc...1 west 42nd street, new york, n.y. 10036 · (212) 564 · 4200

A buying office bulletin. *(Courtesy of Mutual Buying Syndicate, Inc.)*

ers, trends, and special price offerings; and check into general conditions of supply and demand. In addition, buying offices can offer advice on promotions and operations based on the experience of other stores. Buying offices also make group purchases for small stores, so that the total order is large enough to meet the minimum order requirements of large or important manufacturers.

Purchase Orders

Placing an order for merchandise is considered a contract between the store and the vendor. Therefore, writing an order commits the store to take the merchandise, if indeed it meets quality expectations and delivery requirements. Generally, the buyer writes up orders on the store's purchase order forms and has them countersigned by the merchandise manager. Purchase orders specify the date of the order, the name and address of the resource, the terms of sale, shipping instructions, the store's shipping address and name of department, quantity, descriptions and prices of styles ordered, and obligations between buyer and seller.

Terms of Sale   As indicated on the purchase order, *terms of sale* specify how soon after shipment the invoice must be paid. Manufacturers offer cash discounts to retailers if payment is made within this specified period. Discounts are given to encourage prompt payment. The cash discount in the women's apparel industry, for instance, is 8 percent if the invoice is paid within ten days of the end of the billing month.

Pricing

Retail selling prices are based on predetermined store pricing policies and on wholesale costs.

Markup   Markup (sometimes called "markon") is the difference between the wholesale cost and the retail price of the merchandise. It can be figured as a percentage of retail value or calculated on the basis of cost. Most retailers calculate markup as a percentage of retail value rather than wholesale cost. Primarily, this is because expenses and profits are commonly expressed as a percentage of net sales, which are based on retail value. The markup must cover operating expenses and a profit. Store expenses include salaries, sales promotion, and overhead (rent, electricity, store maintenance, etc.). All these expenses are averaged to determine a percentage markup per item.

TABLE 14–1   PRICING OF A TYPICAL $100 DRESS *
(WHOLESALE PRICE = $48.00; RETAIL PRICE = $96.00)

Retailer's Costs

Wholesale cost ($48.00 less 8 percent discount for prompt payment)	$ 44.16
Allowance for markdowns (averaged over all dresses in stock)	6.00
Allowances for shortages and pilferage	2.00
Salaries (averaged per garment)	
Sales staff	5.00
Merchandising and buying staff (including expenses)	4.00
Clerical and stock room (receiving, marking, deliveries, etc., including expenses)	3.00
Advertising, display, sales promotion	5.00
Administrative (executives, credit and accounting offices, including expenses)	8.00
Employee fringe benefits	2.00
Overhead (rent, insurance, utilities, cleaning, security)	9.00
Miscellaneous	1.84
TOTAL	$ 94.00
Taxes	3.00
Profits	3.00
SELLING PRICE	$ 96.00 Retail price
	—44.16 Cost
	$ 51.84 Markup

* These are approximate figures and percentages vary depending on the kind of store.

Price Range   Several price lines are offered in each department or merchandise category. The term *price range* refers to the span between the lowest and highest price line. Merchandise of comparable quality usually falls into the same price range. Within a price range, there must be enough difference between price lines that variations in quality at each level are obvious to customers.

Receiving

When the buyer places an order at the market or with a sales representative, he or she indicates delivery dates to ensure that the merchandise is in the store at the right time to meet consumer demand. Merchandise is accepted by the store in the receiving room or central receiving location, where it is counted and checked for quality. Differences between actual shipment and the purchase order must be reconciled, and a decision made whether to accept or reject a partially filled order or substitutions made by the manufacturer. The buyer must be consulted on any major decision. If the order is unacceptable for any of the above reasons, it must be returned to the manufacturer. The buyer must also check any outstanding orders (those that have not been filled). If an understanding cannot be reached as to why the shipment is late, then the order is canceled.

When the shipping invoice is marked "received," the merchandise is forwarded to the marking room, where merchandise is ticketed according to information stated on the buyer's purchase order. The ticket includes code numbers for vendor, season, classification, department, and of course retail selling price.

Many multiple-unit store groups and chains have central receiving, a separate receiving center where all merchandise is received and then sent either to the flagship store or to each of the branch or chain stores. It is then recounted and rechecked at the store and sent on to a department. The department manager also checks and verifies both the count and the information on the price tag. If approved, the merchandise moves into a stockroom or onto the selling floor.

RECORD KEEPING

Unit Control

The basic tool that helps retailers of all sizes maintain stock in balance with the needs of customers is a unit record system, commonly called a *unit control system*. Unit control is a system for recording the number of units of merchandise bought, sold, in stock, or on order. Records are kept of additions to or subtractions from stock, from the time an order is placed with a manufacturer until that merchandise is sold. Information for unit control comes from purchase orders, sales records, and merchandise transfers (movement of merchandise from one store in a chain or group to another). Many stores now have electronic data processing systems for unit control that automatically collect and process merchandise information.

The buyer is responsible for maintaining current merchandise records, although generally the assistant buyer actually keeps them. These are the records the buyer uses to make adjustments as the selling season progresses. If the records show that an order has not been filled on time, the buyer may cancel; if certain styles are selling quickly, the buyer may make additional purchases or even reorder; if styles are selling too slowly, markdown plans may be made.

The major advantage of unit control systems is that the resulting records enable a buyer to keep track of consumer demand. Unit volume control systems also give a more realistic growth picture in inflationary periods when dollar volume increase may be misleading. Their major drawback is that they cannot determine what styles, colors, or sizes customers wanted but could *not* find at the store. This information can be learned only informally, through customer conversation with, or memos from, sales personnel or department managers.

Inventory Control

To keep tabs on the dollar value of merchandise on hand, stores record all transactions concerning sales, purchases, markdowns, transfers, and returns. As competition continues to increase, the need for accuracy and current factual information compels more and more businesses to convert their record keeping to electronic data processing.

The accounting method used for this purpose is the *inventory control system*. Most stores use the "retail method" of inventory control, which involves figuring inventory at retail values rather than on the basis of the cost price. The "cost method" is more complicated, as each item has to be evaluated separately. The retail method is simpler because an average markup percentage is calculated for all merchandise and subtracted from retail prices to find approximate cost.

Beginning inventory is the dollar value of merchandise on hand at the beginning of an accounting period. The inventory dollar value is established by multiplying unit volume by price. Once the opening inventory has been established, any subsequent transactions—such as purchases, sales, returns, transfer of goods, price changes (markups or markdowns)—are added to or deducted from it to arrive at an ending inventory.

A simplified version of a typical inventory calculation follows:

Beginning inventory
+ Purchases (receipts)
− Net Sales
+ or − Price revisions (markdowns or markups)
− Returns to manufacturer
_____
Ending inventory (actual stock) [1]

[1] René Carrillo, Buyer, Macy's California, interview, February, 1980.

Book inventory is a method of keeping control based on accounting records of transactions obtained from various bookkeeping devices, such as the *purchase journal* (a monthly or semimonthly report of invoices for merchandise received, transfers and returns to vendors) or sales and stock reports.

Physical inventory is taken to confirm the book records and to comply with accounting regulations. It is an actual physical count of all merchandise on hand. In case of discrepancies between the book and the physical inventory, the physical count prevails and the books must be adjusted accordingly.

Stock shortages and overages are the result of any discrepancies between book and physical inventory control. Stock shortages mean a lower physical inventory than book inventory due to theft, damage, or clerical error. Shortages are common, and allowances must be made in initial pricing to cover these losses. Overages are a higher physical inventory than book inventory due to clerical error and are quite rare.

RETAIL SALES

On the Selling Floor

Visual Merchandising   Since many of the same fashions are available in many stores, the presentation of merchandise is important. Visual merchandising must draw the customer to the department most suited to his or her life style. There is no sign that says, "If you are age 38 to 50, live in the suburbs, and wear an average size 10, go to the 'Miss Macy' department." Yet that department was merchandised with those life style statistics in mind. The merchandise itself and the way it is presented must appeal to that sort of customer. Visual merchandising

Designer fashions are often grouped together for effective visual merchandising. *(Courtesy of Marshall Field's, Chicago)*

efforts are coordinated with store planning and display departments (see chapter 15).

Merchandising and design concepts can be destroyed if merchandise is presented incorrectly. For example, sportswear coordinates must be merchandised differently from separates. Coordinates must be shown together in groups by designer or manufacturer, whereas separates are displayed in groups by color, fabric, or related items. Stock is arranged in an orderly, attractive manner to contribute to the visual effect of the department and to help customers quickly find what they want.

As a customer must be able to see fashion in order to buy it, proper display fixtures play an important part in visual presentation. Assortment displays must permit customers to see an entire range of colors or styles in each size. In an apparel department, assortments may be displayed on wall racks, rounders, 4-way (or star) fixtures, or T-stands. While wall racks utilize space well and rounders show off a color story, they are not the most desirable means of display because the customer is confronted with nothing but sleeves (or sides of garments). On frontal projection fixtures, such as the 4-way (with 4 arms) or the T-stand (with 2 arms), the garments face outward, so that the customer can see the fronts of garments. Assortments in accessory areas are presented in display cases or stands. Visual presentation may be rearranged within a department in order to give greater visibility to merchandise which is slow in selling.

The Department   In multiple-unit stores with one buyer in a central location, day-to-day operation —including responsibility for sales and the maintenance of visual merchandising—is generally left in charge of a department manager. This person acts as eyes and ears for the buyer, closely watching and reporting what goods are selling. Department managers may request more stock of a hot item and give the buyer a projected estimate of quantities they expect to sell in a certain period of time. In a small store, the buyer may also function as the department manager.

Sales training   Fashion selling requires special training to give sales personnel merchandise information, confidence, and motivation. In small stores, training is informal, but it can be very effective because personnel are usually familiar with and therefore able to relate to merchandise in all departments. In larger stores, training is likely to take the form of market trip reports and sales meetings. Sales meetings are held by the buyer or department manager, ideally on a daily, weekly, or monthly basis. The new

merchandise is presented, sometimes on models, to show how garments should be worn and accessorized. Vendors often supply sales training programs or aids in such forms as video tapes, slide shows, or brochures.

Buyers instruct salespeople on the selling features of merchandise so that they in turn can point out quality, fashion, and performance features to their customers. Buyers try to infuse enthusiasm into the salespeople, hoping that it will be transmitted to the customer. Motivation for salespeople in "big ticket" departments (such as designer clothes) may take the form of sales commissions.

Selling   Sales, after all, is the basis of success in retailing. The retailer's goal is to beat last year's sales for the same season. Of course, much depends on the buyer's selection of fashion assortments and related merchandising to meet consumer demand. However, success in fashion selling also depends on the ability of salespersons to convey fashion ideas. Salespeople make the important customer contacts for the store. *Personal selling* is the method involving the most customer contact. In this method, a salesperson actively assists customers over the counter or on the floor in choosing merchandise suited to individual tastes and needs. *Salon selling* is a specialized form of selling reserved for stores or departments that offer high-priced, high-quality fashion. Little or no stock is visible on the selling floor. Individual styles are shown to the customer by a salesperson. If a good rapport develops, customers are likely to return repeatedly. For this reason, salon sales personnel often keep files on regular customers, noting style and color preferences, sizes, and other pertinent information. Less personal types of selling include self-selection, self-service, and telephone selling.

Computer Use at Point of Sale   As competition increases, the need for accuracy and current factual information has caused more and more businesses to convert their record keeping to electronic data processing. An electronic computer system is connected to each *point of sale* (the time and place of the sales transaction) via terminals, which replace cash registers. If the correct information is entered, this is the fastest and most accurate way to keep inventory records. By showing exactly what is being sold, computer printouts help fashion executives make decisions about future planning and buying.

At the point of sale the computerized cash register records all the information on the garment ticket: price, department, color, style, vendor, size, and season. It automatically computes sales totals and sales tax and prints the sales slip. For charge purchases,

Point-of-sale transaction. *(Photograph by the author)*

this information is used by the credit department to bill customers.

The information is recorded on magnetic tapes or discs and is processed daily. Processing can immediately determine the day's best sellers. It can show what stock is low and needs to be reordered.

As the planning, pricing, and inventory control of merchandise have become increasingly complex, the computer has helped to organize facts and figures that would otherwise be overwhelming. Because of the accuracy of computer memories, retailers today can do a more precise job of merchandising.

Consumer Acceptance

By comparing current sales with last week's or last month's figures, a buyer can determine whether sales are on the rise or on the decline. If on the rise, then the style is growing more popular; perhaps more of that look should be ordered. If on the decline, those items should be marked down for clearance to make way for new merchandise, thus completing the seasonal buying and selling cycle.

Markdowns   Fashion merchandisers use markdowns to speed the sale of unpopular, damaged, or end-of-season goods, to make room for new merchandise. A markdown is the difference between the original retail price and a reduced price. Ideally, the buyer has made such wise choices in style, color, and size selection that little is left at the end of the season. Yet a certain percentage—about 8 percent in a typical store—of any retail store's stock must be marked down to be sold.[2] Therefore, markdowns must be estimated in advance and reserves added in pricing to make up for the resulting lower gross profits.

Maintained Markup   Maintained markup is the difference between the wholesale cost of the merchandise and the retail price at which it is actually

[2] William Hallerman, vice president and director of stores, Weinstock's, Sacramento, California, "Retailing: Capitalizing on Fashion Trends at the Store Level," lecture, University of California at Davis Extension, November 7, 1979.

sold. Therefore, this markup reflects price adjustments made on the merchandise during the selling period, which are primarily markdowns.

MERCHANDISING EVALUATION

Buyers and management analyze financial and other pertinent information to evaluate the effectiveness of merchandising activities as reflected by consumer acceptance. With the help of this information, they try to measure the merchandising impact on the store's profitability. The analysis can be an ongoing or periodic process.

Daily, weekly, and monthly reports give the buyer an overview of current sales activities. The buyer uses this information to analyze selling trends (see chapter 4). If increased sales point to a trend in a certain silhouette or to certain price points, buyers know to purchase more of the same type of merchandise. On the other hand, buyers do not want to buy more of unpopular merchandise because they do not want too many markdowns. Merchandise can be carried over to the next season, but this practice is dangerous if styles change; the merchandise may not sell at all. Buyers cannot rely totally on computer printouts, however. They must study their customer; they must research the marketplace. "Computers have a function, but they do not have a sense of taste. . . . Computers cannot substitute for thought and intuition." [3]

The buyer may compile a *vendor analysis* showing the initial markup, markdowns, maintained markup, and the resulting profit percentages gained on products from an individual resource. Although a vendor may have one or two bad seasons, the store will most likely drop a resource whose merchandise consistently gives them no profit.

Sales data can also be very revealing in relation to other important information. When compared with last year's data for the same period, the numbers show whether the store's volume grew over the year. When compared to the sales plan, the results show how well the store met its objectives established at the beginning of the period, and therefore how well planning was done. When compared to inventory on hand and on order, as well as to customer returns, the figures can indicate whether merchandising, planning, and promotional activities were successful.

Sales data are also used to determine important ratios such as average gross sales, sales per square foot, and stock or inventory turnover.

Total dollar sales for a given period divided by the number of transactions for the same period provide *average gross sales*. This ratio indicates the dollar volume per transaction. An increase in the ratio can indicate higher prices due to better merchandise, inflation, or larger sales per customer.

Total sales for a period divided by the number of square feet of selling space of a floor or store provide *sales per square foot*, an internationally used indicator on how well and productively a department or store uses its space. In their desire for internal growth, many stores are focusing attention on raising dollars per square foot in existing units, often with physical renovation. As a result, new departments may be created or existing ones may have their display space increased or decreased.

Total sales for a period divided by average inventory or stock value for the same period are called *stock* or *inventory turnover*. For example, if seasonal sales total $1,000,000 and average stock (weekly stock figures divided by the weeks in a season) is 500,000, then the stock turn is 2. Stock turnover is basically how many times the stock is sold out and replaced in a given period. A high turnover ratio is usually very desirable because it speeds the buying and selling cycle and constantly frees funds for renewed use, thus increasing the profitability of the retail operation. A high turnover reduces the inventory risk; it increases the choice and selection available to the customer since new merchandise arrives in the store continually; and it reduces the risk of losses due to outdated styles and patterns.

These sales-related ratios are not only used to evaluate a department or store, but are also very valuable in comparing different stores within a retail chain or in analyzing the success of the competition.

All these indicators are used by buyers and management not only to measure the success of the retail merchandising operation but also to refine and improve the long-range planning of future merchandising activities. Evaluation and the establishing of new and more accurate goals lead to a more profitable, healthier retail operation.

[3] Rose Wells, fashion consultant, quoted in "Rose Wells: Sounding Off on Retailers and Retailing," *Women's Wear Daily*, February 29, 1980, p. 6.

SUMMARY

As merchandisers, retailers must buy the right goods and have them in the store when the customer wants them. Store policies and long-range planning help the retailers do their job effectively. The dollar merchandise plan allocates specific amounts of money to buy fashion assortments. A fashion assortment means that related merchandise is balanced between variation and consistency. Assortment planning is expressed as a buying plan including descriptions of the types, quantities, prices, and sizes of merchandise needed.

Buyers' responsibilities cover both the buying and the selling aspects of retailing. Buyers plan what to buy, search the markets for goods that will meet their customers' needs, work on sales promotion, and supervise merchandising of departments and selling, only to begin the cycle again for a new season.

As merchandise is received in the store, it is ticketed with price and other identification and checked against purchase orders. Records of merchandise in the store or on order are kept by unit control and inventory systems.

Customer acceptance is the basis for success and profitability in retailing. Retailers face a constant challenge to serve their public more efficiently and more effectively, to ensure continued growth and development.

CHAPTER REVIEW

CHAPTER OBJECTIVES

After reading this chapter you should be able to
A. Give evidence of having attained competence in the following areas:
1. Understanding of the buying-selling aspects of merchandising 2. Understanding of the importance of planning and the considerations involved in it 3. Understanding of how the buying-selling cycle relates to the fashion cycle 4. Understanding of buying procedures at the market 5. Understanding of the services of buying offices and the difference between the buying office and the store buyer
B. Define the following terms and concepts in relation to their discussion in the chapter:
1. Merchandising 2. Merchandising policy 3. Dollar merchandise plan 4. Gross margin 5. Stock turnover 6. Assortment planning 7. The buying plan 8. Open-to-buy 9. Buying-selling cycle 10. Supplier, vendor, or resource 11. Shopping the market 12. Line buying 13. Trend buying 14. Buying in breadth 15. Buying in depth 16. Private brands 17. National brands 18. Buying offices 19. Commissionaires 20. Purchase order 21. Terms of sale 22. Markup 23. Retail price 24. Price range 25. Central receiving 26. Unit control 27. Inventory control 28. Beginning inventory 29. Book inventory 30. Physical inventory 31. Stock shortages and overages 32. Visual merchandising 33. Department manager 34. Salon selling 35. Point of sale 36. Consumer acceptance 37. Markdowns 38. Average gross sales 39. Sales per square foot

Questions for Review

1. What are a buyer's responsibilities?
2. Why must a buyer research fashion trends?
3. How is the buying plan calculated?
4. What are the functions of a buying office?
5. Why is record keeping important?

PROJECTS FOR ADDITIONAL LEARNING

1. Visit a retail store contemporary sportswear department. Look at a "rounder" (round display rack) of merchandise. Is it all from one manufacturer, or has the buyer mixed garments from several vendors to carry out a fabric or color theme? Are coordinates displayed together with separates?

   Who are the major vendors in the department? What are the price ranges for jackets, sweaters, skirts, pants, and shirts? Which manufacturers have the most innovative looks? Ask salespeople which groups are selling best. Does the department have a good selection of sizes, colors, and styles? Write a critique of the department.

2. Shop a large department store. Study the three different ways to merchandise the suit look. Compare suits in (a) the missy coat and suit department (suit is priced as a single unit); (b) the sportswear department (components are priced separately); (c) the dress department (components are priced as a unit, usually a dress with jacket). What suit styles do you find in each department? Compare the selection (assortment), price ranges, quality, and fit from one department with the others. Which department has the best value and selection?

3. In a local store, evaluate a sale rack. Is the merchandise marked down or a "special purchase" (garments purchased at a lower price and offered as a promotional event)? Why was the merchandise marked down? Was it because of styling, poor timing, poor construction, poor fit, unattractive colors, or too high a price? Evaluate your findings in a short report.

Saks Fifth Avenue

Viewpoint: The Schoolgirl Knits...And The Arrival Of A New Tradition In Charm and Taste.

Welcome the return of well-bred style. Of fashion that takes its pleasure from delicately defined lines...few, but meaningful details...the unerring classicism of navy and white. Of design reminiscent of Chanel and Dior at their best...when they were working their magic with knits as finely honed, as feminine and charming! as these from Venice Industries. Simple, prophetic statements in basic colors that focus on the form as fashion...and take it to its finest. The look...lady-like, rich.

And ultimately definitive for the Eighties. Left, the detailed, braid-accented cardigan suit. In navy with white, for sizes 6 to 16, $130. Right, the demure navy dress, collared with white lace. For sizes 4 to 14, $110. Both, of a blend of acrylic and polyester. In Sportdress Collections, Third Floor—where we are all the things you are...gifts just right for you! In New York tomorrow, December 17th, meet a special representative from 11 to 4 and see mini-shows of the collection at 12:30 and 1:30.

Saks Fifth Avenue will be open Monday thru Friday 'til 8:30 pm. Saturday 'til 7 pm. White Plains, Garden City and Springfield will be open Monday thru Saturday 'til 9 pm. Bergen 'til 9:30. New York, White Plains and Springfield will also be open Sunday from noon 'til 5 pm, Garden City 'til 6.

RETAIL FASHION PROMOTION

15

A Saks Fifth Avenue
newspaper ad.
*(Courtesy of Saks
Fifth Avenue)*

At each level of the industry, the objective is to sell a product to a particular customer. Promotion, in the broadest sense, is the effort to further those sales by means of advertising, publicity, special events, and display. The main purpose of all phases of fashion promotion is to generate more sales, by inspiring current customers to buy more and by attracting new customers.

Promotion also tries to communicate a store image or the existence of a product to consumers. It attempts to attract the type of customer for whom the merchandise is intended. Therefore, before beginning sales promotion efforts, each fashion business must determine its needs and objectives.

This chapter deals particularly with retail fashion promotion. Most sales promotion in the fashion industry, especially in the form of advertising, is done on the retail level. The methods used by retailers to promote fashion vary considerably. Merchants must choose the approach best suited to their selection of goods and customers, as well as to the size of their business.

PLANNING AND DIRECTION

In planning promotions a store must decide what group of consumers it wants to reach (its target market), and what fashion image it wants to project. Ideally, when a company or store opens, it establishes a policy regarding its image and its customers. However, a store occasionally revamps or updates its fashion image because of changes in the neighborhood or in fashion style and taste.

Sales promotions must be an integral part of the year's merchandising plan. In addition to promoting the six possible fashion seasons (holiday, resort, spring, summer, transitional, and fall), stores schedule traditional activities throughout the retail calendar. These include bridal fashion shows, January and August white sales (sheets, towels, and table linens), special features for Christmas and other holidays, special sales for Washington's Birthday and the Fourth of July, back-to-school sales, and so on.

In small stores, a single person may handle all promotional activities with the help of outside consultants or agencies. In a large store, a sales promotion director manages or coordinates the joint efforts of advertising, special events, display, public relations, and the fashion office. The sales promotion director is responsible for setting goals and making general plans. Together, the sales promotion director, the directors of each promotional area, and buyers must decide what to promote, when to promote it, and how to reach their target market.

FASHION ADVERTISING

The largest part of the sales promotion budget in a retail store is normally allocated to advertising (approximately 1 to 3% of sales), and a large share of the advertising budget goes toward newspaper space. Advertising involves the planning, writing, designing, and scheduling of *paid* announcements to attract customers' attention to a fashion product or event. Thus, advertising is the use of paid time or space in media such as television, radio, newspaper, magazines, billboards, and direct mail.

Kinds of Advertising

Stores use two basic types of advertisement. They try either to sell their image or to sell specific items. *Institutional* or *prestige advertising* draws attention to the store (the institution) rather than to a specific product for sale. The focus is on fashion image, fashion leadership, community goodwill, a new or remodeled store, or a special event. *Merchandise* or *promotional advertising* aims at selling specific items; the store image and goodwill are only incidental.

The best advertising is always planned from the *customer's point of view*. In fashion advertising, the customer should be able to picture how attractive he or she will look wearing the advertised item. Advertising must also be truthful, to build customer confidence and create a good reputation for the manufacturer or the store.

Scheduling and Planning

Ads and promotional events are sometimes planned up to six months ahead of the selling season. Like any other plan, the *advertising plan* is based on past experience, present conditions, and future expectations. An advertising plan is a guide for a specific period of time (such as a week, a quarter of the year, or a season) and for the amount of advertising that a store intends to do in that period to attract customers. A budget is prepared, telling how much money will be allocated for advertising. Advertising space in newspapers or time on radio or television must be contracted. A timetable is developed detailing how the ad production is to be carried out, and by whom, in order to meet media deadlines.

Media

To be effective, fashion advertising has to be noticed. In advertising, *media* is a general term used to cover all methods of transmitting a sales message. Advertisers must choose the medium that will best promote an event or best reach a specific target market. The media include newspapers, magazines, radio, television, billboards, displays, and direct mail. Generally, fashion advertising is visually oriented, the philosophy being "why tell it if you can show it."[1]

Decisions are made not only about which general medium will be used, but also about which particular radio or television station, newspaper, or magazine will reach the appropriate customer for specific merchandise. Each consumer group has unique tastes, ideas, and interests, and consequently responds to different media. Advertising departments or agencies must determine the best possible combination of media to reach a particular target market.

Several ads are usually placed in different media to support each other and strengthen the campaign. To balance the spot radio commercial aimed at the car commuter, the store might also place an ad covering the same material in the newspaper, for bus and train commuters to read.

To maintain public interest, repetition is a necessary part of advertising. Consistency is equally important. The same ad read at the same time every day on the radio, or a fashion ad in the same illustration style every week on the same page in the newspaper, makes people keenly aware of the store or brand name, as well as of the fashion message.

Newspaper Advertising Newspaper advertising is popular among most fashion retailers because (1) it provides visual as well as verbal means of telling consumers what merchandise the company has to offer; (2) it may be offered daily, which is important in the quickly changing fashion business; (3) layouts, art, and copy are relatively easy to produce; and (4) media costs are comparatively low. The retailer buys space in newspapers that reach its potential customers. Day after day, readers in specific geographical areas or trade groups are exposed to the company's fashion message. The producer or retailer can even buy a certain desirable position in the paper, such as the back page of the front section, often paying premium rates to have their ads appear in the same place each day. For example, Macy's San Francisco advertises daily on

---

[1] Jerome Bess, president of Koehler and Reed Advertising, as quoted in "Marketing the Message," *Women's Wear Daily*, January 11, 1979, p. 5.

the front cover of the classified section of the *San Francisco Chronicle*. Preprinted advertising may also be inserted in the newspaper.

Magazine Advertising   Large retailers like Saks Fifth Avenue regularly advertise in fashion magazines because they can benefit from national circulation. Magazines also have regional editions that carry inserted pages of local retail store advertising.

Magazines intended for the general public are referred to as *consumer magazines*; examples are *Vogue* and *Harper's Bazaar*. Each of these magazines aims its editorial fashion coverage to a particular segment of the market, just as stores do; therefore, advertisers use the magazine best suited to reach their target market.

Because of the length of production time, the retailer's fashion message in magazines is usually limited to prestige advertising. Merchandise shown in the ad must be either typical of incoming fashion trends or timeless classics.

Radio and Television Advertising   Television commercials are becoming increasingly popular for fashion advertising. Television has the advantage of being able to show how clothing might fit into a real life situation. However, the major drawback to TV advertising is the cost of air time and production. Excluding time buys, a TV commercial may cost anywhere from $15,000 to $50,000 for a 30-second production. Production costs cover fees for the producer, director, talent, voice-over announcer, camera work, location, editing, music, and expenses for wardrobe, props, lighting, film and developing. Commercials are usually produced by agencies, but less expensive ones can be produced by local TV stations.

The cost of air time is determined by the length of the spot and the time of day it is to be shown. Television prime time—the most expensive—is between 7 and 11 P.M. when the greatest number of adult viewers are watching.

National television advertising is used by large national firms like Sears, which sell and distribute

Retail store art director Bill Watkins discusses the layout for a newspaper advertisement with a member of his staff. *(Photograph by the author)*

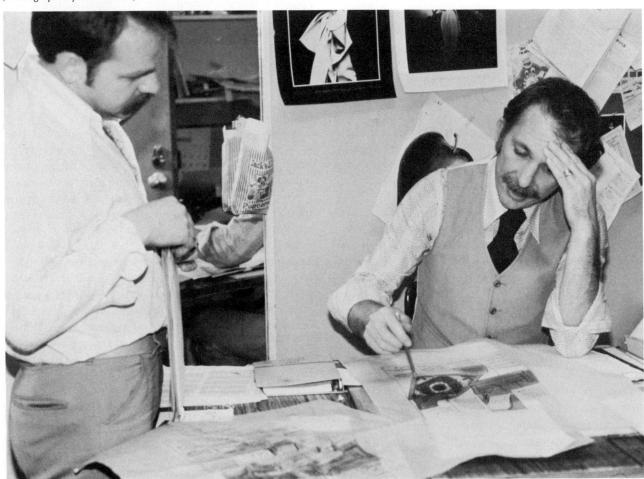

apparel across the country and have the necessarily large advertising budgets to pay for production and buy network television time. A network television show reaches millions of potential consumers throughout the country. Specific time is also set aside on every national show for local "spots" (30- or 60-second commercials), which local retailers use.

Because viewers can see the actual fashion, television has an advantage over radio for apparel advertising. However, radio can make the listener aware of a store location or brand name. Peak radio listening hours, which cost more than others, are during "drive time," the rush hours when commuters listen most to their car radios. Stations are selected for their target market appeal. If the target market for a particular campaign is professional men and women, they might most effectively be reached by spot radio ads on a news program at rush hour, as they commute to or from work. A radio spot would reach teens as well, but a rock music program would be a better choice.

Direct Mail Advertising Direct mail is a highly effective form of advertising because it is personally addressed to each potential customer. Direct mail pieces include catalogs and statement enclosures (provided by manufacturers), often included with monthly billings to charge customers. Mail-order catalogs have become a tremendously popular form of advertising because of the shopping convenience they provide to working women.

Cooperative Advertising

Fiber producers and manufacturers often cooperate financially on advertisements with retailers who feature their merchandise. Co-op allocations are based on a percentage of net sales to the retailer and may provide up to 50 percent of media costs. This additional money enables retailers to make ads larger or to run them more frequently. The additional advertising volume may also help the retailer qualify for a lower media rate. Many retailers would not advertise merchandise without co-op money from producers. A disadvantage of co-op advertising is that buyers may be tempted to select merchandise on the basis of available cooperation allocations; the merchandise, however, may prove to be something that customers do not want.

The Advertising Department in a Retail Store

Because they do so much newspaper advertising, most large retail stores have in-house advertising departments. The advertising department is headed by a director who supervises three divisions: art, copy, and production.

The **art** division is responsible for *layouts*, sketches of how the ad will look. Department or freelance artists execute the final drawings or photographers take pictures. The use of photography is currently popular because its realistic qualities lend themselves to promotional or direct sell advertising. Illustrations are especially appropriate for institu-

Artist Maxi Haun works on the layout for an I. Magnin clearance ad. *(Courtesy of I. Magnin, San Francisco; photograph by the author)*

tional ads where the creation of an illusion is important.

Copywriters produce the word descriptions in an ad, following the layout to make sure that exactly the right amount is written. The good writer pictures the customer who is reading the ad and writes to him or her. Sales copy, which stresses value, is quite different from high-fashion copy, which emphasizes glamour.

The **production** department "pastes up" all parts of the ad into a mechanical composition according to the layout. It is the mechanical technician's responsibility that the finished ad is the same as the original idea and layout. Production is also in charge of "traffic," the flow of art work and copy between the store, printers, engravers, photographers, newspapers, and radio and television stations. Beginning artists often start as paste-up artists in retail production departments.

Advertising Agencies

Stores that have no in-house advertising departments pay commissions or fees to an outside agency to create advertisements and images for them. Agencies also produce television and radio advertisements for stores whose own advertising facilities produce only newspaper ads. An ad agency is usually paid a monthly retainer fee or a commission based on space and time bought in newspapers, magazines, television, and radio. The retainer fee is calculated by the agency, based on the amount of time the ad campaign will take each month. In large agencies, groups of people are assigned to individual accounts under the direction of an account executive, who acts as liaison between the agency and the client. There are also freelance copywriters and illustrators who work for the agencies or directly for retailers.

PUBLICITY

Publicity is the voluntary spreading of information about people, special events, or newsworthy topics through various communications media. Publicity helps promote the sale of fashion merchandise by making a style, manufacturer, retailer, trend, or other aspect of fashion better known to the public. There are no media costs for publicity, but for that very reason it is difficult to obtain. Media editors choose the material they will use because they think it may be of interest to the community. The media

also dictate how, when, and where the message will be used.

Obtaining Publicity

Retailers hope to bring their names to the public eye by calling attention to newsworthy developments in their stores. They may even create events such as fashion shows or celebrity personal appearances to obtain publicity. Stores provide the media with information about such events or topics in the hope that the media will devote time or space to publicizing them.

Retailers send publicity releases to all the media. A news release is a written statement of the important facts about a person, place, or coming event, often accompanied by glossy photographs. Many releases and photographs are provided by merchandise vendors. Publicity material is sent to the media by either the public relations office or the fashion office, whichever is more concerned with the topic or event.

Media That Give Publicity

To achieve maximum benefit from publicity, retailers send publicity material to the media whose audience would be most interested in their message. Retail merchants try to obtain publicity in both print and broadcast media. However, because of the frequency of their publication, newspapers are generally more receptive to publicity than other media. They have pages to fill and may welcome the information.

Fashion magazines give publicity to retail stores in the form of *editorial credits*—the mention of the store name as a source of merchandise that is editorially featured in the magazine.

Radio and television also give some publicity, especially to their advertisers. In fact, one of the drawbacks of publicity in all media is that editorial space or time is given primarily to advertisers.

SPECIAL EVENTS

Special events bring potential customers together at the store or create goodwill. Holding special events that cater to the interests of the public encourages "recreational retailing," shopping with friends or family as a leisure activity. Special events try to replace the personal customer contact that has been lost in many large stores. They build a sense of loyalty and create a community spirit that draws consumers into the store. Well-known retailing special events include Macy's New York Thanksgiving Day Parade. Most special events are planned and carried out by a special events or public relations director.

Fashion Shows

Fashion shows are special events that communicate a fashion story. There are two basic types of fashion shows. The *informal show* is easiest to produce and effective on a personal level. A few models walk around the store, showing the fashions they are wearing to customers who are shopping or having lunch in the store's restaurant. The models can take their time and customers enjoy asking them questions. The *formal* or *runway* show takes a great deal of advance planning: booking models and fittings and arranging for a runway, any scenery, lighting, microphones, music, and seating. Rehearsals are necessary because shows have become increasingly theatrical. Also, there must be advance publicity and advertising to ensure that the show will have a large audience.

If the main objective of a fashion show is sales, it is best to have the show in the store—if possible, in the department whose clothes are being shown. If the primary purpose of the show is goodwill, such as in a charity event, it may be held outside the store in appropriate facilities. Shows may feature styles from one manufacturer or from several sources. Some shows are general in theme; others, such as bridal shows, appeal to special audiences. Clothes are generally grouped according to designer, styling, color, or other visual organization. Models and music are selected to complement the clothes, and a commentary is usually given. There are fewer set formulas in show production today than in the past as one show tries to outdo the other in innovation and imagination. Fashion shows may be organized by the special events office or the fashion office or may be a joint effort between them.

The Fashion Office

The function of the fashion office differs from store to store. In group or chain flagship stores, the fashion office is headed by the *fashion director* (see chapter 13) who has the responsibility of setting the fashion image for the whole store. In a smaller store, or branch store, the head of the fashion office is usually called a *fashion coordinator*. In both cases, however, the fashion office produces fashion shows and works with the display, advertising, and special events departments, as well as buyers, to keep a uniform fashion message throughout the store.

A fashion show at Saks Fifth Avenue, San Francisco.
(Courtesy of Catherine Samperton, the Peninsula Times Tribune, *Ken Yimm photographer)*

DISPLAY OR VISUAL PRESENTATION

Display is the visual presentation of merchandise, communicating store image and fashion ideas to the consumer. In recent years, retailers have been placing greater emphasis on the presentation of merchandise.

Mark Allen, Director of Merchandise Promotion and Store Planning at Donaldson's in Minneapolis, lists three goals of display:

> The number one justification for displays is to inform the customer of the goods we offer and the current fashion trends.
> Second, we seek to entertain the customer in such a way that sets our stores apart from other retailers in the area who may carry the same stock.
> And third, we use displays to tie in with major sales promotions or important trends.[2]

Display artists decorate all store windows and create interior displays of merchandise. An attention-getting window can entice a shopper into the store to look around. The prospective customer is further exposed to fashion and accessory purchase suggestions by interior displays. Donna Wallace (Director of suburban store visual presentation) describes display at the Emporium in San Francisco: "In windows we take a strong direction . . . and feature what we consider our overall best. On the floor, we show what is important in that particular section."[3] Stores in modern shopping malls, however, may have few or no windows, but rather a wide entrance that gives the entering customer a sweeping view of the selling area.

Displays are planned many months in advance in conjunction with other store promotions. From those plans, the display department makes up a seasonal calendar indicating the dates on which specific merchandise is to be featured, and the number and location of windows and interior displays that are to show the merchandise. Buyers compete for window space on the basis of how well their merchandise fits the particular promotional theme.

As with other forms of sales promotion, there should also be consistency between window decoration and in-store displays. Most retailers develop a total store concept for unified presentation.

Window Displays

Window displays are art forms created with merchandise and props, just as garment design is art created with fabric. Display artists use the same elements and principles of good design as garment designers. In planning windows, buyers choose garments that carry out the promotional theme and image of the store. These garments and accessories are usually the most dramatic and fashionable of an assortment.

Windows can set a mood, convey a fashion message, or directly sell merchandise.

Mood windows convey the spirit of a holiday season. Rather than directly promoting purchases, they suggest the idea of gift giving or decorating at Christmas and other holidays.

Fashion message windows feature the newest fashion trends and suggest ways to coordinate accessories for the newest looks. These windows are created to attract attention, to stimulate the customer to buy a new garment and/or accessory.

Direct-sell windows, used mostly by stores that carry popularly priced merchandise, show a representative assortment of the store's merchandise accompanied by prices, to tempt the customer with a possible bargain.

Interior Displays

Interior displays have two purposes: one general, one specific. The first is to have the display generally relate to the area around it and the second is to entice the customer to buy specific merchandise.[4] The main floor or selling area is usually the focal point for display as it makes the strongest impression on the customer.

Interior displays may be located at the entrances to departments to entice the shopper to come in and look, or they may be in the department on ledges, counters, or platforms. They may carry out the theme of window presentations or highlight interesting merchandise from the department.

Interior displays may take the form of *vignettes* or *life style displays* (mannequins posed in a scene and dressed appropriately), or *single items* (shown on a form or stand).

---

[2] "More than Window Dressing," *R-T-W*, March 1979, p. 7.
[3] Ibid.

[4] John Calori, director of visual presentation, I. Magnin, interview, March, 1980.

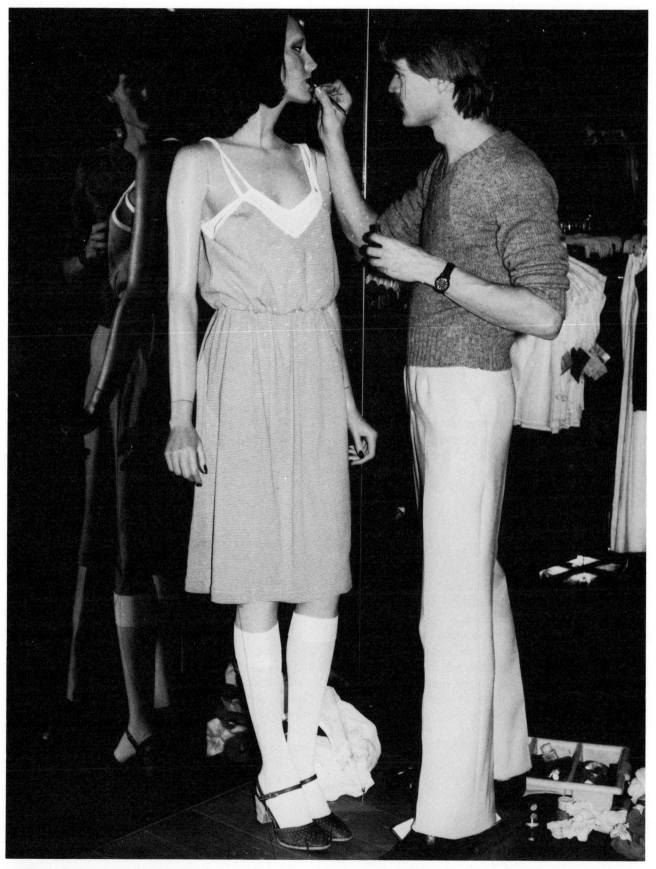

Creating a display at Macy's, New York.
(Photograph by the author)

THE BUYER'S ROLE IN PROMOTION

Plans for promotions are recommended or requested by buyers to the heads of the sales promotion department in conjunction with the projected merchandise plan. Suggestions for advertising, displays, special events, and all other types of promotions are developed with the specialists in these areas and joint efforts must be coordinated.

Advertising

Buyers make requests for ads based on their merchandise plans. They must provide all the information about the merchandise to the advertising copywriter: fabric, colors, styling details, price, and sizes. The garment or accessory itself must be given to the illustrator, layout artist, or photographer.

The buyer or assistant buyer must carefully check the ad for accuracy. Then they must make sure that the merchandise has been delivered and is on the selling floor, with appropriate sign copy, when the ad runs.

Display

Buyers must also request window and in-store displays. They must choose garments or accessories that carry out the promotional theme and image of the store. They must also make sure that there is a good selection of that merchandise on the selling floor for possible customer purchase.

Special Events

Buyers may initiate special events and fashion shows. For example, the buyer of a designer collection might arrange with the fashion office for a trunk show when a designer visits the store on a promotional trip to introduce a new collection in person. Advertising and publicity announce this event to the community, giving the public the opportunity to meet a well-known designer. If the results are favorable, both the designer and the store may win new customers.

EVALUATION

At the end of a promotional event or an advertising campaign, sales are analyzed to evaluate the campaign's effectiveness. Advertising can be evaluated by dollar sales volume. However, it is very difficult to analyze sales results in relation to display or special events. For example, unless a fashion show actually takes place in the middle of a department and people stay afterward to make purchases, who can prove the value of the event? That is why, when budgets are cut, special events are often the first casualties. Management evaluates the effectiveness of a campaign to make recommendations for the next year. Another cycle is complete: a plan made, carried out, and evaluated.

SUMMARY

Advertising, publicity, special events, and display help promote sales in retailing. Advertising is the use of paid time or space in media such as television, radio, newspapers, magazines, or direct mail. Large stores often have their own advertising departments, although outside agencies may produce television or radio commercials. No media costs are paid for publicity, but material used is the choice of the media editors. Special events, such as fashion shows, also attempt to promote products and store image. Display is the visual presentation of the store's merchandising message. Promotional efforts are coordinated with buyers in each merchandising area.

Fashion promotion has a large impact on all levels of the fashion business today. A large fashion promotion campaign can often put over a new fiber, such as Qiana, or a new fashion concept, like Diane von Furstenberg's dresses. It makes the public aware. Otherwise, in the natural course of things, new ideas might never be accepted. The industry is always searching for new and exciting ways to reach and impress the public.

Promotion has its limits, however: it is ultimately the consumer who accepts or rejects a new fashion look. Many stores tried promoting the "Longuette" or midi in 1970. The look caught on to some extent in Europe but was basically rejected by Americans.

CHAPTER REVIEW

CHAPTER OBJECTIVES

After reading this chapter you should be able to

A. Give evidence of having attained competence in the following areas:

1. Understanding of the purpose of sales promotion   2. Ability to explain the purpose, goals, and procedures of advertising, publicity, special events, fashion shows, and display   3. Ability to describe various types of media and their relation to store needs and target customers   4. Ability to describe the buyer's role in promotion

B. Define the following terms and concepts in relation to their discussion in the chapter:

1. Sales promotion   2. Advertising   3. Publicity   4. Special events 5. Display 6. Institutional or prestige advertising 7. Merchandise or promotional advertising 8. Media 9. Radio and television spots 10. Direct mail 11. Cooperative advertising 12. Layouts 13. Copy 14. Ad production   15. Advertising agencies   16. Retainer fee   17. Press release   18. Editorial credits   19. Formal fashion show 20. Informal fashion show 21. Vignettes 22. Promotion evaluation

Questions for Review

1. What is the purpose of fashion promotion?
2. Explain the difference between advertising and publicity.
3. What are the communications media used in fashion promotion?
4. Explain how co-op advertising works.
5. Why must the buyer be involved in retail promotion?

PROJECTS FOR ADDITIONAL LEARNING

1. Find and clip from your fashion magazine collection five examples of co-op advertising. Find the names of the fiber producer, fabric producer (if mentioned), manufacturer, and stores.

2. Analyze the advertising campaign of a large chain store. Search through newspapers over a one-month period and clip the store's advertisements. Are they always on the same page of the newspaper? Do they use photography or an artist's illustrations? Do they have a high fashion image or a popular appeal? Do they show the merchandise to good advantage? Do you feel that the advertisements are effective?

3. Visit a local department store and evaluate its visual merchandising and display. Does display complement and carry out the theme of the merchandise? Describe the decor and display techniques, both in windows and in interiors. Is lighting used effectively? Is merchandise attractively arranged? Do you feel that the total image of the store successfully relates to the merchandise offered?

THE HOME SEWING INDUSTRY

1b

The design department at Burda Patterns in West Germany.
(Courtesy of Verlag Aenne Burda)

An alternative to ready-to-wear is home sewing. Although home sewing is no longer the absolute economic necessity it once was, it does enable many people to have the elegant clothes they could not otherwise afford.

Home sewing has many benefits. Clothes can be made to fit irregular figures (no one is perfect), and home sewing provides the opportunity for quality construction and creative satisfaction.

The home sewing industry has developed into an important additional dimension of the fashion industry. An industry within an industry, home sewing parallels ready-to-wear in many ways. Pattern companies require many of the same talents and skills used in ready-to-wear. They employ designers, pattern makers, sample hands, and other technicians. This chapter covers design development, pattern production, the fabric market, and retailing in sequential order from concept to the home sewing consumer.

PATTERN COMPANIES

The home sewing industry is said to be a $3.5 to $4 billion business in the United States alone. It includes not only fabrics but also sewing machines, patterns, and notions.[1]

The United States now has three major pattern companies: Butterick (incorporating Vogue), Mc-Call's, and Simplicity (the largest). Vogue features high fashion; Butterick is sophisticated; McCall's and Simplicity have traditionally appealed to "middle America," although they have added designer patterns. The largest European pattern company is Burda. Burda also publishes a fashion magazine with a twice-yearly "International" edition. The largest-selling fashion magazine in the world, it includes a pattern foldout in every issue.[2] America's home sewing magazines are basically "home catalogs" from each of the pattern companies.

In addition to their regular line, major pattern companies try to make designer clothes available to the public by offering patterns of best-selling fashions by well-known designers. In many cases they can have the pattern available the same season as the ready-to-wear garment is available in the stores. This is done under a licensing contract arrangement that pays the designer a certain percentage of sales. Even celebrities like Marlo Thomas and Marie Osmond lend their names for their promotional value. Pattern companies also realize that the future of the industry depends on educating people, especially young people, in sewing skills. Therefore, they have established educational divisions to develop teaching aids.

A recent trend in the American pattern industry is the emergence of small, independent companies such as Authentic Patterns, Creative Sewing, Donner Designs, Else, Folkwear Ethnic, Jean Hardy, and Kwik-Sew. These companies attempt to answer the needs of specialized groups of sewers.

[1] Maryann Ondovcsik, "Counter-Points," *Women's Wear Daily*, November 8, 1977, p. 28.

[2] Verlag Aenne Burda, Offenburg, Germany, Press release, March 30, 1977, p. 2.

Developing Patterns and the Pattern Catalog

Pattern companies issue seasonal catalogs showing sketches of each style and sometimes photographs of the garment made up. Ideas for commercial pattern designs originate from many of the same sources used by the apparel industry: shopping the European and American designer and ready-to-wear markets, studying fashion periodicals, and observation. Steps in pattern development are very similar from company to company. First sketches, or *croquis*, are made of the ideas, and in some companies a first pattern and muslin are made up to see how the garment will work.

At this point catalog selections are made. At Burda there are four collections a year, or about 250 new styles a year. In America, major companies usually put out eight to twelve catalogs a year, adding new styles each time, with a total of about 300 new styles per year.

Catalog production is a lengthy process, and companies must strive not to be out of date by the time the patterns arrive on the market. Barbara Larson, Vogue Pattern design director, explains, "We try to pick something that is fashion right in terms of timeliness, although not something that is so specific that it's going to be out of date a year from now.[3]

Pattern companies try to keep their home sewing customer in mind, offering something for every level of taste and sewing ability as well as keeping a balance of different kinds of styles. The design department adds alternate interpretations of each design to give the home sewer more options.

After designs are approved for the catalog, size ranges are determined. In many cases, specific de-

[3] *Vogue Patterns' Designer Notebook* (New York: Butterick Fashion Marketing Company, n.d.), p. 2.

The pattern development and testing studio at Burda Patterns. *(Courtesy of Verlag Aenne Burda)*

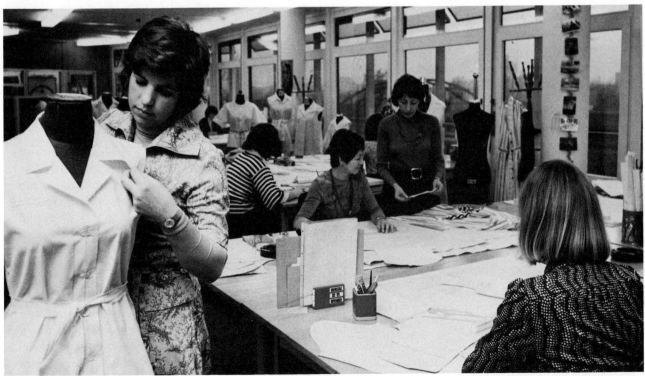

signs are originally done for a particular size range or age group. Sample size patterns must be made and perfected for fit and accuracy.

It is important for pattern companies to know what fabrics will be available to the home sewer. Obviously, a company wants its patterns to be suitable for those fabrics and vice versa. A fabric editor or merchandiser shops the home sewing fabric market and keeps a library of swatches and sources for a complete fabric picture. Pattern designs are tested in some of these fabrics for suitability. Final illustrations for the catalog, often created by freelance artists, are made from these finished garments, and the same illustrations are used on the pattern envelope. Pattern illustrations differ from other fashion illustrations in that they particularly show seams and stitching lines.

Some pattern companies also use photographs to illustrate some or all of their pattern styles. To update new catalogs, photos are often taken of the garments made up in a fabric of the current season.

When a pattern goes into production, the master pattern is made and then graded to other sizes. The pattern pieces are arranged in layouts to figure needed fabric yardage for each fabric width and each size. A diagram or photograph of the pattern layout for cutting is included in the instructions.

Step-by-step instructions are written on how to construct the garment. These directions are often translated into other languages for export. Burda translates its instructions into five languages.

The graphics for the pattern pieces, layout, directions, sketches, and photos, both for the catalog and for pattern envelopes, are prepared and then printed. Catalog pages must be collated and bound. Pattern pieces and directions are folded by a machine, stuffed into envelopes, and sealed. Catalogs and patterns are finally ready to be shipped to the stores.

Pattern companies watch sales, "dropping styles whose sales are declining and adding more when rising sales show an interest in a particular design direction."[4]

Pattern companies work hard to try to make sewing easier and more fun than ever before. Each instruction sheet is carefully worked out at the pattern company. Earlier patterns were merely stamped out with tiny holes as marks for darts and details. Since the 1950s, patterns have been clearly printed, including seam allowances and markings for details.

In Europe, many pattern magazines offer a foldout page of several pattern outlines that overlap each other. The home sewer must find the line (a series of dots, for example) for a particular design, trace it on tissue paper, and add seam allowances. It is a complicated process but one that saves money for the home sewer, as many patterns are included in the price of one magazine. However, European commercial patterns are sold individually and are printed in the same manner as those made in the United States.

Before sizing of patterns became standardized (although pattern sizes still do not match sizing standards in ready-to-wear), size measurements varied greatly from company to company, making fitting a problem. Even today, sizes vary slightly from pattern to pattern.

HOME SEWING SUPPLY RETAILERS

Various types of stores sell fabrics, patterns, and sewing supplies: department stores, small independent stores, and chain stores.

Department Stores

Many leading department stores got their start selling fabrics in the days when nearly everything was made at home or by dressmakers. Even today, huge departments at Liberty's and John Lewis in London, for example, are still devoted to fabrics.

However, fabric departments require a large area to display and sell fabrics effectively. Because other merchandise sells faster, many retailers tend to downplay their yard goods department, giving it less space than is really needed. Also, yard goods customers need special service and it is expensive to train a sales staff especially for one department. For these reasons, many department stores have given up their fabric departments.

Home Sewing Specialty Stores

The market has become more specialized, with small, independent stores cropping up to serve home sewing needs. Some of these stores have merged into large chains. Chain stores have the capital available for volume fabric purchases, which make greater selection and price breaks possible. Even pattern companies cater to them with specially printed catalogs.

Since most fabric producers want to sell only to high-volume customers, and because it is more difficult than ever to establish credit, some small retailers use a buying office. As in ready-to-wear retailing, a buying office represents many stores, enabling them to buy in volume and obtain lower prices.

[4] Ibid., p. 3.

Independent merchants must be innovative. Fashion-oriented fabric stores try to be aware of trends in the ready-to-wear field so that they can obtain the same fabrics for their home sewing customers.

Over-the-Counter Fabrics

Over-the-counter is the term used for fabrics sold in home sewing supply stores. Formerly, fabrics for the home sewing market were totally separate from the textiles supplied to the apparel industry. Today, however, more and more mills and converters are selling both to ready-to-wear manufacturers and the over-the-counter trade. This is a bonus for the home sewer, who can now buy the same fabrics used by well-known manufacturers and designers.

Fabrics are regularly ordered at least six months ahead of season. For example, fabrics for fall are booked in March and are in the store by July and August. *Regular goods* are fabrics purchased directly from the mill's or converter's regular line. They arrive "doubled and rolled" on a bolt, ready for store display. *Off-sale goods* are leftovers from textile firms. The store has to take what is available—perhaps only one color—but at a price savings. Some small stores even buy leftover manufacturers' bolts from jobbers.

Stores make careful decisions about the fabrics they carry because the fabrics reflect the character of the store. Just as in ready-to-wear, fabric buyers must keep up-to-date with fashion forecasts and study the market to find out what is available.

Market and Trend Research

Additional Buying Office Services Market research requires much time and energy. Many independent store owners find it impossible to do market research and run a store as well. Therefore, in addition to providing volume buying power, buying offices can help them by doing research. Buying offices also provide bulletins, seminars, and advice on both buying and marketing. Retail stores pay a membership fee to the buying office that varies according

Edna Goldenberg helps a customer in one of her Yardage Shops. *(Photograph by the author)*

to the size of the store, in both volume and number of store units.[5]

Trade Publications Like those in the ready-to-wear industry, home sewing buyers and retailers subscribe to trade periodicals to keep them abreast of the latest developments in their business. Specialized trade publications include the following:

Home Sewing Trade News, 129 Broadway, Lynnbrook, New York 11536

Fabric News, 360 North Bedford Drive, Beverly Hills, California 90210

Sew Business, Suite 3560, 1271 Avenue of the Americas, New York, New York 10020

In addition, home sewing retailers are interested in *American Fabrics and Fashion* and the special home sewing features in *Women's Wear Daily.*

Trade Shows Retailers of home sewing products attend trade shows like Interstoff, Ideacomo, and TALA. The American Home Sewing Association has two shows a year in New York as well as an annual convention. Each meeting is in a different city, to show the latest fabrics and notions available to its industry.

[5] JoAnn Lulow, "Utilizing a Buying Office," *Home Sewing Trade News*, May 1978, p. 14.

Sales Promotion

Fabric store sales promotion is much like that of any other retail store. Promotional activities include publicity, advertising, display, and special events that bring potential customers into the store, such as fashion shows and sewing classes.

Publicity releases giving information about the store, especially promotional events, are sent to local newspapers, magazines, and radio and television stations.

Advertisements feature new shipments at the beginning of a season, special promotional events, and end-of-season sales. Stores use all media, although only the larger chains can afford television.

Display is also useful because dramatic, visual effects may inspire people to sew. Two examples of display techniques are: showing complementary textures or colors together or grouping blouse and co-ordinating bottom-weight fabrics together.

Promotional events are also used by fabric stores. Many freelance sewing consultants take traveling shows or classes from store to store. Pattern companies may also offer to run promotional programs for stores, in an effort to promote their pattern sales.

Promotions must be timely. For example, when new books on career dressing appeared on the market, many stores responded with in-store clinics on how to sew clothes to wear on the job. Good promotional events are a good selling tool.

One of Krestine Corbin's Creative Sewing fashion clinics, presented at stores across the country.
(Courtesy of Creative Sewing)

THE HOME SEWER

With the disappearance of hand work from ready-to-wear because of rising labor costs, one way to recapture quality craftsmanship is to make clothing at home. The home sewer must learn new techniques to handle, sew, and finish each new fabric that comes on the market. It is important for anyone working in the fashion industry to know how to sew, if only to understand how a garment is put together. This increases awareness of quality construction, even in ready-to-wear. Home sewing can also provide an excellent training and experimental background for a career in the fashion industry.

The home sewer must learn to plan projects carefully. Successful home sewing requires immediate decisions regarding choice of patterns and appropriate fabric. The ready-to-wear designer is able to experiment with many sample garments before perfecting one, whereas the home sewer must make a successful garment in one try. The ability to imagine how the finished garment will look must be developed. It is helpful to first shop clothing stores to analyze the elements that make up a successful and becoming garment.

SUMMARY

The home sewing industry parallels the ready-to-wear fashion industry in the research of fashion trends and the fabric market and the development of styles. Pattern companies such as Vogue-Butterick, McCall's, Simplicity, and Burda offer seasonal catalogs showing sketches and/or photographs of their styles. Pattern development is also similar to that of ready-to-wear except that the patterns themselves are mass produced for consumer use.

Specialty stores have emerged as the most important retailers of patterns and over-the-counter fabrics. Home sewing stores use the same types of resources, services, and promotional activities available to other fashion retailers. And, as in all fashion retailing, it is ultimately the consumer who is responsible for its success or failure—and who completes the cycle of fashion . . . from concept to consumer.

CHAPTER REVIEW

CHAPTER OBJECTIVES

After reading this chapter you should be able to
A. Give evidence of having attained competence in the following areas:
1. Ability to explain the development of styles for the pattern company catalog and considerations in their selection 2. Ability to describe the similarities and differences between ready-to-wear and home sewing textiles, manufacturing, and retailing 3. Ability to explain the reasons for the growth of independent and chain home sewing supply stores 4. Ability to define over-the-counter fabrics
B. Define the following terms and concepts in relation to their discussion in the chapter:
1. Pattern companies 2. Designer patterns 3. Pattern catalog 4. Croquis 5. Over-the-counter fabrics 6. Regular goods 7. Off-sale goods

Questions for Review

1. Why are educational departments important in pattern companies?
2. Discuss the sequential steps in preparing a pattern catalog.
3. Discuss the development of home sewing stores.
4. Discuss the similarities and differences between the home sewing industry and the ready-to-wear apparel industry.

PROJECTS FOR ADDITIONAL LEARNING

1. Evaluate a current pattern catalog. Are the styles offered up-to-date? Do they compare favorably with the styles now in retail stores? Is there a wide selection of styles for a variety of sewing abilities and a variety of customers? Are illustrations or photographs more effective? Is the theme of the catalog consistent? Do you think the pattern company has a particular customer in mind?

2. Visit a local home sewing supply store. Compare fabrics with those seen in ready-to-wear. Are they current? How are fabrics grouped? Do you think the store's visual merchandising entices customers to buy fabrics and make garments?

3. Attend a home sewing promotion. Evaluate the content of the presentation. Was it of educational value? Was it of professional caliber? How does the store benefit from the promotion? How does the customer benefit?

APPENDICES

Dramatic evening fashion by Bill Blass
(Courtesy of Bill Blass, Ltd.)

CAREER GUIDELINES

APPENDIX 1

How will you fit into the fashion business? Choosing a career—not just a job, but work you will enjoy and build on for the future—is one of the most important decisions of your life. We hope that this book and especially this section will help you make that decision.

This appendix tries to give a realistic picture of fashion career possibilities. It surveys job opportunities in textiles, fashion design, marketing, production, retailing, promotion, and the home sewing industry. In planning for your career, you should first understand yourself, your talents, and your ambitions. Then apply those abilities and interests to the field that offers you the best employment opportunities.

THE TEXTILE INDUSTRY

If you enjoy working with fabrics, there are several possibilities for interesting employment in the textile industry. A wide variety of skills and talents is needed, including artists to create new designs, scientists to develop fibers and finishes, technicians to develop and work knitting and weaving processes, and salespeople to market fibers to mills and fabrics to manufacturers. Mechanical skills to run machinery may be obtained in vocational schools; training in art is necessary for a textile design career; and a college education is needed for the scientific and operations areas of the industry. Experienced and able people from the technical as well as the marketing end of the business may advance to management. Relocation may be necessary because most textile operations are located in the South, with marketing and design offices in New York City. However, independent sales representatives are located wherever there are manufacturing centers.

THE HOME SEWING INDUSTRY

Over-the-counter fabrics for home sewing is an important sector of the textile industry. Pattern companies need the services of a fabric expert, but there are very few such positions available. Since they basically parallel the apparel industry, pattern companies also require some of the same skills and talents that are needed in ready-to-wear. However, their greatest needs are in the areas of education (writing pattern directions, for example) and marketing.

Home sewing supply store employees have the same basic qualifications as those of other fashion retailers. However, working for a home sewing supply retailer is an opportunity to combine knowlege of fabrics with education in retailing.

APPAREL MANUFACTURING

For the most part, fashion manufacturers are located in large cities. Those people interested in design positions must be prepared in most cases to relocate to New York or Los Angeles. However, many companies are now opening plants all over the country, and sales representatives are needed to cover territories from coast to coast.

Career opportunities for young people entering the apparel industry vary widely. The most interesting aspect of manufacturing is its diversification. Each person within the company must know something about all areas, so that the company operations run harmoniously. Each of the general branches—merchandising and design, production, and selling—calls for different abilities.

Merchandisers need the ability to prepare the line and present the garments for selling to retailers. The merchandiser works together with the designer in the planning stages, so that the line of samples will be competitive, offering the retailer a varied selection. The merchandiser starts as an assistant merchandiser.

If you have a creative flair, consider becoming a fashion designer. However, designing is not just drawing pretty pictures. Besides being responsible for the original ideas for garments, designers must have a thorough knowledge of fabrics, must be able to make patterns, and must understand how a garment is put together. In some companies, designers are involved in every step of the production of the line, from concept to completed garment.

The prospective fashion designer must be artistically creative, yet understand the technical and marketing aspects of the business as well. Fashion designing is highly competitive. The better aspiring designers are prepared, the broader their opportunities will be. Graduation from a special school for fashion design is considered highly desirable. Upon graduation, the budding designer might start as an assistant in the design or sample department. Any entry-level job will provide useful experience.

If you are interested in fashion design or merchandising, take every opportunity to observe new trends at fashion shows, to visit manufacturers, and to shop all kinds of stores in which garments are sold. Read widely in the many books and magazines that cover fashion (see chapter 4).

If you are technically oriented, you might enjoy a career as a pattern maker. Pattern makers have an important function in the production process: they translate an idea into a pattern for the actual garment. A pattern maker must understand basic mathematics, have a good eye for proportion and line, and be a perfectionist.

To prepare for a career as a pattern maker, it is very important that you learn how to drape a pattern on a dress form and how to draft perfect flat patterns. Your first job may be as an assistant or as a sample cutter or pattern grader.

Production

There are increasingly better opportunities for both men and women as supervisors or managers in fashion production. Production or "operations" heads may have backgrounds in shipping, customer service, and/or piece goods buying. Only a few large manufacturers have management training programs, so a graduate desiring a career in production should seek any entry level position available just to get a start in the field.

Production managers must plan and monitor production to insure that delivery dates are met. Therefore, a well-organized person with a logical mind is best suited for a career in fashion production. Besides technical knowledge, a production manager needs the ability to both manage and motivate people to get the job done. An engineering or business education is an excellent background for a career in this area.

Marketing

If you are outgoing and enjoy working with people, you may like marketing, a career field that is involved with customers and clients. Opportunities are increasing for both men and women to be manufacturers' sales representatives. Sales reps either travel to their territories from New York, or reside within their selling territory. Some college education and merchandising or retailing experience are a good background. A sales rep may start as a showroom model or assistant.

Managers in large manufacturing companies often are people with a background in marketing. Opportunities for advancement in manufacturing are improving as more companies promote from within.

RETAILING

Approximately one of every eight employed persons in the United States works in retailing in some capacity. No matter where you live or where you move, a retail store is nearby. This wide availability of employment is the main reason why retailing and merchandising majors are offered by so many colleges.

You might begin in retailing as a stock room clerk or salesperson, working part-time in a store near your school or home. Work at Christmas time, in the summer, on Saturdays, or after school may provide your initial opportunity and experience.

Another avenue for beginning a retailing career is a management training program. Sizable department stores and specialty stores often provide this type of learning opportunity for those who have graduated from two- and four-year colleges. A typical program consists of work experience in a variety of departments and formal classes conducted by senior executives and training department personnel. All retail stores expect trainees to have selling experience. Unless a person has dealt with customers and heard their comments, questions, and complaints, he or she cannot understand the basis of retailing. Training programs are followed by the opportunity to become a junior executive.

More positions are available in operations than in merchandising. In large stores, there are usually two main tracks to management: one is through buying (merchandising) and the other through operations. Some department stores' training programs combine both tracks, providing a well-rounded experience.

Buying Track

After a training program, the first junior executive position is that of assistant buyer. Assistant buyers aid buyers in all their activities. Assistant buyers spend much of their time maintaining sales and inventory records. In addition, they may accompany buyers on purchasing trips or act for buyers in their absence.

Because the buyer is responsible for the success and profits of the department, he or she must have a combination of merchandising and business training. The buyer might eventually advance to the position of divisional merchandise manager or general merchandise manager. The general merchandise manager is part of top management and sets merchandising policies for the entire store.

Store or Operations Track

The second track in retailing is in store operations. The department manager is responsible for having the goods on the selling floor; for keeping current records of stock; and, in a branch store, for ordering replenishments of stock from the main store. This person needs a background in sales and management training. The department manager is a liaison between salespeople, customers, and buyers. There are also stock room managers and floor supervisors.

The department manager may advance to section manager, assistant store manager, or manager of a branch store. The store manager oversees building maintenance; the movement of goods, employees, and customers within the store; and the general success of the store. Able performers from both merchandising and operations might successfully work their way up to top management. Top management is responsible for the administration and organization of the store, establishing store policies and controlling operations. Obviously, top managers need a solid background in the ranks of lower management.

Other Specialties in Retailing

Some large department and specialty stores employ a fashion coordinator or fashion director. Both work on developing the fashion image of the store, train personnel, and make fashion presentations to customers, which requires public speaking abilities. However, the fashion director's responsibilities are broader. Fashion directors travel to market openings, report on new fashion merchandise, and help buyers to determine what they will order. The fashion director may have a background in styling and coordination or may have been a buyer, depending on store needs. The position of fashion director generally requires a college education in either merchandising or design.

There are also bookkeeping and accounting positions in retailing for those with an education in finance. Such employees keep records of money spent and received, payroll, taxes, and credit. Financial managers must work with top management on budgeting. Other retail opportunities exist in the personnel and training departments, which staff the store with qualified and trained people and handle employee relations. Still other store employees work in sales promotions and advertising, which informs customers about the goods and services available through advertising, publicity, special events, and display.

PROMOTION

If you are creative, you might consider a career in fashion promotion. Fashion promoters communicate a fashion message to the public, to boost sales.

Copywriters work on advertising and publicity for all levels of the industry. They may work directly for producers, manufacturers, and retailers or for agencies. Fashion writers and editors also work for trade and consumer fashion publications. The latter positions are difficult to find and in great demand. They require top writing ability and some experience, perhaps on a college newspaper.

Artists do advertising and publicity layouts and illustrations. Artists are also employed directly by producers, manufacturers, and retailers or work for agencies. Their artistic skills must be technically perfect. Naturally, commercial art training is necessary. Another creative job is that of the display artist in retailing. This position involves decorating the store windows as well as arranging interior displays of merchandise to attract customers.

Imagination and ingenuity are also needed to create special events. Experience in staging shows or running school publicity events is a good background. In most of these areas, a college or technical school training is necessary with a major in journalism or art.

CAREER RESEARCH

After determining how your interests and abilities fit into the fashion business, it is important that you investigate the companies that may be prospective employers. Trade associations will provide lists of companies and valuable information on their respective fields.

There are many different types of companies, both large and small. The advantage of working for a large company is that there is usually opportunity for promotion. However, by working for a small company you can more easily learn every phase of the business.

In design, you can further narrow the field based on your interest in a particular category of fashion—men's, women's, or children's wear—and within each group, based on the style and size range.

In retailing, you must decide whether you would be happiest in a chain store or a single-unit store, a specialty store or a department store. Buying and managerial positions vary with each type and each individual store.

Read about companies that interest you. Directories are available in libraries; annual reports of publicly held companies are available through stock brokers. Before an interview, learn as much as you can about each company: its image, its policies, and so on.

Meet professionals at lectures, fashion shows, Fashion Group meetings, and career seminars. Interview them at their offices for class projects. Continually read trade periodicals to keep abreast of industry news.

HOW TO OBTAIN AN INTERVIEW

Graduating students often feel defeated before they start. However, it is necessary to be persistent and work at getting a job—prospective employers admire people with drive and enthusiasm.

First, you need a résumé listing the highlights of your education, experience, and activities. Be selective. List only the courses, experience, and activities that directly relate to your chosen career. For example, *do not* list the summer you spent as a waitress or waiter at a local resort. On the other hand, *do* list an after-school selling job.

Your résumé should be neatly typed on an electric office typewriter and photocopied or, preferably, printed. You may need to send out as many as 100 résumés to land a job, but don't be discouraged. Each résumé must be accompanied by a letter of introduction asking for an interview and stating where you can be reached by phone or letter and why you want to work for that company. Recommendation letters from teachers and professionals help a great deal.

Many retailers recruit trainees at colleges and junior colleges. However, because textile companies are located largely in New York and the South, you will probably have to write to them unless you live near them. Apparel manufacturing and promotion companies usually respond better to job seekers who contact them in person. They must be convinced by the applicant's enthusiasm that he or she is indeed needed in the company.

In addition to a résumé, the graduate seeking a creative position will need a portfolio to show. The portfolio should look professional, exhibiting only the best examples of your work. Include any projects that won awards or prizes. A design major might include sketches of new ideas (those who are not great artists should do simple technical sketches on graph paper); practice designer work sheets including all the information on fabrics, trimmings, and labor (see the example in chapter 9); large photographs of completed garments worn by professional-looking models; and fabric swatches. Writers should include samples of their work. Especially important is anything that has been published, even in your local or college newspaper.

THE INTERVIEW

A good appearance is absolutely essential for a job interview in the fashion field. You are making a visual statement of what you know about fashion.

Your fashion and company research will be useful during the interview. Brush up on fashion terminology and read current trade periodicals beforehand. Textile and apparel designers should also know up-to-date information on fabric resources. The interviewer will ask questions such as "Why do you want to become a buyer? (designer, etc.)," and "Why do you want to work for this company?" Obviously, without proper research, you could not specifically answer these questions.

No matter what your training or college major, companies will be looking for the following:

A good educational or technical training background

A fashionable appearance

A pleasant personality

A well-developed résumé

Enthusiasm and self-motivation

Awareness and curiosity

The ability to express oneself clearly (except possibly for technical positions)

A professional-looking portfolio (in design or communications)

Leadership ability

THE FIRST JOB

Your first job after school or college should be an apprenticeship, a period of learning on the job. If your employer has no training program, try to set up your own apprenticeship so that you can move around and learn all aspects of the business. Try to learn as much as possible. Think of your first job as paid schooling. Never stop learning and your career will always be rewarding.

The important thing is to obtain experience. Then demonstrate how efficient and talented you are by doing a good job. Companies are always looking for responsible people to promote to better positions. If you are not promoted, at least you have gained experience for moving on to something else. Contacts that you make on the job will be valuable later. For example, fabric salespeople often hear of job openings with apparel manufacturers and spread the word to others.

Be flexible and pleasant with your co-workers. A little humor and diplomacy go a long way toward promoting working relationships. Changes in fashion make the business exciting, but even more so, the creative people involved make it interesting.

Students often talk of opening their own business after graduation, and it seems that working for oneself would be easy. However, many small-company failures are due to lack of experience. Even a specialist with experience in a large company has to take on all the responsibilities in a small one. Before opening your own business, get as much experience as possible, both in a large company and in a successful small one, to see how they are run. Working for yourself is actually harder than working for another company because you must be self-disciplined. There are rewards, of course, for those who have ambition and creativity and are willing to work long and hard.

If you want to move up in the fashion field, give your education, training, and work all the effort and enthusiasm you can. Make the most of each situation. You get out of life what you put into it. Best wishes for a successful and rewarding career.

PROJECTS FOR ADDITIONAL LEARNING

1. Write your résumé. Include information on education, awards, experience, and interests that directly relate to your chosen field.

2. What fashion career do you think would bring you the greatest satisfaction? List the positive aspects of this field as well as the negative. Analyze why you think you will do well and be happy in this career. How is your education preparing you? How will you enter the field, and what are your advancement expectations?

3. Design and communication majors should outline what they plan to include in their portfolios. Ask teachers to help you select your best work. Develop an overall graphic theme for your portfolio.

4. Arrange to interview a professional in your chosen field (designer, retailer, sales representative, etc.). Ask about all aspects of the job. What does he or she like about it, and *not* like? What makes it interesting? How did he or she start in the field, and advance? What valuable advice can he or she give you?

BUSINESS ORGANIZATION AND COMPANY OWNERSHIP

Company ownership is discussed in an appendix because it applies to *all* levels of the fashion industry in the same way.

When a business is formed, a decision must be made about its type of organization. Three basic types of business ownership are common in the United States: the sole or single proprietorship, the partnership, and the corporation. Each has different criteria regarding taxes, management, liability of the owner, and distribution of profits.

A *sole proprietorship* is a business owned by one person; a *partnership* is a business owned by two or more persons under a contractual agreement; and a *corporation* is a separate legal entity formed in accordance with state laws. Corporation ownership is divided into transferable shares of stock that can be distributed among a large number of stockholders or owners.

A small business often begins as an individual proprietorship or partnership, and later, after it has grown, it changes its status into that of a corporation.

SOLE PROPRIETORSHIPS

The most common form of ownership is the single or sole proprietorship. A sole proprietorship is the least complicated business structure to start and the easiest to dissolve. It is the oldest form of business, and the laws regulating it are firmly established.

Legality The structure of a sole proprietorship is very flexible. No federal government approval is necessary, but local authorities may impose some license requirements. There is no legal time limit for a single ownership; the business ends automatically when the proprietor stops doing it.

Administration All policy and day-to-day operations rest with the owner-manager. He or she is in full charge and complete control of organization and profits. The owner has the ability to make quick decisions to adapt to changing market needs, including expanding or contracting the business.

Shortcomings Many single ownerships fail because of inexperience, inept management, undercapitalization, or overdependence on one person, the owner.

Taxes The business profit is taxed as personal income. However, the sole owner is personally liable for all business debt to the extent of his or her entire personal holdings.

Raising Capital A sole owner can raise money to begin or expand a business by purchasing on credit, borrowing, and/or investing personal funds in the business. Since the owner is solely responsible for all business debt, money lenders evaluate the personal wealth of the proprietor as collateral for loans. If a business requires a large investment in equipment or inventory to operate successfully, another type of ownership might be more appropriate.

Example of a Sole Proprietorship

One interesting example of a sole or family proprietorship is Brown's of London. The epitome of "mom and pop" stores, it is owned and operated by Sidney and Joan Burstein. They purchased Brown's, a women's dress shop, in 1970 and made it a mecca for women with discerning taste, for the "outstanding woman who has no wish to stand out."[1] Their designer clothes cater to a rather young, figure-conscious, wealthy clientele. Brown's became so popular that they expanded, but not by the traditional way of adding branches in the suburbs—they simply annexed the shop next door, and eventually other shops on the street. Each shop has a specialty of its own: men's wear (run by their son, Simon), shoes, interior decoration, and even a hair salon.

PARTNERSHIPS

A partnership is a voluntary association of two or more persons to carry on, as co-owners, a business for a profit. Partnership structure has an endless va-

[1] Sidney Burstein, Owner, Brown's, London, personal interview, August 1978.

riation of features. It is easy to begin and terminate. At the beginning the partners should sign an agreement stipulating intentions and buy-sell arrangements in the event that one partner later wants to withdraw. The agreement should also include the contribution of each partner to the business, the division of profit, and the amount of authority for each member.

Legality Partnership brings the same operating flexibility found in a sole proprietorship. There are no federal requirements for starting a partnership, although again local authorities may require some business licenses. Normally, partnership ends by dissolution or the withdrawal of any partner. A partnership is not a separate legal entity, but merely a voluntary association of individuals.

Administration Each partner has equal administrative responsibility, with the various operating functions divided among them. The combined abilities and experience of two or more owners give the business a better chance of succeeding. New business policies and concepts need only the partners' oral agreement to go into effect.

Shortcomings Some disadvantages are obvious. Many partnerships have dissolved or become nonfunctional over disagreements on basic business policies. For a partnership to work, the partners must be compatible and confident that they are working toward a mutual goal. Other serious disadvantages are limited life of partners, unlimited liability, and mutual agency (one partner can make a decision that also binds the other partner or partners).

Taxes The partners are taxed separately on their individual returns. Each partner is fully responsible and liable for all debt and taxes incurred by the business, regardless of the amount of his or her investment in the business, unless a special arrangement (limited partnership) exists limiting the liability of certain partners to their personal investment in the business.

Raising Capital It is easier for two or more people to raise money for their business than it is for one. The combined resources of the partners can be used for collateral when they are seeking investors or applying for a loan. Because of each partner's full liability for business debt, outsiders are more willing to extend credit and grant better terms. The organizational form of a partnership is often used by me-

dium-sized firms and in cases where capital and talent or different specialties work together.

Example of a Partnership Small apparel manufacturing companies often start out as partnerships. Partners bring their specialties into the business. This setup can be ideal since apparel manufacturing has three major divisions. For example, one partner may head design; the second, production; and the third, sales.

CORPORATIONS

A corporation is a complete legal entity unto itself. It is regarded as a legal person, having a continuous existence apart from that of its owners. Unlike a partnership, its existence is not threatened by the death or retirement of a stockholder. Ownership in a corporation is represented by transferable shares of stock whose owners are called stockholders or shareholders. To administer the affairs of the corporation, the stockholders elect a board of directors. The directors in turn select a president and other corporate officers to carry on active management of the business.

Legality A corporation must adhere to formal state laws. The scope and the activities of the company are defined and restricted by a charter. In general, it is necessary to incorporate in the state in which the majority of the business is done. Although no state is legally required to recognize out-of-state corporations, all states permit out-of-state or "foreign" corporations to do business within their borders as long as they comply with state rules and regulations. To incorporate, three or more people must organize and follow certain application and incorporating procedures.

Liability and Other Advantages The main advantage of a corporation over the other business structures is its limited liability. The company is responsible for its debt only to the limit of its assets. The shareholder-owner can lose only the investment.

Because the corporation has a life of its own, retirement, illness, or the death of an owner do not automatically end it. Stock can be transferred from one party to another without interfering with company operations. The ease of disposing of or acquiring stock makes this form of investment very attractive. Both small and large investors find stock ownership a convenient means of partly owning a business enterprise that can be run by professional management.

Administration The shareholders elect a board of directors to administer the affairs of the corporation. The directors in turn select a president and other corporate officers to carry out its active management. Certain stockholders may participate in the policies and day-to-day operation of the companies. They may even control the corporation if they own the majority of stock. But a corporation is not liable for the actions of its stockholders just because they have invested in it.

Shortcomings Sometimes the separation of ownership and control can lead to ineffective management because management has very little at stake in the company's success or failure. In such a case it might be difficult for shareholders to turn out the ineffective officers.

Corporations must accept considerable regulation and limits set by law. A final disadvantage is that corporate income is taxed twice, once in the corporation and again at the shareholder's level.

Taxes Corporations are taxed on their income. Then, if part of the net income is distributed to the owners as dividend, the dividends are considered personal income to the stockholders and are subject to personal income tax. However, the tax code permits small, closely held business corporations (Subchapter S, corporations) under certain circumstances to be taxed at individual rates.

Raising Capital A corporation is generally in the most advantageous position of all the types of businesses to raise capital. It can borrow by putting up corporate assets as collateral. The corporation may "go public," or sell stock to the general public as a means to obtain funds. Funds obtained from selling stock are called equity capital. The risk of the stockholder is limited to the investment; in other words, he cannot lose more than the amount of his investment.

The corporation has become the dominant form of business organization on the American economic scene, probably because of its efficiency in pooling the savings of many individuals and gathering together large amounts of capital. There are still many more sole proprietorships and partnerships than corporations, but in terms of output and dollar volume, the corporations hold an impressive lead. Virtually all large businesses are corporations.

Examples of Corporations in the Fashion Industry
Bloomingdale's in New York City, Bullock's of California, Filene's of Boston, and Rich's in Atlanta are all part of one huge family of retailers, under the name of Federated Department Stores. Federated is one of the nation's largest retail corporations (see appendix XII).

Levi Strauss & Company is an example of an apparel manufacturing corporation (the largest in the world). A family-managed firm, it went public in 1971. Levi Strauss & Co. has divisions to separate various marketing categories such as jeans wear, sports wear, women's wear, and youth wear. They also have foreign subsidiaries to carry out their marketing and manufacturing interests overseas. L. S. & Co. also recently acquired Koracorp Industries, another apparel corporation which was renamed Diversified Apparel Enterprises. True to its name, this new subsidiary encompasses a variety of fashion companies: Koret of California, Koret of Canada, Byer-Rolnick hats, Himalaya sweaters, and Etablissements Fra-For infants wear (in France).

HORIZONTAL AND VERTICAL INTEGRATION

A company may expand by growing horizontally or vertically. Horizontally, companies expand on the same level of the industry. Vertically, companies combine activities on two or more levels of fashion production and/or retailing. Horizontal or vertical expansion may occur in one of three ways: by internal growth, by merger, or by acquisition.

Internal Growth
Most companies grow internally. Internal growth is perhaps the most desirable because it is real growth in terms of creating new products and new jobs.

Horizontally, an apparel company can add new lines to diversify their product offerings; a retail store could open new branches.

A *vertical* apparel company is one that produces its own fabrics, manufactures its own apparel, and retails that apparel in its own stores. The Laura Ashley firm, based in Wales, is an example of a vertical apparel company. Founded by Laura and Bernard Ashley, the firm buys greige goods and prints and dyes them at its own factories. Garments are either cut and sewn in their factories or in a cottage industry arrangement, whereby cut pieces are delivered by truck to neighboring houses to be sewn. Dissatisfied with the merchandising done by their retailer customers, the Ashleys decided to open their own shop in Kensington, a part of London. It was so popular that "at times the doors had to be locked and customers let in a few at a time."[2] They now have over 40 shops around the world selling clothes, accessories, fabrics by the yard, and matching wallpaper.

Not many companies are as vertical as Ashley, but some manufacturers do own and operate retail stores. The manufacturer generally believes so strongly in its merchandising concept that it wants to carry that concept over to the retailing operation or vice versa. An example of this type of organization is Brooks Brothers, the oldest men's apparel retailer in the United States today, founded in 1818 by Henry Brooks. Brooks Brothers now has two manufacturing plants and nineteen men's clothing retail stores across the country.

Mergers and Acquisitions

Companies *merge* to form large corporate organizations for a multitude of reasons. For instance, they may wish to take advantage of a large corporation's purchasing power, or they may want to sell stock to obtain the financial resources needed for expansion.

A store or company may also become part of a corporation by being purchased or *acquired* by that corporation. Sometimes it is cheaper to acquire another company than to develop a new business from scratch. Some parent companies want to be involved in management and financial control; others are content to allow the acquired retail firm to run autonomously, as long as the bottom line on the income statement shows the required profits.

In both cases, operating economies can often be achieved by combining of companies. Duplicate facilities can be eliminated, and marketing, purchasing, and other operations consolidated. Diversification to spread risk can be another motive for a merger or acquisition. Finally, tax considerations and personal reasons can trigger a business combination.

Horizontal Mergers and Acquisitions In a horizontal merger or integration, two companies with the same line of business are combined. Retail stores of relatively equal size often merge to pool their re-

sources. Garfinckel's, incorporating Brooks Brothers, merged with Miller & Rhoads to form a corporation. Miller's of eastern Tennessee; Joseph R. Harris Co. of Washington, D.C.; and Harzfeld's of Kansas City joined later. Today, Garfinckel, Brooks Brothers, Miller & Rhoads, Inc. operates over 90 department and specialty stores from coast to coast, in 17 states and Washington, D.C.

Levi Strauss & Company's purchase of Koracorp is an example of a horizontal acquisition. L. S. & Co. bought another clothing manufacturing corporation in order to further diversify its product range.

Vertical Mergers and Acquisitions In a vertical merger or acquisition, a company expands either forward toward the ultimate consumer or backward toward the source of raw material. Garfinckel's purchase of Brooks Brothers is an example of vertical acquisition. A few textile companies, such as Burlington and J. P. Stevens, have expanded through a combination of mergers and acquisitions (as well as internal growth) to bring all levels of yarn and fabric production together in one corporation.

CONGLOMERATES

Many large conglomerates have moved into the textile and apparel field. A *conglomerate* is a diversified company that owns significantly different lines of business. In a conglomerate merger, two companies in unrelated lines of business are combined. The parent company might be in the apparel industry and own businesses with unrelated product lines, or the parent company might be in a non–apparel-related field and own apparel companies.

General Mills, a food products company, has an apparel division and subsidiaries in the apparel field including The Alligator Company, Eddie Bauer, and Ship & Shore.

Interco, a major diversified apparel manufacturer, also owns a general retail merchandising group that includes department stores, discount stores, and hardware stores.

Conglomerate mergers often lack economic justification, unless the acquiring company can manage more productively the assets of the companies being acquired. Sometimes the diversification of conglomerate ownership can provide advantages to smaller, independent apparel firms through better access to financial resources and managerial talents. The smaller companies may, through conglomerate mer-

[2] "Brief History of Laura Ashley Company," publicity poster (Carno, Wales: Laura Ashley, 1977).

ger, be better able to obtain goods and services in periods of material and energy shortages.

However, there are also many disadvantages for apparel companies associated with a conglomerate. Executives might not be acquainted with the apparel industry. Unsound, hasty decisions can be made in remote corporate headquarters. While a smaller or privately owned apparel firm might fight for survival in a period of adversity, remaining in business until conditions improve, a conglomerate would probably close or liquidate yesterday's successful apparel company if it failed to reach the required profits for a year or two.

BUSINESS ORGANIZATION OUTSIDE THE UNITED STATES

In many other countries the forms of business ownership resemble those in the United States, with variations based on their unique legal, political, social, and economic development.

In socialist and communist countries, the prevailing form of ownership is the government- or state-owned enterprise. In those cases, totally different rules apply.

COMPANY OWNERSHIP TERMINOLOGY IN MAJOR FASHION-PRODUCING COUNTRIES

	Sole Proprietorship	Partnership	Corporation
France	Propriétaire entreprise individuelle	Société en Nom Collectif, Société en Commandite Simple	Société Anonyme (SA), Société à Responsabilité Limitée (SàRL)
Germany	Einzelfirma, Eigentümer	Offene Handelsgesellschaft (OHG), Kommanditgesellschaft (KG)	Aktiengesellschaft (AG), Gesellschaft mit beschränkter Haftung (GmbH)
Italy	Imprese Individuale, Proprietario	Società in Nomo Collettivo, Società in Accomandita Semplice	Società per Azioni (SpA), Società a Responsabilità Limitata
Japan	Jieigyo, Kojin Kigyo	Gomei Kaisha, Yugen Sekinin Kumiai	Kabushiki Kaisha (KK), Yugen Kaisha
Spain	Proprietario	Sociedad Colectiva, Sociedad en Commandita	Sociedad Anonima (SA), Sociedad de Responsabilidad Limitada (SRL)
United Kingdom	Sole Proprietorship	Partnership	Limited Liability Company

THE
25 LARGEST
UNITED STATES
TEXTILE
COMPANIES

APPENDIX 3

Rank	Company *	Sales ($ million)
1	Burlington Industries (Greensboro, N.C.)	2,421
2	J. P. Stevens (New York)	1,651
3	Armstrong Cork (Lancaster, Pa.)	1,244
4	West Point–Pepperell (West Point, Ga.)	885
5	Sperry & Hutchinson (New York)	798
6	Springs Mills (Fort Mills, S.C.)	695
7	Cone Mills (Greensboro, N.C.)	618
8	United Merchants & Manufacturers (New York)	614
9	M. Lowenstein & Sons (New York)	605
10	Congoleum (Milwaukee)	559
11	Cannon Mills (Kannapolis, N.C.)	547
12	Collins & Aikman (New York)	540
13	Dan River (Greensville, S.C.)	530
14	Hanes (Winston-Salem, N.C.)	472
15	Fieldcrest Mills (Eden, N.C.)	464
16	Reeves Brothers (New York)	309
17	Riegel Textile (Greenville, S.C.)	307
18	Albany International (Albany, N.Y.)	289
19	Graniteville (Graniteville, S.C.)	267
20	Avondale Mills (Sylacauga, Ala.)	245
21	Ti-Caro (Gastonia, N.C.)	209
22	Bibb (Macon, Ga.)	207
23	Dixie Yarns (Chattanooga, Tenn.)	200
24	Ludlow (Needham Heights, Mass.)	191
25	Texfi Industries (Greensboro, N.C.)	172

Source: *The 1979 Fortune Double 500 Directory* (Chicago: Time Inc., 1979) (industry code: Textile/Vinyl Flooring).

* Ranked by 1978–79 sales.

THE 25 LARGEST UNITED STATES APPAREL COMPANIES

APPENDIX 4

Rank	Company *	Sales ($ million)
1	Levi Strauss (San Francisco, Cal.)	1,682
2	Interco (St. Louis, Mo.)	1,667
3	Genesco (Nashville, Tenn.)	1,166
4	Blue Bell (Greensboro, N.C.)	872
5	Hart Schaffner & Marx (Chicago, Ill.)	607
6	Cluett, Peabody (New York, N.Y.)	576
7	Kellwood (St. Louis, Mo.)	515
8	V.F. (Wyomissing, Pa.)	488
9	Jonathan Logan (Secaucus, N.J.)	401
10	Warnaco (Bridgeport, Conn.)	398
11	Phillips–Van Heusen (New York, N.Y.)	332
12	Manhattan Industries (New York, N.Y.)	300
13	Oxford Industries (Atlanta, Ga.)	233
14	Palm Beach (Cincinnati, Ohio)	233
15	Salant (New York, N.Y.)	231
16	Russel (Alexander City, Ala.)	176
17	Lesley Fay (New York, N.Y.)	174
18	Bobbie Brooks (Cleveland, Ohio)	151
19	Puritan Fashions (New York, N.Y.)	147
20	Work Wear (Cleveland, Ohio)	144
21	Russ Togs (New York, N.Y.)	143
22	Tultex (Martinsville, Va.)	137
23	Angelica (St. Louis, Mo.)	135
24	William Carter (Needham Heights, Mass.)	130
25	Marlene Industries (New York, N.Y.)	129

Source: *The 1979 Fortune Double 500 Directory* (Chicago: Time Inc., 1979) (industry code: Apparel).

* Ranked by 1978–79 sales.

Levi Strauss & Co.
San Francisco, Cal.

Divisions
    Diversified Products Division, San Francisco, Cal.
    Jeanswear Division, San Francisco, Cal.
    Sportswear Division, San Francisco, Cal.
    Womenswear Division, San Francisco, Cal.
    Youthwear Division, San Francisco, Cal.
Diversified Apparel Enterprises
    Koret of California, San Francisco, Cal.
    Koret of Canada
    Byer-Rolnick Hats
    Himalaya Sweaters
    Etablissement Fra-For
Foreign Subsidiaries
    Numerous foreign subsidiaries under the name
        of Levi Strauss

Interco Incorporated
St. Louis, Mo.

Apparel Manufacturing Group
    Big Yank Corp., New York, N.Y.
    The Biltwell Co. Inc., St. Louis, Mo.
    Campus Sweater & Sportswear Co., New York, N.Y.
    College-Town, Inc., Braintree, Mass.
    Cowden Manufacturing Co., Lexington, Ken.
    Devon Apparel, Inc., Philadelphia, Pa.
    Sidney Gould Co. Ltd., Garden City Park, N.Y.
    International Hat Co., St. Louis, Mo.
    Londontown Corp., Eldensburg, Md.
    Queens Casuals, Inc., Philadelphia, Pa.
    Stuffed Shirt/Stuffed Jeans Inc., New York, N.Y.
Footwear Manufacturing and Retailing Group
    The Florsheim Shoe Co., Chicago, Ill.
    International Shoe Co., St. Louis, Mo.
    Senack Shoes, Inc., St. Louis, Mo.
    INTERCO Savage Ltd., Cambridge, Ont., Canada
General Retail Merchandising Group
    Alberts, Inc., Ferndale, Mich.
    Central Hardware Co., Bridgeton, Mo.
    Eagle Family Discount Stores, Inc., Opa-locka, Fla
    Fine's Men's Shops, Inc., Norfolk, Va.
    Golde's Department Stores, Inc., St. Louis, Mo.
    P. N. Hirsch & Co., St. Louis, Mo.
    Sky City Stores, Inc., Asheville, N.C.
    United Shirt Distributors, Inc., Detroit, Mich.

Genesco, Inc.
Nashville, Tenn.

Operating Companies and Divisions
    Ainsbrooke, Nashville, Tenn.
    Charles H. Bacon Co., New York, N.Y.
    Baker-Cammack Hosiery Mills, Burlington, N.C.
    Big Val Shoe, Nashville, Tenn.
    Burlington Manufacturing Co., Nashville, Tenn.
    Camp Industries, New York, N.Y.
    Capitol Products Co., Nashville, Tenn.
    Cedar Crest Boot Co., Nashville, Tenn.
    Charm Step Shoe Co., Nashville, Tenn.
    Cover Girl Shoe Co., Nashville, Tenn.
    Crestmore Boot Co., Nashville, Tenn.
    Dante, New York, N.Y.
    Dominion Import Co., Nashville, Tenn.
    Dominion Shoe Co., Nashville, Tenn.
    Easy Street Shoe Co., Nashville, Tenn.
    Formfit Rogers, New York, N.Y.
    Fortune Shoe Co., Nashville, Tenn.
    Geisha Robe, New York, N.Y.
    General Shoe Manufacturing, Nashville, Tenn.
    General Shoe Wholesale, Nashville, Tenn.
    Gensole, Nashville, Tenn.
    Gentan, Nashville, Tenn.
    Girltown, Boston, Mass.
    Greensboro Manufacturing Co., New York, N.Y.
    Greif & Co., Baltimore, Md.

Hamilton Sales Co., New York. N.Y.
Hardy Amies of London, New York, N.Y.
Harpeth Apparel Co., Nashville, Tenn.
Hayes Garment Co., Nashville, Tenn.
Haywood Co., Nashville, Tenn.
Jarman Shoe Co., Nashville, Tenn.
Johnston & Murphy Shoe Co., Nashville, Tenn.
Justin Charles Co., New York, N.Y.
Male, Atlanta, Ga.
Mayfair Sportswear, New York, N.Y.
National Vogue Shoemakers, Nashville, Tenn.
Phoenix Clothes, New York, N.Y.
Pleetway, New York, N.Y.
Regatta Sportswear, Nashville, Tenn.
Remuda, Nashville, Tenn.
Republic Shoe Co., Nashville, Tenn.
Robby Len Fashions, New York, N.Y.
Rona/Dalani Dress Co., New York, N.Y.
Rutledge Sleepwear, New York, N.Y.
Sentry Shoe Co., Nashville, Tenn.
Southern Sole, Nashville, Tenn.
Universal Shoe & Apparel, Nashville, Tenn.
Valmore Leather Co., Nashville, Tenn.
Virginia Cutting Co., Nashville, Tenn.
Volunteer Leather Co., Milan, Tenn.
Whitehall Leather Co., Whitehall, Mich.
Wood & Hyde Leather Co., Gloversville, N.Y.
Retail Operations
Baron's, Miami Beach, Fla.
Bell Bros., Nashville, Tenn.
Henri Bendel, New York, N.Y.
Brittain's, Raleigh, N.C.
Burkhardt's, Cincinnati, Ohio
Flagg Bros., Nashville, Tenn.
M. Gilbert & Sons, South Bend, Ind.
Graves, Cox & Co., Lexington, Ken.
Guarantee Shoe Stores, San Antonio, Tex.
Hall-Brown, Knoxville, Tenn.
John-Hardy Shoe Co., Nashville, Tenn.
Innes Shoe Stores, Los Angeles, Cal.
Interstate Shoe Co., Nashville, Tenn.
Jarman Retail, Nashville, Tenn.
Johnston & Murphy Retail, Nashville, Tenn.
S. H. Kress/V. J. Elmdre, New York, N.Y.
Manss, Nashville, Tenn.
McFarlin's, Rochester, N.Y.
Roos/Atkins, San Francisco, Cal.
Sommer & Kaufmann, San Bruno, Cal.
L. Strauss & Co., Indianapolis, Ind.
Valmart, Nashville, Tenn.
Whitehouse & Hardy, New York, N.Y.
Foreign Operations
Agnew-Surpass Shoe Stores, Ltd., Brantford, Ont.,
    Canada
British Rubber Co., Lachine, Que., Canada
General Shoe of Canada, Cambridge, Ont., Canada
Genesco of Canada, Cambridge, Ont., Canada
Genesco International Operations, Cambridge, Ont.,
    Canada
The J. A. Johnston Co., Brackville, Ont., Canada
Charles Jourdan, Romans, France

Blue Bell Inc.
Greensboro, N.C.

Divisions
    Blue Bell Services, Greensboro, N.C.
    Lady Wrangler Division, Greensboro, N.C.
    Red Kap Industries, Nashville, Tenn.
    Retail Factory Outlet Stores, Greensboro, N.C.
    Sedgefield Sportswear, Greensboro, N.C.
    Wrangler Boots, Nashville, Tenn.
    Wrangler Boyswear Division, Greensboro, N.C.
    Wrangler Menswear Division, Greensboro, N.C.
Subsidiaries
    Numerous domestic and foreign subsidiaries under
        the names of Blue Bell and Wrangler

Hart Schaffner & Marx
Chicago, Ill.

Manufacturing Divisions
    Blue Jeans Corp., New York, N.Y.
    Gleneagles/Great Western, Baltimore, Md.
    Hart Schaffner & Marx Clothes, Chicago, Ill.
    Hickey-Freeman Co., Inc., Rochester, N.Y.
    Jaymar-Ruby Inc., Michigan City, Ind.
    Johnny Carson Apparel, Inc., Buffalo, N.Y.
    M. Wile & Co., Inc., Buffalo, N.Y.

Cluett, Peabody & Co., Inc.
New York, N.Y.

Divisions
    The Arrow Company, New York, N.Y.
    Cluett, Peabody International, New York, N.Y.
    Great American Knitting Mills, New York, N.Y.
    Jet Sew, Inc., Barneveld, N.Y.
    Lady Arrow, New York, N.Y.
    The Sanforized Co., New York, N.Y.
    J. Schoeneman, New York, N.Y.
Subsidiaries
    Alatex, Inc., Andalusia, Ala.
    Boyd-Richardson Co., St. Louis, Mo.
    Fischer Mills, Secaucus, N.J.
    Glentex, New York, N.Y.
    Lytton's, Henry C. Lytton & Company, Chicago, Ill.
    The Metropolitan Company, Dayton, Ohio
    RPM Fashions Inc., New York, N.Y.
    Spring City Knitting Co., Royersford, Pa.
    Textest, Inc., New York, N.Y.
Affiliates
    Clupak, Inc., New York, N.Y.
Various foreign subsidiaries

268

Kellwood Company
St. Louis, Mo.

Apparel Groups
    Ashley Group, St. Louis, Mo.
    Calford Group, St. Louis, Mo.
    Glendale Group, Siler City, N.C.
    Kingswell Group, St. Louis, Mo.
    Larchmont, St. Louis, Mo.
    Radcliffe Group, New York, N.Y.
Apparel Subsidiaries
    Perry Manufacturing Co., Mt. Airy, N.C.
    Stahl-Urban Co., Brookhaven, Miss.
    Foreign plant, Mexico
Recreation Group
    American Fiber Lite Inc., Marion, Ill.
    American Waterproofing Co., New Haven, Mo.
    Aquarius Plastics, Washington, Mo.
    Barclay Group, New Haven, Mo.
    Judson Group, New Haven, Mo.
    Stanfield Group, St. Louis, Mo.
    The Wenzel Co., St. Louis, Mo.

Jonathan Logan, Inc.
New York, N.Y.

Selling Divisions
    Act III, New York, N.Y.
    Amy Adams, New York, N.Y.
    Bleeker Street Apparel Corp., Philadelphia, Pa.
    Butte Knitting Mills, New York, N.Y.
    Etienne Aigner, New York, N.Y.
    Fabric Masters, New York, N.Y.
    Harbor Master Ltd., Baltimore, Md.
    Herman, New York, N.Y.
    Hopewell, Philadelphia, Pa.
    Jonathan Logan, North Bergen, N.J.
    Kollection, New York, N.Y.
    Misty Harbor, Baltimore, Md.
    Modern Juniors, New York, N.Y.
    New York Sportswear Exchange, New York, N.Y.
    R & K Originals, New York, N.Y.
    Rosemarie Reid, New York, N.Y.
    Alice Stuart, New York, N.Y.
    Trebor Knitting Mills, Brooklyn, N.Y.
    The Villager, Cornwell Heights, Pa.
Subsidiaries
    Fabric Masters Inc. of Texas, Arlington, Tex.
Manufacturing Plants
    Aero Knit, Baltimore, Md.
    Andrew Knit, Tuscaloosa, Ala.
    Bardstown Manufacturers, Bardstown, Ken.
    Belmont Manufacturing Co., Barnesville, Ohio
    Calhoun Manufacturing, St. Matthews, S.C.
    Clinton Apparel Manufacturing Co., Clinton, S.C.
    Columbus Fashions, Columbus, Ga.
    David Knit, Northumberland, Pa.
    Debra Fashions, Northport, Ala.

Eufaula Fashions, Eufaula, Ala.
Eutaw Manufacturing, Baltimore, Md.
Forest City Fashions, Forest City, Ark.
Greene Manufacturing Co., Greenville, Tenn.
Jay El Dress Co., Philadelphia, Pa.
K & M Dress Co., North Bergen, N.J.
Kim Fashions, Hialeah, Fla.
Kingston Dresses, Fayetteville, Tenn.
Lawrence Manufacturing Co., Walnut Ridge, Ark.
Livingston Fashions, Livingston, Ala.
Lynn Fashions, Brent, Ala.
Margaret Fashions, Panama City, Fla.
Mercer Dress, Burgin, Ken.
Michael Fashions, Miami, Fla.
Misty Manufacturing Co., Baltimore, Md.
Nancy Fashions, Spartanburg, S.C.
Oxford Fashions, Oxford, Ala.
Plaza Manufacturing Co., Spartanburg, S.C.
Roanoke Fashions, Roanoke, Ala.
Ryerson Undergarment, Brooklyn, N.Y.
Sandra Fashions, Sanford, Fla.
Spartan Undies, Spartanburg, S.C.
Steven Fashions, Carrollton, Ala.
Terrence Fashions, Miami, Fla.
Thompson Manufacturing, Bennington, Vt.
Tracy Fashions, Chambersburg, Pa.
Westminster Knit, Westminster, Md.
Woodbury Dress Co., Woodbury, N.J.
York Dress, York, Pa.

Warnaco, Inc.
Bridgeport, Conn.

Edelweiss, Tacoma, Wash.
C. F. Hathaway Co., Waterville, Maine
High Tide Swimwear, Los Angeles, Cal.
Hirsch Weis, Portland, Ore.
Warner's Slimwear, Bridgeport, Conn.
Subsidiaries
CBS Imports Corp., New York, N.Y.
Chaps & Co., New York, N.Y.
San Marcos Corp., Arecibo, Puerto Rico
San Pedro Corp., Inc., Arecibo, Puerto Rico
Jerry Silverman, Inc., New York, N.Y.
Jerry Silverman Sports Inc., New York, N.Y.
Warnaco Men's Sportswear, Altoona, Pa.
Divisions
Puritan Division, Altoona, Pa.
Thane Division, Altoona, Pa.
Warnaco International, Inc., Bridgeport, Conn.
Warnaco Outlet Stores, Inc., Bridgeport, Conn.
White Stag Manufacturing Co., Portland, Ore.

Source: Directory of Corporate Affiliations 1978, 'Who Owns Whom' National Register Publishing Company, Inc., 1979 (Skokie, Ill.)

Fairchild's Financial Manual of Retail Stores 1978, 51st annual ed., (New York: 1978); Fairchild's Publications.

Annual Reports of individual companies

THE TEN LARGEST APPAREL-RELATED RETAILING COMPANIES IN THE UNITED STATES

APPENDIX 5

Rank	Company *	Sales ($ million)
1	**Sears, Roebuck (Chicago)** The world's largest retailer; nationwide chain of selling locations and catalog sales. Simpson-Sears Ltd., Toronto, Canada	$17,946
2	**J. C. Penney (New York)** Nationwide chain of department stores, extensive mail-order business, and other stores	10,845
3	**Federated Department Stores (Cincinnati)** Abraham & Straus, Brooklyn, N.Y. Bloomingdale's, New York, N.Y. Boston Store, Milwaukee, Wisc. Bullock's, Los Angeles, Cal. Bullock's Northern California, Palo Alto, Cal. Burdine's, Miami, Fla. Filene's, Boston, Mass. Foley's, Houston, Tex. Goldsmith's, Memphis, Tenn. Lazarus, Columbus, Ohio Levy's, Tucson, Ariz. I. Magnin & Co., San Francisco, Cal. Rich's, Atlanta, Ga. Rike's, Dayton, Ohio Sanger-Harris, Dallas, Tex. Shillito's, Cincinnati, Ohio	5,405
4	**Montgomery Ward (Chicago)** Nationwide chain of department stores and subsidiaries. Owned by Mobile Corporation, New York	5,014
5	**Dayton Hudson Corporation (Minneapolis)** John A. Brown, Oklahoma City, Okla. Dayton's, Minneapolis, Minn. Diamond's, Phoenix, Ariz. Hudson's, Detroit, Mich. Lipman's, Portland, Ore.	2,981
6	**May Department Stores (St. Louis)** Famous-Barr Company, St. Louis, Mo. G. Fox & Company, Hartford, Conn. The Hecht Company, Washington, D.C. Kaufmann's, Pittsburgh, Pa.	2,623

* Ranked by sales.

Rank	Company	Sales ($ million)
	May-Cohens, Jacksonville, Fla.	
	May–D & F, Denver, Col.	
	May Company, Los Angeles, Cal.	
	The May Company, Cleveland, Ohio	
	Meier & Frank, Portland, Ore.	
	The M. O'Neil Company, Akron, Ohio	
	Strouss, Youngstown, Ohio	
	Venture Stores, Inc., St. Louis, Mo.	
	(discount department stores)	
7	Carter Hawley Hale Stores (Los Angeles)	2,117
	Bergdorf Goodman, New York, N.Y.	
	The Broadway, Los Angeles, Cal.	
	Capwell's, Oakland, Cal.	
	The Emporium, San Francisco, Cal.	
	Neiman-Marcus, Dallas, Tex.	
	Weinstock's, Sacramento, Cal.	
8	Allied Stores (New York)	2,108
	James Black Company, Waterloo, Iowa	
	The Wm. H. Block Company, Indianapolis, Ind.	
	The Bon Marche, Boise, Idaho	
	The Bon Marche, Idaho Falls, Idaho	
	The Bon Marche, Lewiston, Idaho	
	The Bon Marche, Ogden, Utah	
	The Bon Marche, Seattle, Wash.	
	Cain-Sloan Company, Nashville, Tenn.	
	Dey Brothers & Company, Syracuse, N.Y.	
	Donaldson's, Minneapolis, Minn.	
	L. H. Field Company, Jackson, Mich.	
	Gertz, Inc., Jamaica, N.Y.	
	Hardy Herpolsheimer Company, Muskegon, Mich.	
	Heer's, Inc., Springfield, Mo.	
	Herpolsheimer Company, Grand Rapids, Mich.	
	Jordan Marsh Company, Boston, Mass.	
	Jordan Marsh Company, Greensboro, N.C.	
	Jordan Marsh Company, Miami, Fla.	
	Joske Brothers Company, Houston, Tex.	
	Joske Brothers Company, San Antonio, Tex.	
	Levy's of Savannah, Inc., Savannah, Ga.	
	Maas Brothers, Inc., Tampa, Fla.	
	Mabley & Carew, Cincinnati, Ohio	
	Missoula Mercantile Company, Missoula, Mont.	
	The Muller Company, Ltd., Lake Charles, La.	
	The Paris of Montana, Great Falls, Mont.	
	A. Polsky Company, Akron, Ohio	
	Pomeroy's Inc., Harrisburg, Pa.	
	Pomeroy's Inc., Levittown, Pa.	
	D. M. Read Company, Inc., Trumbull, Conn.	
	Stern Brothers, Paramus, N.J.	
	Titche Goettinger Company, Dallas, Tex.	
	Troutman's, Greensburg, Pa.	
	The Edward Wren Store, Springfield, Ohio	
9	R. H. Macy (New York)	1,834
	Bamberger's, Newark, N.J.	
	Davison's, Atlanta, Ga.	
	The LaSalle & Koch Company, Toledo, Ohio	
	(and shopping centers)	
	Macy's, New York, N.Y.	
	Macy's California, San Francisco, Cal.	
	Macy's Missouri–Kansas, Kansas City, Mo.	

Rank	Company	*Sales* *($ million)*
10	Associated Dry Goods (New York)	1,606
	L. S. Ayres and Company, Indianapolis, Ind.	
	The Denver Dry Goods Company, Denver, Col.	
	The Diamond, Charleston, S.C.	
	Goldwaters, Phoenix, Ariz.	
	Hahne & Company, Newark, N.J.	
	The William Hengers Company, Buffalo, N.Y.	
	Joseph Horne Company, Pittsburgh, Pa.	
	Lord & Taylor, New York, N.Y.	
	The H & S Pogue Company, Cincinnati, Ohio	
	Powers Dry Goods Company, Minneapolis, Minn.	
	Robinson of Florida, St. Petersburg, Fla.	
	J. W. Robinson Company, Los Angeles, Cal.	
	Sibley, Lindsay & Curr Company, Rochester, N.Y.	
	Steward Dry Goods Company, Louisville, Ken.	
	Stix, Baer & Fuller, St. Louis, Mo.	

Sources: *The 1979 Fortune Double 500 Directory* (Chicago: Time Inc., 1979); *1978 Directory of Department Stores* (Department Store Guide, Inc., 1978); New York selected annual reports; *Fairchild's Financial Manual of Retail Stores 1978*, 51st annual ed. (New York: Fairchild Publications, 1978); *Directory of Corporate Affiliations 1978, 'Who Owns Whom'* (Skokie, Ill.: National Register Publishing Company, Inc., 1979).

A PROFILE OF IMPORTANT AMERICAN DESIGNER FASHION BUSINESSES

APPENDIX 6

Company	Principal Owners	Operating Heads	Designer	Products and Wholesale Price Ranges
Adolfo, Inc. 538 Madison Ave. New York, N.Y. 10022	Adolfo	Adolfo	Adolfo	Couture suits, dresses, and evening gowns, $175–$1000.
	Leon of Paris	Gary Watenberg, executive vice president	Adolfo	Men's suits and sport coats, $150–$200; Adolfo Sport for men, $30–$75. Licensed products include: Adolfo Sport for women, $30–$100, shirts, ties, furs, shoes, fragrances, hats.
John Anthony, Inc. 550 Seventh Ave. New York, N.Y. 10018	John Anthony	Jerome Uchin	John Anthony	Couture coats, suits, dresses, $150–$400; evening wear to $1,200. Licensed products include: furs, shoes, and Vogue patterns.
Richard Assatly, Ltd. 550 Seventh Ave. New York, N.Y. 10018	Gino deGeorgio, Richard Assatly, Mike Mitchell	Gino deGeorgio, president	Richard Assatly	Dresses, $69–$150; Richard Assatly Additions: evening separates, $39–$69.
Bill Atkinson, Ltd. 514 Seventh Ave. New York, N.Y. 10018	Bill and Jeanne Atkinson	Bill Atkinson, president	Bill Atkinson	Sportswear including coats, $90–$400.
Geoffrey Beene, Inc. 550 Seventh Ave. New York, N.Y. 10018	Leo Orlandi, Geoffrey Beene	Leo Orlandi, executive vice-president	Geoffrey Beene, president	Couture: $600–$2,000. Beene Bag: sportswear, $50–$150. Licensed products including lounge wear, shoes, hosiery, men's sportswear, jeans, active sportswear, neckwear, furs, belts, sheets, and towels.
Bill Blass, Ltd. 550 Seventh Ave. New York, N.Y. 10018	Bill Blass	Bill Blass, president	Bill Blass	Designer clothes, $700–$5,000. Licensed products: furs by Mohl; robes by Royal; tennis clothes by Tennis, Inc.; patterns by Vogue; fragrance by Revlon; scarves; jewelry; men's wear; sheets and towels.
Blassport, Ltd.	Norman Zeiler	Norman Zeiler, president	Bill Blass	Designer sportswear, $30–$150.
Albert Capraro 550 Seventh Ave. New York, N.Y. 10018	Richard Harshman	Carmine Porcelli	Albert Capraro	Coats, suits, dresses, $100–$500; sportswear, $100–$200. Licensed operations: eyewear by Silor Optical; r-t-w in Japan by Hanamura, Ltd.
Bonnie Cashin 866 United Nations Plaza New York, N.Y. 10017	Bonnie Cashin Designs, Inc.	Bonnie Cashin	Bonnie Cashin	The Knittery: sweaters and leather goods.
	Div. of Russell Taylor, Inc.	Bill March, vice president Rhoda Barrett, vice president	Bonnie Cashin	Bonnie Cashin Weatherwear, $40–$150. Cashin Country: coats, suits, jackets, $50–$250.

Company	Principal Owners	Operating Heads	Designer	Products and Wholesale Price Ranges
Liz Claiborne, Inc. 1441 Broadway New York, N.Y. 10018	Liz Claiborne, Arthur Ortenberg, Jerry Chazen, Leonard Boxer	Liz Claiborne, president	Liz Claiborne	Sportswear, $30–$75.
Perry Ellis Sportswear, Inc. 575 Seventh Ave. New York, N.Y. 10018	Manhattan Industries	Perry Ellis	Perry Ellis	Sportswear, $40–$160.
Charlotte Ford, Division of Don Sophisticates 530 Seventh Ave. New York, N.Y. 10018	Herbert Rounick, Charlotte Ford	Herbert Rounick	Charlotte Ford	Don Sophisticate Dresses, $100–$250. The Suit Co., $110–$200. Black Tie: evening separates and dresses, $80–$200. Charlotte Ford II Sportswear, $40–$100. The Blouse Co., $54–$100. The Jean Co., $20–$130. Don Sport by Charlotte Ford: better missy pants, skirts, blouses, sweaters, $40–$80; Princess Sumi petites, $59–$95.
Henry Friedricks & Co. 205 West 39th St. New York, N.Y. 10018	Martin Friedricks	Martin Friedricks, president and chairman	Bill Haire	Sportswear and outerwear under the Bill Haire for Friedricks Sport label, $40–$900.
Diane von Furstenberg Inc. 745 Fifth Ave. New York, N.Y. 10022	Diane von Furstenberg	Sheppard Zinovoy, president	Olivier Gelbsmann	Cosmetics and fragrances, $3.75–$55. Licensed products include dresses, suits, sportswear and children's wear for Puritan Fashions; rainwear for Main Street Fashions, Inc.; eyewear, luggage, home furnishings.
Halston Enterprises Inc. 550 Seventh Ave. New York, N.Y. 10018	Norton Simon, Inc.	Michael Lichtenstein, managing director	Halston	Halston Originals: r-t-w, $280–$1,000. Halston sportswear, $75–$300. Halston made-to-order, avg. price $1,250. Licenses: Halston V (dresses) and Halston VI (sportswear) to Manhattan Inc., $30–$110. Various other licensed products, including accessories, luggage, toiletries, lingerie, men's apparel.
Cathy Hardwick & Friends, Ltd. 530 Seventh Ave. New York, N.Y. 10018	Cathy Hardwick, Patricia Billington	Patricia Billington	Cathy Hardwick	Dresses, $75–$150; separates, $60–$150; coats, $120–$400. Licensed products, including blouses, jeans, sheets, towels.
Holly's Harp, Inc. 950 North Cahuenga Blvd. Los Angeles, CA 90038	Holly Harp, Jim Harp	Holly Harp, president	Holly Harp	Couture, $150–$900. Summertime and Wintertime dresses, $70–$150. Licensed products: Simplicity Patterns, Fieldcrest sheets and towels.
Norma Kamali-OMO 6 W. 56th St. New York, N.Y. 10019	Norma Kamali	Norma Kamali	Norma Kamali	Sportswear, dresses, evening wear, $60–$1,500.
Kasper for J. L. Sports & Joan Leslie 530 Seventh Ave. New York, N.Y. 10018	Division of Leslie Fay	J. L. Sport: Steve Harrison Joan Leslie: Eli Lehrman	Kasper	J. L. Sport: Sportswear, $40–$500. Joan Leslie: Dresses, jackets, skirts, $150–$400.

Company	Principal Owners	Operating Heads	Designer	Products and Wholesale Price Ranges
Anne Klein & Co. Inc. 205 West 39th St. New York, N.Y. 10018	Takihyo, Inc. and Frank R. Mori, Robert P. Oliver, and Tomio Taki	Frank R. Mori	Donna Karan, Louise Dell'Olio	Anne Klein & Co.: designer sportswear, $50–$600. Anne Klein Design Studio licenses various products. Anne Klein International, r-t-w and licensing operations outside United States
Calvin Klein, Ltd. 205 West 39th St. New York, N.Y. 10018	Calvin Klein, Barry Schwartz	Barry Schwartz	Calvin Klein	Women's r-t-w, $84–$280; outerwear, $180–$500; men's wear; cosmetics; blouses, $98–$200; skirts, pants, $84–$180; rainwear, blazers, outerwear, $150–$500; dresses, $94–$280. Licensed products: jeans by Puritan Fashions Corp; furs by Alixandre; scarves; belts; handbags; men's wear; sheets.
L.A. Designs 140 N. La Brea Ave. Los Angeles, Ca. 90036	Lynn La Moine, Carlos Arias	Lynn La Moine	Carlos Arias	Designer knitwear, $65–$850.
Ralph Lauren Inc. 550 Seventh Ave. New York, N.Y. 10018	Bidermann Industries		Ralph Lauren	Women's r-t-w: blouses, skirts, dresses, jackets, $58–$500.
	Polo Fashions Inc. Ralph Lauren	Peter Strom, president	Ralph Lauren	Men's sportswear, $15–$400. Various licensed products include: Chaps men's wear, boots, leather goods, boy's wear, fragrances.
Ron Leal 550 Seventh Ave. New York, N.Y. 10018	Ron Leal, Guido DeNatali	Guido DeNatali	Ron Leal	Designer sportswear, $50–$350, evening wear, coats, and furs.
Frank Masandrea 550 Seventh Ave. New York, N.Y. 10018	Steve Lawrence, Salvatore Giglio, Frank Masandrea	Steve Lawrence	Frank Masandrea	Dresses, $100–$360; bridal apparel, $240–$2,000.
Mary McFadden 264 West 35th St. New York, N.Y. 10018	Mary McFadden, Patrick Lannan	Mary McFadden	Mary McFadden	Couture, $400–$1,400; Licensed products: jewelry, lingerie, fabrics, sheets, perfume; silk dresses for Jack Mulqueen, $130–$150.
Hanae Mori Inc. USA 27 East 79th St. New York, N.Y. 10021	Hanae Mori	Shotaro Hayashi, president	Hanae Mori	Hanae Mori couture, including evening wear, $800–$3,900. Hanae Mori r-t-w: dresses, $190–$700; coats: $400–$700; separates, $400–$700. Licensed products: sheets for West Point–Pepperell.
Albert Nipon Inc. 640 North Broad Street Philadelphia, Pa. 19130	Albert and Pearl Nipon	Albert Nipon	Pearl Nipon	Albert Nipon designer dresses, $100–$200. Albert Nipon Collectibles: designer sportswear, $50–$90. Nipon Boutique: day and evening dresses, $55–$90. Licensed products: r-t-w in Canada and Japan; Swirl (lounge wear); Vogue patterns.

Company	Principal Owners	Operating Heads	Designer	Products and Wholesale Price Ranges
Mollie Parnis, Inc. 530 Seventh Ave. New York, N.Y. 10018	Mollie Parnis, Robert Kaufman	Mollie Parnis	Hubert Latimer Carolyn Simonelli	Mollie Parnis couture, $119–$1200. Mollie Robert dresses, $69–$135.
Rafael Fashion Ltd. 29 West 56th St. New York, N.Y. 10019	Bill Kaiserman	Bill Kaiserman, president	Bill Kaiserman	Dresses, jackets, skirts, blouses, $100–$425; coats, $200–$450; leather and suede, $300–$800.
Oscar de la Renta Ltd. 550 Seventh Ave. New York, N.Y. 10018	Oscar de la Renta, Jerry Shaw	Jerry Shaw, president	Oscar de la Renta	Oscar de la Renta: couture suits, dresses, evening wear, $225–$2100. Miss O: dresses, $75–$150. Licensed products including perfume, men's wear, bathing suits, furs, jewelry, belts.
Dominic Rompollo Inc. 530 Seventh Ave. New York, N.Y. 10018	Ralph Molaro, Jean Roberts, Dominic Rompollo, Gaspare Ciccarello	Ralph Molaro, president	Dominic Rompollo	Dresses, suits, $100–$350.
Gloria Sachs Designs, Ltd. 550 Seventh Ave. New York, N.Y. 10018	Gloria Sachs	Gloria Sachs	Gloria Sachs	Sportswear, dresses, and knitwear under Gloria Sachs Cashmere label, $35–$170; coats, $150–$300.
Giorgio Sant'Angelo for Marger Enterprises 550 Seventh Ave. New York, N.Y. 10018	Mario Lupia	Jerry Guttenberg	Giorgio Sant'Angelo	Dresses, $100–$500. Parts: separates, $25–$100. Licensed products including furs by Michael Forest, home furnishings, and accessories.
Don Sayers 512 Seventh Ave. New York, N.Y. 10018	Division of Russell Taylor, Inc.	Eileen Rubini, division president	Don Sayers	Sportswear, $48–$300.
Jerry Silverman, Inc. 530 Seventh Ave. New York, N.Y. 10018	Warnaco, Inc.	Sheldon Landau	Ted Saulino and Frank Tignino	Dresses, suits, coats, $90–$300.
Adele Simpson Inc. 530 Seventh Ave. New York, N.Y. 10018	Adele Simpson, Joan Raines, Richard Raines	Adele Simpson	Adele Simpson, Donald Hopson	Dresses, $140–$1,000.
Ernst Strauss & Schnell Sports 714 S. Los Angeles Los Angeles, Ca. 90014	Paul Scott, Freddy Diament, Ben Kamm	Paul Scott	Paul Schnell	Tailored daytime suits, $200–$625; coats, $200–$850; fur coats, $550–$1,200; sportswear, $200–$350.
Trigere, Inc. 550 Seventh Ave. New York, N.Y. 10018	Pauline Trigere	J. P. Radley, comptroller	Pauline Trigere	Dresses, suits, coats, $500–$2,000. Licenses: perfume, neckties, furs, costume jewelry.
Adrienne Vittadini 1441 Broadway New York, N.Y. 10018	Adrienne Vittadini, Victor Coopersmith	Victor Coopersmith	Adrienne Vittadini	Knitwear, $20–$80.
Chester Weinberg Sport 530 Seventh Ave. New York, N.Y. 10018	Division of Jones Apparel Group	Susan Van Dine, division president	Chester Weinberg	Sportswear, $30–$90.

Company	Principal Owners	Operating Heads	Designer	Products and Wholesale Price Ranges
Willi Wear, Ltd. 62 West 39th St. New York, N.Y. 10018	Laurie Mallet, Willi Smith	Laurie Mallet, president	Willi Smith, vice-president	Women's sportswear, $15–$150.

Compiled by the author in 1980.

HISTORICAL CHART OF INTERNATIONALLY INFLUENTIAL DESIGNERS

APPENDIX 7

Years Most Influential	Designer and Fashion Directions
1774–93	Rose Bertin, dressmaker to Marie Antoinette
1790–1815	Hippolyte le Roy, dressmaker for the court of Napoleon, creator of the classic revival Empire style
1860s	Charles Worth (b. England), father of modern couture
Late 1800s	Redfern, Cheruit, Doucet, Paquin
Early 1900s	Madame Gerber (house of Callot Sisters), Jeanne Lanvin
1909–11	Paul Poiret, colorful, exotic minaret or lampshade tunic
1912–15	Charlotte Premet
Post–World War I	Madelaine Vionnet, first to do bias cut
1916–21	Coco Chanel, known for the boyish look and for using jersey
1922–29	Jean Patou, known for the Flapper look
1930–35	Elsa Schiaparelli (b. Italy), "hard chic" and unconventional styling
1936–38	Mainbocher (b. United States) and Molyneux (b. Ireland), understatement and broadening shoulders
	(All of the above worked in France.)
1940–45	Claire McCardle (American in America), known for American Look of practical sportswear. The war years made communication with Europe impossible and made Americans begin to appreciate their own designers.
1947–57	Christian Dior. With his New Look, Paris fashion leadership is regained.
1950s–60s	Balenciaga, Givenchy, St. Laurent
	André Courrèges, stark, futuristic
	Italian designers such as Pucci becoming important
1960s	Mary Quant. English designers have international influence.
	Beginning of young designers creating for young people
	Mini skirts and Mod total look
1968–75	Much confusion in fashion direction. Couture is dying due to high cost of labor. Paris influence is waning.
	"Fashion from the streets," young people turn to old clothes and jeans.
	Ethnic influence
1970s	International exchange of fashion and return to traditional fashion
	Major influence from French prêt-à-porter: St. Laurent, Kenzo (b. Japan), Rykiel, Lagerfeld (b. Germany)
	American designers becoming internationally known, such as Beene
	Italian designers important: Armani, Albini, Versace

CHART OF SELECTED MAN-MADE FIBERS, BRAND NAMES, AND PRODUCERS

APPENDIX 8

CELLULOSE FIBERS (made from wood)

Generic Name	Brand Name	Producer
Acetate		
Weaker than most other fibers. When made into fabrics, these fibers drape well and have a lustrous, silklike look. They are fast drying and shrink-resistant. Used mostly in such fabrics as satin, faille, crepe, taffeta, and brocade. Made up in foundation dresses, lingerie, and knitted jerseys.	Ariloft	Eastman Chemical Products, Inc.
	Celanese Acetate	Celanese Corp.
	Chromspun	Eastman Chemical Products, Inc.
	Dicel	Courtaulds
	Estron	Eastman Chemical Products, Inc.
	Lanese	Celanese Corp.
	Loftura	Eastman Chemical Products, Inc.
Rayon		
Weaker than most other fabrics. Popular for dresses, rayon is highly absorbent, soft, easy to dry, economical, and drapable. Use mostly in challis, crepe, and georgette.	Avril	Avtex Fibers, Inc.
	Beau-Grip	North American Rayon Corp.
	Coloray	Courtaulds
	Enkrome	American Enka Company
	Fibro	Courtaulds
	Xena	North American Rayon Corp.
	Zantrel	American Enka Company
Triacetate		
A refinement of acetate, triacetate is also shrink- and wrinkle-resistant, resists fading, and is easily washed. Most important, it has a crisp finish and holds pleating, so it is used in shirts, dresses, and sportswear in such fabrications as sharkskin, taffeta, faille, flannel, and jersey.	Arnel	Celanese Corp.
	Tricel	Courtaulds

NONCELLULOSIC FIBERS

(Made chemically from petroleum, coal, gas, air, and water. Most of these fibers soften at high temperatures, making pleat setting, shape retention, and embossing possible. They are resilient and spring back when crushed, nonabsorbent, and dry quickly. Most are nonallergenic and not affected by moths or mildew. Their nonporous surfaces do not allow dirt to become embedded.)

Generic Name	Brand Name	Producer
Acrylic		
Resembles wool and is warm for its weight. Fabrics made from acrylic are soft and fluffy, making them especially suitable for baby wear, sweaters, dresses, and skiwear. However, acrylic tends to pill.	Acrilan	Monsanto Textiles Company
	Bi-Loft	Monsanto Textiles Company
	Courtelle	Courtaulds
	Creslan	American Cyanamid Company
	Fina	Monsanto Textiles Company
	Orlon	E.I. duPont de Nemours & Co., Inc.
	Zefran	Badische Corp.

Metallic

Composed of metal or metal combined with plastic, metallic threads are often used decoratively in fabrics of other fibers.

Lurex	Dow Badische Co.

Modacrylic

A nonallergenic fur substitute, these fibers are made from resins and are used mostly for fake furs, deep pile coats, and hairpieces.

Acrilan	Monsanto Textiles Company
SEF	Monsanto Textiles Company
Verel	Eastman Kodak Company

Nylon

Nylon is exceptionally strong, elastic, lustrous, and easy to wash. Nylon yarns made from filaments are smooth and soft; spun nylon yarns give light-weight warmth. There are two types of nylon: 6 and 66.

Anso	Allied Chemical Corp.
Antron	E.I. duPont de Nemours & Co., Inc.
Beaunit Nylon	North American Rayon Corp.
Blue "C"	Monsanto Textiles Company
Cadon	Monsanto Textiles Company
Cantrece	E.I. duPont de Nemours & Co., Inc.
Caprolan	Allied Chemical Corp.
Captiva	Allied Chemical Corp.
Celanese Nylon	Celanese Corp.
Celon 6	Courtaulds
Cordura	E.I. duPont de Nemours & Co., Inc.
Crepeset	American Enka Company
Cumuloft	Monsanto Textiles Company
Enkaloft	American Enka Company
Enkalure	American Enka Company
Enkasheer	American Enka Company
Monvelle	Monsanto Textiles Company
Multisheer	American Enka Company
Nyesta	Roselon
Qiana	E.I. duPont de Nemours & Co., Inc.
Shareen	Courtaulds
Ulstron	Monsanto Textiles Company
Ultron	Monsanto Textiles Company
Vecana	Chevron Chemical Company
Zeflon	Badische Corp.
Zefran	Badische Corp.

Olefin

Olefin can draw body moisture away from the skin to the outside of the fabric. It is used in sweaters and hosiery.

Herculon	Hercules Inc.
Marvess	Phillips Fibers Corp.
Polyloom	Chevron Chemical Company
Vectra	Chevron Chemical Company

Polyester

One of the major fibers in apparel today, polyester dries quickly and can retain heat-set pleats and creases. It is therefore used for permanent press.

Avlin	Avtex Fibers Inc.
Blue "C"	Monsanto Textiles Company
Caprolan	Allied Chemical Corp.
Dacron	E.I. duPont de Nemours & Co., Inc.
Encron	American Enka Company
Fortrel	Celanese Corp.
Hollofil	E.I. duPont de Nemours & Co., Inc.
Kodel	Eastman Chemical Products, Inc.
Lirelle	Courtaulds
Silesta	Roselon
Spectran	Monsanto Textiles Company
Strialine	American Enka Company
Terrylene	I.C.I.
Trevira	Hoechst Fibers Inc.
Twisloc	Monsanto Textiles Company
Vycron	North American Rayon Corp.
Zefran	Badische Corp.

Synthetic Rubber

Synthetic rubbers are used where stretch is necessary, such as in elastic and foundation garments.

Uniroyal

Uniroyal

Spandex

Light, soft, and smooth, some Spandex is even stronger than rubber. The fibers do not deteriorate from perspiration, lotions, or detergent, making Spandex ideal for swimsuits.

Lycra
Monvelle

E.I. duPont de Nemours & Co., Inc.
Monsanto Textiles Co.

Source: Man-Made Fiber Producers Association, Inc.

NATIONAL TRADE ASSOCIATIONS AND LABOR UNIONS IN THE FASHION INDUSTRY

APPENDIX 9

Amalgamated Clothing Workers of America (ACWA)
15 Union Square
New York, N.Y. 10003

American Apparel Manufacturers Association, Inc.
1611 North Kent Street, Suite 800
Arlington, Va. 22209

American Footwear Industries Association
1611 North Kent Street
Arlington, Va. 22209

American Printed Fabrics Council, Inc.
1440 Broadway
New York, N.Y. 10018

American Textile Manufacturers' Institute, Inc. (ATMI)
Wachovia Center
400 South Tryon Street
Charlotte, N.C. 28285

American Wool Council
200 Clayton Street
Denver, Colo. 80206

American Yarn Spinners Association, Inc.
P.O. Box 99
Gastonia, N.C. 28052

California Fashion Creators
110 East 9th Street
Los Angeles, Ca. 90015

Cotton, Inc.
1370 Avenue of the Americas
New York, N.Y. 10019

Council of Fashion Designers of America
32 East 57th Street
New York, N.Y. 10022

The Fashion Group Inc.
9 Rockefeller Plaza
New York, N.Y. 10020

International Ladies' Garment Workers' Union (ILGWU)
1710 Broadway
New York, N.Y. 10019

International Silk Association, USA (ISA)
299 Madison Avenue
New York, N.Y. 10017

Knitted Textile Association
51 Madison Avenue
New York, N.Y. 10010

Man-Made Fiber Producers Association, Inc.
1150–17th Street, N.W.
Washington, D.C. 20036

Men's Fashion Association of America (MFA)
1290 Avenue of the Americas
New York, N.Y. 10019

Millinery Institute of America
10 East 49th Street
New York, N.Y. 10016

National Cotton Council of America
P.O. Box 12285
Memphis, Tennessee 38112

National Knitted Outerwear Association
51 Madison Avenue
New York, N.Y. 10010

National Knitwear Manufacturers Association
350 Fifth Avenue
New York, N.Y. 10001

National Retail Merchants' Association (NRMA)
100 West 31st Street
New York, N.Y. 10001

United Garment Workers of America (UGW)
31 Union Square
New York, N.Y. 10003

Wool Bureau, Inc.
360 Lexington Avenue
New York, N.Y. 10017

FASHION INDUSTRY TERMINOLOGY

Learning the terminology of the fashion industry is an important part of a fashion education. By using correct terminology, you show that you are familiar with the business. Many fashions terms are from the French language, since France has long been the capital of fashion innovation. For further clarification, check the index and refer to the text to see how the term was used.

accessories Articles worn or carried to complete a fashion look, such as jewelry, scarves, hats, handbags, or shoes.

advertising Any paid message in the media used to increase sales, publicize services, or gain the acceptance of ideas by potential buyers.

advertising director The person in charge of personnel and activities of the advertising department.

alta moda Italian couture.

apparel Clothing, not necessarily fashionable.

apparel industry The manufacturers, jobbers, and contractors engaged in the manufacture of clothing (also called the *garment trade*, the *needle trades*, *cutting-up trades*, the *rag business*).

artisans People who do skilled work with their hands.

atelier (ah'-tel-yay') French word for designer workshop. Ateliers are classified as *flou* (for soft dressmaking) or *tailleur* (for tailoring suits and coats).

avant-garde (a'-vahnt guard') French term describing a design that is ahead of its time or unconventional.

base goods Main solid fabric of a group.

book inventory The dollar value of inventory, as stated in accounting records.

boutique (boo-teek') French word for a small shop with unusual clothing and atmosphere.

branch store Store owned and operated by a parent store; generally located in a suburban area under the name of the parent store.

branch store manager Person responsible for the overall operation of a branch store in a department store group.

brand name A trade name that identifies a certain product made by a particular producer.

buyer A merchandising executive with the responsibility of planning, buying, and selling merchandise.

buying office An independent or store-owned office located at a market center, which buys for one chain or for many stores.

buying plan A general description of the types and quantities of merchandise a buyer expects to purchase for delivery within a specific period.

caution fee (cow-see-on') An admission or entrance fee charged by haute couture houses to commercial customers as a preventive measure against copying, but which may be applied to any purchases.

chain store organization A group of stores that sell essentially the same merchandise and are centrally owned, operated, and merchandised.

checking Describes a style selling well at retail.

chic (sheek) French word meaning stylish.

classic A fashion that is long-lasting.

classification An assortment of related merchandise that is grouped together within a department of a store.

collection A designer's or manufacturer's group of garments for a specific season. (Moderately and lower-priced collections are referred to as *lines*.)

commissionaire (ko-me'-see-ohn-air') Store representative in foreign cities.

confinement A fabric, line, label, or style that is sold by a producer or manufacturer on some exclusive basis in the trading area.

conglomerate A group of companies that may or may not be related in terms of product or marketing level, but that are owned by a single parent organization.

consumer A user; sometimes used to denote a person who makes a buying decision.

consumer demand The quantity of goods or services the consumer is willing to buy.

consumerism The rights of consumers to protection against unfair marketing practices.

consumer obsolescence The rejection of present ownership in favor of something newer, even though the "old" still has utility value.

contemporary styling Sophisticated, updated styling; originally designed for the age group that grew out of juniors.

contractor An independent manufacturer who does the sewing (sometimes the cutting) for other producers; an "outside shop."

converter A textile producer that buys greige goods or unfinished fabric from mills and dyes, prints, and finishes it before selling it to a manufacturer.

co-operative advertising Advertising costs shared by a textile producer and/or a manufacturer and/or a retailer.

cotton A vegetable fiber from the boll of the cotton plant.

Coty American Fashion Critics Award Annual award given since 1942 for outstanding fashion design.

couture (ko-tour') Literally, French for dressmaking; applied to fashion businesses that make clothes to order.

couturièr (koo-tu'-ree-ay') Male French dress designer, for example, Yves St. Laurent, Marc Bohan, and Hubert de Givenchy.

couturière (koo-tu'-ree-air') Female French designer, for example, Alix Grès.

custom made Apparel made to a customer's special order; cut and fitted to individual measurements; opposite of ready-to-wear.

cutter The person who cuts material during the manufacturing process.

department store General merchandise store, including apparel, household goods, and furniture.

designer Person employed in creating ideas for garments or accessories in the fashion industry.

design reports Reports and ideas available on a subscription basis to manufacturers and retailers. For example, I. M. International, Faces, Nigel French, Promostyl, Here and There, Tobé.

design resource Any resource from which a designer obtains ideas. Can be trade newspapers, design reports, fashion magazines, museums, historic costume books, nature, theater, films, fabrics, etc.

direct-mail advertising Any printed advertising distributed directly to specific prospects by mail.

discount merchandising Low-margin retailing, selling merchandise below normal price levels and offering reduced services.

discretionary income Income left after basic necessities have been paid for.

display Visual presentation of merchandise or ideas.

disposable income Income minus taxes; a person's purchasing power.

divisional merchandise manager A person in middle management of a retail store; executive responsible for merchandising activities of a related group of departments; supervises buyers and assistants.

dollar merchandise plan A budget or projection, expressed in dollars, of the sales goals of a merchandise classification, a department, or an entire store for a certain period, including the amount of stock required to achieve those sales.

dossier (dose'-ee-ay') French for press packet.

draping A method of making a pattern by draping fabric on a dress form.

fabrication Selection of the appropriate fabric for a garment.

fad A short-lived fashion.

fashion The prevailing style of any given time; implies change in style.

fashion consultant A person who gives professional fashion advice or services.

fashion coordinator or director The fashion expert of an organization who keeps it current with fashion developments and works with designers or buyers to form the fashion image of the company.

fashion cycle Fashion change; refers to the introduction, acceptance, and decline of a fashion.

fashion editor The head fashion reporter at a magazine or newspaper who analyzes the fashion scene and interprets it for the readers.

fashion forecast A prediction of forthcoming fashions.

fashion goods New goods that have a relatively short life but are of interest temporarily to many people.

Fashion Group An international association of professional women in the fashion business; founded in 1931.

fashion innovation New ideas in fashion styling.

fashion merchandising The planning required to have the right fashion merchandise available in the proper quantities and place, at the right time and price to meet consumer demand.

fashion press Reporters of fashion news for magazines and newspapers.

fashion retailing The business of buying fashion merchandise from a variety of resources and re-selling it to ultimate consumers at a convenient location.

fashion trend The direction in which fashion is moving.

Federation Française de la Couture French couture trade association composed of three main membership classifications (each called a *Chambre Syndicale*) and associated groups of manufacturers and artisans.

fibers Strands or filaments of natural or synthetic sources from which yarns are made.

filament A continuous strand of fiber.

findings Trade term for functional trimmings needed to complete a garment, such as zippers and elastic.

finishing The last treatments given to fabrics; the final hand work or final touches done to a garment.

first pattern Trial pattern made in the design department for the sample garment.

general merchandise stores Retail organizations including department stores, most mail-order houses, and variety stores.

generic name Family name given to each type of fiber.

grading Process of making a sample size pattern larger or smaller to make up a complete size range.

greige goods Unbleached, unfinished fabrics bought by converters.

gross margin The difference in dollars between net sales and the net cost of merchandise during a period of time.

hard goods Major appliances: refrigerators, deep freezers, electric and gas ranges, washing machines, dryers, air conditioners (opposite of soft goods).

haute couture Those dressmaking houses in Paris that belong to the *Chambre Syndicale* and meet the criteria to be on its *Couture-Creation* list (see chapter 2).

high fashion The newest fashion designs worn by fashion leaders.

horizontal integration The joining of companies that function on the same marketing and production level.

hot item A best seller; also known as a *runner* or a *ford*.

Ideacomo Italian fabric producers' trade fair, held each November and May in Como, Italy, followed by presentations in New York.

ILGWU International Ladies' Garment Workers' Union.

import merchandise Goods made in a foreign country.

inside shop An apparel company that does all its manufacturing processes in its own factory.

intensity The brightness or paleness of a color.

Inter-Color A twice-yearly meeting in Paris of fashion industry representatives from all over the world to discuss color directions for the future.

Interstoff German term meaning "inter-fabric" International fabric trade fair, held each November and May in Frankfurt, Germany.

Jacquard loom (jah-kard') A loom invented by Joseph Jacquard in France in 1801 that weaves an elaborate pattern (such as damask, brocade, or tapestry) by controlling each warp thread separately.

jobber A middleman between producer and commercial consumer.

juniors Size scale of female apparel. Range is in odd numbers, 3 to 15.

knock-off A copy of a higher-priced style.

leased department Within a store, a department that is actually run by an outside company.

licensing Giving a manufacturer permission to use a designer's name or designs in return for a fee or percentage of sales.

line An apparel manufacturer's collection of styles. Also, visual direction in a design caused by seams, details, or trimming.

line-for-line copy Exact copy of a style originated by a foreign couturier.

linen A vegetable fiber from the woody stalk of the flax plant.

loss leader An item sold at less than regular wholesale price for the purpose of attracting retail buyers to other merchandise.

man-made fibers Synthetic fibers made from cellulose in wood or plant life or from chemicals derived from petroleum, gas, and coal.

markdown The difference between the original retail price and a reduced price.

marker A pattern layout put on top of the fabric for the cutter to follow.

market A group of potential customers; or the place, area, or time at which buyers and sellers meet to transact business.

marketing A total business interaction that includes the planning, pricing, promotion, and distribution of consumer-wanted goods.

markup (mark-on) Difference between cost price and selling price.

mass production The production of merchandise in quantity (factory made), as opposed to custom made, one at a time.

media Means of communication: newspapers, magazines, radio, TV, trade publications.

missy Size range in feminine apparel in even numbers, 6 to 16.

moda pronta Italian ready-to-wear.

mode Synonym for fashion; used mainly in Europe.

national brands Manufacturers' brands that are available nationwide.

natural fibers Fibers that nature provides: cotton, wool, silk, and flax.

off-price A price lower than the original wholesale price, or below normal wholesale price.

offshore production Garments designed in one country but produced in another where labor is cheaper.

open-to-buy The amount of money a buyer can spend on merchandise to be delivered within a given period, minus the amount allocated to merchandise on order.

operations Steps in production; activities of running a business.

overhead The costs of operating the store or company that do not vary with the number or value of the specific items being sold.

over-the-counter trade Fabrics sold to home sewing retailers.

outside shop Contractors used by apparel producers to sew garments, sometimes to cut fabric.

parent store The downtown or centrally located store where the executive, merchandising, and promotional staffs are located.

physical inventory A physical count of stock on hand.

piece goods The trade term for fabrics.

piece work Rate by which most factory workers are paid.

prestige or institutional advertising Advertising to promote a store's image or goodwill rather than specific merchandise.

prêt-à-porter French for ready-to-wear; literally, "ready to carry."

price line A specific price point at which an assortment of merchandise is offered for sale.

price range The range between the lowest and highest price lines carried.

production pattern The final pattern made to company size standards.

promotion An activity designed to encourage the purchase of a product.

promotional or merchandise advertising Advertising to promote the sale of specific merchandise.

promotional stores Stores that stress special sales, bargains, and price reductions, and claim to undersell competitors.

proportion An important principle of garment design; the relation of one part of the design to another.

publicity Nonpaid messages about a company, its policies, personnel, activities, or services.

purchase journal A monthly or semimonthly report listing all invoices for merchandise received, transfers of merchandise, or returns to vendors as entered in a store's book inventory.

ready-to-wear Apparel that is mass produced (opposite of custom made).

receiving The point in the store where packages are opened, checked, and marked.

resource Term used by retailers; synonymous with manufacturers, wholesalers, distributors. A company that sells goods in the market of finished apparel.

retailing The business of buying goods at wholesale markets and selling them at retail to the ultimate consumer.

retail method of inventory A method of inventory evaluation in which all merchandise transactions are recorded at retail value.

retail price The wholesale price plus a markup covering the retailer's operating costs and a profit.

sales promotion director Supervises advertising, display, special activities or events, press, and/or public relations.

sample The model or trial garment that is shown to the trade.

sample cut A three- to ten-yard length of fabric used by the design department to make up a trial sample garment.

Savile Row Street in London famous for its men's tailors.

Seventh Avenue The main street of New York City's garment district; term used to represent the whole area.

showing Formal presentation of styles, usually in connection with showing the season's new merchandise.

showroom A place where salespersons show a line of merchandise to potential buyers; called *salon de presentations* in France.

silhouette Outline of a garment.

silk An animal fiber from the cocoons spun by silkworms.

soft goods Fashion and textile merchandise (opposite of hard goods).

special events Activities set up to attract customers to a selling place.

specialty store A retail establishment that handles fairly narrow categories of goods, such as men's apparel, female apparel, or shoes.

spinning The process of drawing and twisting fibers together into yarns or threads.

staple goods Goods for which there is a demand that continues over many seasons. Staple goods should always be carried in stock.

stock turnover The number of times that a store's merchandise stock is sold and replaced in a given period.

store image The character or personality that a store presents to the public.

style Certain characteristics that distinguish a garment from other garments; a subdivision within a fashion.

style ranges Categories of styles that appeal to different consumers.

stylist A fashion expert; generally selects colors, prints, or styles for presentation or prepares fashion merchandise for photographic presentation in an advertisement or catalog.

tanning The process of transforming animal skins into leather.

target market The group of consumers to whom a producer, manufacturer, or retailer aims products, services, and advertising.

textile fabrics Cloth made from textile fibers by weaving, knitting, felting, crocheting, laminating, or bonding.

texture The surface interest in a fabric.

toile (twahl) French word for muslin or muslin sample garment.

trademark Company's individual registered mark and name for a product.

trend setter A designer or fashion leader who sets a fashion direction that others follow.

trunk show Show of designer clothes that moves from store to store, often accompanied by a personal appearance of the designer.

ultimate consumer The end user; one who uses the product for personal purposes.

unit control Systems for recording the number of units of merchandise bought, sold, in stock, or on order.

value The lightness or darkness of a color.

vendor A seller, a resource, a manufacturer, a supplier.

vertical integration The joining of companies at different levels of production and marketing, such as a fiber producer with a fabric mill.

warp knitting Knitting fabric in loops running vertically.

weaving The process of forming fabric by interlacing yarns on looms.

weft knitting Knitting fabric in loops horizontally or in a circle.

wholesale market Market where commercial consumers buy from producers.

wholesale price Price paid by commercial consumers for supplies and products.

Women's Wear Daily Trade publication of the women's fashion industries.

wool An animal fiber from the hair of sheep or certain other animals.

yarn A continuous thread produced by twisting or spinning fibers together.

SELECTED BIBLIOGRAPHY

Adburgham, Alison, *Liberty's, A Biography of a Shop.* London: George Allen & Unwin, Ltd., 1975.

All about Textiles. Charlotte, N.C.: American Textile Manufacturers Institute, 1978.

"Apparel Manufacturing," *Small Business Reporter,* 10, no. 3. San Francisco: Bank of America N.T. & S.A., 1971.

Brockman, Helen L., *The Theory of Fashion Design.* New York: John Wiley & Sons, Inc., 1965.

Calasibetta, Charlotte, *Fairchild's Dictionary of Fashion.* New York: Fairchild Publications, Inc., 1975.

Carter, Ernestine, *The Changing World of Fashion.* London: Weidenfeld and Nicholson, 1977.

The Changing American Woman—200 Years of American Fashion. New York: Special edition of *Women's Wear Daily,* Fairchild Publications, Inc., 1976.

Coleman, Elizabeth Ann, "The Pattern of Male Fashion," in *Of Men Only.* New York: The Brooklyn Museum, 1975.

Cobrin, Harry, *Men's Clothing Industry: Colonial Through Modern Times.* New York: Fairchild Publications, Inc., 1970.

Fleece to Fabric. Denver: American Wool Council, 1977.

Frings, Virginia Stephens, *Apparel Manufacturing from the Inside Out* (audio-visual). San Francisco: Canfield Press; Harper & Row, Publishers, Inc.; and Design West, 1975.

Frings, Virginia Stephens, *Design in Clothing* (audio-visual). San Francisco: Canfield Press; Harper & Row, Publishers, Inc.; and Design West, 1977.

Frings, Virginia Stephens, *Your Career in Design and Merchandising* (audio-visual). San Francisco: Design West, 1977.

Garland, Madge, *The Changing Form of Fashion.* New York: Praeger Publishers, 1970.

Grace, Evelyn, *Introduction to Fashion Merchandising.* Englewood Cliffs, N.J.: Prentice-Hall, Inc., 1978.

Lambert, Eleanor, *World of Fashion—People, Places, Resources.* New York: R. R. Bowker Company, 1976.

Lyman, Ruth, *Couture: An Illustrated History of the Great Paris Designers and Their Creations.* New York: Doubleday & Company, Inc., 1972.

Quant, Mary, *Quant by Quant.* London: Cassell and Company Ltd., 1965.

Ross, Ishbel, *Crusades and Crinolines.* New York: Harper & Row, Publishers, Inc., 1963.

"Signature of 450,000." New York: International Ladies' Garment Workers' Union, 1965.

Tate, Sharon Lee, *Inside Fashion Design.* San Francisco: Canfield Press, Harper & Row, Publishers, Inc., 1977.

Textiles from Start to Finish. Charlotte, N.C.: American Textile Manufacturers Institute, 1978.

Walz, Barbra, and Bernadine Morris, *The Fashion Makers.* New York: Random House, Inc., 1978.

INDEX